**PROPERTY OF
PUBLIC INTEREST
INSTITUTE**

PROPERTY OF
PUBLIC INTEREST
INSTITUTE

Models of Strategic Choice in Politics

Models of
Strategic Choice
in Politics

Edited by Peter C. Ordeshook

Ann Arbor
The University of Michigan Press

Copyright © by The University of Michigan 1989
All rights reserved
Published in the United States of America by
The University of Michigan Press
Manufactured in the United States of America

1992 1991 1990 1989   4 3 2 1

Library of Congress Cataloging-in-Publication Data

Models of strategic choice in politics / edited by Peter C. Ordeshook.
   p.   cm.
  Bibliography: p.
  ISBN 0-472-10122-6 (alk. paper)
  1. Political science—Decision making—Mathematical models.
2. Elections—Mathematical models. 3. International relations—
Mathematical models. 4. Legislative bodies—Mathematical models.
I. Ordeshook, Peter C., 1942-   .
JA74.M63 1989
320′.01′51—dc20   89-32107
                                                                                CIP

Contents

Introduction ... 1

Elections

Information Aggregation in Two-Candidate Elections ... 7
John O. Ledyard

Voters, Investors, and the Consumption of Political
Information ... 31
Brian E. Roberts

Political Investment, Voter Perceptions, and Candidate
Strategy: An Equilibrium Spatial Analysis ... 49
Melvin J. Hinich and Michael C. Munger

A Mathematical Proof of Duverger's Law ... 69
Thomas R. Palfrey

Service-Induced Campaign Contributions, Incumbent
Shirking, and Reelection Opportunities ... 93
David P. Baron

Electoral Accountability and Incumbency ... 121
David Austen-Smith and Jeffrey Banks

International Relations

The Dynamics of Longer Brinkmanship Crises ... 151
Robert Powell

Uncertainty, Rational Learning, and Bargaining in the
Cuban Missile Crisis ... 177
R. Harrison Wagner

Bargaining in Repeated Crises: A Limited Information
Model ... 207
James D. Morrow

Stability in International Systems and the Costs of War ... 229
Emerson M. S. Niou and Peter C. Ordeshook

The Road to War Is Strewn with Peaceful Intentions 253
Bruce Bueno de Mesquita and David Lalman

Legislative Processes

Reciprocity among Self-Interested Actors: Uncertainty, Asymmetry, and Distribution 269
Randall L. Calvert

Collective Choice without Procedural Commitment 295
Thomas W. Gilligan and Keith Krehbiel

Condorcet Consistent Binary Agendas under Incomplete Information 315
Joon Pyo Jung

The Power to Propose 343
David P. Baron and John Ferejohn

References 367

Introduction

Peter C. Ordeshook

The intent of this volume is to offer a sample of contemporary political theory that draws on the rational choice paradigm in general and game theory in particular. No collection of fifteen essays can, of course, provide an exhaustive summary of research agendas, but together they reveal several important and general facts. First, applications of game theory to politics now extend beyond the simple adaptations of those games introductory texts have made so familiar—the Prisoners' Dilemma, Chicken, and simple majority-rule voting games. Sequential games, games of incomplete information, stochastic games, and the application of ideas such as Bayes's equilibria, subgame perfection, rational expectations, and sequential equilibria now permeate the literature, allowing us to explore previously inexplicable processes and phenomena. For example, the formalization and application of games with incomplete information, illustrated by the contributions of Jung, Austen-Smith and Banks, Powell, and Ledyard, move us toward an understanding of the role of reputation, of the possibility of deception as a strategy, of the mechanisms whereby people learn about the preferences of others, of the ways in which the details of political processes provide opportunities for signaling one's intentions, and of the distortions in outcomes that occur when information is not universally shared.

The second fact this volume demonstrates is that although the usual domain of research employing the most sophisticated and mathematically elegant tools has been elections and legislative voting, the field of international relations is now an especially fertile area of inquiry. The early preoccupation with elections and voting stemmed, doubtlessly, from the fact that well-specified processes, whose descriptions mapped readily into the representations employed by game theorists, were the easiest to model, to manipulate, and to solve. But contemporary advances in game theory—in particular, in the analysis of extensive-form and sequential games—allows research into less well-defined processes such as bargaining, coalition formation, and the threats and counterthreats that seem a part of international politics. Rather than limit their explorations to processes in which rules and procedures are self-evident and determined exogenously, political theory, as illustrated by the several contributions to the study of international politics, is now increasingly concerned with endogenously determined processes or, as in the Ferejohn and Baron essays, with legislative processes in which the modeling of form is a primary analytic task.

This volume also demonstrates that understanding politics requires sophisticated tools of deduction. Readers unfamiliar with mathematical notation will find several essays difficult to comprehend. Some persons may complain that substantive detail is being obscured by formalism while others may assert that the specificity of assumptions these essays employ limit their substantive relevance. It is, however, a grievous error to assume that these essays report mere mathematical manipulations without substantive content, and that less formal approaches allow a simpler and more general understanding. Strategic interaction among people with dissimilar interests is the core of politics, and these essays, which seek to shed light on aspects of politics that had previously been obscured from view, reveal the complexities inherent in explorations of that core. Joining the debate over Duverger's Law, Palfrey asks: What are the consequencess for multi-party competition if voters reason carefully about how they should vote in single-member districts, given that they are uncertain about the preferences of other voters? What general lessons can we draw from the Cuban missile crisis, asks Wagner, if we carefully detail the strategic alternatives available to key decision-makers? How, asks Calvert, are vote trading agreements sustained in a legislature when there are no exogenously determined enforcement mechanisms? What evidence is there, asks Roberts, that voters appropriately utilize indirect information about candidates' issue positions in deciding how to vote in mass elections? If the reasoning that these and the other essays offer is complex and if the assumptions they employ seem restrictive, that is because the processes of politics are complex and require, for their understanding, an explicit specification of their character. The simplifications offered by seemingly more understandable and general verbal argument are inadequate. With such argument it is too easy to misperceive so simple a situation as the interactions of two people whose interests are incompletely revealed to the other, and where individual choices not only move toward certain outcomes, but also reveal something about oneself that can be used to advantage by the other. Learning how such circumstances are reflected in political processes and how people respond to them requires careful, deductive analysis. If mathematics is a necessary part of that analysis, then such mathematics is necessarily a part of political theory.

The contributions to this volume are divided into three areas: elections, international relations, and legislative processes. That the tools we use to formulate models in one area apply to the others demonstrates a fourth and most important fact—contemporary political theory is an integrated subject. Specific models may employ different assumptions about individual preferences or about the structure of strategic interaction, but the logic of game theory is a thread that unites all of them. Thus, although the research this volume reports looks quite unlike the writings of classical political theorists such as Hobbes, Madison, Locke, and Rousseau, there is at least one commonality. Classical theorists rejected the notion that different constructs are required to study the various facets of politics (and economics). Similarly, although personal interests and a familiarity with substantive details yield specialization, the primitive concepts and constructs employed in contemporary theory to study one area often apply equally well to others. Thus, those who study legislatures, voting, international conflict, or any of the myriad topics falling under the rubrics of public choice and political economy can contribute to research in other subfields. What we learn about how to best represent unstructured choices in a legislature, about the ways in which voters use information in elections and how candidates might manipulate that information, or about the nature of the enforcement of agreements in international politics has general applicability. In this sense, contemporary theory is Theory.

Elections

Information Aggregation in Two-Candidate Elections

John O. Ledyard

It has been difficult to explain the relevance of public opinion polls, reporters, and interest-group endorsements in an election campaign—indeed it is difficult to understand the purpose of a campaign itself—within the context of standard spatial competition models. The problem is that these mechanisms have no role in the election process when every voter and candidate is fully informed from the beginning of the process. Only in the presence of imperfectly and asymmetrically informed agents can campaigns and their associated events have an impact on election processes and outcomes.[1]

To date, modeling of elections with imperfectly informed players has generally[2] taken one of two approaches I refer to as the (1) naive and (2) rational expectations models. Neither, however, allows a complete and wholly consistent analysis of information processes in elections. In the naive approach, illustrated by Ledyard (1984) and Palfrey (in this volume), voters and candidates are modeled as Bayesians who use common knowledge about each other's priors and rationality to anticipate all actions and to compute their expected utility maximizing strategies. These are normal form models that sidestep issues that would arise in an extensive form. Although the equilibrium strategies can be complex contingent plans, such models are naive because they ignore an important possibility for the acquisition of information by uninformed agents. They assume that players do not look at the actual actions of the others and use that data, and the knowledge of the equilibrium strategy, to make better inferences about what the others know and, therefore, better inferences about the true state of the world. This assumption makes sense if all players move only once and simultaneously. However, as in most elections, if candidates can continually revise campaign strategies up to the actual vote and if voters can change intentions on the basis

---

I would like to thank John Ferejohn, who once asked me whether elections aggregated information like markets do. (The answer, John, is no.) I would also like to thank Richard McKelvey for helpful comments.

1. For an excellent survey of models of imperfect information in politics, as of 1985, see Calvert (1986).

2. Banks (1987*a*) and Harrington (1988*b*) are exceptions.

of endorsements and polls and other information about voter preferences and candidate plans, then it is necessary to recognize that a standard normal form model, which does not incorporate the possibility of sequential adjustment in the specification of strategies, is not sufficiently rich.

Recognizing the fact that voters and candidates can learn from each other's actual moves, but trying to preserve as much as possible from the complete information spatial competition model, McKelvey and Ordeshook (1985) take a second approach by adapting the rational expectations model of markets[3] to elections. Both strategies and expectations are required to be in equilibrium simultaneously. That is, strategies are best replays given expectations and expectations are fully conditioned on the information revealed in the strategic choices.[4] For example, if one candidate knows the median voter's ideal point then this candidate chooses the median as her platform. But the uninformed candidate will know, after observing that choice, exactly what the median position is and by choosing that median will ensure a tie with the informed candidate. The equilibrium is the same as that in the complete information model. This property of many rational expectations equilibria, that in equilibrium even initially uninformed players are fully informed, leads to the seeming paradox that there is no incentive to be informed because the other candidate will apparently be able to free ride on that information.[5] The source of the paradox is the omission of an important strategic consideration in the equilibrium concept. In particular, there is no recognition of the fact that the informed candidate, knowing that the uninformed candidate will use the information in her strategy choice, may act to mask that information in an effort to mislead by choosing some position other than the median. Rational expectations equilibria may not remain as equilibria if a wider range of strategies is recognized.

In this essay we attempt to remedy the omission and to study elections in which candidates and voters can be imperfectly and privately informed, with a particular emphasis on the strategic effects of asymmetric information. We want to know whether information is aggregated,[6] whether uninformed voters and candidates become informed, and to

---

3. In the economics literature on rational expectations in markets, players use prices to make inferences about others' information. See, e.g., Lucas (1972) or Plott and Sunder (1982).

4. For those not familiar with the rational expectations approach, the method by which information is revealed will be discussed in more detail below.

5. This paradox has also been noted in the economics analysis of markets and caused some problems for the efficient markets hypothesis.

6. We say information is aggregated when the behavior of agents, including their information inference activities, lead them to act together as if they are fully informed.

what extent information asymmetries cause outcomes to differ from those predicted by the models with completely informed players. As we will see below the answers depend on the institutional structure that is in place.

The essay is organized as follows. In sections I and II we introduce the model, while sections III–V contain the analysis. In section I, we summarize the structure needed from standard, complete information spatial competition models and give examples to illustrate the notation. In section II, we introduce the model of asymmetric information and define an equilibrium for the naive approach in which candidates can choose strategies conditional on their private information but not conditional on the strategy choice of the other candidate. In this simple context information is valuable because the better informed candidate will generally have a higher probability of winning the election. In section III, we look at what happens if candidates can make inferences about the other's private information from the other's strategic choices or, loosely, campaign behavior. We are especially interested in the sequence of strategy choices when there are no direct costs to changing positions, since when one candidate is fully informed and the other is not, the process is a signaling model. In section IV, we introduce a poll in order to generate public information in the midst of the strategic choices of the candidates. Again this is viewed as costless. In section V, we replace the poll with another election, so that there is a real opportunity cost to be paid if a candidate wants to mask his information. The current election can be lost trying to protect future chances. A summary of all the results and some observations are provided in section VI.

I. The Standard Election Model—Complete Information

To introduce notation and to provide a basis for the analysis we begin by summarizing the standard spatial competition model of two-candidate elections. Two *candidates*, A and B, are presumed to compete by selecting *strategies* in a space X, where X is a subset of the n-dimensional Euclidean space. These strategies are often called platforms but can include anything that affects voter behavior such as campaign strategies, speech topics and locations, expenditure decisions by state or category, timing of announcements, etc. Using a somewhat abusive notation we also let A be the strategy of candidate A and let B be the strategy of candidate B. Candidates are assumed to choose strategies to *maximize the probability of winning*.[7] The aggregate behavior of individual voters

---
7. For these models, it can be shown that this is equivalent to the maximization of expected utility.

is captured in a function identifying the effect of candidate strategies on the probabilities of winning. Let prob {A wins} = $\Pi(A,B,m)$ = 1 − prob {B wins} = 1 − $\Pi(B,A,m)$ where m parameterizes the voters' behavior.[8] The zero-sum game, denoted by $G = \{A,B,X,\Pi,m\}$, is *the candidates' game.* An *equilibrium* of the game G is a pair of strategies (A',B') such that each is a best reply to the other. That is, $\Pi(A,B',m) \leq \Pi(A',B',m) \leq \Pi(A',B,m)$ for all $A,B \in X$. Note that $\Pi(A',B',m) = \frac{1}{2}$.

To see how most specific spatial competition models fit into this framework let us examine three. In each, voters are assumed to have preferences over the strategy space captured in a utility function $U(x,e)$ where e are the parameters identifying each particular voter. One interpretation of U is that it is the indirect expected utility to the voter if the candidate using strategy x were to win. The entire collection of voters is then described by a density function $f(e,m)$, parameterized by m, where $f(e',m')$ describes the proportion of the voters whose preferences are defined by e' when the true parameter is m'. With this notation in mind we can turn to the examples and derive Π for each.

Example 1: The Median Voter (Downs 1957; Enelow and Hinich 1984b)

Strategies and the parameters e and m are real numbers where e is interpreted to be the ideal point of the voter and m is the median of the distribution of the ideal points. The utility functions are assumed to be single-peaked at e or, more specifically, $U(x,e) = -\|x - e\|$. It is also assumed that there are no abstentions. For this model of voter behavior, it is easy to show that

$$\Pi(A,B,m) = \begin{Bmatrix} 1 \\ \frac{1}{2} \\ 0 \end{Bmatrix} \text{if } \|A - m\| \begin{Bmatrix} < \\ = \\ > \end{Bmatrix} \|B - m\|.$$

In equilibrium $A = B = m$. If the strategy space has more than 1 dimension an equilibrium rarely exists.

Example 2: Rational Abstentions (Ledyard 1984)

The strategy space is n-dimensional and the utility function of a typical voter is $U(x,e) = V(x,d) - c$ where $e = (d,c)$, c is the cost of voting for this voter, and d parameterizes the voters' preferences. If we assume that $f(e,m) = g(d,m)h(c)$ and if abstentions are rational (that is, a voter

---

8. The last equality assumes that the candidates' names are unimportant. The entire theory presented below can be easily generalized to the case in which names are important and the last equality does not hold.

abstains if and only if the expected benefits from voting do not outweigh the cost) then it can be shown that

$$\Pi(A,B,m) \begin{cases} > \frac{1}{2} \text{ if } \int V(A,d)g(d,m)dd > \int V(B,d)g(d,m)dd \\ = \frac{1}{2} \qquad\qquad\qquad\qquad = \\ < \frac{1}{2} \qquad\qquad\qquad\qquad < \end{cases}$$

In equilibrium $A = B = \operatorname*{argmax}_{x} \int V(x, d)g(d,m)dd$. In equilibrium, no one votes but the threat of turnout still drives the candidates. A sufficient condition for equilibrium to exist is that the density of the costs of voting is uniform on $[0,C]$ where $C > 0$. Equilibrium also exists for other densities.

Example 3: Probabilistic Voting (Coughlin and Nitzan 1981)

The strategy space is n-dimensional. It is assumed that voters vote randomly but systematically and that prob $\{e$ votes for $A\}$/prob $\{e$ votes for $B\} = U(A,e)/U(B,e)$. There are no abstentions. For this model of voter behavior,

$$\Pi(A,B,e) = \int \text{prob } \{e \text{ votes for } A\} f(e,m) d\,e.$$

In equilibrium $A = B = \operatorname{argmax} \int [lnU(x,e)] f(e,m)de$. Equilibrium exists for a wide range of densities.

II. The Standard Election Model—Incomplete Information

We want to study what happens if the candidates do not know m but instead have only some private and possibly indirect information about voters.[9] The basis for the private information could be privately commissioned polls, local knowledge, prior beliefs, experience, etc. We use an approach that is standard in game and auction theory and model the election by assuming that candidates A and B privately observe signals, a and b. The triple (a,b,m) is assumed to be distributed according to the density function $g(a,b,m)$, which is common knowledge (as is Π). This is

---

9. We do not explicitly consider what the voters know but include their information in the function Π. Those interested in models with uninformed voters, and in the strategic revelation of information by candidates to voters, should consult Banks (1987a) and Harrington (1988b). Another model with uninformed voters can be found in McKelvey and Ordeshook (1985). They do not deal with strategic issues but instead postulate a rational expectations model of equilibrium behavior.

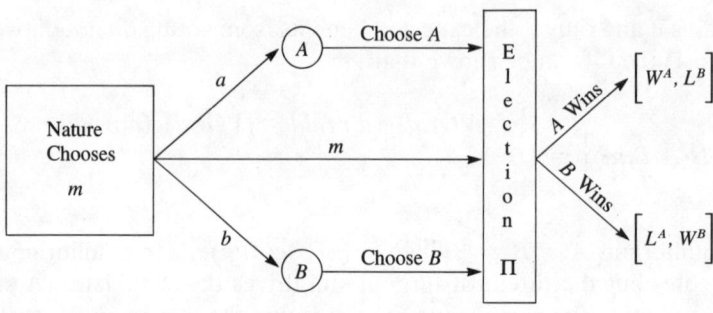

Fig. 1

a game with imperfect information in which nature moves first and picks a particular value of (a,b,m). A and B, after seeing a and b respectively, simultaneously select their strategies, A and B. Voters then vote according to the function $\Pi(A,B,m)$ which yields the outcome—someone wins. An equilibrium is a strategy for each player describing what that candidate will do conditional on his or her private information (see fig. 1).

More formally, the (Bayes) game is $G = \{A,B,\Pi(A,B,m),g(a,b,m)\}$. A (contingent) strategy for candidate A is a function $A(a)$; for B it is a function $B(b)$. A (Bayes) equilibrium of G is a pair of functions $A^*(a), B^*(b)$ such that for every a

$$A^*(a) \in \operatorname*{argmax}_A \int \Pi(A, B^*(b), m) g(m,a,b) dm db \qquad (1.1)$$

and for every b

$$B^*(b) \in \operatorname*{argmin}_B \int \Pi(A^*(a), B, m) g(m,a,b) dm da. \qquad (1.2)$$

To develop a feel for this model let us look at three special cases: (1) symmetric information, (2) no information, and (3) extremely asymmetric information.

Example 4: Symmetric Information

To model a situation in which A and B are in symmetric situations, *ex ante*,[10] with respect to information we assume that a and b are independently and identically distributed, *given m*. That is, we assume that $g(m,a,b) = g^1(a,m)g^1(b,m)$. For this informational structure there is a symmetric equilibrium in which $A^*(s) = B^*(s) = C^*(s)$ for every signal s. Further, the ex ante expected probability that A wins is

$$\int \Pi[C^*(a), C^*(b), m] g^1(a,m) g^1(b,m) da db dm.$$

---

10. *Ex ante* refers to the situation before a and b are known.

It is easy to see that this probability equals ½ in the absence of any other asymmetries. It is also true, however, that the *interim*[11] expected probability that A wins given a, defined as

$$\int \Pi(A^*(a), B^*(b), m) g(a,b,m) db\, dm$$

can be anything between 0 and 1. A similar observation can be made with respect to the *ex post*[12] expected probability that A wins given a and b, which is

$$\int \Pi[A^*(a), B^*(b), m] g(a,b,m) dm.$$

Example 5: No Prior Information

To model a situation in which neither candidate possesses information we assume that a and b are distributed independently and identically and that both a and b are independent of m. In this case, $g(a,b,m) = r(a)r(b)t(m)$ and in equilibrium $A^*(a) = A^*$ and $B^*(b) = B^*$. That is, optimal strategies ignore the signals because, for example, given the signal a

$$A^*(a) \in \underset{A}{\text{argmax}} \int \Pi(A, B^*(b), m) r(b) t(m) db\, dm$$

and the objective function is independent of a. One can simply redefine the probability of winning as $\Pi^*(A, B) = \int \Pi(A, B, m) t(m) dm$. The game is now as in section I with complete information. Neither player knows anything of importance that the other does not.

Example 6: Asymmetrically Informed Candidates

To illustrate the extent to which information about the electorate can be valuable for a candidate, consider a case in which A is well informed and B knows very little. This might occur because A is the incumbent and knows the district while B is the challenger with very little experience. To capture this asymmetry we let $g(a,b,m) = r(a,m)t(b)$. B's signal provides no information while A's signal tells A something about m. In effect, the marginal density on m captures what both A and B know about the distribution of voters while the correlation between a and m, described by $r(\ )$, determines the extent to which A is better informed than B. In equilibrium, $B^*(b) = \hat{B}$ and for every realization of a,

---

11. *Interim* refers to the situation that exists when A knows a but not b or m and B knows b but not a or m.

12. *Ex post* describes the situation after a and b are known.

$\int \Pi [A^*(a), \hat{B}, m] r(m, a) dm \geq \frac{1}{2}$ (for most examples it is $> \frac{1}{2}$). In an extreme case, if A is fully informed, then

$$A^* = \hat{A} \text{ and } \hat{A} \in \underset{A}{\operatorname{argmax}} \Pi[A, \hat{B}, m].$$

Because

$$\hat{B} \notin \underset{B}{\operatorname{argmax}} \Pi[\hat{A}, B, m], \Pi[\hat{A}, \hat{B}, m] > \frac{1}{2},$$

and, therefore, information is valuable. This example illustrates that an incumbency advantage can be derived from the possession of better *private* information about the voting tendencies of the constituency to be served.

Since A's equilibrium strategy depends on a, an outside observer could invert the relationship after observing the action A^*, compute $A^{*-1}(A^*) = \{a \mid A^*(a) = A^*\}$, and then use that information to update his prior. If $A^{*-1}(A^*) = a^*$, then the outside observer would know everything A does. If B could do this *before the election*[13] then B could, presumably, minimize A's informational advantage. The election process would be aggregating privately held information and the equilibrium might look like a rational expectations equilibrium. Counteracting this tendency is the fact that A, as a strategic player, will recognize that B can gain from information leakages and A will act to minimize the loss by choosing a different strategy.

There are at least two questions to be studied. Do elections aggregate information? Do informational considerations distort the strategic choices of candidates from those predicted by the standard model? As we will see, the answers to such questions depend on institutional features like the timing of strategic choices, the existence of public polls, and the existence of future elections.

III. The Timing of Strategic Choices

If the candidates can react to each other's electoral strategies they may be able to infer each other's private information which leads to information aggregation. This is the intuition behind rational expectations equilibria. To ascertain whether this intuition is valid in elections, we begin with the simplest election scenario. First candidates A and B simultaneously pick, respectively, strategies α and β. After observing each other's choices, they choose again by simultaneously picking, respectively, A and B, at which point the voters vote. The timing structure is shown in figure 2. The

---

13. We have assumed in (1.1) and (1.2) that A and B move simultaneously, so that any chance to infer A's information arises too late to help B strategically.

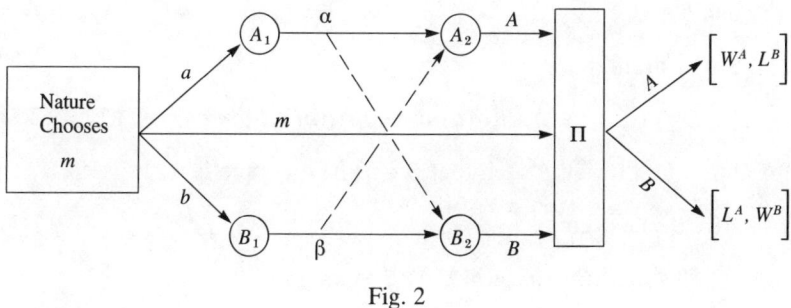

Fig. 2

crucial assumption, which generates the main theorem in this section, is that the first moves, (α,β), are free in the sense that voters vote only on the basis of A and B. In the economics literature this type of move has become known as *cheap talk* and its use can affect the outcome.[14] To analyze this new game, we need a tighter equilibrium concept than Bayes equilibrium, which allows us to see what occurs when one agent can infer something about the other's private information. We use the idea of a sequential equilibrium, the main feature of which is a requirement of subgame perfection—a form of dynamic rationality.

More formally, the game is $G = \{A, B, \Pi(A,B,m)g(a,b,m)\}$. A (contingent) strategy for candidate A is a pair of functions $\alpha(a)$ and $A(\alpha,\beta,a)$, and a (contingent) strategy for B is a pair of functions $\beta(b)$ and $B(\alpha,\beta,b)\}$. A (sequential[15] Bayes) equilibrium of G is the 4-tuple of functions $\alpha(a), \beta(b), A(\alpha,\beta,a), B(\alpha,\beta,b)$ such that for each a

$$\alpha(a) \in \operatorname*{argmax}_{\alpha}$$

$$\int \Pi[A\ (\alpha,\beta(b),a),\ B(\alpha,\beta(b),b), m]g(m,a,b)dmdb, \qquad (2.1)$$

---

14. The usual example of a nonfree move is a change in platform so radical that voters switch to the other, more dependable, candidate. Banks (1987a) uses a somewhat *ad hoc* cost proportional to the distance $\|\alpha - A\|$ to model this. In our context an "opportunity cost" would arise if x were time indexed as $(x_1, x_2) = x$. Then the moves α and A would constitute parts of the strategy (α, A). At time 2, α is fixed and can affect voters' reactions to A since $\Pi = \Pi[(\alpha, A),(\beta, B), m]$. We assume below in (2) that voters ignore the moves α, β, and let $\Pi = \Pi(A, B, m)$ to emphasize the signaling nature of the first moves. In section V, we allow the first moves to be costly.

15. Relations (2.1) to (2.4) are necessary but not sufficient for a sequential equilibrium. An additional criterion must be met that specifies how candidates will react to zero-probability events. That is, $A\ (\alpha,\beta,a)$ must also be defined on β for which there are no b such that $\beta = \beta(b)$. We do not do that here since the results we are interested in below do not depend in any crucial way on this extension. The reader is free to apply his or her favorite refinement.

16   Models of Strategic Choice in Politics

for each b

$$\beta(b) \in \underset{\beta}{\operatorname{argmin}}$$

$$\int \Pi[A\ (\alpha(a),\beta,a),\ B(\alpha(a),\beta,b),\ m]g(m\,a,b)dmda, \qquad (2.2)$$

for all α,a and for all β such that $\beta = \beta(b)$ for some b,

$$A(\alpha,\beta,a) \in \underset{A}{\operatorname{argmax}}$$

$$\int \Pi[A, B(\alpha,\beta,b), m]g(m,a,b\ |\ \beta = \beta(b))dmdb, \qquad (2.3)$$

and such that for all β,b and for all α such that $\alpha = \alpha(a)$ for some a,

$$B(\alpha,\beta,b) \in \underset{B}{\operatorname{argmin}}$$

$$\int \Pi[A(\alpha,\beta,a),B,m]g(m,a,b\ |\ \alpha = \alpha(a))dmda. \qquad (2.4)$$

The key fact that we will observe in this model is that the equilibrium electoral outcomes are exactly the same as in the model of the previous section when no reaction is possible. That is, no information aggregation occurs and no advantage or disadvantage accrues to either candidate from her ability to react to the other. This is true since the equilibrium functions $\alpha(a)$ and $\beta(b)$ are constant (termed *pooling strategies*) and no inferences can be made about private information. The intuition is this: if, say, A were to choose α differently in different states of information, then B, knowing this and being able to condition on that information, would be able to use that information and do better. Since this is a zero-sum game, when B does better A does worse. Anything A says can and will be used against her. Of course, A can anticipate that B will use the information and can scramble the signals by permuting the strategic choice of α across signals. If B does not anticipate this then A will be better off because A would have misled B into using a suboptimal strategy for the true state. Of course, B prevents this by ignoring A's α strategy. In equilibrium, A cannot gain by separating (choosing different α in different information sets) but can lose if B uses the information. In equilibrium, B cannot lose by ignoring any separation and can lose if A uses any attempt at inference by B against B.

For the reader who is unfamiliar with the machinery of Bayesian games, an example is helpful. Consider a simple form of Down's model (example 1 in section I) in which there are only two possible medians: $m \in \{L,R\}$. Assume that each candidate has only two strategies. That is, $A, B, \alpha,$ and β belong to the set $\{l,r\}$. (It is not necessary that either $l = L$ or $r = R$ but they can be interpreted as such.) Finally, assume that B knows the value of m and that A does not. A believes the probability that $m = L$ is ¼. The payoff function can be summarized in a payoff table for A.

$$\Pi(A,B,L) = \begin{array}{c|c|c} A\backslash B & l & r \\ \hline l & ½ & 1 \\ r & 0 & ½ \end{array}$$

and

$$\Pi(A,B,R) = \begin{array}{c|c|c} A\backslash B & l & r \\ \hline l & ½ & 0 \\ r & 1 & ½ \end{array}$$

The two-move game can then be thought of as follows:

Move 0: Nature Chooses m
Move 1: B picks $\beta \in \{l,r\}$, A's choice is unimportant since A is uninformed,
Move 2: A picks $A \in \{l,r\}$, B chooses $B = m$.

Those who are familiar with the literature will note that this is just a very simple signaling game whose game tree and information sets are given in figure 3. It is easy to compute that, even if mixed strategies are allowed (as long as A can differentiate between different mixtures), the only equilibria involve B pooling at move 1 and A picking r at move 2. B can pool by picking l whether the true state is L or R or by picking r whether the true state is L or R. Both strategies leave A uninformed. The equilibrium outcome is that B wins if $m = L$ and there is a tie if $m = R$. This is identical to the outcome of a one (simultaneous) move game. The ex ante probability that B wins, calculated before B receives information, is ⅝ and the ex ante probability that A wins is ⅜. One can interpret this as the advantage from being informed. It also indicates that there are gains from the acquisition of private information and suggests that an interesting variation, not studied in this essay, would be to let candidates buy information (e.g., pay for private polls) rather than simply begin with their information in hand.

To capture the simple intuition from this example in a more general theorem, we first need to handle some minor technical details that arise from the possibility of multiple equilibria. We will show that pooling at the first stage is an equilibrium strategy. That is, there are constant functions $\alpha(a) = \alpha'$ and $\beta(b) = \beta'$ which are the first part of a sequential equilibrium. There may also be other equilibria, but both candidates will

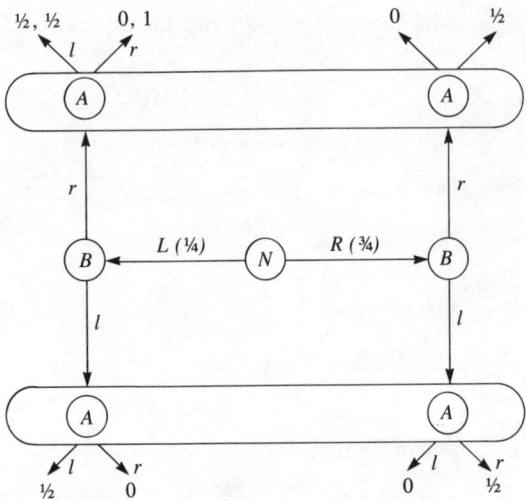

Fig. 3

be indifferent between these and the pooling equilibrium. To establish this, we must identify when nonpooling is inessential.

DEFINITION. *Let $\alpha^*, \beta^*, A^*, B^*$ be an equilibrium satisfying (2). We say that α^* is an* essentially pooled *strategy (a symmetric definition applies for β^*) if and only if, for every $a, b, \alpha', \beta', \alpha''$ such that $\alpha' = \alpha^*(a), \beta' = \beta^*(b)$, and $\alpha'' = \alpha^*(a'')$ for some a'',*

$$\int \Pi[A^*(\alpha',\beta',a), B^*(\alpha',\beta',b),m]g(m,a,b \mid \beta' = \beta^*(b))dmdb$$

$$= \int \Pi[A^*(\alpha'',\beta',a), B^*(\alpha',\beta',b),m]g(m,a,b \mid \beta' = \beta^*(b))dmdb \quad (3.1)$$

and

$$\int \Pi[A^*(\alpha',\beta',a), B^*(\alpha',\beta',b),m]g(m,a,b \mid \alpha' = \alpha^*(b))dmda$$

$$= \int \Pi[A^*(\alpha',\beta',a), B^*(\alpha'',\beta',b),m]g(m,a,b \mid \alpha' = \alpha^*(a))dmda. \quad (3.2)$$

That is, both A and B are indifferent between using the second-move strategy generated by α' and that generated by α''. Also both candidates are indifferent between the original equilibrium and that created by replacing α' with α''.

We can now state the principal result of this section.

Information Aggregation in Two-Candidate Elections 19

THEOREM 1. *If $<\alpha(a),\beta(b),A(\alpha,\beta,a),B(\alpha,\beta,b)>$ is an equilibrium of the election game satisfying (2), then $\alpha(\cdot)$ and $\beta(\cdot)$ are essentially pooled strategies.*

Proof. Let α^*,β^*,A^*,B^* satisfy (2). We prove α^* is essentially pooled. The proof for β^* follows a symmetric argument. Let $Z = \{\alpha \mid \alpha^*(a) = \alpha \text{ for some } A\}$. If Z is a singleton then $\alpha^*(\ )$ is a pooled strategy and we are done. So let $\alpha',\alpha'', \epsilon\, Z$ with $\alpha' \neq \alpha''$, let $\alpha^*(a') = \alpha'$ and let $\alpha^*(a'') = \alpha''$. From (2.4) it follows that

$$\int \Pi[A^*(\alpha',\beta',a),B^*(\alpha',\beta',b),m]g(m,a,b \mid \alpha'=\alpha^*(a))dmda$$
$$\leq \int \Pi[A^*(\alpha',\beta',a),B^*(\alpha'',\beta',b),m]g(m,a,b \mid \alpha'=\alpha^*(a))dmda \quad (4.1)$$

for all $<\beta',b>$ such that $\beta' = \beta^*(b)$. If we integrate (4.1) over all b we get (remembering that $\beta' = \beta^*(b)$),

$$\int \Pi[A^*(\alpha',\beta^*(b),a),B^*(\alpha',\beta^*(b),m]g(m,a,b \mid \alpha'=\alpha^*(a))dmdadb$$
$$\leq \int \Pi[A^*(\alpha',\beta^*(b),a),B^*(\alpha'',\beta^*(b),m)] \times$$
$$g(m,a,b \mid \alpha'=\alpha^*(a))dmdadb. \quad (4.2)$$

Now (2.3) implies that, for all β' such that $\beta' = \beta^*(b)$ for some b,

$$\int \Pi[A^*(\alpha',\beta',\bar{a}),\beta^*(\alpha'',\beta',b),m]g(m,\bar{a},b \mid \beta' = \beta^*(b))dmdb$$
$$\leq \int \Pi[A^*(\alpha'',\beta',\bar{a}),B^*(\alpha'',\beta',b),m] \times$$
$$g(m,\bar{a},b \mid \beta' = \beta^*(b))dmdb. \quad (4.3)$$

Integrating (4.3) over all b implies

$$\int \Pi[A^*(\alpha',\beta^*(b),\bar{a}),B^*(\alpha'',\beta^*(b),b),m]g(m,\bar{a},b)dmdb$$
$$\leq \int \Pi[A^*(\alpha'',\beta^*(b),\bar{a}),B^*(\alpha'',\beta^*(b),b,m)g(m,\bar{a},b)dmdb. \quad (4.4)$$

Integrate (4.4) over $\{a \mid \alpha^*(a) = \alpha'\}$ and use (4.2) to get

$$\int \Pi^*[A^*(\alpha',\beta^*(b),a),B^*(\alpha',\beta^*(b),b),m] \times$$
$$g(m,a,b \mid \alpha' = \alpha^*(a))dmdbda$$
$$\leq \int \Pi[A^*(\alpha'',\beta^*(b),a),B^*(\alpha'',\beta^*(b),b),m] \times$$
$$g(m,a,b \mid \alpha' = \alpha^*(a))dmdbda. \quad (4.5)$$

Now we must consider two cases.

Case 1. $\exists\, b',\beta',a',a'',\alpha',\alpha''$ such that $\alpha^*(a') = \alpha' \neq \alpha^*(a'') = \alpha''$ and

$\beta' = \beta^*(b')$ and at least one of the inequalities (4.1) or (4.3) is strict. Then (4.5) is strict and ∃ at least one a^* such that $\alpha' = \alpha^*(a^*)$ and

$$\alpha' \notin \underset{\alpha}{\operatorname{argmax}} \int \Pi[A^*(\alpha,\beta^*(b),a^*),B^*(\alpha,\beta^*(b),b),m]g(m,a,b)dmdb.$$

Therefore, (2.1) is contradicted which proves the theorem.

Case 2. For all $a',a'',\alpha',\alpha'',\beta',b'$ such that $\alpha' = \alpha^*(a'), \beta' = \beta^*(b'), \alpha'' = \alpha^*(a'')$ the inequalities (4.1) and (4.3) are equalities. Then by (3.1) and (3.2), $\alpha^*(\cdot)$ and $\beta^*(\cdot)$ are essentially pooled strategies.

(Q.E.D.)

Although the ability to react to the strategy of one's electoral opponent and to take advantage of inferences about the opponent's private information is *potentially* beneficial, in equilibrium no leakage of information occurs because a candidate can only lose by allowing that to happen. The outcome of the electoral process is the same as it was in the one-move model of section II. No aggregation of information occurs. It can also be shown that increasing the number of allowed responses or moves in the election process to more than two will not change the conclusions. The only strategy choice that will depend, in equilibrium, on one's private information is that last one. Nothing important happens until the last move. Rational expectations are *not* an equilibrium.

COROLLARY 1.1. *The outcome of a T-move election (for T finite) is the same as the outcome of a one-move election.*

Finally, it is important to observe that the simultaneity of the moves is crucial to some of the conclusions. Returning to the simple signaling example with two medians, if B had to choose B first and A could choose A after observing B's choice then there are two equilibria.

Equilibrium 1. B pools and picks r, A reacts by picking r also. In this case, the probability that A wins is ½ for each value of m. B's informational advantage has been lost because of the first move.

Equilibrium 2. B separates and chooses m. A matches B. Again the probability that A wins is ½ for each value of m and B has lost the informational advantage.

Candidate A can guarantee at least a tie by matching B's move and, therefore, B neither gains nor loses from the revelation of the information. Whether information is aggregated in this case is indeterminate.

IV. Polls

A very natural question to ask is whether the existence of public polls effect the aggregation of information. We modify the model in section III by having a poll taken and the results publicly announced between the candidates' first and second moves. First, nature determines the

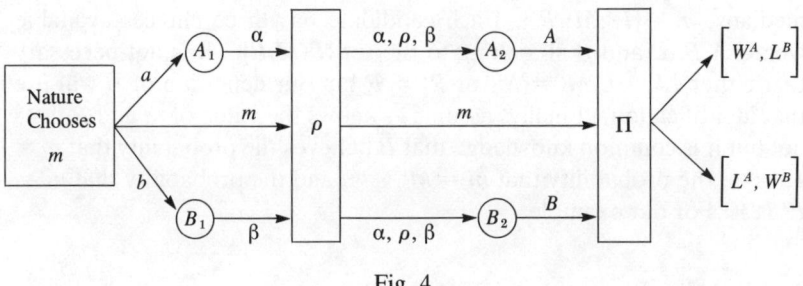

Fig. 4

private information by picking a and b. Next A and B simultaneously choose and announce α and β. Then a poll is taken and the result p, which is the proportion of the voters who would vote for A, is announced. While it would not be difficult to allow for polling errors, we avoid the extra notation and assume that the poll result is governed by a nonrandom relationship $p = \rho(\alpha,\beta,m)$ which is common knowledge. After the poll results are announced, A and B choose strategies A and B, respectively. In accordance with the timing sequence shown in figure 4, the election is then held and the outcome occurs.

A (sequential) equilibrium is a 4-tuple of conditional strategies $\alpha(a),\beta(b),A(\alpha,\beta,p,a),B(\alpha,\beta,p,b)$ where

$A(\cdot) \in \operatorname*{argmax}_{A} \int \Pi(A,B(\cdot),m) \times$

$g(m,a,b \mid \beta = \beta(b), p = \rho(\alpha,\beta,m))dmdb$ (5.1)

$B(\cdot) \in \operatorname*{argmin}_{B} \int \Pi(A(\cdot),B,m) \times$

$g(m,a,b \mid \alpha = \alpha(a), p = \rho(\alpha,\beta,m))dmda$ (5.2)

$\alpha(a) \in \operatorname*{argmax}_{\alpha} \int \Pi[A(\alpha,\beta(b),\rho(\alpha,\beta(b),m),a),B(\alpha,\beta(b),$

$\rho(\alpha,\beta(b),m),b),m]\, g(m,a,b)dmdb$ (5.3)

$\beta(b) \in \operatorname*{argmin}_{\beta} \int \Pi[A(\alpha(a),\beta, \rho(\alpha(a),\beta,m),a),B(\alpha(a),$

$\beta,\rho(\alpha(a),\beta,m),b),m]\, g(m,a,b)dmda.$ (5.4)

The only difference between these relations and those in (2) is the fact that the choice of A and B is now conditioned on the information in the poll result, p, which can be affected by the choices of α and β.

Since the equilibrium conditions (5) are notationally complex and since the result we want to highlight is easier to understand in an example, we turn to a special case of the median voter model which is a bit more complex than that of section III in that we allow three possible medians, $m \in \{L', M', R'\}$. Each candidate has three choices available where A, B, α, and β all belong to the set $\{L, M, R\}$. (It is not necessary that either $L' = L, M' = M$, or $R' = R$ but our definition of Π will use that identification.) Finally, assume A knows the value of m and B does not but it is common knowledge that B believes the probability that $m = L'$ is $\frac{1}{8}$, the probability that $m = M'$ is $\frac{1}{2}$, and the probability that $m = R'$ is $\frac{3}{8}$. For our example,

$\Pi(A,B,m) =$

	if $m = L'$			if $m = M'$			if $m = R'$		
A\B	L	M	R	L	M	R	L	M	R
L	½	1	1	½	0	½	½	0	0
M	0	½	1	1	½	1	1	½	0
R	0	0	½	½	0	½	1	1	½

Finally, let the function that determines the poll result be the same as the function that determines the electoral outcome. That is, let[16] $p = \rho(\alpha,\beta,m) \equiv \Pi(\alpha,\beta,m)$.

To provide a benchmark, let us first examine the outcome when there is no poll. Using the model in section III, it is easy to compute that the equilibrium would involve A pooling in the choice of α. At the second move, A chooses L if $m = L', M$ if $m = M'$, and R if $m = R'$. B's choice of β is unimportant (B is uninformed). B chooses M at the second move. The ex ante probability that A, the informed candidate, wins is $\frac{3}{4}$.

To understand the equilibrium with the poll, we need to work our way back from the last move to the first. At the second move, A chooses m no matter what has happened earlier. B extracts as much information as possible from the signals b, α, β, and p and then chooses the position with the highest probability of being the true median. More formally, for each possible pair of first period choices, α and β, we can calculate B's information after the poll and, therefore, B's strategy choice in period 2. B's information and strategy choices are summarized thus:

---

16. In the Downs model and the Coughlin-Nitzan model this identification makes some sense if voters correctly reveal their intention to vote. In the Ledyard model of voter behavior it would not make sense since voting in the poll (without costs of participation) would follow the median voter model while voting in the election would not.

Information Aggregation in Two-Candidate Elections

α\β	L	M	R
L	LMR	L **L** MR	L M **R**
M	L **M** R	LMR	**L**M R
R	L M **R**	L **M** R	LMR

where, for example, the entry for $(\alpha,\beta) = [L,M]$ means that if $m = L$ then B knows that $m = L$ and B plays L, but if $m = M$ or R then B knows that $m \in \{M,R\}$ and B plays M. (The horizontal configurations are the information sets and the bold-faced letter is the strategic choice.)

Given that we know A's and B's second move choices conditional on the true state m and the first move choices, we can now compute the best first move choices for each. The following table summarizes the best responses by A to a choice of β for each possible median.

median\β	L	M	R
L'	L	MR	RM
M'	LMR	LMR	LMR
R'	LM	LM	R

Thus, if A knows that the median is R' and B has chosen β equal to L then A is indifferent between responding with an α of L or M. Since A is "better off" if B can learn nothing from A's choice of α, A should pool. A quick examination of the previous table will show that A can pool with a best response by matching B's choice. For example, if β is R then α should be R, no matter what the true median is. This matching and pooling choice also minimizes the information that B can extract from the process since $p = \frac{1}{2}$ for every m when the first moves are the same. B learns nothing from the first moves or from the poll.

We can also calculate B's best response to any α given that A pools. The following table summarizes the payoffs to A for each pair of first move choices.

α\β	L	M	R
L	$3/4^x$	$11/16$	$8/16^o$
M	$11/16$	$12/16^x$	$9/16^o$
R	$8/16^o$	$9/16$	$3/4^x$

We have identified A's best response in each column with an x and have identified B's best response in each row with an o. The important observation is that *there is no pure strategy equilibrium!* A always moves to prevent B from learning anything by matching B's position and B always moves to separate his position from A's to generate information. There is, however, a *mixed strategy* equilibrium to this game. In particular one can show, using the previous table, that if the probability that A chooses α equal to L is ½ and equal to R is ½, and if B uses the same mixed strategy, then that is an equilibrium. A still pools but B can extract, with positive probability, some information by using a mixed strategy. When α and β are different (which will happen ½ the time) B will be able to infer the true median. The ex ante probability that A wins is ⅝ which is less than the probability without the poll. A still retains an advantage from being better informed and A can still mask her private information by using a pooling strategy but her advantage is reduced through the existence of the public poll. An interesting study, which we do not pursue here, would analyze the tradeoffs between private and public polls, and the incentives for the provision of either, especially if polling is costly.

In the more general model the main features of the example survive. That is, as long as there are some first period moves by one candidate given the first move of the other candidate, which lead the poll to generate useful information for some m, then (1) there are no pure strategy equilibria, (2) candidates mask their own private information up to the election, but (3) information aggregation does occur. Let

$$\psi(\alpha',\beta',a) = \int \Pi[A(\alpha',\beta',\rho(\alpha',\beta',m),a),B(\alpha',\beta',\rho(\alpha',\beta',m),b),m] \\ g(m,a,b)dmdb$$

where $A(\cdot)$ and $B(\cdot)$ satisfy (5.1) and (5.2). Hence ψ is the indirect utility to A of the last period game given a. If there are multiple equilibria in (5), each candidate is indifferent between them because of the zero-sum nature of the game. Therefore, ψ is well defined.

DEFINITION: *We say that the poll can generate useful information for* A *if for all* β *there is an* α *such that*

$$\int \psi(\alpha,\beta,a)da > \int \psi(\beta,\beta,a)da.$$

For example, if ρ were constant for all α and β then it could generate no useful information. If there is some β, such that (6) is false for all α then B can, by choosing that β, ensure that the probability that he wins is at least as high as it would be without the poll. A poll such that ρ is identical to Π, as in the example, can generate useful information for one of A or B as long as both are not already fully informed.

THEOREM. *If $\rho(\alpha,\alpha,m)$ is constant in m and if ρ can generate useful information then there is no equilibrium where α and β are pooled pure strategies.*

Proof. Suppose that α' and β' are part of an equilibrium. Then

$$\int \psi(\alpha',\beta',a)da \geq \int \psi(\beta',\beta',a)da = \int \phi(a)da,$$

where

$$\phi(a) = \int \Pi[A(a),B(b),m]g(m,a,b)dmdb$$

and where $A(\cdot)$ and $B(\cdot)$ satisfy (1). Also, using a symmetric construction for B,

$$\int \psi(\alpha',\beta',a)da \leq \int \psi(\alpha',\alpha',a)da = \int \phi(a)da.$$

Therefore

$$\int \psi(\alpha',\beta',a)da = \int \phi(a)da.$$

But if $\rho(\ )$ can generate useful information, there is an $\hat{\alpha}$ such that

$$\int \psi(\hat{\alpha},\beta',a)da > \int \psi(\beta',\beta',a)da = \int \phi(a)da$$

Therefore there is $\hat{\alpha}$ such that

$$\int \psi(\alpha',\beta',a)da \geq \int \psi(\hat{\alpha},\beta',a)da > \int \psi(\beta',\beta',a)da,$$

which contradicts (7). (Q.E.D.)

COROLLARY. *Under the hypothesis of the theorem there is an equilibrium where α and β are mixed strategies and, for some realizations of those strategies, information is aggregated.*

With public polling, candidates that are not initially fully informed make their second period moves with more information than in the one-shot election analyzed in section II. An interesting question is whether a sequence of free moves, say $\alpha_1,\alpha_2,\ldots$, and a sequence of polls, $\rho_1,\rho_2,\ldots$, converge to full information revelation and, therefore, to a fully informed rational expectations equilibrium. This remains an open question.

V. Sequences of Elections

To this point, all preliminary moves of the candidates are free of commitment or cost. That fact plus the zero-sum nature of the game leads candidates to choose pooling strategies up to the last move so as not to leak information to an opponent. If, on the other hand, an election is held after each move, opportunity costs become important. A candidate must assess the trade-off between the increase in the probability of winning the current election, by being responsive to the private information, and the decrease in the probability of winning the next elections, by revealing the information to the opponent. In contrast to our previous models, the existence of the trade-off can lead a candidate to a nonpooling strategy that allows some private information to pass to the opponent. The trade-off may also lead a candidate to not exploit fully an informational advantage today so as to preserve that advantage for tomorrow.

To see how nonpooling strategies are sustained, we use the simplest modification of the earlier models that allows us to study the phenomenon. The election scenario, described in figure 5, has A and B first choosing positions α and β, respectively. An election is then held and the outcome occurs according to the function $\Pi(\alpha,\beta,m)$. The outcome is common knowledge. The candidates then choose A and B, respectively, and another election determines the outcome according to $\Pi(A,B,m)$. We assume that m does not change between elections, although it is easy to accommodate a situation in which the m in period 1 and the m in period 2 are believed to be correlated.

Since sequences of elections have not been regularly analyzed in the literature, we must make some assumptions to complete the model. In particular we assume that (1) candidates have no time preference, (2) the value of winning is constant over time, and (3) the value of losing is constant over time. Taken together these imply that each expected utility-maximizing candidate wishes to maximize the sum of the probabilities of winning.

The equilibrium of the game is a 4-tuple of strategies $< \alpha(a)$, $\beta(b), A(\alpha,\beta,p,a), B(\alpha,\beta,p,b) >$ where p is the outcome of the first election, such that for all p such that $p = \Pi(\alpha,\beta,m)$ for some $\alpha = \alpha(a)$ and $\beta = \beta(b)$, it is true for all α,a, for all β such that $\beta = \beta(b)$ for some b

$$A(\cdot) \in \underset{A}{\operatorname{argmax}} \int \Pi[A, B(\alpha,\beta,p,b),m] \times$$

$$g(m,a,b \mid \beta = \beta(b), p = \Pi(\alpha,\beta,m))dmdb$$

Information Aggregation in Two-Candidate Elections

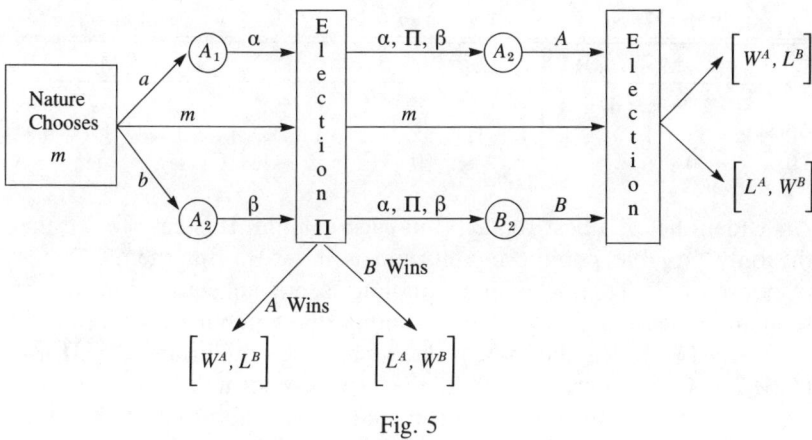

Fig. 5

for all β,b, for all α such that $\alpha = \alpha(a)$ for some a,

$$B(\cdot) \in \underset{B}{\operatorname{argmax}} \int \Pi[A(\alpha,\beta,p,a),B,m] \times$$

$$g(m,a,b \mid \alpha = \alpha(a), p = \Pi(\alpha,\beta,m))dmda$$

for all a

$$\alpha(\cdot) \in \underset{\alpha}{\operatorname{argmax}} \int \Pi(\alpha,\beta(b),m) + \Pi[A(\alpha,\beta(b),\Pi(\alpha,\beta(b),m),a),$$

$$B(\alpha,\beta(b),\Pi(\beta(b),m),b),m]g(m,a,b)dmdb$$

for all b

$$\beta(\cdot) \in \underset{\beta}{\operatorname{argmax}} \int \Pi(\alpha(a),\beta,m) + \Pi[A(\alpha(a),\beta,\Pi(\alpha(a),\beta,m),m),$$

$$B(\alpha(a),\beta,\Pi(\alpha(a),\beta,m),m)g(m,a,b)dmda.$$

To keep the analysis as simple as possible, we reexamine the example used in section III to see what new behavior can occur. Recalling that candidate A was fully informed as to which of three possible medians was the true one, it is easy to see that in the second election A will still fully exploit that information and will choose $A = L$ if $m = L'$, etc. The question is what will A do in the first election?

Suppose A follows a pooling strategy in equilibrium. We can compute A's total payoff from each pair of first election strategies, α and β, where the computations of the choices A,B and the payoffs for the second election are identical to those in section IV. The total payoffs to A, conditional on α,β, and m, are

28   Models of Strategic Choice in Politics

	if $m = L'$			if $m = M'$			if $m = R'$		
α\β	L	M	R	L	M	R	L	M	R
L	½ + 1^x	1 + ½^x	1 + ½	½ + ½	0 + ½	½ + ½	½ + 1	0 + 1	0 + ½
M	0 + ½	½ + 1^x	1 + 1^x	1 + ½^x	½ + ½^x	1 + ½^x	1 + 1^x	½ + 1^x	0 + ½
R	0 + ½	0 + 1	½ + 1	½ + ½	0 + ½	½ + ½	1 + ½	1 + ½^x	½ + 1^x

An x identifies A's best replay(s) in each column. It is easy to see that the only possible pooling equilibrium is $\alpha = M$. But then, B's best response is R. Therefore, pure pooling is not an equilibrium of the sequential election game. There is one partially pooling equilibrium: $\beta = M$, $\alpha = (M,M,R)$, and there is one separating equilibrium: $\beta = M, \alpha = (L,M,R)$. In this example, then, the private information held by A is simply not valuable enough to protect and so A chooses α to maximize the probability of winning election number 1. This tendency to separate would be reinforced if candidate A had a time preference (a discount rate less than 1) since then $\beta = M, \alpha = (L,M,R)$ is the only equilibrium.

It is not generally true, however, that candidates necessarily follow separating strategies in the first election. To see why, consider our example but with different prior beliefs. In particular, suppose it is common knowledge that B believes the prob $(m = L') = ½$, the prob $(m = M') = ⅜$, and the prob $(m = R') = ⅛$. Now the unique sequential equilibrium has first election components of $\beta = L$ and $\alpha = (L,M,M)$. This is a partially separating strategy since $\alpha(R) = M$. If A were to separate, then A would win the first election (if $m = M'$ or R') but A would reveal the information and tie the second. If A pools, then A wins the first when $m = M'$ or R' and also wins the second if $m = R'$ since B would choose M in the second.

In general, with many possible medians (say the whole real line) A can, by choosing just to the side of B on which the real median lies, protect her information *and* win the current election. Whether this can go on forever is unknown.

It does seem to be a general result that the informed candidate will not completely pool since full separation would be preferred to full-pooling. The intuition is simple for the case of a fully informed candidate versus an uninformed candidate. In a pooling equilibrium (since A must act as uninformed) the probability A wins in period 1 is ½. Further, since some information may leak, the probability that A wins in period 2 is less than what it would be if no information leaked. If A were to fully separate in equilibrium then the probability A wins the first election is the same as if no information has leaked. The probability A wins the second is ½ since both candidates are fully informed. A is therefore better off separating. Complete pooling is not an equilibrium.

A sequence of elections, then, can lead to the aggregation of information both from the election results and from a leakage of information from candidates who cannot afford to risk losing today's election in order to protect that information for the next election. A theorem remains to be provided for the general case.

VI. Summary and Observations

We have learned several facts about information in elections. First, and perhaps least surprising, we have seen that private information is valuable to candidates because it can raise the probability of being elected, in a symmetric equilibrium, to above .5.

Second, we found that, even if candidates can react to their opponent's strategic choices and make inferences about their opponent's private information, no information aggregation occurs because no candidate will follow a strategy that will allow her information to leak. They all follow an essentially pooling strategy. The positive benefit due the private information and the constant-sum nature of the election game provide strong incentives to each candidate to conceal whatever they know from the other. Even when a large, finite number of moves are available, the outcome remains identical to that which occurs when the candidates can move once simultaneously and, therefore, cannot react to their opponent's choices. Rational expectations equilibria will not occur. We also noted that if one candidate must move before the other then that candidate loses any informational advantage. If the informed candidate must move first then rational expectations equilibria may arise.

Third, we found that adding a public poll to the election process affects strategic choices and outcomes. Although each candidate continues to be able to prevent leakage of her private information through her (pooling) strategic choice, she cannot prevent her opponent from learning through the poll. One might think that the informed candidate could match exactly the strategy of her opponent and cause the poll to predict a tie and, therefore, to provide no useful information, but her opponent can defeat this tactic with a mixed strategy. Since the poll provides both candidates with the same information and since candidates can successfully hide their private information, the election outcome with a poll is the same as that of the single choice model in section II if we update each candidate's prior with the poll.

Fourth, however, the candidates will not be able to hide private information by using a pooling strategy in a sequence of elections. Doing so may lead the candidate to lose the current election; so there is a cost to hiding information as well as a cost to revealing it. Although we prove no general results, we do provide an example that suggests two phenomena: (1) Some information aggregation will occur since it will be too costly to fully pool, and (2) candidates will skew their behavior in the sense that they will follow different strategies than those which would be best in a one-move model. A sequence of two elections with two privately informed candidates is not equivalent to two single elections and rational expectations may not occur.

Necessarily, we have several questions unanswered, and these questions are of three types. First, what occurs if the acquisition of the candidates' private information and the public polling information is costly? Because information aggregation is not complete, contrary to the assumption of a rational expectations equilibrium, there remains a benefit to its acquisition. What happens if the collection of private information is endogenous? If, in a simple model we allow private polls, in which reliability increases with the amount of money spent on it, we could compare the benefits from public polls to those of the private polls.

Second, what occurs if the moves of the candidates are costly? For example, we assume throughout that if a candidate uses a sequence of moves $A_1, A_2, \ldots, A_T$, then the probability that the candidate wins is $\Pi(A_T, B_T, m)$ which does not depend on the early moves. That is, all early moves are "cheap talk." An alternate assumption is to suppose that the probability of winning is $\Pi(A_1, \ldots, A_T, B_1, \ldots, B_T, m)$. While partial answers are given by the example of sequential elections in section V and by Bernhardt-Ingberman (1985), Banks (1987a), and Harrington (1988b), a more thorough and less ad hoc analysis is required. This would allow us, for example, to better understand the informational benefits from incumbency as well as the costs of being "locked" into positions. We also need to explicitly merge models of uninformed candidates with models of uninformed voters, which requires a much better understanding of the process by which voters acquire information.

Third, what occurs if the number of moves in each sequence is increased? For example, we might conjecture that as the number of polls prior to the election is increased, the election outcome approaches the outcome predicted by a rational expectations equilibrium. A similar result might be available for a large sequence of elections but, since candidates distort their strategies, it may be more difficult to establish.

Voters, Investors, and the Consumption of Political Information

Brian E. Roberts

The ignorance of the rational voter is a hallmark of modern political theory. As Downs (1957) suggests, a calculation of the private return on an investment in costly political information leads the rational voter to remain uninformed or ignorant. A similar calculation of the opportunity costs incurred in its digestion and interpretation limits the amount of even "costless" political information (that is, information that is freely made available) the rational voter chooses to assimilate.

It comes as little surprise then that modern political models of voter behavior are predicated on assumptions of uncertainty, ambiguity, or more generally, asymmetric information. What is generally not made explicit in such models is the availability and (discriminating) use of "costless" political information.[1] In a notable departure from this norm, McKelvey and Ordeshook (1985) present a rational choice election model that takes explicit account of the use of "costless" information by uninformed voters. The costless information is conveyed by the actions of *informed* voters who, by definition, have invested in costly information. Uninformed voters are not directly privy to the information guiding informed voters, but inferences drawn (without cost) from the behavior of informed voters ultimately permit uninformed voters to act *as if* they possess the same, costly information acquired by informed voters.

This essay examines empirically the theoretical proposition that, given enough exposure to the behavior of informed voters, uninformed voters will act as if they too possess costly political information. The analysis first addresses questions related to the existence and behavior of an informed voting population. This is followed by explicit consideration

---

The valuable comments of William Marshall, Barry Weingast, Arthur Denzau, Keith Krehbiel, and Mathew McCubbins are gratefully acknowledged.

1. There is a large empirical literature that addresses the issue of voter ignorance. Kinder and Sears (1982) review the empirical evidence and find Downs's conjecture to be well founded. The impact of various sources of costless information on voter behavior and how voters process what political information they do have is also the subject of extensive research (MacEuen 1984; Gant and Davis 1984).

of the ability of uninformed voters to infer indirectly otherwise costly information from the actions of informed voters. Ultimately this ability is manifested in decisions by uninformed voters that are made as if they possessed costly political information.

Providing motivation for the existence of an informed subset of voters is imperative in light of the compelling incentives for voters to remain rationally ignorant. In principle this is not a difficult task. Downs (1957), cited above as championing the rationally ignorant voter, suggests the prerequisites for a rational investment in costly information. Like any investment, it is made in expectation of earning some positive rate of return, pecuniary or otherwise. Downs states, "Naturally, the men who stand most to gain . . . are the ones who can best afford the expense of becoming expert. . . ." (1957, 254).

In practice, the opportunities to profit from, and thus best afford an investment in political information must be identified. This process is made easier with the recognition that the value of information about, for instance, the likely outcome of an election or the true policy preference of candidates is not derived solely by direct participants in the political process. For example, the prices of financial claims (e.g., stocks) whose values are contingent on the outcome of an election will reflect capital market participants' expectations about election outcomes: first, about who will win the election; second, about the economic consequences (policies) of the election if a given candidate wins. The prices of such politically sensitive assets thus provide a costless source of political information for the (otherwise) ignorant voter.[2] The expectations that market participants form derive from prior investments in political information.

The following empirical analysis exploits the existence of politically sensitive securities and tests whether voters' candidate preferences, as measured by opinion polls, change in accordance with new and valuable political information reflected in the prices of relevant securities. The analysis is not predicated on the ability of voters to infer directly the political information underlying security price changes. Rather, the relevant question is whether voters act as if they have access to the same costly information acquired by investors. The 1980 presidential election provides the backdrop to this analysis.

---

2. An unfortunate paradox arises in that other market participants may also view prices as a costless source of information and attempt to free ride on any original investment in costly information. In this case, the incentive for any investment in such information disappears. See Grossman and Stiglitz (1980) and Green (1977).

I. Expectations and Asymmetric Information

The salient feature distinguishing rational expectations models of the sort underlying both the McKelvey-Ordeshook model and the following empirical analysis from their ad hoc predecessors is the presumed existence of an underlying model of the economy that agents use to forecast prices or other such state contingent variables. Rational forecasts (expectations) are simply conditional expectations, given all past realizations of the variable in question (e.g., prices). These past realizations are viewed as having been generated by the underlying model. Given this forecasting heuristic, if all agents have the same information and use the same underlying model of the economy then, as Muth (1961) showed, the current conditional expectation of, for example, a future price is an unbiased predictor of that price.

Much of the work in rational expectations subsequent to Muth's has explored the implications of relaxing the strong assumptions in his basic model. An important branch of this research focuses on the homogeneity of information.[3] Particular attention is paid to the role of prices as a medium through which information is disseminated among differentially informed agents. A popular approach, first employed by Green (1973), is to assume an informational dichotomy wherein agents are either "informed" or "uninformed." Green shows that, in equilibrium, uninformed agents are able to inform themselves by inverting prices that impound the informed agents' information.[4] Grossman and Stiglitz (1980), and work by Grossman (1976,1977,1981), show the robustness of Green's result and explore the conditions under which agents seek to become informed.

There is no need to restrict the notion of an aggregate signal to an explicit market price for the results of Green and of Grossman and Stiglitz to obtain. Under the assumptions of rational expectations models such as Green's, any signal that aggregates heterogeneous information can be inverted to infer the values of the market parameters generating it. The McKelvey-Ordeshook model incorporates this feature of the rational expectations model and extends the logic to political markets. In their model an uninformed subset of a voting population inverts the results of an opinion poll (aggregate signal) taken over the entire voting population and infers informed voters' information about candidates'

---

3. See Grossman (1981) for a review of this literature.

4. Lucas (1972) was the first to describe how knowledge of the parameters of the underlying forecasting model could be inferred from the prices generated by the model.

policies.[5] In equilibrium, the uninformed voters vote as if they possess the information of the informed voters. This equilibrium is described as a fulfilled expectations equilibrium. It is in the spirit of a rational expectations equilibrium, though technically different. For although there does not exist an underlying stochastic process (model) of which poll results are realizations, voters infer the information content of polls and behave rationally with respect to the impounded information.

Prior to the McKelvey-Ordeshook model, uncertainty with respect either to candidates' policies or to voter preferences was usually described in terms of probability distributions or lotteries.[6] Equilibrium conditions were established only by imposing restrictions on the allowable classes of distributions or lotteries. As Austen-Smith (1983) points out, a particularly appealing aspect of the McKelvey-Ordeshook model is that the focus need not be on the nature of such restrictions because, "it is evidently not the information structure *per se* which 'induces' . . . equilibrium: it exists with full information."

While the McKelvey-Ordeshook model is an interesting contribution to the expectations literature, its major impact is felt in the study of political models of rational choice under uncertainty.[7] Informational issues, particularly those related to asymmetric information, dominate the two prominent sources of uncertainty in political models: voter uncertainty about candidate positions and, with inevitable symmetry, candidates' uncertainty about voters' preferences.

The expectations equilibrium in the McKelvey-Ordeshook model incorporates both kinds of uncertainty. Empirical evidence supports the theoretical underpinnings of Downsian rational voter ignorance that provide motivation for modeling voters as uncertain. Candidate uncertainty about voters' preferences is thought to be more intuitively plausible and does not require justification (Enelow and Hinich forthcoming *a*).

Beyond showing the equilibrium properties of their model, McKelvey and Ordeshook also consider the dynamic problem of how such an equilibrium is achieved.[8] The rate at which the voting population con-

---

5. Coincidentally, candidates learn about voter preferences from the polls and alter their policy positions in an effort to attract a majority of voters at the election.

6. For examples see Davis and Hinich (1968), Zeckhauser (1969), Davis, Hinich, and Ordeshook (1970), Shepsle (1972), Coughlin and Nitzan (1981), Enelow and Hinich (1982), Campbell (1983), Enelow and Hinich (1984*a*), Coughlin (1984), Enelow and Hinich (forthcoming *a*).

7. See Austen-Smith (1983).

8. The dynamics of achieving a rational expectations equilibrium is an important topic in its own right. See Cyert and DeGroot (1974) and Townsend (1978).

verges to a "fully informed" population depends on the relative size and distribution of the informed subset of voters. The possibility of voters revising their beliefs on the basis of past political events (elections, polls, etc.) is a necessary component of their model and provides the foundation for the following analysis.

II. Empirical Evidence

The following analysis is presented in two stages. The initial analysis identifies what are to be labeled as politically sensitive assets. Such assets have the characteristic of having payoffs that are contingent on the outcome of presidential elections. The value of such claims, if they exist, will vary prior to an election outcome as either the probability of the outcome changes or if the payoff is expected to differ from prior expectations. The second stage in the analysis tests two hypotheses implicit in the theoretical model of McKelvey and Ordeshook discussed above. The first hypothesis is that the values of politically sensitive assets reflect the information about voters' intentions found in public opinion polls. The second hypothesis is that opinion polls, in turn, reflect information about candidates impounded in the prices of politically sensitive assets.

The Identification of Politically Sensitive Assets

The existence of politically sensitive assets is implicit in Schwert's advocacy of capital market analysis in the study of regulatory policy changes (Schwert 1981). If government policy has systematic effects on the value of particular firms, then capital markets will reflect the impact of changes in government policy. By extension, if elected officials play a predictable role in government policy, then one can assume that any new information about either the likelihood of a policy change (election outcome) or the magnitude of the effects of any probable policy change will be capitalized expeditiously in an efficient capital market. On the strength of the preceding argument, tests for the existence of politically sensitive assets make use of capital market analysis.[9]

Ultimately, we wish to identify those assets that were particularly sensitive to the policy agenda before the voters in the 1980 presidential election. An analysis of the competing party platforms, which subjectively determines the relevant assets, is rejected in favor of an empirical filtering process that is designed to eliminate as much subjectivity as

---

9. In the context of this essay, capital market analysis studies the reaction of asset values to the release of new information.

possible. The use of capital market analysis effectively makes the decision to allow any asset to pass on to the next stage one that is based on the informed decisions of thousands of capital market participants.[10]

The methodology employed at this stage is based on capital market event-time analysis (Fama, Fisher, Jensen, and Roll 1969; Brown and Warner 1980, 1985). The model employed was a simple market model of the form:

$$R_{pt} = \alpha_p + \beta_p R_{mt} + \varepsilon_{pt},$$

where, R_{pt} = Daily rate of return on an equal-weighted industry portfolio, and R_{mt} = Daily rate of return on a value-weighted market index portfolio.[11]

The specification of this model presumes the existence of an underlying return generating process. In particular, this model maintains that the expected return on an asset (portfolio) is directly related to the covariance of the asset's return with the return on a market portfolio. Such a model is consistent with the Capital Asset Pricing Model (CAPM), a general equilibrium pricing model that underlies most modern financial theory (Sharpe 1964; Lintner 1965; Mossin 1966; Black 1972).

The rationale for using the market model is the desire to isolate the idiosyncratic effects of certain events (e.g., election outcomes) on the returns of specific assets. Idiosyncratic effects are those that cannot be attributed to market wide movements in stock prices. Estimates of the model's coefficients (α, β) prior to the events (e.g., elections) provide a benchmark for the behavior of returns in response to unanticipated outcomes. The extent to which an asset's return differs from its expected return (based on the market model) is a measure of a specific event's effect on the value of the asset. This idiosyncratic response, known as the asset's abnormal return, is proxied by the prediction error of the market model. Analysis of the error terms of the market model on or around election dates makes it possible to gauge the differential sensitivity of assets to the resolution of uncertainty in political markets.

In this study, a separate set of coefficients (α, β) from the market model was estimated for each of twenty-nine industry portfolios prior to

---

10. Reliance on capital market analysis does restrict the domain of potential assets to those that are traded as financial claims (equity) in organized markets (NYSE, AMEX). The diversity of the real assets underlying these claims is so great as to make this restriction of little consequence.

11. The index was constructed by the Center for Research on Stock Prices (CRSP) at the University of Chicago.

TABLE 1. Industry Portfolio Descriptions

Portfolio	SIC Code	Industry Description
1.	1040	Gold & Silver Ores
2.	1310	Petroleum & Natural Gas
3.	2040	Grain Mill Products
4.	2060	Sugar & Confectionery Products
5.	2080	Beverages
6.	2620	Paper Mills (Except Building)
7.	2810	Industrial Inorganic Chemicals
8.	2830	Drugs
9.	2840	Soap, Detergent, & Cleaners
10.	2910	Petroleum Refining
11.	3010	Tires & Inner Tubes
12.	3310	Blast Furnaces, Steel Works, & Rolling Mills
13.	3530	Construction, Mining, Mat. Handling Equip.
14.	3550	Special Industrial Machinery
15.	3570	Office, Computing, & Accounting Machines
16.	3620	Electrical Industrial Apparatus
17.	3630	Household Appliances
18.	3660	Communication Equipment
19.	3670	Electronic Components & Accessories
20.	3710	Motor Vehicles & Parts
21.	3720	Aircraft & Parts
22.	4010	Railroads
23.	4510	Air Transportation: Certified Carriers
24.	4920	Gas Production & Distribution
25.	4930	Utilities (Combined)
26.	5310	Department Stores
27.	5410	Grocery Stores
28.	6710	Holding Offices
29.	6720	Investment Offices

each general (presidential) election from 1964 to 1980. The resignation of Richard Nixon on August 8, 1974, was treated as an election. The twenty-nine portfolios were selected using the following criteria. Each portfolio consists of at least ten firms. Each firm in a given portfolio had the same three-digit primary Standard Industrial Classification (SIC)[12] code and had securities traded daily from 1964 to 1981. Satisfaction of these criteria was based on data from the computer files of CRSP at the University of Chicago (see table 1 for a list of industries).

Sets of coefficients were estimated using CRSP daily return data over a 175-day period ending 50 days prior to the election involved. The

---

12. The Standard Industrial Classification code classifies firms on the basis of their primary line of business. At the three-digit level of classification used in this study there are approximately 300 separate industies identified in the United States.

TABLE 2. Capital Market Filter Results: Surviving Industry Portfolios

Portfolio	SIC Code	Industry Description	P-Level*
1.	1310	Petroleum & Natural Gas	.959
2.	2040	Grain Mill Products	.996
3.	2060	Sugar & Confectionery Products	.980
4.	3010	Tires & Inner Tubes	.978
5.	3560	General Industrial Machinery	.980
6.	3630	Household Appliances	.983
7.	3720	Aircraft & Aircraft Parts	.990
8.	4930	Utilities (Combined)	.980
9.	5410	Grocery Stores	.995

*The reported P-Level is that associated with S, as defined below.

$Ho: P_i \sim U[0,1] \quad i = 1, \ldots, 6$

$S = \sum_n - 2Ln(P_i) \sim \chi^2(2n)$

coefficients and the actual return of the market portfolio on the first trading day following an election were used to generate a predicted return for each industry portfolio. The difference between predicted and actual returns measures the abnormal performance of the industry portfolios on the first day of trade after the election. In an efficient capital market all residual uncertainty about the outcome of an election will be capitalized with the opening of the financial markets.[13]

Abnormal returns were measured for each of the six elections. The hypothesis that the abnormal performance of any particular portfolio differed from zero for all six elections was tested.[14] The results of these tests are presented in table 2. Nine of the twenty-nine portfolios had abnormal performances that differed from zero at a 5 percent level of significance. These nine portfolios were carried forward to the next stage of the analysis.

The filter survived by nine portfolios was coarse. Elections were treated as homogeneous events. No account was taken of the outcome of an election, or the positions and party of the winning candidate. The filter is likely to exclude some politically sensitive assets because of the

---

13. The NYSE opened for the first time on an election day for the November, 1984, general election.

14. The abnormal returns were standardized by dividing them by the standard deviation of the model errors over the estimation period (see Brown and Warner 1980). The standardized abnormal returns are distributed student-t under the assumption of no abnormal performance. The null hypothesis was that the P-levels associated with the standardized abnormal return test statistic were distributed uniformly over the unit interval. Thus $S_p = \Sigma 2\ln(1 - P_{pt}) \sim \chi^2(2n)$.

simplistic empirical model employed. However, the use of such a naive filter avoids subjectivity in both appropriately characterizing elections and in constructing portfolios. Moreover, the portfolios that did emerge are probably quite sensitive to political events and, therefore, are potent subjects for the subsequent analysis.

The Impact of Poll Results on Stock Returns

The second stage of the analysis focuses exclusively on the 1980 U.S. presidential election. This stage provides a test of the hypothesis that voters' intentions as reflected in opinion polls affect the prices of politically sensitive assets. Recall from the theoretical model that the price of the election contingent claim reflects traders' assessment of voters' preferences. Opinion polls are of such great potential value to traders that it is doubtful that investors would settle for the information in the polls released to the national media at irregular intervals prior to an election. In fact, the market for private polls (the bread and butter of most pollsters) is so extensive that it is plausible to believe that investors who wish it are provided with almost continuous polling data. The availability of such data to investors poses a problem for the researcher with access to the results of public, media polls only. If, as the theory maintains, market prices reflect continuous polling, how is it possible to verify empirically such price behavior with discontinuous poll data?

The approach taken in this study is to view media polls as providing redundant information. Viewing the private poll data as continuous (daily), it is then reasonable to believe that on the days that media polls are conducted (but rarely reported) private polls are both conducted and reported. On these days both the media and private polls are drawing from the same distribution of voter preferences. The information that is eventually reported by the media, therefore, is available to investors via private polls on the day the media polls are conducted. Fortunately, the dates of the media polls are identified.

The data used in this study are based on the three-way Gallup Presidential Trial Heats. The raw poll data were transformed to provide a measure of the implied probability of a Reagan victory (See fig. 1).[15]

---

15. The poll results were assumed to be drawn from a binomial distribution with an unknown probability of success, p. This parameter, p, was assumed to have a beta distribution. Investors were assumed to have diffuse, flat priors on the parameter's location. Investors are portrayed as Bayesians using poll results to revise their (initially diffuse) priors on the probability of a Reagan victory. The use of the beta/binomial conjugate pair has a long history in applied statistics (Hornsnaell 1957). A conjugate pair is appealing in the case of diffuse priors because the functional form of the posterior distribution remains the same as that of the prior distribution. In this case, the investors' posterior distribution

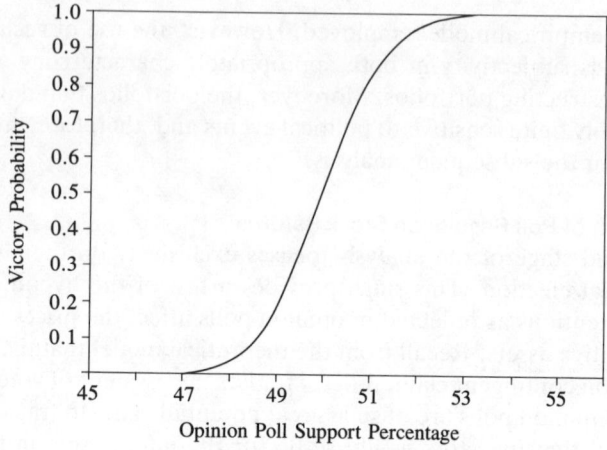

Fig. 1. Implied probability of a Reagan victory

Investors are assumed to react to the change in implied probability from one poll to the next.

The empirical model is designed to overcome the problems presented by the use of discrete poll data. As discussed above, political information is available on a continuous basis to market participants. Media poll data provide only snapshots of the political climate, while between any two media polls volumes of new political information can reach and are priced in the capital market. The discrete poll data can be used to explain cumulative market effects between successive polls. The possibility exists of missing large but offsetting movements in the value of politically sensitive assets in the interim. The dates and frequency of media polls are to some extent, however, endogenous with respect to events that may substantially influence voters' preferences, e.g., party conventions, debates, etc.

---

of p (following an observed poll result) remains a beta distribution. The beta density is of the form: $f(p) = (\alpha + \beta + 1)! p^{\alpha}(1 - p)^{\beta}/(\alpha!\beta!)$, where, $0 < p < 1$, and $\alpha, \beta > 1$. The assumption of diffuse priors implies that $\alpha = \beta = 0$. Each poll constitutes a sample from a binomial distribution with a draw of r successes in n trial, where n is the sample size of the poll (typically around 2,000) and r is the number of voters preferring Reagan. Because the Gallup polls included a third candidate (and undecided voters) the data was modified to accommodate the binomial distribution by attributing to Reagan the proportion: (Reagan/ Reagan + Carter)). The likelihood of p is $1(p|r,n)pr(1 - p)n - r$, and the posterior density of p is $f(p|r,n)f(p)1(p|r,n)$, where $f(p|r,n) = (n + 1)! p^r(1 - p)^{n-r}/[r!(n - r)!]$, $E[p] = (r + 1)/(n + 1)$, $E[p^2] = [(r + 2)(r + 1)]/[(n + 3)(n + 2)]$, and $\sigma_p^2 = E[p^2] - \{E[p]\}^2 = \{[(r + 2)(r + 1)]/[(n + 3)(n + 2)]\} - \{[(r + 1)(r + 1)]/[(n + 1)(n + 1)]\}$. Thus, the implied probability of a Reagan victory $Pr(p < .5)$ equals $Pr(Z < (E[p] - .5)/\sigma_p)$. Given the large sample size, the beta distribution is approximately normal. Therefore Z is $N(0,1)$.

The Empirical Model

A two-step process is used to test the hypothesis that the returns of politically sensitive assets can be explained, in part, by changes in voters' preferences. The first step uses the same techniques employed in the capital market filter. For each of the nine portfolios surviving the filter, the estimated coefficients (α, β) of a market model were used to generate daily residual series over the time period spanned by the Gallup poll data.[16] The estimated model is of the form:

$$R_{pt} = \alpha_p + \beta_p R_{mt} + \varepsilon_{pt} \quad p = 1, \ldots, 9 \quad (1)$$

As in the model used for the capital market filter, R_{pt} is the daily rate of return on an industry portfolio (p), and R_{mt} is the daily rate of return on the CRSP value-weighted market index.

The second step tests the explanatory power of poll data. The nine residual series (ε_p) from the first step were used to construct dependent variables for separate estimates of the following model:

$$ERCUM_{p,t} = \alpha_p + \delta_{p1} P_t + \delta_{p2} P_{t-1} + v_{p,t} \quad p = 1, \ldots, 9 \quad (2)$$

where, $ERCUM_{p,t}$ is the cumulative estimated residual for portfolio p between successive poll dates. In other words, the estimated daily residuals, ε_{pt}, were summed over the trading days between consecutive polls. This process yielded nine observations for each of the nine portfolios. P_t is the implied probability of a Reagan victory from the poll taken at the end of the interval over which the daily residuals comprising $ERCUM_{p,t}$ were summed. P_{t-1} is the implied probability of a Reagan victory from the poll that precedes that cumulative residual interval of $ERCUM_{p,t}$.

Note that the theory suggests that the portfolio returns should be explained by changes in the implied probability of a Reagan victory, yet the above model uses the levels of two successive polls (P_t, P_{t-1}). The latter specification is used in light of the Bayesian characterization of investors that allows for the possibility that information in previous polls is not entirely discounted. If, in fact, investors derive information solely from strict changes this would be indicated by the special case of $\delta_1 = -\delta_2$. The coefficient estimates, presented below, do not support this hypothesis.

---

16. The model was estimated over a 150-day period ending the day before the first poll was taken.

Econometric Considerations

Estimation of Equation (2) presents a number of econometric difficulties. First, under the assumption of constant daily variance of stock returns, the irregular number of days between polls introduces, by construction, a violation of the OLS assumption of constant error variance. Therefore, the model was estimated using a weighted least squares technique.[17]

The second difficulty arises from the paucity of observations. The analysis is limited to the results of ten poll samples. The model itself was estimated with nine observations; the presence of a lagged term (P_{t-1}) forced the loss of one observation. The main statistical consequence of so few observations again relates to the model's error structure. Only a limited appeal can be made to the Central Limit Theorem to bolster claims of normally distributed error terms. Using the Shapiro-Wilk W statistic, normality was not rejected for of any of the nine residual series.

The potential misspecification of the model represents a third difficulty. Because this relates to observed coefficient estimates, discussion of it follows the presentation of results.

Results

Equation (2) was estimated separately for each of the nine portfolios that survived the initial capital market filter. The regression results are presented in table 3.

Two aspects of these results are of interest. First, the joint significance of the poll parameters, δ_1 and δ_2, provides direct evidence on the hypothesis being tested. Recall that our interest was on the ability of poll data to explain, in part, the rate of return on politically sensitive assets. The dependent variable in Equation (2) is constructed, for any given portfolio, from the estimated error series from the market model, Equation (1). By definition this variable encompasses those aspects of the portfolio's return that cannot be explained by market-wide movements. Estimation of Equation (2) is a test for the existence of an industry-specific political component in those error terms. An F-Test was performed for each regression to test the joint hypothesis that $\delta_1 = \delta_2 = 0$. This hypothesis was rejected at a 10 percent level of significance for four of the nine portfolios. These results are also presented in table 3.

A finding of four significant portfolios is encouraging. Recall that the nine portfolios surviving the first stage did so on the strength of their

---

17. The weights (W_t) were defined as: $W_t = 1/\sqrt{N_t}$, where N_t is the number of trading days between polls (t) and ($t + 1$) (see Johnston 1963, 228–38).

TABLE 3. Estimates of Asset Sensitivity to Poll Results $ERCUM_{p,t} = \alpha_p + \delta_{p1}P_t + \delta_{p2}P_{t-1} + V_{p,t}$ (Eq. 2)

Portfolio[a]	δ_1 (t-test)	δ_2 (t-test)	F(2,6)	P-Level
1.	−.0113 (−.329)	.0169 (−.509)	.251	.7858
2.	.0044 (.388)	.0108 (.985)	.724	.5228
3.	.0393 (.590)	−.0127 (−.199)	.175	.844
4.	−.0151 (−.593)	−.0171 (−.701)	.584	.5867
5.	.0146 (2.159)	.0249 (3.829)	12.995**	.0066
6.	.0152 (.951)	.0395 (2.57)	4.818*	.0565
7.	.0242 (1.284)	.0381 (2.103)	4.114*	.0750
8.	.0035 (.293)	−.0223 (−1.947)	1.931	.2252
9.	.0244 (1.789)	.0185 (1.406)	3.572*	.0951

*significant at .1
**significant at .01
[a]From table 2.

sensitivity across six elections. The tests at the current stage are limited to only 1980 election data. The emergence of four significant portfolios suggests that certain policy issues are raised repeatedly in general elections; other issues are election specific.

A second interesting aspect of the above results relates to the sign and magnitude of the poll parameters. As suggested above, these parameters provide information about the use of poll information by capital market participants. Focusing on the significant equations (5, 6, 7, and 9), it is evident that the special case of investors using first differences ($\delta_1 = -\delta_2$) does not hold. Furthermore, because the parameters are consistently of the same sign, information seems to be drawn from polls preceding the two most recently conducted. Thus the poll parameters indicate that the lag structure specified in Equation (1) is truncated. This is the misspecification problem mentioned above. Given no strong priors on the appropriate lag structure and given the limited degrees of freedom with which to explore more elaborate structures, no respecification was undertaken.

44 Models of Strategic Choice in Politics

The Sensitivity of Polls to Capital Market Signals

The second hypothesis generated by the theoretical model maintains the existence of a reciprocal flow of information between economic and political markets. The hypothesis is that political information reflected in the value of politically sensitive assets will subsequently be reflected in polls.

Many of the results from rational expectations models are relevant to this issue. Lucas (1972) suggests that an aggregate signal, such as a price, can be inverted to learn the underlying, exogenous determinants of the signal. The results of Green (1973) and of Grossman and Stiglitz (1980) are based on this intuition. In the problem at hand, voters may be conceived of as having in mind a model that they use to predict an asset's response to a given poll announcement. For instance, consider the model that was used above to explain asset returns partly as a function of poll data. Voters may be viewed as having prior beliefs about the value of the parameters δ_1 and δ_2—the asset's sensitivity to poll data. The extent to which the actual asset return differs from the voters' prediction—based on assumptions about voters' perceived parameter values—is a measure of the (informed) market's information about candidates' policy positions. Rational voters will revise estimates of δ_1 and δ_2 on the basis of their prediction errors.

As an example, suppose the politically sensitive asset in question is an acre of land that yearly produces 100 bushels of wheat. Furthermore, suppose that the winning candidate will choose a subsidy to the production of wheat, ranging from \$0.00 to \$1.00 per bushel. Voters believe that candidate D is pro-farming and will choose a subsidy of \$1.00. Candidate R is known to be extremely free-market and will choose $S = \$0.00$ with certainty. The value of land is: $V = \text{prob}(D)*\$100.00$. The most recent poll showed p ($\text{prob}(D)$) to be .5 and $V = \$0.50$. A subsequent poll showed p to be .8 and in the interim V rose to .72. Were SD believed by the market to be \$1.00 then for $p = .8$, $V = .8$. In order for p to be .8 and V to be .72, it must be that $SD = .9$. Traders must have uncovered information indicating a moderation of D's position. At the margin some voters will change their candidate allegiance in light of this market information and the next poll will show a change in p.

Such a scenario is consistent with a rational expectations model but must seem far-fetched to champions of the rationally ignorant voter. To claim that voters, as a matter of habit, read the daily financial press to learn about candidates' policy positions is a tenuous proposition.

The approach here is to view voters as heterogeneous rather than as uniformly unable to make use of capital market information. The dichotomy proposed by McKelvey and Ordeshook (1985), with some voters informed and some uninformed, is a less general characterization of a voting population. In this light, the distinction between a voter and a trader (capital market participant) loses some precision. The decision to become informed is also a decision to consider trading. Those voters with a comparative advantage in the collection of costly political information have an incentive to do so given an opportunity to trade profitably on such information. The profitability of such transactions depends on the subsequent dissemination of the relevant information. The observed capitalization of this information is evidence of informed voters/traders. This subset of informed voters is the foundation upon which the entire voting population is informed in the McKelvey-Ordeshook model. In that model, the number of informed voters does not have to be large in order to generate convergence of a voting population to a fully informed equilibrium.

The Empirical Model and Results

The model used in these tests is based on the rational expectations scenario described above. The prediction errors from Equation 2 (v_{pt}) are used to construct explanatory variables for changes in implied probabilities. These variables are designed to reflect changes in the perceived sensitivity of politically sensitive assets.

The model is specified as

$$DPRON_{t+3} = \alpha_p + \sum_{p=1}^{4} \beta_{p,t} EPORT_t + \mu \qquad (3)$$

where $DPRON_t$ is the change in probability of a Reagan victory between successive polls ($P_{t+1} - P_t$). $EPORT_{p,t}$ is the measure of voters' changed perceptions of Reagan's policy positions. These perception changes are induced by information impounded in the prices of politically sensitive assets. There are four explanatory variables, each derived from one of the four portfolios whose value was found sensitive to poll data in Equation (2).

Each of the independent variables was constructed as follows:

Let $X_{p,t} = [v_{p,t} / DPRON_t] = [v_{p,t} / (P_{t+1}-P_t)]$,

then, define

$$EPORT_{p,t} = \Delta X_{p,t}$$
$$= X_{p,t+1} - X_{p,t+1}$$
$$= [v_{p,t+1}/DPRON_{t+1}] - [v_{p,t}/DPRON_t]$$
$$= [v_{p,t+1}/(P_{t+2}-P_{t+1})] - [v_{p,t}/(P_{t+1}-P_t)].$$

$v_{p,t}$ is the estimated error for portfolio p (at time t) from Equation (2). $DPRON_t$ is as defined above. The variable $\Delta X_{p,t}$ is a naive estimate of the sensitivity of portfolio p to changes in implied probabilities.[18] Thus, $EPORT_{p,t}$ represents changes in assessed sensitivity of particular portfolios induced by capital market reevaluations of candidates' policy positions.

The ability of changes in the political sensitivity of four industry portfolios to explain changes in implied probabilities of a Reagan victory is tested by the estimation of Equation (3). The four industry portfolios were chosen on the basis of the sensitivity of their returns to opinion poll data in Equation (2). The specification of the variables and the timing of events precluded a simultaneous estimation of equations (2) and (3). Estimation of Equation (3) yielded the following results:

$$DPRON_t = -.207 + 7.776\ EPORT_{1,t} + 3.076\ EPORT_{2,t}$$
$$(.039)\quad (.721)\qquad\qquad (.639)$$

$$+\ 8.672\ EPORT_{3,t} + 8.008\ EPORT_{4,t}$$
$$(1.342)\qquad\qquad (.971)$$

(standard error)
$$\bar{R}^2 = .9850$$

The uniformly low standard errors of the above estimation are very encouraging. Equations (2) and (3) were estimated separately, yet the returns of the four portfolios found to be sensitive to poll data in Equation (2) are sources of explanatory power for changes in subsequent polls as evidenced by the above results.

The specification of Equation (3) introduces a potentially serious statistical problem. Although related in a highly nonlinear fashion, there is a common term in the dependent and independent variables.[19] The nature of this relationship may have induced a nonobvious enhancement of the statistical significance of the linear relationship specified in the equation. To assuage the doubts raised by this problem, Equation (3) was reestimated without the scaling factors on the independent vari-

---

18. Voters naively attribute the error terms (v_t) in Equation (2) to a model of the form: $v_t = X_t P_t$. In other words the error is naively explained as a function of changes in the probable outcome of the election. The coefficient, ΔX_t, thus represents the voters' new assessment of the sensitivity of the candidate's policy position (election payoff) to changes in probabilities.

19. In the following expansion of Equation (3) note the presence of the term P_{t+2} in both the dependent and independent variables: $DPRON_{t+3} = EPORT_t$, and $[P_{t+3} - P_{t+2}] = [v_{t+1}/(P_{t+2} - P_{t+1})] - [v_t/(P_{t+1} - P_t)]$.

ables—the source of the specification problem. The results were quite robust; all the coefficients were significant at a 5 percent confidence level and the adjusted R^2 was .8663. The slight loss in explanatory power may be attributable to either the conviction that the second equation was not correctly specified (i.e., the scaling factor was integral to the relationship) or to statistical problems introduced to the original equation through the inclusion of the common factor.

Summary and Conclusion

This essay studies political information. Empirical evidence is presented on the use of political information by participants in both the political process and economic markets. The hypotheses that are tested follow from formal models of elections that predict a full information equilibrium when the electorate is initially comprised of both informed and uninformed voters. The testable implications of such models explored in this essay are (1) that the prices of assets whose values are contingent on the outcome of an election will, prior to an election, reflect changes in voters' candidate preferences; and (2) that voters' candidate preferences are influenced by political information conveyed by changes in the values of politically sensitive assets. The empirical evidence is convincing in tests of both hypotheses and thus suggests some interesting conclusions.

Scholars of the electoral process will note that the evidence suggests that voters have a fairly sophisticated sensitivity to changes in the economic consequences of elections. The results are not meant to suggest that voters are sensitive to multiple economic dimensions of an election. A more realistic interpretation is that particular subsets of voters are sensitive to particular or industry-specific issues rather than (or in addition to) macroeconomic issues. Furthermore, this sensitivity is of a distinctly prospective character. Voters are reacting to anticipated policy changes, not to retrospective reevaluations of incumbent performance.

While it is difficult, both theoretically and empirically, to say whether or not voters react directly to financial information (prices), it is clear that both voters and investors react to similar information about policy changes; investors simply expend greater resources to acquire and to respond to political information more quickly. This apparent sensitivity to anticipated policy changes (a purely prospective reaction) is further testimony to the sophistication of voters in the processing of political information. Evidence from more elections and a more sophisticated filtering process for the identification of politically sensitive assets should further substantiate the results of this study.

Political Investment, Voter Perceptions, and Candidate Strategy: An Equilibrium Spatial Analysis

Melvin J. Hinich and Michael C. Munger

Clearly, contributors offer dollars and other resources in exchange for political favors. But why do legislators seek such contributions? Alternatively, why does it cost so much to campaign? Existing work in the formal literature is not capable of offering answers to these questions, primarily because it presents no clear representation of how voters use information in deciding among candidates. If voters have complete information, spending on advertising should not influence their relative assessment of candidates. But then money does a campaign no good, so candidates seeking reelection should not offer any valuable favors in exchange for contributions. The usual alternative approach is predicated on the rational ignorance of voters. Yet, if voters are entirely (though rationally) ignorant, whoever spends the most money should win.

We do not find either of these two predictions to be empirically satisfying: candidates allocate much of their time and resources to the pursuit of contributions, but spending more money does not guarantee victory by any means. In the following pages we investigate the relationship between campaign expenditures, voter reactions, and candidate strategies in determining pluralities. The results we present add to the understanding of legislative institutions in two ways: (1) we present an explicit spatial depiction of the political process, including campaign expenditures directly in the perceptions of voters in making political choices; and (2) we present a strategic Cournot-Nash duopoly game between the candidates in influencing this choice, and are able to characterize the equilibria of this game. The basic logic of the model has pessimistic implications about the effectiveness of campaign reform and

---

The authors wish to thank Henry Chappell, Allan Meltzer, Peter Ordeshook, Keith Poole, Thomas Romer, and the participants of workshops at the University of Texas, the California Institute of Technology, and the Carnegie Conference on Political Economy for many helpful comments. Any errors that remain are our responsibility.

electoral competition. We predict a constantly increasing spiral of expenditures, but with no electoral gain by candidates, and no informational benefits to citizens in making their voting decisions.

The paper is organized as follows: section I reviews previous work on the electoral process with contributions and rational investors. Section II presents our spatial model of voter choice between candidates. The third section outlines a model of investor contributions as contingent claims. Section IV investigates the form of the simple expenditure game between candidates, and the fifth section presents the equilibrium result of this game. Section VI considers some extensions to account for the impact of incumbency and campaign finance laws. The final section presents concluding remarks.

I. Previous Work

Existing research on the impact of campaign spending on voter choice between candidates has typically taken one of two approaches, both of which extend Downs's (1957) conception of "net party differential." The first presumes that voters are paid implicit or explicit bribes to participate, and choose between candidates or parties based only on a comparison of the contingent wealth positions (Barro 1973; Becker 1983). The second includes expenditures directly in the function aggregating votes across individual voters (Ben-Zion and Eytan 1974; Bental and Ben-Zion 1975; Denzau and Munger 1986).

The difficulties with these uses of information by voters are articulated by Denzau and Munger in their comparison of rational ignorance and "civics class" full information assumptions about voters. If voters were ignorant, and neither candidate possessed some additional advantage in credibility, then the candidate spending the most must win, and elections become fund-raising contests. The alternative of full information is even less palatable: advertising can have no effect whatsoever. The fundamental question, then, is precisely *how* money matters in electoral campaigns.

Austen-Smith (1987a) presents a partial answer. In his theory of electoral competition interest groups compete for political favors by contributing to candidates. Candidates in turn spend money to affect the vote. Austen-Smith succinctly states what we believe to be the most important issues:

> ... while candidates adopt and state the positions with which they contest the election, they cannot do so without ambiguity. People learn of candidates' positions through the various media, in political debate, and so on.

Such intervening variables *introduce noise into the signal* sent by a candidate, who must then devote resources to articulating a position. (P. 126; emphasis added)

The role of campaign contributions/expenditures is to reduce the variance of voters' perceptions of candidate positions. Austen-Smith does not fully develop this insight, because he restricts the focus of each candidate's expenditures to reducing his own variance. In the next two sections we set forth a game theoretic model where expenditures influence the noise associated with voter perceptions of both candidates, and voters vote probabilistically.

II. Probabilistic Model of Spatial Voter Choice

The spatial model of voter choice derives from Downs (1957) and Black (1958). The more formal subsequent model of Davis and Hinich (1966, 1967) allows us to flesh out and make rigorous the ambiguous concept of "voter desires." The clearly defined and fixed preferences of voters in the model give precise meaning to the well-known prediction of Hotelling (1929) that voters will prefer the candidate "nearest" to them in terms of policy.

The classical spatial model of voting rests on several key assumptions. First, voters possess complete and transitive preferences over the set of policies. Second, voters use certain indices to measure policy, both for expressing their own preferences and for judging the positions of candidates. Third, all voters use the same, and only these, indices to measure any given policy. Finally, since (absent utter homogeneity) every voter cannot obtain his most preferred set of public goods, voters evaluate candidates according to a loss function based on the divergence between the candidate's proposed platform and the voter's ideal point.

This model, by assuming voters react only to policy platforms, makes two rather extreme implicit presumptions about voter behavior. First, there exists a sharp discontinuity in the likelihood a voter votes for a particular candidate, based on a knife-edge comparison of the weighted Euclidean distance between the voter's ideal and each platform. Except in the case of absolute indifference, where the voter flips a coin, behavior is deterministic. Second, all of the candidates' attributes other than their asserted platforms are irrelevant to the voting decision. Candidates cannot differ in terms of the credibility of their commitments to a particular platform. Voters do not choose a candidate because his character and leadership qualities make him appear well-suited to react competently in times of crisis or respond to unforeseen issues.

A more realistic treatment of voter choice, relaxing several of the restrictive assumptions of the classical model, is probabilistic voting (Hinich, Ledyard, and Ordeshook, 1973; and Hinich, 1977). The probabilistic model modifies the classical model by treating choice as a utility function that is monotonic in utility. Voters choose according to the classical model, but an observer cannot determine with certainty how a population will behave. An important advantage of this approach is that it incorporates nonpolicy characteristics of candidates, such as character, credibility, and leadership. Empirical research on the importance of nonpolicy characteristics argues strongly for its inclusion, and the probabilistic approach appears to be the most parsimonious way of accomplishing this (Enelow and Hinich 1982, 1984b). The likelihood of voting for the "closest" candidate is a continuous, monotonically decreasing function of the difference between the voter's ideal and the positions of the two candidates, rather than a step function. This approach has proved fruitful in several contexts (e.g., Coughlin and Nitzan 1981; Enelow and Hinich forthcoming a; Coughlin 1982; and Austen-Smith 1987a).

Our use of probabilistic voting in conditions of voter uncertainty dictates the following assumptions be made explicit.

A1. Connectedness: Voters possess preferences over all issues in the N-dimensional *policy space, denoted* Ω, where preferences are represented by an ideal point, or Nx1 column vector of preferred positions $X_i = (x_{1i}, x_{2i}, \ldots, x_{Ni})'$.

A2. Loss Function: Each voter evaluates the candidates according to the spatial closeness of the projected (mapped from Π) candidate positions to his *ideal point, denoted* X_i.

A3. Uncertain Candidate Ideology: Two candidates, Theta and Psi, have fixed, though from voters' perspective uncertain, positions upon the classical left-right Downsian *economic dimension, denoted* Π.

A4. Predictive Dimension: Voters have accurate, common perceptions of the *vector of mappings, denoted* v, from the economic dimension Π (where the origin is the status quo) onto the policy space Ω.

We can now write the positions of Theta and Psi as vectors in the policy space Ω (Enelow and Hinich 1989b), assuming certainty of candidate positions on Π. For each voter i:

$$\theta_i = \Pi_\theta v = (\Pi_\theta v_1, \Pi_\theta v_2, \ldots, \Pi_\theta v_N), \text{ and} \tag{1}$$

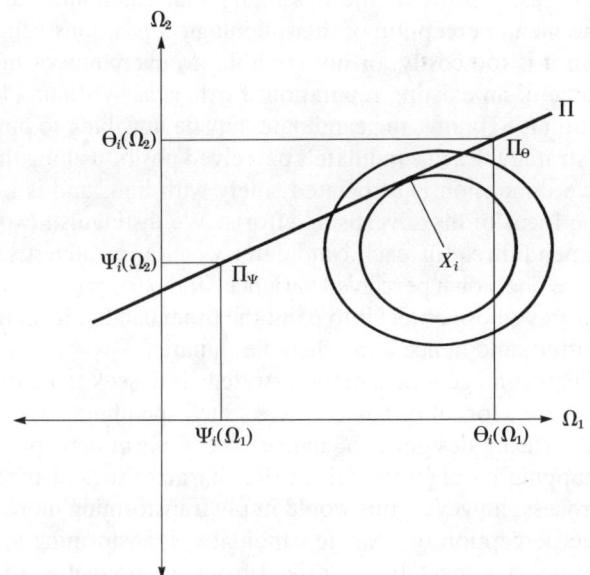

Fig. 1. Mapping from the economic dimension Π onto policy Ω

$$\Psi_i = \Pi_\Psi v. \tag{2}$$

The relation between candidate position on the predictive dimension and his imputed policy stand is depicted in figure 1 for the case of two dimensions, where Π is projected onto the two dimensions Ω_1 and Ω_2.

The more interesting case, and our focus, is where voter perceptions exhibit specific and idiosyncratic error γ. For i, Theta's position is:

$$\theta_i = (\Pi_\theta + \gamma_{i\theta})v \tag{3}$$

$$E(\gamma_{i\theta}) = 0 \tag{4}$$

$$E(\gamma^2_{i\theta}) = \sigma^2_{i\theta}. \tag{5}$$

Thus, each voter has an unbiased, but imperfect, perception of the candidate's behavior once he is in office. Given this model of voter perception, candidates have two conceptual alternatives in conducting their campaigns:

a) Change the mean or variance of the perception of Π_θ or Π_Ψ: As noted above (A3), we do not presently allow (though the model can easily address) the possibility that candidates can change the mean perception of their ideological positions.[1] In the short run it is too costly, or not credible, to overcome or modify the force of an existing reputation; further, as Wittman (1977) and Lott (1987) note, the candidate may be unwilling to pursue such a strategy. Each candidate's perceived position along the predictive dimension is associated solely with him, and is as a result the focus of his advertising efforts. We distinguish two types of expenditures for each candidate: s (self), or advertising to reduce one's own perceived variance, and o (opponent), or expenditures whose object is to paint the other candidate as an uncommitted, and hence unpredictable, lunatic.

b) The second general electoral strategy is to seek to modify one or more v_k, for all or some voters. Such spending would promote advertising designed to change voters' *mean* perceptions of the mapping parameters. Given the characteristics of the mapping process, however, this would imply transforming more than just the perception of a single candidate. Transforming v_j modifies *all* policy expectations derived from the predictive dimension. The mapping vector v is therefore a commonly held perception, induced in voters' minds by experience over a wide array of party and ideological affiliations. No individual could much affect either the mean or variance of v, though groups such as parties and phenomena exogenous to our model (particularly realignments) may sharply transform the mapping parameters.

Fortunately, even a model restricted to the first strategy (changing variance along the predictive dimension) has rich implications for an electoral game. We rewrite (5) to account for the four campaign strategy variables (s_θ, o_θ, s_Ψ, and o_Ψ) of the two candidates:

$$E(\gamma^2_{i\theta}) = \sigma^2_{i\theta}(s_\theta, o_\Psi), \quad \text{and} \quad E(\gamma^2_{i}\Psi) = \sigma^2_{i\Psi}(s_\Psi, o_\theta). \tag{5'}$$

We assume s expenditures reduce the candidates' "self" variance, and o expenditures increase that of the opponent. "Self" variance decreases concavely in s and opponent's increases concavely in o (see fig. 2).

---

1. There are important theoretical and empirical reasons to be careful in modeling candidate movements along the predictive dimension. Dougan and Munger (1989) and Lott (1986, 1987) provide compelling reasons to doubt the efficacy of the mean movement strategy, particularly in the short run (i.e., any single election). A long-run (repeated election game) model, or a treatment of nomination procedures, would be more appropriate for credible movements along Π. Chappell (1988) questions the voters' abilities to gauge candidate credibility unless they know the candidates' motivations.

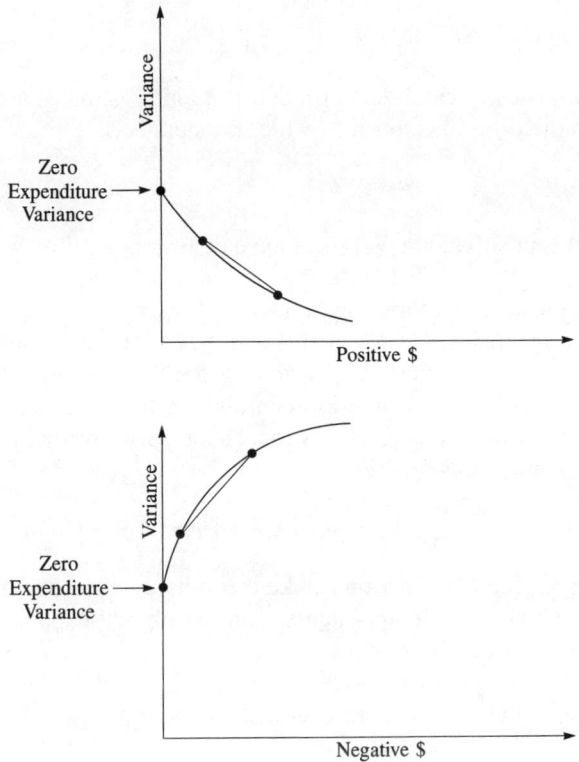

Fig. 2. Response of perceived variance of a candidate's position to positive self (*s*) negative opponent (*o*) advertising

Next, we define the *i*th voter's deterministic spatial utility function and net candidate differential NCD:

$$U_i = U_i[\theta_i - X_i] \tag{6}$$

$$NCD_i = (U_i[\theta_i - X_i] - U_i[\Psi_i - X_i]) \tag{7}$$

Allowing perceptual errors according to (4) and (5′), assuming quadratic utility, and using the notation $[\theta - X]^2 = \Sigma_k(\theta_k - X_k)^2$ for the Euclidean distance squared between θ and X:[2]

$$U_i[\hat{\theta}_i - X_i] = -[\hat{\theta}_i - X_i]^2, \; U_i[\hat{\Psi}_i - X_i] = -[\hat{\Psi}_i - X_i]^2, \tag{8}$$

---

2. In the present paper we implicitly assume identical issue salience. This assumption is made solely for notational convenience; allowing the salience matrix to be other than some scalar multiplied by an identity matrix simply transforms the indifference curves into ellipses, as Enelow and Hinich (1984) have shown.

$$E(U_i[\theta_i - X_i]) = -E([\theta_i - X_i]^2) - v^2_\theta \sigma^2_{i\theta}(\cdot) \tag{9}$$

$$E(NCD_i) = -[\theta_i - X_i]^2 + [\Psi_i - X_i]^2 + v^2\delta_i. \tag{10}$$

For the purposes of candidate strategies the interesting part of this expression is the difference term δ_i, which we define as:

$$\delta_i = \sigma^2_{i\Psi}(s_\Psi, o_\theta) - \sigma^2_{i\theta}(s_\theta, o_\Psi). \tag{11}$$

If $E(NCD)$ is positive, and voters behave deterministically, i votes for θ; if negative, for Ψ, and abstains if the expected difference is zero. Candidates seek electoral victory, implied by $V(\cdot) > .5$, where $V_\Psi(\cdot) = 1 - V_\theta$. The interpretation Hinich (1977) attaches to this distribution is the proportion of voters with ideal X_i who vote for Theta, summed across all ideal points.[3] If F is a population cumulative density function for the likelihood a particular voter votes for Theta, given NCD_i, then Theta seeks to maximize this function:

$$V_\theta(s_\theta, o_\theta, s_\Psi, o_\Psi) = \sum_i [F(-[\theta_i - X_i]^2 + [\Psi_i - X_i]^2 + v^2\delta_i)]. \tag{12}$$

The expected plurality function is, like the individual variance terms that are its most important components, concave in self-expenditures and convex in those of the opponent.

Finally, we must identify the source of the funds to be spent. We assume candidates have no funds of their own, and cannot borrow, but must solicit contributions C_J from the M contributor/investors. Total campaign expenditures e (the sum of o and s, for each candidate) are constrained by total contributions:

$$e_\theta \leq \sum_{J=1}^{M} C_{\theta J}, \text{ and } e_\Psi \leq \sum_{J=1}^{M} C_{\Psi J}. \tag{13}$$

III. Contributors

The contributors' problem is to maximize the net expected return from political investment, assuming that the investor can borrow additional money beyond the budget, or that leftover budget can be invested at the next best rate of return. Of course, if this "next best" rate of return exceeds that available in political activity, then the investor contributes nothing to either candidate.

---

3. Voters who are closer to θ are more likely to vote for Theta than for Psi, but given the other, unobservable, characteristics of the candidate (character, integrity, commitment, leadership ability) we cannot treat voter choice as being determined solely by the weighted Euclidean distance.

Political Investment, Voter Perceptions, and Candidate Strategy 57

We posit four characteristics of political participation relevant to the Jth $(J = 1, \ldots, M)$ investor's utility function ϕ_J: (1) perceived positions θ_J, Ψ_J; (2) private benefits offered in exchange for contributions; (3) borrowing/leftover budget; and (4) probability each candidate will win. Let us consider each of the four in turn.

1. *Perceived positions θ_J, Ψ_J.* Similar to voters, we assume investors map candidate positions along the predictive dimension onto the policy space with transformation vector W_J and with (unbiased) error α_J:[4]

$$\theta_J = (\Pi_\theta + \alpha_{J\theta}) W_J, \text{ and } \Psi_J = (\Pi_\Psi + \alpha_{J\Psi}) W_J. \tag{14}$$

2. *Private benefits $\beta_{\theta J}(C_{\theta J})$, $\beta_{\Psi J}(C_{\Psi J})$.* Each candidate makes available to investors private benefits that affect their wealth positions. These benefits might range from access, in a transaction similar to that discussed by Ferejohn and Noll (1984), to votes on particularistic benefits such as a favorable procurement contract or private tax exemptions (Chappell 1982). While the level of provision of such benefits may correlate with candidate ideologies Π_θ and Π_Ψ, private benefits are decidedly *non-public*. Each β_J must therefore be excludable (the candidate can with some cost withhold the benefit from some or all potential recipients), and have a positive marginal cost of provision, if only in that each candidate has only a fixed stock, $\overline{\beta}_\theta$ and $\overline{\beta}_\Psi$, of private benefits to allocate. We assume, however, that at the margin such particularistic benefits (particularly access) create only a negligible increment to the total tax bill, and that we can ignore the β's as components of public policy Ω.

3. *Borrowing/leftover budget B'.* Define the investor's budget as:

$$B'_J = I_J - C_{\theta J} - C_{\Psi J}, \tag{15}$$

where I_J is the total amount allocated by the investor J to political activity. Thus, if $B'_J < 0$ the investor has borrowed money ($C_{\theta J} + C_{\Psi J} > I_J$); if $B'_J > 0$ then J has B' dollars to invest in other races or the next most profitable business investment.

4. *Probabilities of election p_u and p_Ψ.* Each prospective investor judges the likely election outcomes as one of the events θ wins (occurring with probability p_θ) or Ψ wins ($p_\Psi = 1 - p_\theta$). Because of differences in information sets these assessments may differ across investors. Further, though p_θ and p_Ψ are endogenous to the model we assume the

---

4. Because of the greater resources of interest groups and other potential investors, it is likely $\alpha_{J\theta} << \gamma_{i\theta}$, and $\alpha_{J\Psi} << \gamma_{i\Psi}$, which is to say that voters are relatively less well informed. At present we make no such restriction, but allow for future examination by building such a distinction directly into our notation.

marginal electoral impact of each contribution is negligible. Hence p_θ and p_Ψ are *exogenous* inputs to the decision calculus of investors acting alone or in small coalitions.

Thus, the investor's problem (dropping the J subscript to simplify notation) is to invest his funds to maximize net expected return G:

$$G(C_\theta, C_\Psi) = P_\theta \; \phi(\theta, \beta_\theta(C_\theta), B') + p_\Psi \; \phi(\Psi, \beta_\Psi(C_\Psi), B'), \qquad (16)$$

where ϕ is concave in β_θ and β_Ψ.

In order to establish the concavity of the objective function, we take first and second derivatives with respect to C_θ (the case for C_Ψ is of course symmetric):

$$\frac{\partial G}{\partial C_\theta} = p_\theta \; \frac{\partial \phi}{\partial \beta_\theta} \frac{\partial \beta_\theta}{\partial C_\theta} - \frac{\partial \phi}{\partial B'}, \geq 0. \qquad (17)$$

$$\frac{\partial^2 G}{\partial C^2_\theta} = p_\theta \; \frac{\partial^2 \phi}{\partial \beta_\theta^2} \left[\frac{(\partial \beta_\theta)}{\partial C_\theta} \right]^2 + p_\theta \; \frac{\partial \phi}{\partial \beta_\theta} \frac{\partial^2 \beta_\theta}{\partial C_\theta^2} - p_\theta \frac{\partial^2 \phi}{\partial \beta_\theta \partial B'} \frac{\partial \beta_\theta}{\partial C_\theta} + \frac{\partial^2 \phi}{\partial B'^2} \qquad (18)$$

For the first derivative Equation (17) establishes nonnegativity. Either G is increasing in C_θ or the opportunity cost rate of return ($\partial \phi / \partial B'$) is so high that the result is a nonparticipating corner solution. The situation for the second derivative is more complex: the first, second, and fourth terms are negative, as required, but the cross-partial for β_θ and B' may be positive. This term captures the influence of private favors on the opportunity cost rate of return. If private favors raise (or reduce only slightly) the opportunity cost rate of return, Equation (18) is sufficient for strict concavity.

We turn now to a consideration of the strategic interactions of candidate activities, given the behavior of voters and contributors outlined above.

IV. The Structure of the Game and Characterization of Equilibrium

Two aspects of the game between candidates require further exposition before we proceed to the existence results in the next section. (1) Fixed candidate positions. Candidates are not free to choose voters' perceptions; instead, Theta and Psi must rely on attempts to depict their fixed records in a more propitious light. Whether we believe candidates possess personal policy preferences in fact (Wittman 1983; Lott 1986) or as a competitive necessity (Bernhardt and Ingberman 1985; Dougan and

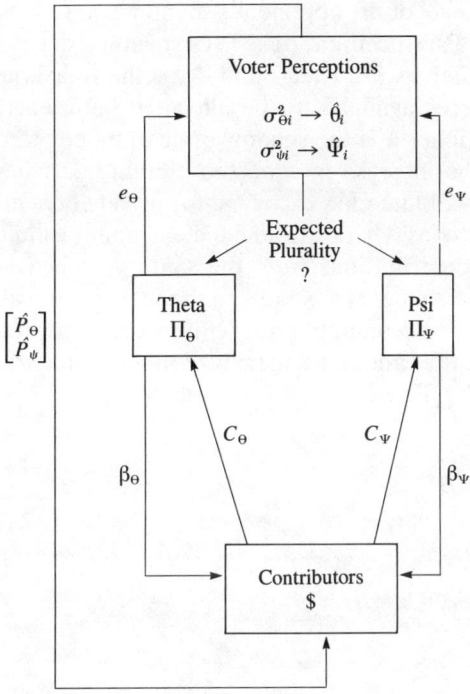

Fig. 3. The conceptual variance/expenditure game between candidates

Munger 1989), candidates are not able to vary public positions without large electoral costs. (2) Fixed election probabilities from the perspective of contributors. We treat election probabilities as invariant to the individual contribution decisions, though clearly in the aggregate contributions partly determine the plurality ex post. Thus, there is no game among contributors. Although economic interests may not be indifferent between outcomes, the election is beyond their individual control, and there are no strategic factors in the contribution decision except maximization of wealth.

The conceptual form of the game is depicted in figure 3. To cast the complex political interaction outlined above as a game, we must formally characterize the objective functions and strategy sets of Theta and Psi. Assuming Cournot-Nash behavior, and focusing on Theta, the candidate seeks to maximize:

$$V_\theta(s_\theta, \bar{s}_\Psi, o_\theta, \bar{o}_\Psi) + \lambda(e^*_\theta - s_\theta - o_\theta), \qquad (19)$$

where $\bar{s}_\psi$ is the level of the opponent's spending on reducing the variance associated with Psi's position, $\bar{o}_\psi$ is Psi's spending devoted to increasing the noise associated with Theta, and e^*_θ is the (maximum) quantity of electoral resources available to be allocated between these two functions. The multiplier λ is the shadow price of money to be spent on the campaign, or the increase in expected plurality deriving from a $1 increase in money obtained in exchange for private benefits.

We do not consider the strategic elements of candidate pledges in competing for contributions from the same prospective investors, but such competitive elements are likely to shape real world allocation strategies and should be accounted for in future work. For present purposes it is sufficient that the candidates maximize the resources e^*_θ and e^*_ψ available to them. For Theta:

$$e^*_\theta = \sum_{J=1}^{M} C_{\theta J}(\beta^*_{\theta j}). \tag{20}$$

$$\hat{\beta}_\theta \geq \sum_{J=1}^{M} \beta^*_{\theta J} = \beta^*_\theta. \tag{21}$$

The formal solution to the problem takes the form of an M-dimensional vector of private benefit allocations and the associated shadow price:

$$\beta^*_\theta = (\beta_{\theta 1}{}^*, \beta_{\theta 2}{}^*, \ldots, \beta_{\theta m}{}^*, \lambda^*), \tag{22}$$

where * denotes optimal level. This allocation represents the contribution-maximizing strategy, but is not strategic in any useful sense. Rather, the candidate takes these resources and turns to the next stage of his campaign: how to allocate the resources between "self" and "opponent" expenditures.

The existence of the solutions β^*_θ and β^*_ψ is easily demonstrated. The strategy set of private benefits available for allocation among competing potential contributors is compact and convex, so that we need only show that the vote function is concave in its argument. This result follows from Enelow and Hinich (forthcoming b, 8), Theorem I, assuming the following four conditions hold: (1) The voter utility functions $U_i(\cdot)$ are jointly concave in all arguments; (2) The cumulative distribution function F is defined over any of the broad class of densities known as $PF2$ densities (which includes the normal, exponential, gamma, binomial, poisson, and virtually every other density function used in the statistics or modeling literature); (3) Additionally, the contributor objective functions must be strictly concave, but this was demonstrated by (17) and (18) above; and (4) The variances associated with voter perceptions of the two candidates must be jointly concave in its arguments (the four expenditure variables) as we assumed above in (5).

Having informally demonstrated the existence of a set of solutions to the individual maximization problems of θ (given arbitrary C_Ψ) and Ψ (given arbitrary C_θ), we now turn to the main existence result. We formally state our assumptions and the existence theorem, as well as two corollaries, the proofs of which are presented in the appendix to this essay.

A1. At least one contributor contributes to at least one candidate.
A2. ϕ_J is concave in C_θ, given $\overline{C}_\Psi$, and in C_Ψ, given $\overline{C}_\theta$, for each contributor.
A3. The choice sets e_θ and e_Ψ are convex and compact.
A4. $F[\cdot]$ is strictly concave in s_θ, o_θ, s_Ψ, and o_Ψ, implying $V_\theta(\cdot)$ and $V_\Psi(\cdot)$ are also concave.[5]

The only additional assumptions (beyond existence of individual maxima) are $A1$ and $A3$; $A1$ is necessary for any game to exist at all (since candidates strategize over spending), and $A3$ follows from the definition of the e_θ, e_Ψ sets as the sums over the (nonempty, by $A1$) sets of $C_{\theta J}$, $C_{\Psi J}$.

EXISTENCE THEOREM. *A1–A4 imply the existence of a unique Nash equilibrium to the campaign expenditure game.*

The following two corollaries are extensions of the main existence theorem. In examining these results, we seek only to illustrate some immediate consequences rather than exhaustively explore the implications of the model. We assume candidates perceive voters as voting probabilistically so that (as suggested by Enelow and Hinich, 1984a, 10) platforms converge to $\Pi_\theta = \Pi_\Psi$. This assumption allows us to focus on the gaming aspects of the process, and is not crucial to the applicability of the model.

COROLLARY I. *If $\Pi_\theta = \Pi_\Psi$, $\beta_\theta = \beta_\Psi$, $\sigma_{\theta i}^2(.) = \sigma_{\Psi i}^2(.)$, and A1–A5 are true, then $e^*_\theta = e^*_\Psi$, $o^*_\theta = o^*_\Psi$, $s^*_\theta = s^*_\Psi$, and $\delta_i = 0$ for each voter.*

---

5. Enelow and Hinich (1989b) provide plausible conditions on the utilities and the standard deviation of F such that the assumption ($A4$) holds.

In other words, if neither has an advantage in terms of policy, the technology of affecting variance, or the private benefits he has to offer, then the allocational strategies must be the same. In game theoretic terms, we have defined a symmetric game. The result is a continuous strategy Prisoner's Dilemma: each candidate exhausts his electoral resources (private benefits) for exactly zero net gain. In short, Corollary I suggests that in the absence of differentiation between candidates each is faced with the frustrating situation of Alice in Wonderland: they must run as fast as they can just to remain where they are in the race. The reason is that each can respond to expenditures by the other with exactly matching, offsetting spending. Since strategies are defined over a difference term (δ) and strategies are symmetric, the net impact is zero and candidates cannot improve their expected pluralities.

COROLLARY II. *If $\Pi_\theta = \Pi_\Psi$, $\beta_\theta = \beta_\Psi$, $\sigma_{\theta i}^2(.) = \sigma_{\Psi i}^2(.)$, for each voter, A1–A5 are true, and $f(.)$ is symmetric around $f(0)$, then once again all expenditures and strategy variables are identical, $\delta_i = 0$, and the optimal strategies yield $V^*_\theta = V^*_\Psi = .5$, or equal expected vote totals for each candidate.*

We turn now to a consideration of the comparative statics of the model. In particular, we seek to examine the impact of incumbency and campaign finance laws (both contribution limits and expenditure ceilings).

VI. Incumbency and Campaign Finance laws

In this section we write the full solution to the candidates' maximization problem, and examine the sensitivity of this solution to the effects of incumbency and attempts to regulate campaign finance. The predictions of the model in this regard are simple and intuitive: First, incumbents always win, unless the perceptions of voters, and hence the probability distributions describing their behavior changes, or there is a political realignment. Second, campaign finance laws primarily help incumbents.

Reproducing Equation (19) above, but writing out each of the terms, the maximization problem of Theta is:

$$\text{Max: } \Sigma_i \left[F\left((\Psi_i - X_i)^2 - (\theta_i - X_i)^2 + \sigma_{i\Psi}^2 (\bar{s}_\Psi, o_\theta) - \sigma_{i\theta}^2 (s_\theta, \bar{o}_\Psi)\right)\right] + \lambda \left([\Sigma_j C_j (\beta^*_{\theta j})] - s_\theta - o_\theta\right), \qquad (23)$$

where as before β^* is the solution vector to the contribution maximization problem, and the contribution supply ($C_j(\beta_{\theta j})$) functions are the inverses of the demand for policy functions in the contributor objective functions:

$$G(C_\theta, C_\Psi) = p_\theta \, \phi(NCD_i, \beta_\theta(C_\theta), B')$$
$$+ p_\Psi \, \phi(NCD_i, \beta_\Psi(C_\Psi), B'), \qquad (24)$$

To solve this problem, we take the first derivatives with respect to the two strategy variables o_θ and s_θ and the shadow price λ. The three first order conditions of this problem are then set equal to zero, implying that at a maximum:

$$\partial \sigma_{\theta i}^2 / \partial o_\theta = -\partial \sigma_{\Psi i}^2 / \partial s_\theta = \lambda. \qquad (25)$$

This expression implies that the last dollar allocated by the candidate must increase the opponent's variance by the same amount that it reduces his own, and that the electoral value of this last dollar is the shadow price of additional funds λ. Equation (25) is true of any maximum, but it is of particular interest to us in this section in our consideration of incumbency and campaign finance laws.

In the existence theorem and corollaries above we assumed that the technologies of reducing one's own variance and increasing that of one's opponent were concave, symmetric, and identical. There is no reason to believe that these conditions are general, or even likely. First, there may be differences between two candidates in the expenditures required to convince voters of the plausibility of a given reduction or increase in the noise associated with the two positions. Second, as Alesina and Cukierman (1987), Page (1976), and Shepsle (1972) suggest, the symmetry condition is unlikely to hold. It is easier (for our purposes, cheaper) to cloud the likely position of an opponent than to illuminate and focus on one's own position, implying a strategy of "ambiguity." To the extent that it is comparatively cheaper to campaign negatively (i.e., attacking one's opponent), then Equation (25) above indicates that positive, self-oriented campaigning will be observed (if at all) only if the available budget e^* is large enough to equalize the marginal electoral gains. It is entirely possible that for poorly financed campaigns with a candidate known to voters the equalities in Equation (25) do not hold, and all money is spent on negative campaigning o_θ and o_Ψ. Alternatively, if the candidate is unknown, the opposite corner solution is implied: all money in a limited campaign is spent on establishing some name recognition and reducing the very large variance associated with a political tyro. In what follows we will not consider either of these two corner solutions, but certainly do not rule them out as empirical possibilities.

We seek now to investigate in turn the effects of incumbency and the impact of campaign finance laws.

Incumbency. There are at least two ways that incumbency can be imbedded in the model. First, it seems plausible to imagine that incumbents could promise greater levels of private benefits to potential contributors, primarily because incumbents have known, secure committee assignments and seniority. Even if a challenger is fortunate enough to be named to the same committee as the person he defeated, he will have none of the experience and institutional assets associated with seniority. Second, the incumbent has a known record, a set of votes, and a reputation for delivering on previous promises of private benefits. Further, the incumbent is likely to be able to deliver immediately, while challengers will almost certainly have to wait until they are in office. For either case, the variance of the challenger's position will always be higher for a given level of expenditure. Challengers must spend more money to achieve a similar level of variance, even if the marginal reduction of variance for challengers may be higher from each dollar spent.

In the context of the model, and allowing Theta to be the incumbent and Psi the challenger, we have

$$\hat{\beta}_\theta \gg \overline{\beta}_\psi, \text{ and} \tag{26}$$

$$\sigma_{i\theta}^2(.) \ll \sigma_{i\psi}^2(.) \text{ for equivalent expenditures.} \tag{27}$$

In either case, the incumbent must win ($V_\theta > .5$) as long as the two platforms are approximately equal ($\Pi_\theta \approx \Pi_\psi$).

However, a dramatic change in either of two areas can force incumbents out of office. First, individual voters' perceptions of a candidate's character, performance, or other volatile factors influencing the shape of the voting probability distribution can remove a candidate who was once perceived as a front-runner (witness the precipitous decline of Gary Hart's popularity). Second, a "realignment" (exogenous change in the mapping parameters v_i) will cause incumbents to lose, because they have difficulty changing their perceived positions along the predictive dimension. Thus our prediction is that incumbents should never lose if they maintain their image as being trustworthy and consistent, or they should lose in bunches.

Campaign Finance Laws. The avowed goal of campaign finance laws is to reduce the public's perception of corruption of the political process. There are three basic types of campaign finance regulation: (1) contribution limits by investors, (2) expenditure limits for candidates, and (3) disclosure provisions. We will consider only the first two; for a discussion of the impact of disclosure provisions, see Aranson and Hinich (1978).

Both contribution limits and expenditure restrictions benefit incumbents. A characteristic of our model is its "Prisoner's Dilemma" for expenditure: if the two candidates are otherwise equal, and spend the same amount, they always tie, as demonstrated by Corollaries I and II above. But if one has a lead in terms of the level of variance with which he starts the race, equal spending implies whoever starts ahead stays ahead. Since, as discussed above, incumbents are generally expected to possess such advantages as name recognition and a reputation, a binding restriction on *either* spending or contributions protects incumbents. Restrictions on spending have this impact immediately if they impose the same limit on both challenger and incumbent. Contribution limits accomplish the same object more indirectly, by forcing the challenger to promise private benefits to many more potential contributors, and preventing him from making any single promise of any value.

VII. Conclusions

It is important to emphasize the explicit game framework that underlies the predictions of the model outlined above. The three sets of agents we consider are wealth/utility maximizing contributors, utility maximizing voters, and two expected plurality maximizing candidates with fixed positions along a left-right ideological or predictive dimension. Voters map the candidates' positions along this single dimension onto the policy space over which they have preferences and a well-defined ideal point. This mapping, however, is accomplished only with idiosyncratic, candidate- and voter-specific error. It is the variance of these errors that candidates seek to affect through their campaign expenditures, with the money for these efforts coming from contributors.

The explicit game matches candidates seeking to influence the difference in voters' perceptions of the errors associated with the two candidate positions. In this regard, expenditures on affecting variance have symmetric effects on expected plurality: an increase in the opponent's variance is exactly the same as a similar decrease in your own. Our results suggest that there exist reasonable conditions under which such a game has at least one equilibrium. Further, if the two candidates are identical, each will spend the same amount, and if the probability distribution describing voter behavior is symmetric, then the two candidates will split the vote. This suggests, for example, that open-seat elections will be very close and spending will be very high, unless one or the other candidate has a clear and established reputation acquired in other office or public life.

On the other hand, if one candidate is an incumbent, there may be no amount of spending that will cause the challenger to win, provided the incumbent can match it. The game in our model implies that electoral competition can result in extremely close races at either high or low levels of expenditure, but that the individual incentive to spend more will create an upward spiral of spending and response spending. Thus, our results do not paint an optimistic picture for the chances for reform of the campaign finance process. Restrictions on spending or contributions tend to benefit incumbents, reducing competition and insulating officials from the electoral forces that assure accountability. The alternative is little better, however, since the absence of such restrictions imply an ever-expanding quantity of resources will be spent on elections. Worse, such a result implies no real consequent increase in competitiveness, because incumbents can still win simply by matching the challenger's spending.

APPENDIX: PROOFS OF THE EXISTENCE THEOREM AND COROLLARIES

Existence Theorem: Given A1–A5, we know from Owen (1982, Theorem IV.6.2), that a pure strategy equilibrium exists; if the expected plurality function V is strictly concave then a unique pure strategy equilibrium exists in expenditures. Thus, we must only justify A4 and the theorem follows immediately.

Enelow and Hinich demonstrate the concavity of the expected plurality function in policy choices. The relevant expected plurality for the present proof is:

$$V_\theta(s_\theta, o_\theta, s_\Psi, o_\Psi) = \sum_i [F(-(\theta_i - X_i)^2 + (\Psi_i - X_i)^2 + v^2\delta_i]. \tag{A.1}$$

Since the summation is over voters, and the sum of concave functions is itself concave, we need only establish that (A.1) is concave for arbitrary i. For any particular voter, the concavity of $f(\cdot)$ is established by Enelow and Hinich (forthcoming b) if $\delta_i = 0$. This result will still follow so long as δ_i is itself concave in the strategy variables e_θ and e_Ψ. Recall that δ_i is:

$$\delta_i = \sigma^2_{i\Psi}(s_\Psi, o_\theta) - \sigma^2_{i\theta}(s_\theta, o_\Psi). \tag{A.2}$$

where:

$$\frac{\partial V_\theta}{\partial s_\theta} > 0; \quad \frac{\partial V_\theta}{\partial s_\psi} < 0; \quad \frac{\partial V_\theta}{\partial o_\theta} > 0; \quad \frac{\partial V_\theta}{\partial o_\psi} < 0, \quad \text{and}$$

$$\frac{\partial^2 V_\theta}{\partial s_\theta^2} > 0; \quad \frac{\partial^2 V_\theta}{\partial s_\psi^2} < 0; \quad \frac{\partial^2 V_\theta}{\partial o_\theta^2} > 0; \quad \frac{\partial^2 V_\theta}{\partial o_\psi^2} < 0. \tag{A.3}$$

But (A.2) is therefore the sum of products involving scalars and concave functions of the strategy variables, and is concave. (Q.E.D.)

Corollary I: Suppose the corollary is false, or that $e_\theta \neq e_\psi$. Given that the two variances, both functions of expenditures, are concave, we know that δ, a sum of concave functions, is concave, and $V(\cdot)$ is therefore concave in expenditures. Suppose Theta spends less; then $\sigma_\theta^2(\cdot) > \sigma_\psi^2(\cdot)$, $\delta < 0$, and $V(\cdot) < .5$ indicating a loss for Theta. Since Theta could spend more if he allocated more of his private benefits to attracting funds, this cannot be an equilibrium.

Theta can do better than Psi only if he spends more, yet both have the same quantity of resources to allocate. As long as the ability of the two candidates to affect their own variance and that of their opponent is identical ($\sigma_\theta^2(\cdot) = \sigma_\psi^2(\cdot)$ for the same $(\cdot)$), each candidate must dissipate all his resources.

Alternatively, suppose $s_\theta \neq s_\psi$; one candidate must then not be maximizing his plurality, since the first order conditions of the maximization problem imply equal marginal impacts for s and o spending, and if the two candidates are identical they must arrive at the same solutions.

Corollary II: Assuming that f is symmetric around $f(0)$ means that equal departures in either direction from zero expected policy difference ($E(NCD_i) = 0$) are equivalent in probability terms. The only addition to the equilibrium in II, above, is then that the two candidates tie in expected vote, or:

$$1 - F(NCD_i = 0, \delta = 0) = F(NCD_i = 0, \delta = 0) = .5. \tag{A.4}$$

A Mathematical Proof of Duverger's Law

Thomas R. Palfrey

It is not just coincidence that Duverger's Law has established itself as one of the premier empirical regularities in political science. With only minor caveats,[1] it is not only a stylized fact, but also a well-documented fact[2] that single-member-district electoral systems in which winners are decided by simple plurality rule usually produce two-party systems. It is, as far as I know, the only such regularity in political science that is widely referred to as a "law."

What seems surprising, and what motivates this essay, is that in spite of the revolutionary ascent of formal modeling to the forefront of political theory methodology, this clear empirical regularity which has extremely intuitive informal explanations seems to have miraculously escaped the grips of an unambiguous mathematical theorem. If it is as true a law as many seem to believe, then there should be a simple theoretical explanation for it that formalizes the informal stories and rationalizations that have been repeatedly offered for over a century. I hope this would also help identify and illuminate the rare circumstances in which departures from the most sweeping versions of the law might be

---

California Institute of Technology. The author would like to thank the National Science Foundation for financial support. This paper was prepared for delivery at the Economic Theories of Politics conference in Haifa, Israel, June, 1988, and has benefited from discussions with Bruce Cain, John Ledyard, and Richard McKelvey.

1. The most well-known exception is Canada, where provincial party systems are bipartisan, but not all provinces have the same two dominant parties. This produces a patchwork national party system that is a conglomeration of strong regional parties, but in which there are still two dominant national parties. The only contradiction to the law here is that the minor parties do not completely disappear. Apparently, and not surprisingly, parties that have heavily concentrated local support can compete for national office in their regions. It is very important to note, however, that within those regions the local party systems tend to be bipartisan. Furthermore, only the two major parties (the Tories and the Liberals) have controlled the national government. A second exception is India (see Weiner 1957), where there is only one dominant party, but third parties seem to be able to survive. Riker (1976b) argues that this can happen when historical circumstances produce a consensus party that is centrally located on the political spectrum and has wide popular appeal: the Congress Party of India.

2. See Rae (1971) and many of the references in Riker's (1982b) excellent survey of Duverger's Law.

expected. This essay offers such a model that explains Duverger's Law and indicates some unusual circumstances in which the law might not hold up.

What do all the informal explanations have in common? We are fortunate that Riker (1982b) has already collected many of these, so I will give only a few representative examples. One of the earliest is presented by Droop (1869) who says that unpopular parties do not receive votes because voters do not want to waste their votes:

> Each elector has practically a choice between two candidates or sets of candidates . . . . (T)he electors usually find out that their votes will be thrown away, unless given in favor of one or the other of the parties between whom the election really lies.

This is a remarkable statement that is really a claim about equilibrium behavior of rational voters. It says that voters are making calculating decisions that weigh the chances of affecting the outcome given how other voters vote. It states that strategic voting is rational behavior, that voters are rational and do this, and that it results in a stable equilibrium configuration with only two parties. Thus voters are not only rational in his explanation, but they have rational expectations. His early conjecture about this type of strategic voting has been widely confirmed.[3]

Earlier this century, Schattschneider (1942, 82) stated:

> (P)eople who vote for minor opposition parties *waste their votes*. All who oppose the party in power are made to feel a certain need for concentrating their support behind the party most likely to lead a successful opposition. As a consequence, the tendency to support minor parties is checked. The tendency of the single-member district system to give the second major party a great advantage over all minor parties is extremely important. In this way it is possible to explain the *longevity* of the major parties and the instability of the minor parties. (Emphasis as in original)

These two explanations coincide almost exactly with what Duverger (1951, 226) himself called the "psychological factor" leading to two dominant parties:

> In cases where there are three parties operating under the simple majority single-ballot system the electors soon realize that their votes are wasted if they continue to give them to the third party: hence their natural tendency

---

3. See, for example, Cain (1978), Duverger (1950), Bensel and Sanders (1979), Spafford (1972), and others.

to transfer their vote to the less evil of its two adversaries in order to prevent the success of the greater evil.

Duverger's psychological factor is then, quite simply, rational strategic voting.

There have been two different formal theoretical approaches which have begun to address the question of what is the stable number of parties in a winner-take-all system. Both approaches are innovative and move a step beyond the standard Downsian models of electoral competition by opening up the possibility of multiparty equilibria.

The first approach captures the aspect of multicandidate competition for a single seat that is the focus of traditional explanations for Duverger's Law. With more than two candidates, voters have a significantly more difficult decision problem, since they may be better off voting for a candidate other than their first choice, if it appears that their first choice stands no realistic chance of victory.[4] This is the direction we pursue here.

The first attempt to formalize this connection between Duverger's Law and rational voting behavior appears in Riker (1976). Ironically, a major point of that essay is to construct a theoretical model that can explain the experience in India with persistent third parties, what Riker (1976, 94) refers to (perhaps overenthusiastically) as "an egregious exception" to Duverger's Law.[5] Cox (1987) adopts a similar approach but embeds the strategic decision making by voters into a probabilistic equilibrium model based on the theory of Bayesian games (Ledyard 1981, 1984). He shows that the only circumstances in which strategic voting might lead voters to abandon their most preferred candidate is if their second most preferred candidate is expected to receive more votes. However, even that is not a sufficient condition for strategic voting. He uses this result to show that there will be a marginal effect of strategic voting to help candidates who are expected to do well and to hurt candidates who are expected to do less well.

This essay obtains a much stronger result. Using the same basic model of voter decision making as Ledyard (1981) and Cox (1987), we show that when the number of voters in the electorate is large, the

---

4. In fact, this is not only true for single-member district simple-plurality rule systems, but for most other multicandidate rules as well. Cumulative voting, proportional representation, the Borda count, the Hare system, and virtually any other method have this difficulty. For a general statement about the widespread problems of eliciting "sincere" behavior, see Gibbard (1973).

5. As we will show later in the essay, this "egregious exception" is in fact a theoretically predicted exceptional case: the proverbial exception that proves the rule.

equilibrium share of the "third-party vote" must necessarily be small. Moreover, this equilibrium share of the vote declines to zero in the limit as the size of the electorate grows. This result is true under very general assumptions about the heterogeneity and distribution of voter preferences over candidates, and the total number of candidates in the election, and possibilities for abstention.

The necessity of examining large electorates seems reasonable, if one interprets Duverger's Law as describing a property of national electoral systems. In fact, Riker argues that a *large* electorate should be included as one of the conditions for plurality voting to have such a forceful impact on the party systems (1982*b*, 755). It is this essay's focus on the asymptotic properties of strategic voting that enables this stronger result to be obtained.

The second of these approaches (Brams and Straffin 1982; Palfrey 1984) is quite different and brings in dynamic, intertemporal factors by investigating whether two established parties will be able to adopt issue positions to preempt the successful entry of any third party. Palfrey (1984) shows in a simple one-dimensional spatial model that an equilibrium configuration of the two established parties in a winner-take-all system (when it exists) will have one leftist party and one party right of center, which are jointly situated so that no third party can enter the competition and win. The intuition is that by positioning themselves neither too close together nor too extreme, the two established parties are located so that there is no "room" for an entrant. Thus, given two established parties, additional parties are not viable.[6] The weakness of this approach is that it assumes no strategic voting.

The rest of the paper is organized as follows. Section II presents the model of three-candidate elections, following the assumptions of Cox (1987). Section III proves the central result of the essay, that in equilibrium, the share of the vote for the third party declines to zero as the number of voters increases. Section IV explores the extent to which these results generalize when candidates are free to select platforms, as opposed to when the distribution of voter preferences over candidates is exogenously fixed.

---

6. A related model is analyzed by Greenberg and Shepsle (1987). They define an axiomatic notion of stability that is somewhat different from the noncooperative game-theoretic equilibrium used in Palfrey (1984), but that retains the basic idea that established parties are situated in a way that deters entry of new parties. However, they apply their stability notion to election systems with multiple member districts, not winner-take-all systems.

II. The Model

There are three candidates, A, B, C. There are n voters. Each voter has a (strict) preference ranking over the three candidates and we represent a voter's preferences for each candidate by a Von Neumann–Morgenstern utility number. These utilities are normalized so that voter i receives a utility of 1 if his (or her) first choice wins, a utility of 0 for his least preferred candidate and a utility of v_i for his middle-ranked candidate. The distribution of voter preferences is represented by $<q_{AB}, q_{AC}, q_{BA}, q_{BC}, q_{CA}, q_{CB}>$ and $<F_{AB}(\cdot) F_{AC}(\cdot), F_{BA}(\cdot), F_{BC}(\cdot), F_{CA}(\cdot), F_{CB}(\cdot)>$.

Each q_{ij} equals the probability a randomly selected voter ranks candidate i first and j second, or alternatively, the average frequency of each possible preference ranking in the electorate. We assume each voter's preference is independently drawn from this distribution. A voter who ranks i first and j second is henceforth referred to as an ij-type. Below, we make two assumptions about the distribution. That these assumptions are relatively innocuous is argued later in the essay.

ASSUMPTION 1. $q_{ij} > 0$ for all $i,j = A,B,C$.

In other words, we assume that every ranking of the candidates can occur (but, possibly, with very low frequency). Each $F_{ij}(\cdot)$ is the cumulative distribution function (*cdf*) of Von Neumann–Morgenstern utility values of j (the second-ranked candidate) for a randomly selected ij-type. An ij-type who values j at v will be called an ij-v-type.

ASSUMPTION 2. *For all $i,j, F_{ij}(\cdot)$ is twice continuously differentiable, where,*

$F_{ij}(0) = 0$
$F_{ij}(1) = 1$
$f_{ij}(v) \equiv F'_{ih}(v) > 0$ *for all* $v \varepsilon [0,1]$.

Assumption 2 rules out mass points of voters and assumes that the probability that two randomly selected voters will have exactly the same ranking and exactly the same "intensity of preference" (v) is negligible. Finally, we assume that each voter's preferences are independently drawn from the probability distribution given

$$P = <q_{AB}, \ldots, q_{CB}, F_{AB}, \ldots, F_{CB}>.$$

Now that we have specified voter preferences, we can specify the voting game. Each voter simultaneously chooses one of the candidates to vote for, taking as given the voting strategies of other voters, in order to maximize the expected utility of the outcome of the election. Recall that since we are talking about election of a *single* candidate, ties will have to be broken if two (or all three) candidates tie for the most votes received. How these ties are broken does not affect the results in section III, so we will simply assume that ties are broken alphabetically (e.g., A beats B in a tiebreaker).

Each voter knows only his own preferences between A,B, and C and that the other voters are independently distributed according to P. Therefore, a voter views the strategies of the other voters as functions that specify what each other voter would do for every type he might be. We can represent such a strategy for one voter as a measurable function

$$\sigma^i : \{AB, AC, BA, BC, CA, CB\} \times [0,1] \to \{A, B, C\}.$$

To simplify the proofs, we will only investigate properties of "symmetric" equilibria. In other words, we will investigate stable behavior in which only two *identical* voters will make identical voting decisions. This restriction enables us to suppress the i-index on σ. Therefore, a voter views the strategy of each other voter as the *same* function σ. This symmetry assumption could be dispensed with, but it would be at considerable cost in notation.

The careful reader will have also noticed by now that we assume all voters vote. Thus, in contrast to Ledyard (1981) or Palfrey and Rosenthal (1985) we do not consider the possibility of abstentions.

So far, we have accumulated a number of assumptions that potentially might restrict the scope of the theorem. Summarizing, these are:

1. All preference types are possible.
2. Distribution of preferences has no mass points.
3. Voter preferences are independent.
4. No abstention.
5. Symmetric equilibrium.

We will discuss relaxing these assumptions later in the essay.

Let D_A, D_B, and D_C denote the set of voter types who vote for A, B, or C, respectively under σ. The probability a randomly selected other voter will vote for A, B, or C, is denoted π_A, π_B, or π_C, respectively where $\pi_A + \pi_B + \pi_C = 1$ and $\pi_j \geq 0 \ \forall j$. Then π_j is the probability that a randomly selected voter other than i has a type in D_j. For shorthand, we can denote a strategy $\sigma = (D_A, D_B, D_C)$.

Given (D_A, D_B, D_C) and (π_A, π_B, π_C), voter i adopts a strategy to maximize expected utility. This strategy is characterized below for an AB-v-type voter. Optimal strategies against (D_A, D_B, D_C)—"best responses"—for other types of voters are similar.

Finally, we assume no one votes for the candidate ranked last in preference. Thus, an AB voter never votes for C, etc. This is quite reasonable, as a voter can never gain by doing so. A strategy that calls for voting for one's *least* preferred candidate would be a *weakly dominated strategy*. Ruling out weakly dominated strategies is usually considered reasonable, and the logic of doing so in the present context is compelling.[7]

The following lemma states that any equilibrium strategy must have the property that a voter will vote sincerely (i.e., for his top-ranked candidate) for small values of v (i.e., if his second-ranked and third-ranked candidates both produce relatively low utility levels). A voter will only vote insincerely in equilibrium if v is relatively large (i.e., his second-ranked candidate is sufficiently close in utility to his top-ranked candidate). Furthermore, insincere voting requires that the likelihood of switching the outcome from one's worst candidate to one's second-choice candidate by voting insincerely instead of sincerely exceeds the probability that insincere voting switches the outcome from one's most preferred candidate to one's least preferred candidate.

LEMMA 1. *If other voters use (D_A, D_B, D_C), generating probabilities (π_A, π_B, π_C), and if i is a type AB–voter, then i's best response is:*

(i) Vote for A if:

$$p_{AB}^n (1 - v) + p_{AC}^n > p_{CB}^n v$$

(ii) Either vote for A or B if (i) holds with equality.
(iii) Vote for B if $p_{CB}^n v > p_{AB}^n (1 - v) + p_{AC}^n$.

where

$p_{AB}^n =$ probability that voting for A yields A, but voting for B yields B
$p_{AC}^n =$ probability that voting for A yields A, but voting for B yields C
$p_{CB}^n =$ probability that voting for A yields C, but voting for B yields B.

---

7. Exceptions to the "reasonableness" of eliminating dominated strategies seem to arise in Prisoners' Dilemmas and related games where there are clear group gains to coordinating behavior. That is, everyone benefits when *everyone* adopts a dominated strategy. Such gains are not present in the voting game considered here. For further discussion of the appropriateness of eliminating dominant strategies see Palfrey and Srivastava (1986).

These probabilities are computed using trinomial formulas, with parameters π_A, π_B, π_C, and n. They are derived below:

p_{AC}^n = probability that out of $(n-1)$ other voters, a vote for A, b vote for B, c vote for C, and $b < a = c - 1$

= probability$\{b < a = c - 1\}$

$$= \sum_{k=\lceil\frac{n-1}{3}\rceil}^{\lceil\frac{n}{2}\rceil - 1} \frac{(n-1)!}{k!(k+1)!(n-2k-2)!} (\pi_A)^k (\pi_B)^{n-2k-2} (\pi_C)^{k+1}$$

where $[X]$ is the least integer greater than or equal to X. Similarly,

p_{CB}^n = probability $\{a < b = c - 1\}$

$$= \sum_{k=\lceil\frac{n-1}{3}\rceil}^{\lceil\frac{n}{2}\rceil - 1} \frac{(n-1)!}{k!(k+1)!(n-2k-2)!} (\pi_A)^{n-2k-2} (\pi_B)^k (\pi_C)^{k+1}$$

and

$p_{AB}^n =$ probability $\{a = b \geq c - 1\}$

+ probability $\{a = b - 1 \geq c - 1\}$

$$= \sum_{k=\lceil\frac{n+1}{3}\rceil - 1}^{\lceil\frac{n-1}{2}\rceil} \frac{(n-1)!}{k!k!(n-2k-1)!} (\pi_A)^k (\pi_B)^k (\pi_C)^{n-2k-1}$$

$$+ \sum_{k=\lceil\frac{n}{3}\rceil - 1}^{\lceil\frac{n-1}{2}\rceil - 1} \frac{(n-1)!}{k!(k+1)!(n-2k-2)!} (\pi_A)^k (\pi_B)^{k+1} (\pi_C)^{n-2k-2}.$$

Analogous formulas for the voters with other preference orders over candidates can also be derived. We say σ is a *Symmetric Bayesian-Nash Equilibrium* (or simply *Equilibrium*) if for every i, $\sigma(t_i)$ maximizes i's expected utility when i is type t_i and when all other voters use the strategy σ.

From Lemma 1, if either p_{ij}^n or p_{kj}^n is positive, we may rewrite the inequality in (i) as:

$$v_{ij}^n \geq \frac{p_{ij}^n + p_{ik}^n}{p_{ij}^n + p_{kj}^n} \qquad (2)$$

Consequently insincere voting not only requires v to be relatively large, but also requires that the voter is more likely to be pivotal between his second and last choices than between his first and last choices ($p_{kj}^n > p_{ik}^n$). Therefore, an equilibrium can be written as a set of six *cut points*, $v_n^* = (v_{AB}^n, v_{AC}^n, v_{BA}^n, v_{BC}^n, v_{CA}^n, v_{CB}^n)$, each of which must either equal 1 or satisfy (2) with equality. A cut point has a convenient and simple interpretation. A voter votes for his second choice if and only if his intensity of preference for that second choice (v) is sufficiently high. Inequality (2) is a precise statement of what "sufficiently high" means. For some ij-types, there is no $v \in (0,1)$ that is sufficiently high, in which case no voter with this order of preference for the candidates will vote strategically. This happens for an ij-type when $p_{ik}^n > p_{kj}^n$.[8]

Lemma 1, then, specifies six inequality conditions that must hold at an equilibrium. However, this is only a partial description of an equilibrium. A further requirement of *Bayesian* equilibrium is that π_A, π_B, and π_C are in fact generated by the voters all adopting the decision rule given by the equilibrium cut points. This is sometimes referred to as the "rational expectations" property of Bayesian equilibrium, because it means that if all voters share expectations that other voters vote for A, B, and C with probabilities π_A, π_B, and π_C, then the optimal behavior by voters, given these expectations, will produce the expected voting pattern—i.e., expectations (or beliefs) are self-fulfilling. This produces three additional equilibria conditions:

$$\pi_A = q_{AB}F_{AB}(v_{AB}^n) + q_{AC}F_{AC}(v_{AC}^n)$$
$$+ q_{BA}[1 - F_{BA}(v_{BA}^n)] + q_{CA}[1 - F_{CA}(v_{CA}^n)] \quad (3A)$$

$$\pi_B = q_{BA}F_{BA}(v_{BA}^n) + q_{BC}F_{BC}(v_{BC}^n)$$
$$+ q_{AB}[1 - F_{AB}(v_{AB}^n)] + q_{CB}[1 - F_{CB}(v_{CB}^n)] \quad (3B)$$

$$\pi_C = q_{CA}F_{CA}(v_{CA}^n) + q_{CB}F_{CB}(v_{CB}^n)$$
$$+ q_{AC}[1 - F_{AC}(v_{AC}^n)] + q_{BC}[1 - F_{BC}(v_{BC}^n)] \quad (3C)$$

Possible Equilibria

We distinguish between three possible types of equilibria, depending upon the configuration of voter strategies. These are called *one-party equilibrium, two-party equilibrium,* and *three-party equilibrium,* and are defined by the number of parties whose candidate receives a positive expected vote. The form of Duverger's Law that we intend to prove is that, within the confines of our model, only two-party equilibrium occur.

---

8. Cox (1987) has pointed out that one case where this happens is when $\pi_i > \pi_j$.

Several observations can now be made about equilibrium with at least four voters. First, there will exist an equilibrium. In fact there exists *at least three equilibria* where in each of these equilibria there is substantial strategic voting, in the sense that some voters do not vote for their first choice. To see this, take any pair of parties, assume all voters vote for their preferred one of these two, and consider the implications of Lemma 1: A voter should vote for his first choice unless his first choice is not one of the two candidates receiving votes, in which case he should vote for his second choice. (This argument requires that the population of voters be at least four.) This is an equilibrium.

Next, consider a possible one-party equilibrium in which the candidate of one of the parties receives all of the votes. Why is this not an equilibrium? The probability of casting a decisive vote is 0, so each voter is indifferent between voting for any candidate, since his vote cannot affect the outcome (assuming the population of voters exceeds two). However, for a voter who ranks the unanimous winner *last*, voting for either other candidate is guaranteed to generate at least as high an expected utility as voting for the candidate who is expected to get all the votes, and, for some (out of equilibrium) configuration of strategies by other voters, generates strictly higher expected utility. Thus such equilibria rely on the use of dominated strategies. This eliminates the "unanimous" equilibria.

To summarize, Lemma 1 and the assumption that voters do not use dominated strategies together immediately imply that:

1. There is no equilibrium in which only one party's candidate receives votes.
2. There are three two-party equilibria.

We next turn to the central question of this paper: In large electorates, (as $n \to \infty$) will there ever exist any three-party equilibrium? The answer is no, except for knife-edge cases.

III. Strategic Voting with Many Voters

The objective of this section is to show that in large electorates with simple-plurality, single-ballot elections there do not exist any equilibria in which all parties are viable. In particular, except for knife-edge cases, the only equilibria that can exist in large electorates involve exactly two parties with candidates who receive a positive fraction of the vote, if we assume voters do not use dominated strategies (i.e., they never vote for their *last* choice).

With three candidates and *any* number of voters, the critical element in the voter calculus is the probability of casting a decisive vote, and in particular, the relative probabilities of casting a decisive vote between one's first and last choices versus one's second and last choices. Consequently, the key aspect of "proving" Duverger's Law in large electorates involves identifying the asymptotic properties of these probabilities. The following lemma turns out to be very important in establishing these properties:

LEMMA 2. *Assume* $\pi_A < \min\{\pi_B, \pi_c\}$. *Then* $\lim_{n\to\infty} \left(\dfrac{p_{AC}^n}{p_{CB}^n} \right) = 0$.

Proof. The proof consists of a messy formalization of the following intuitive argument. Without loss of generality, assume $\pi_B \le \pi_C$. Then p_{AC}^n is the probability that the least popular candidate and the "favorite" are tied for the most votes and p_{CB}^n is the probability that the second most popular and the favorite are tied for the most votes.[9] Thus p_{AC}^n / p_{CB}^n is equivalent to the ratio of likelihoods that the least popular candidate is tied for victory with the favorite compared to the second most popular candidate being tied with the favorite, *conditional* on one of these two ties occurring. The lemma states that *with many voters, if some candidate ties the favorite it will almost certainly have to be the second most popular candidate*. The implication of this is that if your *personal* favorite is the least popular candidate then, regardless of your relative valuation, v, of your second choice, with enough voters in the electorate you will be better off voting for your second choice.

Outline of Formal Proof (Details in Appendix)

For each n, denote by E_{AC}^n and E_{CB}^n the expected winning share of the two candidates who receive the most votes, conditional on A and C being tied for the most, or B and C being tied for the most,[10] respectively, and define $E_{AC} = \lim_{n\to\infty} E_{AC}^n$ and $E_{CB} = \lim_{n\to\infty} E_{CB}^n$. The proof next proceeds through a series of steps:

---

9. Actually, because of the tie-breaking rule, P_{AC}^n equals the probability that, with $n - 1$ voters, C receives the most votes and A receives *one less* vote than C; P_{CB}^n equals the probability that C receives the most votes and B receives one less vote than C; P_{AB}^n equals the probability A and B tie for the most votes or B gets one more vote than A.

10. See note 9.

Step 1: Prove that

$$E_{AC} = \begin{cases} 1/3 & \text{if } (\pi_B)^2 > \pi_A \pi_C \\ \dfrac{1}{2 + \dfrac{\pi_B}{\sqrt{\pi_A \pi_C}}} & \text{if } (\pi_B)^2 < \pi_A \pi_C \end{cases}$$

$$E_{CB} = \dfrac{1}{2 + \dfrac{\pi_A}{\sqrt{\pi_B \pi_C}}}$$

Step 2: Let

$$\overline{P}^n_{AC} = \dfrac{(n-1)! \, (\pi_A \pi_C)^{[(n-1)E_{AC}]} \pi_C \pi_B^{[n-2-2E_{AC}(n-1)]}}{[(n-1)E_{AC}]![1+(n-1)E_{AC}]![n-2-2E_{AC}(n-1)]!}$$

$$\overline{P}^n_{CB} = \dfrac{(n-1)! \, (\pi_B \pi_C)^{[(n-1)E_{CB}]} \pi_C \pi_A^{[n-2-2E_{CB}(n-1)]}}{[(n-1)E_{CB}]![1+(n-1)E_{CB}]![n-2-2E_{CB}(n-1)]!}$$

Prove:

$$\lim_{n \to \infty} \left(\dfrac{\overline{P}^n_{AC}}{\overline{P}^n_{CB}} \right) = 0$$

Step 3:

$$\lim_{n \to \infty} \left(\dfrac{\overline{P}^n_{AC}}{\overline{P}^n_{CB}} \right) = 0 \iff \lim_{n \to \infty} \left(\dfrac{p^n_{AC}}{p^n_{CB}} \right) = 0$$

These three steps are proved in the appendix and establish the lemma in case $\pi_C \geq \pi_B$. If $\pi_B \geq \pi_C$, the entire proof goes through identically with the only change being that $E_{AC} = 1/3$ for *all* values of (π_A, π_B, π_C), such that $\pi_B \geq \pi_C$.

THEOREM. *Fix F. There does not exist a sequence of equilibria $\{v_n^*\}_{n=1}^{\infty}$ such that $0 < \pi_A^* < \min\{\pi_B^*, \pi_C^*\}$, where $\pi_j^* = \lim_{n \to \infty} \pi_j(v_n^*), j = A, B, C$, where $\pi_j(v_n^*)$ is given by equation (3j).*

Proof. Without loss of generality, let $\pi_B^* = \min\{\pi_B^*, \pi_C^*\}$ and hypothesize $0 < \pi_A^* < \pi_B^*$. Then for some profile, there must exist some subsequence of $\{v_n^*\}$, call it $\{v_m^*\}$, such that at least one of the following limits holds:

$$\lim_{m \to \infty} v_{AB}^{*m} \equiv v_{AB}^* > 0$$

$$\lim_{m \to \infty} v_{AC}^{*m} \equiv v_{AC}^* > 0$$

$$\lim_{m \to \infty} v_{BA}^{*m} \equiv v_{BA}^* < 1$$

$$\lim_{m \to \infty} v_{CA}^{*m} \equiv v_{CA}^* < 1.$$

In other words, there must be some region with a positive measure of voters who vote for A in the limit. We will now apply Lemma 1 to prove that v_{AB}^* and v_{AC}^* must equal 0 and v_{BA}^* and v_{CA}^* must equal 1. From Equation (2), we have

$$v_{AB}^{*m} = \frac{p_{AB}^m + p_{AC}^m}{p_{AB}^m + p_{CB}^m} = \frac{p_{AB}^m/p_{CB}^m + p_{AC}^m/p_{CB}^m}{p_{AB}^m/p_{CB}^m + 1}$$

(Note that for large m $p_{CB}^m > 0$, by the hypothesis that $\pi_B^* > 0$ and $\pi_C^* > 0$.) If limits exist, then

$$v_{AB}^* = \lim_{m \to \infty} v_{AB}^{*m} = \frac{\lim_{m \to \infty}(p_{AB}^m/p_{CB}^m) + \lim_{m \to \infty}(p_{AC}^m/p_{CB}^m)}{\lim_{m \to \infty}(p_{AB}^m/p_{CB}^m) + 1}.$$

From Lemma 1, each of the limits on the right-hand side of the equation above exists and equals 0, so $v_{AB}^* = 0$. By the same argument, $v_{AC}^* = 0$. That $v_{AB}^* = 1$ follows simply from the observation that if every voter who prefers A to B (and C is last) will never vote for A, then no voter who prefers B to A (and C is last) will ever vote for A. Similarly $v_{CA}^* = 1$. Therefore, $\pi_A^* = 0$, a contradiction. (Q.E.D.)

An alternative statement of the proof is the following.

THEOREM. *Fix F and fix $\pi_A > \pi_B > \pi_C > 0$. Then there is an electorate size N such that for all $n \geq N$ and for all equilibria $\{v_n^*\}$, $(\pi_A^*(v_n^*), \pi_B^*(v_n^*), \pi_C^*(v_n^*)) \neq (\pi_A, \pi_B, \pi_C)$, and $\pi_C^*(v_n^*) < \pi_C$.*

In other words, the least popular party's equilibrium share of the vote must converge to 0 as the electorate becomes large, if all voters are acting strategically.

Exceptional Cases

The above theorem does not completely rule out three-party equilibria since there is the possibility that $\pi_A = \min\{\pi_B, \pi_C\}$. There are two cases to consider here. First, if $\pi_B = \pi_C$, then we must have $\pi_A = \pi_B = \pi_C = \frac{1}{3}$. In this case, for large n, all voters vote for their first choice, since the right-hand side of inequality Equation (2) converges to 1. This can be sustained as an equilibrium only if $q_{AB} + q_{AC} = q_{BA} + q_{BC} = q_{CA} + q_{CB}$, a knife-edge case.

Second, if $\pi_B = \pi_C$, then $\pi_A > \pi_B = \pi_C$. In this case, inspection of inequality Equation (2) for large n shows that in equilibrium we must have all voters voting for their first choice, so such an equilibrium can occur in large electorates only if either $q_{AB} + q_{AC} = q_{BA} + q_{BC}$ or $q_{AB} + q_{AC} = q_{CA} + q_{CB}$ or $q_{BA} + q_{BC} = q_{CA} + q_{CB}$. Again, these are exceptional cases.

The exceptional cases have interesting interpretations. The first case, where $\pi_A = \pi_B = \pi_C = \frac{1}{3}$ can occur in one of two ways. The obvious way it can occur is ruled out by assumption and might arise if all voters evaluate all candidates identically. While this may not seem to be a likely thing to happen from an empirical standpoint, and it may seem intuitively implausible, it certainly cannot be ruled out theoretically; in fact some recent versions of the Downsian model of candidate competition make such a theoretical prediction. We return to this in the next section.

This case can also arise if the parties take positions so that voters are equally split in their preferences between the parties. While there maybe some rare historical instances where this has happened, such situations seem inherently unstable because of the delicate balance on which *exactly* equal three-way division hangs.

The second exceptional case arises when there is one very popular party and two (or more) equally minor parties. Again I would argue that is relatively unlikely to happen, but here we do have a specific empirical case that seems to fit: India. The discussion in Riker (1976*b*) and some of the references he cites support this theoretical explanation quite convincingly. The Congress party is clearly dominant relative to a collection of lesser parties, the strongest of which are roughly equal in strength. The lesser parties are of significant size and do not disappear, but are just too disparate to unify into a single, effective opposition party.

IV. Extensions and Generalizations

More Than Three Possible Parties

The basic idea of the results in the last section was that if exactly three parties put up candidates for election when there are many voters, then equilibrium voting patterns will end up eliminating *exactly one* party in the sense that its candidate must receive an order of magnitude fewer votes than the runner-up. One (of several) artificial features of the model was that only three parties were considered. Suppose $m > 3$ parties competed. Then is it possible that perhaps more than 2, say $m - 1$, parties could be viable in equilibria? The answer is no. *Two* is unequivocally special in this regard. Suppose we wanted to see if the expected vote shares, $\pi_A \geq \pi_B > \pi_C \geq \pi_D \geq \cdots > 0$, in an m-party race could possibly be a limit point of equilibrium expected vote shares as the number of voters became large. As before, we find (by a similar argument) that the probability of a voter being decisive between A and B will become (in the limit) infinitely greater than the probability of a voter being decisive between A and any other pair. Thus, in the natural generalization of this model to plurality voting between candidates from m parties, Duverger's Law remains intact.

It is probably instructive to sketch the proof. What has to be shown is that in large electorates, equilibrium voting behavior implies that a voter will always vote for the most preferred candidate of the two frontrunners. To see this, consider a voter with utility v_1 for his or her first choice, v_2 for second, etc., up to v_m for his least-preferred candidate. That is $v_1 \geq v_2 \geq \cdots \geq v_m$. Let v_k denote the utility of his first choice among the frontrunners (i.e., k equals either A or B) and let v_l denote the utility of his second choice among the frontrunners, and assume $v_k > v_l$.[11] Let j be any candidate other than k. We can write down a condition analogous to inequality Equation (2) that specifies when such a voter is better off voting for k than j. Using the same notation as before, we get for given n:

$$v_k > v_j \left[\frac{\sum_{i \neq j} p^n_{ij}}{\sum_{h \neq k} p^n_{kh}} \right] + \sum_{i \neq j,k} v_i \left[\frac{p^n_{ki} - p^n_{ij}}{\sum_{h \neq k} p^n_{kh}} \right]. \quad (2')$$

This can be rewritten as:

$$v_k > v_j \left[\frac{\sum_{i \neq j} \left(\frac{p^n_{ij}}{p^n_{kl}}\right)}{\sum_{h \neq k} \left(\frac{p^n_{kh}}{p^n_{kl}}\right)} \right] + \sum_{i \neq j,k} v_i \left[\frac{\frac{(p^n_{ki} - p^n_{ij})}{p^n_{kl}}}{\sum_{h \neq k} \left(\frac{p^n_{kh}}{p^n_{kl}}\right)} \right]. \quad (2'')$$

---

11. By assumption $v_k > v_l$ for all except a measure zero set of voters.

The limiting argument now proceeds in the familiar fashion. Fixing $\pi_k \geq \pi_l > \ldots > 0$, we get $p_{ij}^n/p_{kl}^n \to 0$, for all $ij \neq kl$. Thus, the right-hand side of Equation (2″) converges to v_l, independently of j.

Spatial Party Competition

A natural question to ask is whether the model presented here is consistent with a spatial model of voter behavior. The answer is yes, but with a caveat. If the voters are drawn from a continuous distribution of "reasonable" (say, Euclidean) preferences and parties offer candidates at different points in the policy space then the results go through directly. If the parties generate candidates over which all voters are indifferent the result will be false. Therefore, the caveat is that the theorem applies only to differentiated parties.

Several remarks about this implicit assumption that three candidates do not converge are in order. First, even if parties do converge in policy space, the results will still go through as long as voters systematically misperceive the locations of the candidates, or if candidates have nonpolicy attributes that distinguish them (age, looks, voice quality, ethnic background, regional base, etc.). The failure of the result to hold *at convergence of candidates* is appropriately viewed as a knife-edge case.

Second, this knife-edge feature suggests that the next step to take is to embed a game of party competition within the structure of the n-party voter equilibrium studied here. This would generate a model somewhat like Ledyard (1984), with two important exceptions. First, we have three candidates, not two. Second, Ledyard allows for abstention. While the abstentions are easy to incorporate, the complications generated by more than two candidates are subtle and difficult because of the inevitability of strategic voting. In Ledyard's (1984) model,[12] the formal structure is a two-stage game. The first stage of the game is a simultaneous choice of platforms (or nomination of candidates) by each party. In the second stage, the voters get to observe (perfectly) these choices by candidates but have incomplete information about the preferences of the other voters. Voters then choose simultaneously which candidate to vote for. The second-stage subgames correspond exactly with the analysis in the body of this essay. However, as we pointed out earlier, there are multiple voter equilibria in *any* subgame (i.e., for any location of the candidates). These multiple equilibria make the equilibrium behavior in

---

12. This is also the case in other models in which candidates *and* noncandidates are both treated as strategic actors (see, for example, Austen-Smith 1987a and Ingberman 1986, in the context of campaign financing).

the first stage of the game essentially indeterminate—i.e., there will be many candidate equilibria that can be supported by some configuration of voter equilibria in the subgames. (By *configuration* we mean a function that assigns party platforms into equilibrium voting strategies.) This indeterminacy needs to be investigated more thoroughly, but such an investigation is clearly beyond the scope of this essay.

The spatial interpretation of the model presented in section II also relates to Assumption 1, that all preference orders have positive probability. In one dimension with single-peaked preferences, some preferences are impossible. Nontheless, the theorem goes through even if $q_{jk} = 0$ for some orderings. Similarly, with respect to the details of Assumption 2, it is not necessary that the density function be positive for all $v \in [0,1]$. The only important part of Assumption 2 is the requirement that there be no mass points.

Abstention

Any model of voting that explores the implications of rational strategic behavior in *large electorates* is obliged to consider the implications of abstention. It is established by Palfrey and Rosenthal (1985) using a very similar Bayesian game approach that in large electorates rational voters with positive net costs of voting will not turn out. This means, simply, that we must restrict analysis to the portion of the electorate who have nonpositive net costs of voting. There are many reasons why net costs may not be positive: consumption value from voting, feelings of citizen duty or obligation, fear of reprisals or sanctions for not voting (badgering by spouse, union official, friends, party activists), to name a few that are often suggested. In fact, as long as any strictly positive fraction of the electorate has nonpositive net costs of voting, and therefore vote, all of the results of the essay hold.

In an extreme case, if all voters were to have strictly positive net voting costs then the prediction would be that nearly 0 percent turnout would occur with large elections. While this will undoubtedly change the theorems in this essay (I have not worked out the details), the implication of no turnout is wildly out of sync with the significant numbers we observe voting.

Dynamics

The results in this essay have been interpreted as implying that if three parties are competing in a single-ballot winner-take-all system, eventually (i.e., in an equilibrium) one of the parties will be weeded out. However, the model is static, even though the interpretation has dynamic overtones. A dynamic model would probably serve two very useful purposes here. First, the equilibrium expectations of voters, which drive their equilibrium voting decisions in multicandidate elections do not emerge from thin air. These expectations are the product of past electoral outcomes, polls, media commentary, and other factors. Polls, past outcomes, etc. themselves are endogenously a function of voters' expectations and decisions. This suggests that it would make more sense from a standpoint of realism to explicitly model expectations and strategies as evolving over time. (For examples of this approach in dynamic economic models, see Marcet and Sargent 1985 and Woodford 1986.)

The second potential contribution of a dynamic model would be to lead toward a resolution of the indeterminacy of multiple equilibria in the static model. The static model in this essay went a long way in this regard, by essentially eliminating all equilibria in the voting game except for two-party equilibria. However, there are still (at least three) multiple two-party voter equilibria, and these in turn produce a plethora of equilibria in the larger game of party competition, as argued above. A well-formulated model of the dynamics of the formation of expectations and beliefs about when a party is a "viable" one (worth expending one's vote on) might shed some light on the indeterminacy issue.

Other Electoral Systems

The original statement of Duverger's Law actually has more components than the one examined here. In fact, Duverger asserts a partial converse (which he does not refer to as a "law") of the result proved here, that "the single-majority systems with *second ballot* and *proportional representation* favor multi-partisan" (1951, 239). This presents some new problems from a theoretical standpoint, as the modeling of proportional representation systems is much harder because of more of a need to explicitly study the coalition formation process. This is not to say that in simple majority, single-ballot, non-PR systems, the coalition formation process among legislators is inconsequential. In fact, this is an aspect of the problem we have glossed over in this essay. Usually a party runs a slate of candidates, often across a range of political "districts" to produce a legislature as a concoction of regional winners. The representative system modeled in this paper consisted of but a single "at large" district with a single representative.

Duverger claims that an additional (beside strategic voting) reinforcing feature in preventing more than two parties is the underrepresentation of small parties (share of seats much less than share of votes) that results as a consequence of single-ballot winner-take-all elections at the district level. Since this "mechanical" (Duverger 1951, 226) factor would seem to reinforce the strategic voting factor analyzed in this essay, its absence from the model does not seem to detract significantly from the results.

On the other hand, the entire notion of PR makes little sense at all in the context of electing a one-member government. The fact that a party can win some seats with less than a majority only makes sense if there are several seats up for grabs. Thus any model of PR will require a model of multimember assemblies. This is a more difficult issue. There are many variations on PR and majority-based electoral systems, as well as completely different types of systems (approval voting, cumulative voting, etc.) for which the implications of strategic voting are not well understood.

APPENDIX

Proof of Step 1 of Lemma 2. This problem is equivalent to the following one. A total of n balls are drawn with replacement from an urn containing a large number of red balls, white balls, and green balls that occur with frequencies $0 < p_1 < p_2 \le p_3$, respectively. Let X_n^{13} denote the random variable taking on values between ⅓ and ½ equal to the proportion of red balls conditional on exactly k red balls being drawn, exactly $(k + 1)$ green balls being drawn, and exactly $(n - 2k - 2)$ white balls being drawn from a sample of $n - 1$ balls and $k \ge (n - 1)/3$. Then

$$E_{13}^n = \frac{1}{n} \sum_{k=\lceil \frac{n-1}{3} \rceil}^{\lfloor \frac{n}{2} \rfloor - 1} k \bar{p}_{13}^{kn}, \text{ where } \bar{p}_{13}^{kn} = \text{prob}(X_n^{13} = k/n - 1).$$

Think of the red balls as being votes for A, the green balls as being votes for C, and the white balls as being votes for B.

Standard results in probability theory tell us that the distribution of X_n^{13} is asymptotically normal. Therefore, since in our problem p_{13}^{kn} is unimodal in k for each n and that mode converges to a limit, then the limit of the modes must equal E_{13}.

The limit of the modes is simple to compute because X_n^{13} has a distribution similar to a binomial. In particular,

$$\bar{p}_{13}^{kn} = \frac{p_{13}^{kn}}{\sum_{j=\lceil \frac{n-1}{3} \rceil}^{\lfloor \frac{n}{2} \rfloor - 1} p_{13}^{jn}}$$

where

$$p_{13}^{jn} = \frac{(n-1)!}{j!(j+1)!(n-2j-2)!} p_1^j p_2^{n-2j-2} p_3^{j+1},$$

$$j = [\frac{n-1}{3}], \ldots, [\frac{n}{2}] - 1.$$

Therefore, $\tilde{p}_{13}^{kn}$ is unimodal in k if and only if p_{13}^{kn} is unimodal in k. To see that p_{13}^{kn} is unimodal look at first differences, $\Delta p_{13}^{kn} = p_{13}^{kn} - p_{13}^{k-1n}$. This gives

$$\Delta p_{13}^{kn} = \left[\frac{(n-2k)(n-2k-1)}{k(k+1)}\left(\frac{p_1 p_3}{p_2^2}\right) - 1\right]\frac{(n-1)!}{(k-1)!k!(n-2k)!} p_1^{k-1} p_2^{n-2k} p_3^k.$$

So $\Delta p_{13}^{kn} > 0$ if

$$\frac{p_1 p_3}{(p_2)^2} > \frac{k(k+1)}{(n-2k)(n-2k-1)}.$$

Rewriting this expression using the notation of the lemma, we get $\tilde{p}_{AC}^{kn}$ is increasing if

$$\frac{\pi_A \pi_C}{(\pi_B)^2} > \frac{k(k+1)}{(n-2k)(n-2k-1)}.$$

The right-hand side is strictly increasing in k, so $\tilde{p}_{AC}^{kn}$ is unimodal in k, as desired. If the mode is interior to $(\frac{1}{3}, \frac{1}{2})$, then for large n, it occurs at k which approximates

$$\frac{\pi_A \pi_C}{\pi_B^2} = \frac{k^2}{(n-2k)^2}$$

or

$$\frac{\pi_A \pi_C}{\pi_B^2} = \frac{(k/n)^2}{[1 - 2(k/n)]^2}.$$

Solving, gives

$$\frac{k}{n} = \frac{1}{2 + \pi_B / \sqrt{\pi_A \pi_C}}$$

if $\pi_B^2 > \pi_A \pi_C$.

Since k/n is constrained to be at least ⅓, we must have

$$\frac{k}{n} = \frac{1}{3}$$

for $\pi_B^2 > \pi_A \pi_C$. Consequently, we get

$$E_{AC} = \begin{cases} \frac{1}{3} & \text{if } \pi_B^2 > \pi_A \pi_C \\ \frac{1}{2 + \pi_B / \sqrt{\pi_A \pi_C}} & \text{if } \pi_B^2 < \pi_A \pi_C \end{cases}.$$

An identical argument proves that $E_{CB} = \frac{1}{2 + \pi_A/\sqrt{\pi_B \pi_C}}$ because $\pi_A^2 < \pi_B \pi_C$ by hypothesis. (Recall $\pi_A < \pi_B \leq \pi_C$.)

Proof of Step 2 of Lemma 2: Let

$$\bar{\bar{p}}_{CB}^n = \frac{(n-1)! \, (\pi_B \pi_C)^{[(n-1)E_{AC}]} \pi_C \pi_A^{n-2-2[(n-1)E_{AC}]}}{[(n-1)E_{AC}]!(1 + [(n-1)E_{AC}])!(n-2-2[(n-1)E_{AC}])!}.$$

Then

$$\frac{\bar{p}_{AC}^n}{\bar{\bar{p}}_{CB}^n} = \left[\frac{\pi_A}{\pi_B}\right]^{1+3[E_{AC}(n-1)]-(n-1)}$$

which, for large n is bounded above by 1. By construction, $\bar{\bar{p}}_{CB}^n < \bar{p}_{CB}^n$, and it is easy to show that

$$\frac{\bar{\bar{p}}_{CB}^n}{\bar{p}_{CB}^n} \quad \text{converges to 0,}$$

so:

$$\lim_{n\to\infty} \frac{\overline{p}^n_{AC}}{\overline{p}^n_{CB}} = \lim_{n\to\infty} \left(\frac{\overline{p}^n_{AC}}{\overline{p}^n_{CB}}\right)\left(\frac{\overline{\overline{p}}^n_{CB}}{\overline{p}^n_{CB}}\right) = 0.$$

Proof of Step 3 of Lemma 2. The central limit theorem insures that for any $\varepsilon > 0$, $p^n_{AC}(\varepsilon)$ and $p^n_{CB}(\varepsilon)$ converge to p^n_{AC} and p^n_{CB} in the sense that $\lim_{n\to\infty}(p^n_{AC}(\varepsilon)/p^n_{AC}) = 1$, and $\lim_{n\to\infty}(p^n_{CB}(\varepsilon)/p^n_{CB}) = 1$, where

$$p^n_{AC}(\varepsilon) = \sum_{max\{\frac{n-1}{3},[(n-1)(E_{AC}-\varepsilon)]\}}^{min\{\frac{n-1}{2},[(n-1)(E_{AC}+\varepsilon)]\}} \frac{(n-1)!}{k!(k+1)!(2n-2k-2)!} \pi_A^k \pi_B^{n-2k-2} \pi_C^{k-1}$$

$$p^n_{CB}(\varepsilon) = \sum_{k=max\{\frac{n-1}{3},[(n-1)(E_{CB}-\varepsilon)]\}}^{min\{\frac{n-1}{2},[(n-1)(E_{CB}+\varepsilon)]\}} \frac{(n-1)!}{k!(k+1)!(n-2k-2)!} \pi_A^{n-2k-2} \pi_B^k \pi_C^{k-1}.$$

Since E_{AC} and E_{CB} are both *strictly* less than ½, we may choose ε so that

$$\left(\frac{n-1}{2}\right) - [(n-1)(E_{AC}+\varepsilon)] \quad \text{and} \quad \left(\frac{n-1}{2}\right) - [(n-1)(E_{CB}+\varepsilon)]$$

both diverge to ∞ in the limit. Since E_{CB} is strictly greater than ⅓, ε can also be chosen so that

$$[(n-1)(E_{CB}-\varepsilon)] - \frac{n-1}{3}$$

diverges to ∞ in the limit. Therefore, we may rewrite $p^n_{AC}(\varepsilon)$ and $p^n_{CB}(\varepsilon)$ for n sufficiently large and ε sufficiently small as:

$$p^n_{AC}(\varepsilon) = \sum_{k=[(n-1)(E_{AC}-\varepsilon)]}^{[(n-1)(E_{AC}+\varepsilon)]} \frac{(n-1)!}{k!(k+1)!(n-2k-2)!} (\pi_A^k \pi_B^{n-2k-2} \pi_C^{k+1} \delta_k)$$

$$p^n_{CB}(\varepsilon) = \sum_{k=[(n-1)(E_{CB}-\varepsilon)]}^{[(n-1)(E_{CB}+\varepsilon)]} \frac{(n-1)!}{k!(k+1)!(n-2k-2)!} (\pi_A^{n-2k-2} \pi_B^k \pi_C^{k+1})$$

where

$$\delta_k = 0 \text{ if } k < \frac{n-1}{3}$$
$$= 1 \text{ if } k \geq \frac{n-1}{3}.$$

For each n both of these sums contain equal numbers of terms that can be matched up. For given n, call the terms on the right-hand side of the $p_{AC}^n(\varepsilon)$ equation $a_1, \ldots, a_{m_n}$ and the terms on the right-hand side of the $p_{CB}^n(\varepsilon)$ equation $b_1, \ldots, b_{m_n}$. By construction, we have $\lim a_l/b_l = 0$ uniformly in l. We also have

$$\lim_{n \to \infty} \frac{p_{AC}^n(\varepsilon)}{p_{CB}^n(\varepsilon)} = \lim_{n \to \infty} \frac{a_1 + \ldots + a_{m_n}}{b_1 + \ldots + b_{m_n}}$$

but

$$\frac{a_1 + \ldots a_{m_n}}{b_1 + \ldots b_{m_n}} \leq \max_{l \leq m_n} \frac{a_l}{b_l}.$$

Since $\frac{a_l}{b_l} \to 0$ uniformly, we get

$$\lim_{n \to \infty} \frac{p_{AC}^n(\varepsilon)}{p_{CB}^n(\varepsilon)} = 0.$$

Therefore

$$\lim_{n \to \infty} \frac{p_{AC}^n}{p_{CB}^n} = 0.$$

Service-Induced Campaign Contributions, Incumbent Shirking, and Reelection Opportunities

David P. Baron

I. Introduction

The relationship between candidates for office and the contributors to their election campaigns is central to the understanding of elections. In the past two decades, interest groups have become an increasingly important feature of this relationship by providing campaign funds that most candidates are unable, or unwilling, to risk doing without. Some interest groups make contributions to influence the outcome of elections, but others are interested in obtaining something more tangible from the winner in exchange for their contributions. Some seek specific policy outcomes and hope that campaign contributions will give them access to officeholders so that they will have the opportunity to try to convince them of the merits of their cause or policy objective. In addition, as Fiorina (1977) has emphasized, members of Congress can be important in intervening in the bureaucracy on behalf of constituents and contributors. As he argues (43), "Congressmen possess the power to expedite and influence bureaucratic decisions. This capability flows directly from congressional control over what bureaucrats value most: higher budgets and new program authorizations. In a very real sense each congressman is a monopoly supplier of bureaucratic unsticking services for his district." He adds (47), "In fact, it is probable that at least some congressmen deliberately stimulate the demand for their bureaucratic fixit services."

The focus of this essay is the relationship between the ability of elected officials to provide access and services to constituents and interest groups and their ability to solicit campaign funds. The perspective adopted here is not that interest groups and other contributors force contributions on candidates but that candidates use their quasi-monopoly position to extract contributions from groups that have a demand for services that only successful candidates can provide. The emphasis is on

---

This research has been supported by National Science Foundation grant no. SES-8808211.

the incentive of interest groups to make contributions in anticipation of the provision of services and how candidates can structure contributions to their election and reelection campaigns to provide assurances to the interest groups that the promised services will be delivered.

The model may be interpreted as pertaining to two categories of services. The first includes services that provide a nonrivalrous private benefit to individuals or groups without imposing a direct cost on others. Such services might include support or opposition for certain types of particularistic legislation or intervention in cases before regulatory commissions, public works agencies, government loan agencies, and other administrative bodies that allocate funds. These services are such that either candidate is likely to be willing to provide them, so contributors may give to both candidates. The second category pertains to services that benefit one set of potential contributors and impose costs on another set. Labor, trade, and tax legislation has this property as might intervention with the National Labor Relations Board and the Environmental Protection Agency. Here, each candidate may be aligned with a distinct set of potential contributors and interest groups, who would then give only to the candidate aligned with their interests. Similarly, if the services represent efforts on behalf of policy outcomes that benefit one set of interest groups at the expense of another set of interest groups, candidates may solicit contributions from those interest groups that are aligned with their ideology, party, or policy position.

The interest groups considered here are thus in the spirit of those characterized by Jacobson and Kernell (1983, 36), "Economic interest groups—corporate political-action committees, professional and trade associations, labor unions—are commonly assumed to be motivated by hopes of tangible if unspecified payoffs, as are private individuals who donate substantial sums. Their rational strategy is to contribute to candidates who are likely to be in a position to help or harm them. . . . Contributions intended to curry favor are not made with an eye to electoral utility; the idea is to buy influence, not affect the outcome. If an incumbent is certain to win, so much the better." The value of the services desired by interest groups is likely to be idiosyncratic, so candidates are likely to know those values only imperfectly. The candidates thus must determine their campaign contributions-solicitation strategy and their service promises based on incomplete information.

Baron (1989) presents a model in which candidates compete for an elected office by raising funds to finance their campaigns by promising to provide, conditional on winning the election, access and services to interest groups that contribute to their election campaign. Once elected, however, the incumbent may have an incentive to shirk on those promises, since the provision of services and the granting of access is costly. The present essay addresses the role of contributions to an incumbent's reelection campaign as a means of discouraging shirking on promised services.

Shirking in this setting can be of two forms. First, the successful candidate may choose to provide no services at all. This, of course, would easily be detected and certainly would be opposed by the candidate's party and might end the future prospects of the candidate. Nevertheless, an incumbent may decide not to stand for reelection and may well be willing to go against his party and his contributors by consuming the benefits of office rather than performing as promised. This form of shirking, which will be referred to as quitting, should be treated as endogenous in a theory of service-induced campaign contributions. Second, once elected, the successful candidate may provide some, but not as many, services as had been promised. The successful candidate may attempt to justify or explain this by claiming that due to factors beyond his control the services were more difficult to provide than had been anticipated. Even though they may be able to observe the services actually provided, interest groups are likely to be less well informed than is the incumbent about how difficult or costly it is to deliver the promised services. Interest groups thus cannot verify whether the incumbent's explanation is true or is merely an excuse. Shirking by excuses is an inherent feature of the contributor-candidate relationship.

The incentive to shirk is mitigated by the candidate's interest in reelection, since he will need contributions for his reelection campaign. Interest groups, of course, recognize this and have an incentive at the time of their initial contribution to pledge to make a contribution, contingent on the promised services actually being provided, to the candidate's reelection campaign. As will be indicated, the candidate may have an incentive to borrow against the interest group's pledge as a means of obtaining greater contributions to the initial campaign. The understanding between a candidate and interest groups is thus a promise to provide services if elected in exchange for a contribution to the initial campaign and a pledged contribution to the reelection campaign to be made if he becomes the incumbent and the services are actually performed. Unless it is against the incumbent's interest to misrepresent the true cost of providing services, however, interest groups will doubt any claim by the incumbent that costs were higher than expected and hence will be willing to contribute less to the initial election campaign. The incumbent thus will wish to structure the interest groups' reelection campaign contributions to assure them that he will provide the promised services rather than make excuses.

The model demonstrates how the incentives to shirk can be eliminated by appropriately structuring the contributions provided by interest groups and the services promised by candidates. The setting is an electoral competition between two candidates with a continuum of interest groups that have private information about their valuation of the services. The interest groups and the candidates have symmetric but incomplete information about the cost or difficulty of providing the services, but the successful candidate, who becomes the incumbent, will privately observe that cost prior to the time at which he delivers the promised services. If that cost is high, the incumbent may have an incentive to quit, and when he prefers to remain in office, he has an incentive to make excuses. The analysis demonstrates how the incentives to shirk can be dealt with in electoral competition.

Although the model considered here addresses the shirking problem, the resolution of that problem requires that candidates and interest groups be able to make credible commitments to their promises and pledges. Thus, at the time of the initial election, candidates are assumed to commit to a campaign contributions-services schedule that specifies for contributors the services promised to be provided as a function of the contributions and of the cost of providing the services. Those promises and pledges are observable to both the candidates and the interest groups, so the issue of commitment is different in nature from that of shirking. That is, shirking by excuses cannot be observed by an interest group because it is unable to observe the cost or difficulty of providing the services. Candidates, however, are not allowed to renege on the contributions-services schedules they announce to the interest groups. That is, once elected, the winner cannot renege by announcing a new reelection contributions-services schedule.[1] Similarly, interest groups are not allowed to renege on their pledged contributions to the reelection campaign. One reason that such commitment may have a degree of credibility is that interest groups can call reneging to the attention of challengers to the incumbent who can be expected to call it to the attention of voters and to use that reneging as a basis for their own campaign solicitations.

Downs (1957) provided the seminal treatment of elections by viewing political parties as choosing policies so as to be elected rather than seeking election in order to choose policies. Downs thus formulates the party's objective as winning office. Many of the subsequent models

---

1. The candidates are also assumed to be able to commit to deny service to any group that does not contribute to the initial campaign.

follow in this tradition by specifying candidate objectives in terms of maximizing votes, the probability of winning, or plurality.[2] Ledyard (1984) extends such an electoral model to consider explicitly voters' strategies, and he characterizes a voter-candidate equilibrium in which candidates choose a platform that maximizes the aggregate expected utility of voters. Wittman (1983) argues that candidates in elections do not seek to maximize the probability of winning but instead have policy preferences that affect their platform choices.[3] The present essay represents candidate preferences in terms of the value of being in office, which may derive from the subsequent opportunity to affect policy outcomes. Contributors play a role similar to that of voters and provide campaign resources that are used to increase the probability of winning the election. Candidates, however, bear the cost of serving their campaign contributors.

The strategic nature of electoral competition and campaign contributions is analyzed by Jacobson and Kernell (1983). Aranson and Hinich (1979) consider the contributor's problem and focus on the effect of disclosure of, and limits on, individual contributions. Their model, however, is not closed, since candidate competition and the effect of contributions on that competition are not considered. The model considered here allows a characterization of a contributor-candidate equilibrium that relates contributions to the election outcome. Ferejohn and Noll (1985) consider the relationship between contributors and candidates in a model in which candidates offer one unit of service and choose the contributions required in exchange. This restriction is relaxed by Baron (1989), who focuses primarily on explanations for the incumbency advantage. The present model emphasizes the role of reelection opportunities in mitigating the incentives to shirk.

The model and the notation are introduced in section II, and the analysis of the incumbent's problem is presented in section III. Campaign contributions solicitation for the initial election campaign is then analyzed in section IV. Electoral competition is characterized in section V, and to obtain a closed-form characterization of the equilibrium, an example is analyzed in section VI under the assumption that the incumbent does not quit. The issue of shirking by quitting is then addressed in section VII, and conclusions are offered in the final section.

---

2. These objectives lead to a zero-sum game between the candidates. See Ordeshook (1986, chap. 4) for a presentation of this class of models. Calvert (1986) surveys the literature on electoral models involving uncertainty or imperfect information.

3. Wittman (1988) surveys models in which candidates have policy preferences.

II. The Model

A two-candidate election is considered, and aligned with each candidate is a set of interest groups that may contribute to his campaign. In addition, there may be interest groups that are willing to contribute to both candidates.[4] Since attention will be restricted to a symmetric equilibrium, the candidates and the sets of potential contributors to each candidate will be assumed to be identical. As indicated in section I, the perspective taken here is that the candidates have power relative to interest groups, so candidates extract contributions from them rather than interest groups forcing contributions on unwilling candidates. A candidate, however, must not only decide how much to promise contributors but also how to assure them that he will not shirk on the promised services. To deal with this shirking, the approach developed by Riordan and Sappington (1987) will be employed.

The model incorporates two informational asymmetries. First, candidates are not assumed to know the value of the services to individual interest groups. Second, at the time of the initial election neither candidates nor interest groups know how difficult, or how costly, it will be to provide services. That cost includes the effort of the incumbent, the opportunity cost of staff time, and the expenditures of the perquisites of office.

At the beginning of the initial election campaign each interest groups knows a parameter $\theta \in [\theta^-, \theta^+]$ of its valuation of the services, and the candidates have only incomplete information about θ as represented by a density function $f(\theta)$ that is positive on $[\theta^-, \theta^+]$.[5] The parameter θ might, for example, represent the number of members of the interest group who will benefit from the services. Since candidates do not know the value of the services to individual interest groups, they cannot practice first-degree price discrimination. They can, however, use self-selection by offering interest groups a set of service-contribution alternatives from which they can select. One task of a candidate is thus to choose that set to extract as much in contributions as possible, consistent with the cost of providing the promised services.

Prior to the election, both candidates and the interest groups are assumed to have symmetric, but imperfect, information, represented by a density function $h(\omega)$, about the marginal cost $\omega \in [\omega^-, \omega^+]$ of providing services. The successful candidate will privately observe ω after tak-

---

4. Contributions may be monetary or in terms of campaign labor, endorsements, or other resources. For modeling purposes, all contributions will be expressed in the same numeraire.

5. The number of interest groups is thus normalized to one.

ing office and at that point will be better informed than are the interest groups. Because services are costly to provide, the candidate prefers to promise fewer services for the event in which the cost is high than when it is low. The services provided are observable by the interest groups, but since they are unable to observe ω, they are concerned about the incumbent's opportunity to shirk by excuses.

To simplify the analysis, ω and θ are assumed to be statistically independent. This might correspond to a case in which all the interest groups demand the same type of service but value it differently.

Characterization of the electoral competition and campaign contributions solicitation is facilitated by the formulation of the candidate's problem as a direct revelation game in which each candidate chooses a contributions-services schedule for the initial election and a contributions schedule for the reelection campaign. Interest groups then select from that schedule, and the winning candidate subsequently determines the services to provide once he has observed the cost. The revelation principle states that there exists a schedule that is optimal for the candidate and induces both the winner and the interest groups to reveal their private information truthfully. The candidates thus can be considered to compete by choosing contributions-services schedules that are incentive compatible.

The candidates want the contributions to be a function of the valuation parameter θ of the interest group and thus employ a nonlinear "pricing" policy that offers potential contributors a set of contributions-services alternatives from which they can select. The contributions to the initial campaign are thus a function $c(\hat{\theta})$ of the choice $\hat{\theta} = \hat{\theta}(\theta)$ made by interest group θ. The services $s(\hat{\theta},\hat{\omega})$ and the contributions $Q(\hat{\theta},\hat{\omega})$ to the reelection campaign can be a function of both $\hat{\theta}$ and the choice $\hat{\omega} = \hat{\omega}(\omega)$ by the incumbent. Consequently, candidates offer contributions-services schedules

$$\{(c(\hat{\theta}),s(\hat{\theta},\hat{\omega}),Q(\hat{\theta},\hat{\omega})),\hat{\theta} \in [\theta^-,\theta^+], \hat{\omega} \in [\omega^-,\omega^+]\}$$

from which interest groups select by choosing $\hat{\theta} = \hat{\theta}(\theta)$. That is, interest groups contribute $c(\hat{\theta})$ in exchange for the promise that services $s(\hat{\theta},\hat{\omega})$ will be delivered when the incumbent announces $\hat{\omega}$.[6] When the services are delivered, the interest group completes the exchange by making a contribution $Q(\hat{\theta},\hat{\omega})$ to the incumbent's reelection campaign. The assumption of commitment means that both the functions s and Q are

---

6. This formulation is equivalent to a formulation in which candidates announce schedules $(s(c,\omega),Q(c,\omega))$ and interest groups choose contributions $c = c(\theta)$.

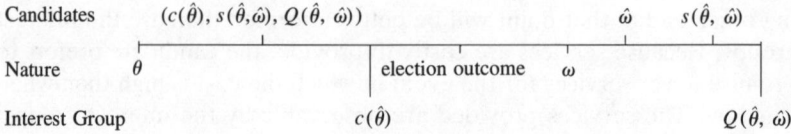

Fig. 1. Sequence of actions and events

announced prior to the initial campaign and that the candidate will not renege on those choices.

An interest group's contribution to a candidate depends on the likelihood that that candidate will win, since a contribution to a loser is wasted. Interest groups will be assumed to have expectations about which candidate will win, and those expectations are denoted by the probability p that candidate 1 will win. The election outcome is assumed to depend stochastically on the campaign expenditures of the candidates, and thus the probability that candidate 1 will win will be represented by a function $P(X_1,X_2)$, where X_i denotes the campaign expenditures, which are assumed to equal the contributions, of candidate i. In the context of the model of McKelvey and Ordeshook (1985), the campaign contributions may be viewed as informing a subset of voters, with uninformed voters "learning" in a rational expectations sense from polls and endorsements. An equilibrium requires that the expectations p of interest groups equal $P(X_1,X_2)$.

The equilibrium sought involves both a Bayesian-Nash equilibrium among the candidates and the contributors and a rational expectations equilibrium for interest group beliefs about the probability that a candidate will win the initial election. The characterization of the equilibrium proceeds by considering in sequence the contributions to the reelection campaign, the contributions to the initial election campaign, the candidate's choice of the services to promise, and then the electoral competition between the candidates. The sequence of actions and events is presented in figure 1.

The notation employed in the model is presented in table 1.

III. The Incumbent's Problem

Consider first the incumbent's problem of assuring the interest groups that he will not shirk by excuses: i.e., provide fewer services by reporting a marginal cost $\hat{\omega}$ different from the true ω that he observes upon taking office. To understand the incentive to shirk by excuses, note that the services $s(\theta,\hat{\omega})$ provided would be expected to be a decreasing

TABLE 1. Notation Employed in the Model

θ	Private information on the value of services to group $\theta \in [\theta^-, \theta^+]$
$\hat{\theta}(\theta)$	Selection or response function of interest group θ
$s(\theta,\omega)$	Services promised, conditional on becoming the incumbent
$\omega s(\theta,\omega)$	Incumbent's cost of providing services $s(\theta,\omega)$
ω	Incumbent's marginal cost of providing services; ω is private information received after taking office
$\hat{\omega}(\omega)$	Response function of the incumbent
$R(s(\theta,\omega))\theta$	Value of the service to group θ; $R(0) = 0$; $R'(\cdot) > 0$; $R''(\cdot) \leq 0$
$f(\theta)$	Density function of θ with $f(\theta) > 0$ for $\theta \in [\theta^-,\theta^+]$
$F(\theta)$	Distribution function of θ
$h(\omega)$	Density function of ω with $h(\omega) > 0$ for $\omega \in [\omega^-,\omega^+]$
$H(\omega)$	Distribution function of ω
$c(\theta)$	Contributions to the initial campaign by interest group θ
$C(\theta)$	Expected contributions to both campaigns by interest group θ
X_i	Total contributions to candidate i's initial campaign
$P(X_1,X_2)$	Probability that candidate 1 wins the initial election; $P_1 > 0$; $P_2 < 0$; $P_{11} < 0$; $P_{22} > 0$
$Q(\theta,\omega)$	Pledged contributions to the reelection campaign
$Y(\omega)$	Total pledged contributions to the reelection campaign
V	Value to the candidate of occupying the office
$U(Y(\omega))$	Value to the incumbent of having contributions $Y(\omega)$ at the beginning of the reelection campaign; $U'(Y(\omega)) > 0$
p	Interest groups' expectation of the probability that candidate 1 will be elected
$Z(\omega)$	Performance value conditional on ω
T	Incumbency value
EW	Expected value of the election opportunity
$\delta(\omega)$	Probability that the incumbent quits when ω is observed

function of the marginal cost of providing the service. The incumbent has an incentive to shirk by announcing $\hat{\omega} > \omega$ to contributors as a means of reducing the amount of services he has to deliver. This incentive to shirk reduces the value to the interest group of the anticipated services, which reduces the contributions it is willing to make. The incumbent, however, can assure the interest group that he will not misrepresent ω, and hence not shirk by excuses, by choosing an incentive-compatible reelection contributions function $Q(\theta,\hat{\omega})$ that induces himself to announce $\hat{\omega} = \omega$.[7]

To characterize the set of incentive compatible policies for the incumbent, let $Z(\hat{\omega};\omega)$ denote the "performance value" defined as the value, once in office, of providing services and receiving contributions to

---

7. Since the schedules are chosen ex ante, the incumbent cannot practice first-degree price discrimination based on what he learns from the interest group's contribution to the initial election campaign.

his reelection campaign when he realizes ω and announces that it is $\hat{\omega}$. The performance value is thus[8]

$$Z(\hat{\omega};\omega) \equiv -\omega \int_{\theta^-}^{\theta^+} s(\theta,\hat{\omega})f(\theta)d\theta + U(Y(\hat{\omega})), \tag{1}$$

where $\omega s(\theta,\hat{\omega})$ is the cost of providing the services and $U(\cdot)$ is the value of beginning the reelection campaign with contributions $Y(\hat{\omega})$, where

$$Y(\hat{\omega}) = \int_{\theta^-}^{\theta^+} Q(\theta,\hat{\omega})f(\theta)d\theta \tag{2}$$

is the reelection contributions from all the interest groups. For any schedule $(s(\theta,\hat{\omega}), Q(\theta,\hat{\omega}))$ the incumbent will choose $\hat{\omega}(\omega) \in \arg\max_{\hat{\omega}} Z(\hat{\omega};\omega)$.

The revelation principle implies that the candidate can choose a reelection campaign contributions schedule $Q(\cdot,\cdot)$ that will induce him not to shirk if he wins the election; i.e., to choose $\hat{\omega}(\omega) = \omega$. The analysis proceeds by characterizing the class of service functions that can be implemented; i.e., for which $\hat{\omega}(\omega) = \omega$. The performance value resulting from a response function $\hat{\omega}(\omega) = \omega$ can be determined by differentiating $Z(\hat{\omega};\omega)$ with respect to ω, evaluating the derivative at $\hat{\omega} = \omega$, and using the first-order condition for the choice of θ. That is,[9]

$$\frac{dZ(\hat{\omega};\omega)}{d\omega}\bigg|_{\hat{\omega}=\omega} = \frac{\partial Z(\hat{\omega};\omega)}{\partial \hat{\omega}} \frac{d\hat{\omega}(\omega)}{d\omega}\bigg|_{\hat{\omega}=\omega} + \frac{\partial Z(\hat{\omega};\omega)}{\partial \omega}\bigg|_{\hat{\omega}=\omega}$$

$$= \frac{\partial Z(\hat{\omega};\omega)}{\partial \omega}\bigg|_{\hat{\omega}=\omega}$$

$$= -\int_{\theta^-}^{\theta^+} s(\theta,\omega)f(\theta)d\theta. \tag{3}$$

The performance value $Z(\omega) \equiv Z(\omega;\omega)$ then is obtained by integrating (3), which yields

$$Z(\omega) = \int_{\omega}^{\omega^+} \int_{\theta^-}^{\theta^+} s(\theta,\tilde{\omega})f(\theta)d\theta d\tilde{\omega} + Z(\omega^+). \tag{4}$$

---

8. This assumes that θ is reported truthfully, which will be assured by the choice of $c(\theta)$ as characterized in the next section.

9. This derivative exists almost everywhere.

This is a strictly decreasing function of ω, so the performance value is lower the higher the costs of delivering the service are.

The service function $s(\theta,\omega)$ then can be implemented by choosing the reelection contribution schedule Q to equate (1) evaluated at $\hat{\omega} = \omega$ with (4). That is, the service function $s(\theta,\omega)$ can be implemented by choosing $Q(\theta,\omega)$ to satisfy

$$-\omega \int_{\theta^-}^{\theta^+} s(\theta,\omega)f(\theta)d\theta + U(Y(\omega)) = Z(\omega^+)$$

$$+ \int_{\omega}^{\omega^+} \int_{\theta^-}^{\theta^+} s(\theta,\tilde{\omega})f(\theta)d\theta d\tilde{\omega}. \tag{5}$$

Note that one function $Q(\theta,\omega)$ that satisfies (5) is that which satisfies it pointwise on θ. To permit a closed-form solution to be obtained, the function $U(Y)$ will be assumed to be linear or $U(Y) = \alpha Y$, where $\alpha > 0$ is the marginal value of a dollar of contributions to the reelection campaign.[10] The contributions $Y(\omega)$ to the reelection campaign thus are from (5)

$$Y(\omega) = \int_{\theta^-}^{\theta^+} Q(\theta,\omega)f(\theta)d\theta$$

$$= \frac{1}{\alpha}\left(Z(\omega^+) + \omega \int_{\theta^-}^{\theta^+} s(\theta,\omega)f(\theta)d\theta + \int_{\omega}^{\omega^+} \int_{\theta^-}^{\theta^+} s(\theta,\tilde{\omega})f(\theta)d\theta d\tilde{\omega}\right). \tag{6}$$

To verify that a reelection contributions function $Q(\theta,\omega)$ satisfying (6) will cause the winner to choose $\hat{\omega} = \omega$ given a service function $s(\theta,\hat{\omega})$, substitute $\int_{\theta^-}^{\theta^+} Q(\theta,\hat{\omega})f(\theta)d\theta$ from (6) into (1) to obtain

$$Z(\hat{\omega};\omega) = -\int_{\theta^-}^{\theta^+} (\hat{\omega} - \omega)s(\theta,\hat{\omega})f(\theta)d\theta$$

$$+ \int_{\hat{\omega}}^{\omega^+} \int_{\theta^-}^{\theta^+} s(\theta,\tilde{\omega})f(\theta)d\theta d\tilde{\omega} + Z(\omega^+). \tag{7}$$

It is straightforward to show that for any service function $s(\cdot,\cdot)$ the $\hat{\omega}$ that satisfies the first-order incentive compatibility condition for the maximi-

---

10. The linearity assumption is made to facilitate characterization of the equilibrium.

zation of $Z(\hat{\omega};\omega)$ in (7) equals ω. Incentive compatibility also requires that $s(\theta,\omega)$ satisfy the local second-order condition[11]

$$\int_{\theta^-}^{\theta^+} \frac{\partial s(\theta,\omega)}{\partial \omega} f(\theta)d\theta \leq 0, \forall \omega \in [\omega^-,\omega^+]. \tag{8}$$

The global incentive compatibility condition is

$$\int_{\theta^-}^{\theta^+} s(\theta,\omega)f(\theta)d\theta \geq \int_{\theta^-}^{\theta^+} s(\theta,\hat{\omega})f(\theta)d\theta, \forall \hat{\omega} > \omega, \forall \omega \in [\omega^-,\omega^+]. \tag{9}$$

Consequently, any service function $s(\theta,\omega)$ that is nonincreasing in ω can be implemented by choosing $Q(\theta,\hat{\omega})$ to satisfy (6). A service function satisfying (9) is said to be implementable by the incumbent.[12] The incumbent thus can assure the interest groups that he will not shirk by making excuses. The following characterization of the reelection contributions schedule summarizes this development.

PROPOSITION 1. *A service function $s(\theta,\omega)$ is implementable by the incumbent using the reelection contributions function $Q(\theta,\omega)$ in (6) if and only if it satisfies (9). For any implementable service function $s(\theta,\omega)$, the contributions $Y(\omega)$ to the reelection campaign and the performance value $Z(\omega)$ are decreasing functions of ω.*

These properties of the services and reelection campaign contributions functions are as expected. The set of service functions that can be implemented is composed of those functions that provide fewer services the higher is the cost of providing them. Similarly, the contributions to the incumbent's reelection campaign are a decreasing function of the cost of providing services and hence of the services provided. The value of incumbency is also decreasing in the cost of providing services.

An increase in the constant $Z(\omega^+)$ in (4) and (6) shifts upwards the incumbency value and the reelection contributions, but as will be indicated below, this reduces the contributions the interest groups are willing to make to the initial campaign. The candidate thus faces a trade-off between contributions to the reelection campaign and contributions to the initial campaign.

---

11. This condition is obtained by differentiating $Z(\hat{\omega};\omega)$ in (7) twice and using the first-order condition.

12. Implementation conditions on s as a function of θ are characterized in the next section.

The development in this section has addressed the issue of shirking by excuses. The incentive to shirk by quitting is present if the incumbency value $Z(\omega)$ in (4) is negative. The analysis will proceed under the assumption either that the incumbency value is nonnegative or that forces external to the model, such as party considerations, honor, or future rewards ensure that the incumbent will not quit. Shirking by quitting will then be addressed in section VII.

IV. Contributions to the Initial Election Campaign

In section III the properties required for the function $s(\theta,\omega)$ to be implementable by the incumbent were characterized as a function of ω. In this section the properties required on $s(\theta,\omega)$ as a function of θ are characterized. Prior to the initial election, a candidate chooses a campaign contributions-services schedule

$$\{(c(\theta),s(\theta,\omega),Q(\theta,\omega)),\ \forall \theta \in [\theta^-,\theta^+],\ \forall \theta \in [\omega^-,\omega^+]\},$$

and an interest group with valuation parameter θ selects a campaign contributions-services triple from that schedule. Interest group θ thus chooses $\hat\theta$, thereby making contributions $c(\hat\theta)$ to the initial election campaign and the associated contributions $Q(\hat\theta,\omega)$ to the reelection campaign in exchange for the promise of services $s(\hat\theta,\omega)$. Given a service function $s(\hat\theta,\omega)$ implementable by the incumbent, the expected gain $G(\hat\theta;\theta)$ to interest group θ from $(c(\hat\theta),s(\hat\theta,\omega),Q(\hat\theta,\omega))$ is

$$G(\hat\theta;\theta) = p \int_{\omega^-}^{\omega^+} [R(s(\hat\theta,\omega))\theta - Q(\hat\theta,\omega)]h(\omega)d\omega - c(\hat\theta), \qquad (10)$$

where $R(s)\theta$ is the value of the services to group θ, $Q(\theta,\omega)$ satisfies (6), $s(\theta,\omega)$ satisfies (9), and p is the perceived probability of winning. The function R is assumed to be strictly increasing and strictly concave is s with $R(0) = 0$. Each interest group is assumed to take p as given, and not as a function of its contribution, which is consistent with each group's contribution being small relative to total contributions. The revelation principle implies that the candidate can choose an incentive-compatible campaign contributions-services schedule $(s(\theta,\omega),c(\theta),Q(\theta,\omega))$ which induces interest group θ to choose the triple designed for it; i.e., $\hat\theta(\theta) = \theta$.

Proceeding in a manner analogous to that in section III, the class of implementable incentive compatible service functions will first be characterized. Incentive compatibility implies that the gain $G(\theta) \equiv G(\theta;\theta)$ satisfies, using the approach in Equation (3),

$$\frac{dG(\theta)}{d\theta} = \frac{\partial G(\hat{\theta};\theta)}{\partial \theta}\bigg|_{\hat{\theta}=\theta} = p \int_{\omega^-}^{\omega^+} R(s(\theta,\omega))h(\omega)d\omega, \qquad (11)$$

and integrating yields

$$G(\theta) = G(\theta^-) + p \int_{\theta^-}^{\theta} \int_{\omega^-}^{\omega^+} R(s(\tilde{\theta},\omega))h(\omega)d\omega d\tilde{\theta}. \qquad (12)$$

This gain is the portion of the value of the services to the interest group that cannot be extracted due to the candidate's incomplete information about the parameter θ. The gain is an increasing function of θ, so groups with higher valuations have greater gains from any implementable contributions-services schedule. The gain is also higher the more likely the candidate is to win. The interest group will contribute only if

$$G(\theta) \geq 0, \forall \theta \in [\theta^-, \theta^+]. \qquad (13)$$

Since $G(\theta)$ in (12) is an increasing function of θ, (13) is satisfied if $G(\theta^-) \geq 0$ and $s(\theta,\omega)$ is incentive compatible.

The service function $s(\theta,\omega)$ must satisfy the local second-order condition

$$\int_{\omega^-}^{\omega^+} R'(s(\theta,\omega)) \frac{\partial s(\theta,\omega)}{\partial \theta} h(\omega)d\omega \geq 0, \qquad (14)$$

so $\partial s(\theta,\omega)/\partial \theta \geq 0 \,\forall\, \omega \in [\omega^-, \omega^+]$ is a sufficient condition for local incentive compatibility. Global incentive compatibility requires that $s(\cdot,\cdot)$ satisfy

$$\int_{\omega^-}^{\omega^+} R(s(\hat{\theta},\omega))h(\omega)d\omega \leq \int_{\omega^-}^{\omega^+} R(s(\theta,\omega))h(\omega)d\omega, \forall \hat{\theta} > \theta,$$

$$\forall \theta \in [\theta^-, \theta^+]. \qquad (15)$$

This condition is satisfied if $s(\theta,\omega)$ is a nondecreasing function of θ.

Given the service function $s(\theta,\omega)$ and the contributions $Q(\theta,\omega)$ satisfying (6), equating (12) and (10) evaluated at $\hat{\theta} = \theta$ yields the contributions function $c(\theta)$ that will implement $(s(\theta,\omega), Q(\theta,\omega))$ by ensuring that $\hat{\theta} = \theta$, or

$$c(\theta) = p \int_{\omega^-}^{\omega^+} \left[R(s(\theta,\omega))\theta - Q(\theta,\omega) \right] h(\omega)d\omega - G(\theta^-)$$

$$- p \int_{\theta^-}^{\theta} \int_{\omega^-}^{\omega^+} R(s(\tilde{\theta},\omega))h(\omega)d\omega d\tilde{\theta}. \tag{16}$$

This expression indicates the trade-off between the pledged contributions to the reelection campaign and the contributions to the initial campaign. Contributions to the initial campaign are reduced in a one-to-p ratio by the expectation of the contributions $\int_{\omega^-}^{\omega^+} Q(\theta,\omega)h(\omega)d\omega$ to the reelection campaign conditional on the candidate winning. A candidate thus faces a trade-off between contributions to the initial election campaign and contributions to the reelection campaign. The parameter $G(\theta^-)$ fixes the terminal point of the gain $G(\theta)$ of the interest groups, and thus a candidate can increase contributions $c(\theta)$ by choosing a lower $G(\theta^-)$. Since group θ will contribute only if $G(\theta) \geq 0$, $G(\theta^-)$ will be set to zero.

The contributions X to the initial campaign are

$$X = \int_{\theta^-}^{\theta^+} c(\theta)f(\theta)d\theta$$

$$= p \int_{\theta^-}^{\theta^+} \int_{\omega^-}^{\omega^+} \left[R(s(\theta,\omega))m(\theta) - Q(\theta,\omega) \right] h(\omega)f(\theta)d\omega d\theta$$

$$- G(\theta^-), \tag{17}$$

where $m(\theta) \equiv \theta - \frac{1-F(\theta)}{f(\theta)}$. The effect of the candidate's incomplete information about θ is reflected in the term $m(\theta)$. If the candidate could practice first-degree price discrimination and extract all the value from the interest groups, contributions would be

$$p \int_{\theta^-}^{\theta^+} \int_{\omega^-}^{\omega^+} R(s(\theta,\omega))\theta h(\omega)f(\theta)d\omega d\theta.$$

Given the candidate's incomplete information, only self-selection can be used, and this results in an inability to extract

$$p \int_{\theta^-}^{\theta^+} \int_{\omega^-}^{\omega^+} R(s(\theta,\omega)) \frac{1-F(\theta)}{f(\theta)} h(\omega)f(\theta)d\omega d\theta$$

in contributions from the interest groups.

The expression in (17) can be rewritten in terms of the total expected contributions to both the initial election and the reelection campaigns or

$$X + p \int_{\theta^-}^{\theta^+} \int_{\omega^-}^{\omega^+} Q(\theta,\omega)h(\omega)f(\theta)dwd\theta$$

$$= p \int_{\theta^-}^{\theta^+} \int_{\omega^-}^{\omega^+} R(s(\theta,\omega))m(\theta)h(\omega)f(\theta)dwd\theta - G(\theta^-). \tag{18}$$

Total contributions thus depend only on the services offered by the candidate and on interest group beliefs about the probability that the candidate will win the initial election.

The total contributions X to the initial campaign can be rewritten by taking the expectation of the reelection contributions $Y(\omega)$ in (6), integrating by parts, and substituting into (17) to obtain

$$X = p \int_{\theta^-}^{\theta^+} \int_{\omega^-}^{\omega^+} \left[R(s(\theta,\omega))m(\theta) - \frac{1}{\alpha} s(\theta,\omega)n(\omega) \right] h(\omega)f(\theta)d\omega d\theta$$

$$- \frac{p}{\alpha} Z(\omega^+) - G(\theta^-), \tag{19}$$

where $n(\omega) \equiv \omega + H(\omega)/h(\omega)$. An increase in the services $s(\theta,\omega)$ increases contributions through the return function $R(s(\theta,\omega))$ but reduces it by $\frac{1}{\alpha} n(\omega)$ because the contributions Y to the reelection campaign are also increasing in $s(\theta,\omega)$ (as indicated in (6)) and X is decreasing in the reelection contributions as indicated in (17). The term $H(\omega)/h(\omega)$ is the marginal "assurance cost"; i.e., the cost of assuring the interest groups that if he wins he will not shirk by excuses.

The results of this section are summarized in the following proposition.

PROPOSITION 2. *A service function $s(\theta,\omega)$ is implementable by a reelection contributions function $Q(\theta,\omega)$ satisfying (6) and a contributions function $c(\theta)$ satisfying (16) if and only if it satisfies (9) and (15). The gain to the interest group is an increasing function of θ, so interest groups that value the services more highly gain more from their campaign contributions.*

V. The Candidate's Problem

In sections III and IV, the relation between campaign contributions and the promised services was characterized. The candidate, say candidate

1, then must choose $s(\theta,\omega)$, given his opponent's strategy, to maximize the expected value EW of his election opportunity, which is given by

$$EW = P(X_1,X_2) \int_{\omega^-}^{\omega^+} [V + Z(\omega)]h(\omega)d\omega, \tag{20}$$

where V is the candidate's personal valuation of the office and $P(X_1,X_2)$ is the probability that candidate 1 wins the election when candidate i's campaign expenditures are X_i.[13] Taking the expectation of $Z(\omega)$ in (4), integrating by parts, and substituting into (20) yields

$$EW = P(X_1,X_2) \cdot$$

$$\int_{\theta^-}^{\theta^+} \int_{\omega^-}^{\omega^+} \left[V + Z(\omega^+) + s(\theta,\omega)\frac{H(\omega)}{h(\omega)} \right] h(\omega)f(\theta)d\omega d\theta. \tag{21}$$

The candidate maximizes EW with respect to $(s(\theta,\omega), Z(\omega^+), G(\theta^-))$, taking his opponent's expenditures X_2 as given, subject to (9), (15), and (17) and the participation constraint $G(\theta^-) \geq 0$. The contributions X_1 are reduced by the gain $G(\theta^-)$ to the interest group with the lowest valuation, so the optimal $G(\theta^-) = 0$. The remaining controls of the candidate are $s(\theta,\omega)$ and $Z(\theta^+)$. The constraints in (9) and (15) will be ignored initially, and then the properties of $s(\theta,\omega)$ will be investigated.

The first-order conditions for $s(\theta,\omega)$ and $Z(\omega^+)$, respectively, are obtained by pointwise differentiation of (21), which yields

$$P_1 \cdot p\left(R'(s(\theta,\omega))m(\theta) - \frac{1}{\alpha}n(\omega) \right) \cdot$$

$$\int_{\theta^-}^{\theta^+} \int_{\omega^-}^{\omega^+} \left[V + Z(\omega^+) + s(\theta,\omega)\frac{H(\omega)}{h(\omega)} \right] h(\omega)f(\theta)d\omega d\theta$$

$$+ P \cdot \frac{H(\omega)}{h(\omega)} = 0 \tag{22}$$

and

$$- P_1 \cdot \left(\frac{p}{\alpha}\right) \int_{\theta^-}^{\theta^+} \int_{\omega^-}^{\omega^+} \left[V + Z(\omega^+) + s(\theta,\omega)\frac{H(\omega)}{h(\omega)} \right]$$

$$h(\omega)f(\theta)d\omega d\theta + P = 0, \tag{23}$$

---

13. Baron (1989) considers contributions in addition to those made by interest groups seeking access and services.

where P_1 denotes the partial derivative with respect to X_1.

Substituting (23) into (22) indicates that the optimal services function satisfies

$$\begin{cases} s(\theta,\omega) = 0 & \text{if } R'(0)m(\theta) - \frac{\omega}{\alpha} \leq 0 \\ s(\theta,\omega) > 0 & \text{if } R'(s(\theta,\omega))m(\theta) - \frac{\omega}{\alpha} = 0. \end{cases} \quad (24)$$

A necessary condition for the candidate to offer services is thus $m(\theta) \geq 0$. When $m(\theta) < 0$ and $s(\theta,\omega) = 0$, the interest group contributes nothing to either campaign as indicated by (6) and (16). When $m(\theta) \geq 0$, the equilibrium service function in (24) is independent of the value V of office, of the beliefs p of the interest groups, of the expenditures of the opponent, and of the distribution of ω. The control $Z(\omega^+)$ and both contribution functions, however, depend on V, p, and $h(\cdot)$.

For θ such that $m(\theta) > 0$, and hence $R'(s)m(\theta) - \frac{\omega}{\alpha} = 0$, then $R'(s)m(\theta) - \frac{n(\omega)}{\alpha} < 0$ for $\omega > \omega^-$. Thus, from (22) the incumbency value

$$\int_{\theta^-}^{\theta^+} \int_{\omega^-}^{\omega^+} \left[V + Z(\omega^+) + s(\theta,\omega) \frac{H(\omega)}{h(\omega)} \right] h(\omega) f(\theta) d\omega d\theta$$

is positive.

To determine if the service function $s(\theta,\omega)$ satisfying (24) is implementable, it is necessary to verify the second-order incentive compatibility conditions in (9) and (15). When no services are offered, those conditions are trivially satisfied. When services are offered, differentiating (24) with respect to ω yields

$$R''(s(\theta,\omega)) \frac{\partial s(\theta,\omega)}{\partial \omega} m(\theta) - \frac{1}{\alpha} = 0 \quad (25)$$

and with respect to θ yields

$$R''(s(\theta,\omega)) \frac{\partial s(\theta,\omega)}{\partial \theta} m(\theta) + R'(s(\theta,\omega)) \frac{\partial m(\theta)}{\partial \theta} = 0. \quad (26)$$

Since $R(\cdot)$ is strictly concave, $\partial s(\theta,\omega)/\partial \omega < 0$ which satisfies (9). The condition in (15) is satisfied if $\partial m(\theta)/\partial \theta \geq 0$, which is satisfied for any distribution with an increasing hazard rate. This condition is satisfied for most commonly used distributions and will be assumed to hold throughout the remainder of the analysis.[14]

Since R is a strictly concave function of the services received, the candidate will offer more services the higher is the marginal value α of a contribution to the reelection campaign and will offer fewer services the higher is the marginal cost ω. More services are offered to interest groups with higher valuations, and groups with low valuations ($m(\theta) < 0$) will receive no services and will make no contributions.

The results of this section are summarized in the following proposition.

PROPOSITION 3. *If $m(\theta)$ is nondecreasing in θ, the equilibrium service function $s(\theta,\omega)$ satisfying (24) is implementable. If services are offered, the service function is decreasing in the marginal cost ω and is increasing in the valuation parameter θ. The service function is an increasing function of the marginal return α of a dollar of contributions to the reelection campaign and the service function is independent of the value of office, the beliefs of the interest groups about the likelihood that the candidate will win, the contributions to the opponent, and the distribution $h(\cdot)$ of the marginal cost of providing services.*

VI. A Symmetric Equilibrium

An equilibrium in the electoral game is (1) a contributions-service schedule

$$\{(c(\theta),s(\theta,\omega),Q(\theta,\omega)), \forall \theta \in [\theta^-,\theta^+], \forall \omega \in [\omega^-,\omega^+]\}$$

for each candidate who maximizes EW in (20); (2) a response function $\hat{\omega}(\omega) = \omega, \forall \omega$, for each candidate; (3) a response $\hat{\theta}(\theta)$ for each interest group θ that maximizes $G(\hat{\theta};\theta)$ in (10) given the candidates' schedules and satisfies $\hat{\theta}(\theta) = \theta$, $\forall \theta$; and (4) the rational expectations condition that the beliefs p of the interest groups equal the probability of winning $P(X_1,X_2)$ determined by the campaign expenditures generated from the equilibrium contributions-services schedules and interest group strategies. Since the candidates are identical as are the set of interest groups contributing to each candidate, a symmetric equilibrium will be considered.

---

14. If $m(\theta)$ is decreasing on some interval, then it can be flattened to satisfy (15). See Myerson (1981).

To provide a closed-form characterization of the equilibrium, the following specifications will be made

$$P(X_1,X_2) = \frac{X_1}{X_1 + X_2} \tag{27}$$

$$R(s) = rs^{1/2}. \tag{28}$$

The probability of winning is thus given by the candidate's expenditures relative to total expenditures.[15] The following specifications will be made to simplify the expressions for the equilibrium strategies:

$$f(\theta) = \begin{cases} 1 & \text{if } \theta \in [0,1] \\ 0 & \text{if } \theta \notin [0,1] \end{cases} \tag{29}$$

$$h(\omega) = \begin{cases} 1 & \text{if } \omega \in [1,2] \\ 0 & \text{if } \omega \notin [1,2]. \end{cases} \tag{30}$$

Consequently, $m(\theta) = 2\theta - 1$ and $n(\omega) = 2\omega - 1$.

The specifications in (28) and (29) imply from (24) that

$$s(\theta,\omega) = \begin{cases} 0 & \text{if } \theta < \frac{1}{2} \\ \left(\frac{\alpha r m(\theta)}{2\omega}\right)^2 & \text{if } \theta \geq \frac{1}{2}. \end{cases} \tag{31}$$

Since $m(\theta) < 0$ for $\theta < \frac{1}{2}$, the candidate does not offer services to, or raise funds from, the half of the interest groups with the lowest valuation of the services. Contributions are thus obtained from the interest groups with high stakes in the services. When services are offered, the candidate provides more services the higher are the parameters r and θ of the interest group's valuation of the services and the higher is the marginal value α of a dollar of contributions to the reelection campaign. The services are a strictly convex function of θ, so groups with higher θ get proportionately higher services. Services are a strictly decreasing and strictly concave function of the marginal cost ω.

The contributions X_1 in (19) to the initial campaign of candidate 1 then are

$$X_1 = \frac{p\alpha r^2}{48} - \left(\frac{p}{\alpha}\right)Z(\omega^+). \tag{32}$$

---

15. Baron (1989) considers asymmetric election contests in which one candidate has an incumbency advantage.

To determine $Z(\omega^+) = Z(2)$, substitute X_1 into (23) and solve for $Z(2)$ to obtain

$$Z(2) = -\frac{(1-p)}{(2-p)}\left[V + \frac{\alpha^2 r^2}{24}\log 2\right] + \frac{\alpha^2 r^2}{48}. \tag{33}$$

Substituting $Z(2)$ into (32) yields

$$X_i = \frac{p(1-p)}{\alpha(2-p)}\left[V + \frac{\alpha^2 r^2}{24}\log 2\right], \tag{34}$$

so the higher the candidate values the office, the greater are the contributions. This results not because more services are offered as a function of V but because lower contributions to the reelection campaign are demanded. The contributions to the initial campaign are an increasing function of the value V of the office and an increasing function of the valuation parameter r. The contributions to the initial election campaign are strictly convex in the value α of contributions to the reelection campaign. For low values of α, contributions are decreasing in α and for $\alpha > \alpha^0 \equiv [24V/(r^2 \cdot \log 2)]^{1/2}$ are increasing in α. As the value of a contribution to the reelection campaign increases, the candidate offers more services and substitutes contributions to the reelection campaign for contributions to the initial election campaign. Beyond α^0 the substitution is reversed.

The corresponding contributions for candidate 2 are given in (34) with p replaced by $1 - p$. The equilibrium p^* is then determined from the rational expectations condition

$$p^* = \frac{X_1}{X_1 + X_2} = \frac{\frac{p^*(1-p^*)}{\alpha(2-p^*)}\left[V + \frac{\alpha^2 r^2}{24}\log 2\right]}{\left[\frac{p^*(1-p^*)}{\alpha(2-p^*)} + \frac{(1-p^*)p^*}{\alpha(1+p^*)}\right]\left[V + \frac{\alpha^2 r^2}{24}\log 2\right]}. \tag{35}$$

Evaluation yields $p^* = \frac{1}{2}$, so the equilibrium is symmetric and unique. The following characterization is made at p^*.

The performance value $Z(\omega)$ in (4) conditional on the realized marginal cost is

$$Z(\omega) = \frac{\alpha^2 r^2}{24\omega} - \frac{1}{3}\left(V + \frac{\alpha^2 r^2}{24}\log 2\right), \tag{36}$$

which is negative for

$$\omega > \frac{3\alpha^2 r^2}{\alpha^2 r^2 \log 2 + 24V}. \qquad (37)$$

The right side of (37) is increasing in α, so the higher the value of contributions to the reelection campaign the more likely the performance value is to be positive. If $\alpha^2 \geq 48V/r^2(3 - 2\log 2)$, then $Z(\omega) \geq 0$ $\forall \omega$. If $\alpha^2 \leq 24V/r^2 (3 - \log 2)$, then $Z(\omega) \leq 0$ $\forall \omega$. A negative performance value $Z(\omega)$ means that the incumbent will have an incentive to shirk by quitting. In the next section this incentive will be addressed and for the remainder of this section, forces external to the model will be assumed to prevent the incumbent from quitting.

The contributions function $Q(\theta,\omega)$ for the reelection campaign can be obtained from (6) as

$$Q(\theta,\omega) = \begin{cases} 0 & \text{if } \theta < \frac{1}{2} \\ \left(\frac{1}{\alpha}\right)\left[Z(2) + \frac{\alpha^2 r^2 m(\theta)^2}{2}\left(\frac{1}{\omega} - \frac{1}{4}\right)\right] & \text{if } \theta \geq \frac{1}{2}. \end{cases} \qquad (38)$$

The reelection contributions function $Q(\theta,\omega)$ for $\theta \geq \frac{1}{2}$ is an increasing and strictly convex function of θ, so groups with higher valuations provide greater contributions. Since $Z(2)$ is decreasing in V, a higher valuation of the office leads the candidate to substitute contributions to the reelection campaign for contributions to the initial campaign. The total contributions $Y(\omega) = E_\theta Q(\theta,\omega)$ to the reelection campaign are

$$Y(\omega) = \left(\frac{1}{\alpha}\right)\left[Z(2) + \frac{\alpha^2 r^2}{12}\left(\frac{1}{\omega} - \frac{1}{4}\right)\right]$$

$$= \left(\frac{1}{\alpha}\right)\left[\frac{\alpha^2 r^2}{12\omega} - \frac{1}{3}\left(V + \frac{\alpha^2 r^2}{24}\log 2\right)\right], \qquad (39)$$

which can be positive or negative depending on the parameter values. A successful candidate thus may begin his reelection campaign with a deficit. Negative reelection contributions $E_\theta Q(\theta,\omega)$ represent a "credit" to the interest groups. Candidates thus in equilibrium may borrow from the future. This, however, does not mean that the winner of the election will be unable to finance his reelection campaign, since the incumbent can offer to provide services in the subsequent term in exchange for contributions to his reelection campaign and the subsequent reelection campaign.

The performance value in (36) can be written in terms of the contributions $E_\theta Q(\theta,\omega)$ to the reelection campaign as

$$Z(\omega) = -\frac{\alpha^2 r^2}{24\omega} + \alpha E_\theta Q(\theta,\omega). \tag{40}$$

The performance value of the incumbent thus may be negative due both to credits given to interest groups and to the cost of providing services.

The value T of incumbency is defined as

$$T \equiv \int_{\theta^-}^{\theta^+} \int_{\omega^-}^{\omega^+} [V + Z(\omega)] h(\omega) f(\theta) d\omega d\theta. \tag{41}$$

The expectation $EZ(\omega)$ at a symmetric equilibrium is

$$EZ(\omega) = \int_{\theta^-}^{\theta^+} \int_{\omega^-}^{\omega^+} Z(\omega) h(\omega) f(\theta) d\omega d\theta = -\frac{1}{3}\left(V - \frac{\alpha^2 r^2}{12} \log 2\right), \tag{42}$$

and thus the incumbency value is

$$T = \frac{2}{3}\left[V + \frac{\alpha^2 r^2}{24} \log 2\right]$$

$$= 4\alpha X_1. \tag{43}$$

This is increasing in the value V of office and increasing and strictly convex in αr. The expected value EW of the election opportunity is then $EW = \frac{1}{2}T$, which inherits the properties of T. The candidates thus earn rents from the opportunity to stand for office.

The gain $G(\theta)$ to the interest groups is

$$G(\theta) = \begin{cases} 0 & \text{if } \theta < \frac{1}{2} \\ \dfrac{\alpha r^2 \log 2}{16}(2\theta - 1)^2 & \text{if } \theta \geq \frac{1}{2}, \end{cases} \tag{44}$$

which is a strictly increasing and strictly convex function of their valuation parameters r and θ, for $\theta \geq \frac{1}{2}$. If θ represents the size of an interest group, larger interest groups gain more from their contributions than do smaller interest groups. The gain is also an increasing linear function of the marginal value α of a contribution to the reelection campaign, since the more valuable contributions are to the reelection campaign, the more services the candidates offer.

The contributions function $c(\theta)$ for the initial campaign is

$$c(\theta) = \begin{cases} 0 & \text{if } \theta < \tfrac{1}{2} \\ \left(\dfrac{\alpha r^2 \log 2}{4}\right)\left[\theta^2 - \dfrac{1}{4}\right] - \dfrac{\alpha r^2 m(\theta)^2}{4}\left(\log 2 - \dfrac{1}{4}\right) - \dfrac{p}{\alpha} Z(2) \\ \quad \text{if } \theta \geq \tfrac{1}{2}. \end{cases} \qquad (45)$$

Groups with higher valuations θ for the services thus contribute more to the initial election campaign and more to the reelection campaign. The expected total contributions $C(\theta)$ by group θ to a candidate are, from (38) and (45),

$$C(\theta) = c(\theta) + \frac{1}{2} E_\omega Q(\theta,\omega) = \begin{cases} 0 & \text{if } \theta < \tfrac{1}{2} \\ \left(\dfrac{\alpha r^2 \log 2}{4}\right)\left[\theta^2 - \dfrac{1}{4}\right] & \text{if } \theta \geq \tfrac{1}{2}. \end{cases} \quad (46)$$

The expected total contributions are an increasing and strictly convex function of the valuation parameters r and θ of the services to the interest group, so higher θ groups contribute more in total. The expected total contributions are increasing in the marginal value α of a contribution to the reelection campaign but are independent of the value V of the office being contested.

The expected total contributions $EC(\theta)$ to the candidate from all the interest groups are

$$EC(\theta) \equiv X_1 + pEY(\omega) = \frac{\alpha^2 r^2 \log 2}{24} = E_{\theta,\omega} \omega s(\theta,\omega). \qquad (47)$$

Thus, the total contributions are equal to the expected cost of providing the service. Consequently, the interest groups contribute exactly as much as the cost of the services they receive. This is a form of efficiency in the service-induced campaign contributions relation.

The properties of the equilibrium for the example are summarized in the following proposition.

PROPOSITION 4. *For the example, contributions are solicited only from the half of the interest groups with the highest valuations of the services. The services offered to those groups are a strictly increasing and strictly convex function of r, α, and θ and a strictly decreasing and strictly concave function of ω. The expected total contributions to the candidate equal the expected cost of the promised services.*[16] *The performance value may be negative in equilibrium, so shirking by quitting may be a problem if it is not precluded exogenously.*

VII. Precluding Quitting

The above analysis has assumed either that the candidate could credibly commit not to quit or that forces outside the model were sufficient to prevent the winner from quitting in the event that the cost of delivering the services turns out to be sufficiently high that the performance value $Z(\omega)$ in (4) and (36) is negative. When quitting cannot be prevented, the interest groups will expect fewer services to be delivered and hence will contribute less. Characterization of the equilibrium in this case is a straightforward extension of the above analysis.

Let $\delta(\omega) \in [0,1]$ denote the probability that the winner will quit when he observes ω. The expression for EW in (20) is thus

$$EW = P(X_1,X_2) \int_{\omega^-}^{\omega^+} [V + \delta(\omega)Z(\omega)]h(\omega)d\omega. \tag{48}$$

The contributions X in (19) are

$$X = p \int_{\theta^-}^{\theta^+} \int_{\omega^-}^{\omega^+} \left[\delta(\omega)\left(R(s(\theta,\omega))m(\theta) - \frac{1}{\alpha}s(\theta,\omega)n(\omega)\right)\right]$$
$$\times h(\omega)f(\theta)d\omega d\theta - \frac{p}{\alpha}Z(\omega^+)\int_{\omega^-}^{\omega^+}\delta(\omega)h(\omega)d\omega - G(\theta^-). \tag{49}$$

The necessary optimality conditions for $s(\theta,\omega)$ and $Z(\omega^+)$ are then (22) and (23) multiplied by $\delta(\omega)$, so the promised services are as characterized in (24). Then, since $Z(\omega)$ is decreasing in ω, there is an interval $[\omega^-,\omega^*]$ on which $\delta(\omega)$ equals one and an interval $(\omega^*,\omega^+]$ on which it equals zero. The highest cost ω^* for which the incumbent will not quit is defined by

$$Z(\omega^*) \equiv 0.$$

---

16. This result does not hold in general.

For the example,

$$\omega^* = \frac{\alpha^2 r^2}{8\left(V + \frac{\alpha^2 r^2}{24}\log 2\right)}, \qquad (50)$$

so if $\omega^* < \omega^+$ the ex ante probability is positive that the incumbent will quit.

The resulting contributions X^* when $\omega^* < \omega^+$ are

$$\begin{aligned}X^* &= p(\omega^* - 1)\left[\frac{\alpha r^2}{24}\left(\frac{1}{\omega^*} - \frac{1}{2}\right) + \frac{1}{3\alpha}\left(V + \frac{\alpha^2 r^2}{24}\log 2\right)\right]\\ &= p(\omega^* - 1)\left[\frac{\alpha r^2}{24}\left(\frac{1}{\omega^*} - \frac{1}{2}\right) + X\right].\end{aligned} \qquad (51)$$

Contributions are thus lower when quitting cannot be precluded. The expected value EW^* of the election opportunity in equilibrium is[17]

$$EW^* = \frac{1}{3}\left[V + \frac{\alpha^2 r^2}{16}\left(\log \omega^* - \frac{1}{3}\log 2\right)\right]. \qquad (52)$$

The expected services are

$$E_{\theta,\omega}s(\theta,\omega) = \frac{\alpha^2 r^2}{24}\left(\frac{\omega^* - 1}{\omega^*}\right). \qquad (53)$$

Compared with the case in which quitting is precluded exogenously, the expected services are lower and hence total contributions by the interest groups and the contributions to the initial campaign are lower. The interest groups are worse off and the candidates are better off when the incumbent can quit when the cost becomes too high.

The results of this section are summarized in the following proposition.

PROPOSITION 5. *When quitting cannot be precluded, the candidate quits when $Z(\omega)$ in (4) is negative. The equilibrium contributions-services schedule is given in (24),(16), and (6). The resulting contributions are lower than when quitting can be precluded, and the interest groups are worse off. The candidates are better off.*

---

17. It is straightforward to verify that EW is strictly concave in ω^* and is maximized at the ω^* in (50).

VIII. Conclusions

The model of campaign contributions solicitation is based on the promise of services to be provided by the successful candidate. Promises, however, are not enforceable because of the inability of contributors to assess how difficult, or how costly, the services are to provide. Candidate promises are thus subject to shirking. One form of shirking involves making excuses by telling contributors that the services promised are more difficult to deliver than they actually are and thus that only some of the promised services will be delivered. The possibility that the candidate may shirk in this manner reduces the return to contributors and thus produces fewer contributions for the candidates. This shirking can be eliminated, but at a cost to the candidates and to the interest groups, by the candidates structuring the contributions to their reelection campaigns so that an incumbent has the incentive to deliver the promised services. Because that structuring reflects a cost of avoiding shirking, fewer services are provided than would result under complete information.

In a symmetric equilibrium, the services provided are an increasing function of the value of the services to the interest groups and a decreasing function of the cost of providing services. The greater the value of contributions to the reelection campaign, the more services are provided. The candidate faces a trade-off between the contributions to his initial campaign and contributions to his reelection campaign. The higher the value of the office for the initial term relative to the value of the reelection opportunities, the more the candidate will structure the contribution-service schedule to favor contributions to the present campaign at the expense of future campaigns. If that valuation is sufficiently high, the candidate may offer credits to interest groups and thus may begin his reelection campaign with a deficit.

In the event that upon taking office the winner learns that the cost of providing the services is high, he may prefer to quit by refusing to provide any services. This makes the candidates better off because they know they will quit if the performance value is negative. Quitting, however, reduces the expected services provided and hence reduces campaign contributions. The interest groups are then worse off than if the incumbent were precluded from shirking by quitting.

The principal limitation of this model is that the candidate is assumed to commit to the contributions-services schedule $(c(\theta), s(\theta, \omega), Q(\theta, \omega))$. For example, in the absence of commitment, once in office the incumbent could announce a different policy $(\tilde{s}(\theta, \omega), \overline{Q}(\theta, \omega))$, since he then knows the type of each individual interest group. Knowing their type the incumbent could then extract all the gain from the interest groups. Recognizing this, the interest groups would have no incentive to make contributions to the initial campaign. A means of assuring reliance on promises is thus required to support the equilibria characterized here, but it should arise endogenously in the model instead of being imposed exogenously. A fully dynamic model without commitment may be successful in yielding such reliance.

Electoral Accountability and Incumbency

David Austen-Smith and Jeffrey Banks

Loosely speaking, the concept of electoral accountability refers to the ability of a legislator's constituents to oust that legislator from office if his or her legislative performance is found wanting (H. Pitkin 1967; W. Riker 1982a). The threat of losing the next election is supposed to provide incentives for representatives to act in the interests of their electorate, irrespective of any personal objectives. However, the extent to which this threat is effective and, therefore, the extent to which elected officials are electorally accountable, is moot.

In a world of perfect and complete information, there is little problem with accountability (R. Barro 1973); it is the presence of imperfect and incomplete information on the part of voters that generates difficulties. There are two principal ways in which informational deficiencies are manifest here. First, it is hard, if not wholly impossible, to monitor much of elected legislators' behavior. Although roll-call votes and so forth are easily recorded, legislators' efforts to promote issues and decisions favoring their particular constituents are not so readily observed. Legislatures are complex institutions in which many different types of agents engage in a wide variety of activity under various degrees of uncertainty. In such circumstances, to ascribe responsibility for any policy outcome to some particular legislator is often impossible. Second, policy outcomes from the postelection legislative stage need have no structural relationship either to candidates' announced electoral platforms or to their previous legislative histories, if any. Announcements are "mere words" whereas voters care about concrete outcomes, and to affect outcomes requires positive legislative action on the part of the elected representative. Similarly, even when monitoring difficulties are not severe, if some representative's term of office proves disappointing to his or her electorate, it is not clear that electing a challenger will lead to any better results. Since policy-oriented voters at any election are concerned with future outcomes, the fact that the past was disappointing

---

We are grateful for the comments of participants in the Politics and Organizations Workshop at Stanford University. This work is supported by National Science Foundation (NSF) grant no. SES-8700468. The usual caveats apply.

is not a sufficient reason to remove the current incumbent. In other words, threats to replace lax incumbents may not be credible.

Given the ex post difficulties of monitoring an incumbent's legislative performance, and the ex ante problems of inferring any candidate's legislative intent from his electoral platform or legislative history, it is not evident that "electoral accountability" has much bite when voters are sequentially rational and policy oriented. Concern over the issue has been manifest at least since Stokes and Miller (1962) who argued that, to all intents and purposes, constituents were unaware of the activities of their congressional representatives (see also A. Abramowitz 1980). On the other hand, a huge literature has recently appeared on the apparent increase in tenure of House and Senate incumbents (cf. Erikson 1970; Tufte 1973; Mayhew 1974a; Collie 1981; Krehbiel and Wright 1983; Jacobson 1987; Ansolabehere, Brady, and Fiorina 1987; inter alia). Of course, the fact that incumbents appear relatively secure, or even that there has been a jump in such security, does not in itself imply incumbents are less accountable and more free from electoral competition; they may be getting better at delivering more of what their constituents want. More important for our purposes, however, is that this phenomenon demonstrates a systematic bias, or incumbency effect, in voter behavior in elections with an incumbent. If voters care about policy outcomes (and there is evidence that they do; see Wright and Berkman 1986) then, because of the monitoring and inference problems discussed above, such voting strategies must take into account incumbents' incentives to avoid costly legislative activities that might benefit their constituents. Thus, the extent to which the electoral mechanism serves as an instrument of accountability is unclear. This issue is the central concern for the present essay.

We approach the problem of electoral accountability through a simple spatial voting model. In this model policy outcomes are the result of incumbents providing effort to influence the determination of the final legislative decision, where this effort is costly in terms of some resource (e.g., time) available to incumbents. This differs from the usual spatial model of elections in which the announced platform of any candidate is equated with the expected policy outcome that she would implement if elected. In contrast, our model provides no a priori reason to presume that the electoral rhetoric of the successful candidate has anything to do with final policy outcomes; any such relationship will be determined endogenously. Voters in any election will attempt to deduce which of the candidates seeking office would exert the preferred amount of effort, where this preference is induced by voters' underlying preferences over policy outcomes. Candidates, however, are not assumed to have policy preferences; all that candidates care about is electoral success (Downs 1957; Mayhew 1974*b*). So when legislative effort is costly and unobservable, how can electoral accountability provide incentives for incumbents to expend such effort?

Our answer relies on two substantive assumptions. The first is that an incumbent will run for office in future elections. This assumption is neither novel nor exceptional (Barro 1973; Ferejohn 1986); although incumbents do not run for office indefinitely, representatives typically seek at least two consecutive terms, and in our model this is sufficient. The second assumption is that there exist challengers possessing similar attributes to the incumbent; in particular, for no candidate does there exist a strategy that guarantees electoral success. In the basic model below, this feature is generated by imposing complete symmetry across candidates. Thus differences in legislative experience, bargaining skills, and so forth, are ruled out. However, as we argue in a later section, such symmetry is sufficient but not necessary for the assumption. Further, it turns out that despite imposing candidate symmetry, an incumbency effect emerges endogenously in the model. From a methodological perspective, this demonstrates that ex ante candidate asymmetries (beyond the titles of Incumbent and Challenger, per se) are not necessary to explain ex post asymmetries in legislative tenure patterns (Bernhardt and Ingberman 1985; Baron 1988).

Together, these assumptions imply that, in equilibrium, voters will be indifferent between the candidates for office at every election. In the usual formulation of rational choice voting models, whenever a voter is indifferent between two candidates, he is presumed to flip a fair coin to determine his vote. However, given no abstention, there is no reason why the voter should choose to flip a fair, rather than a biased, coin if he is truly indifferent, any probabilistic voting scheme will do. In particular, in each election the voter can allow the probability of reelecting the current incumbent to be determined by such historical data as the incumbent's previous electoral platform, and the realization of the previous legislative policy outcome. This sort of retrospective voting strategy then gives the voter the ability to influence the legislative behavior of incumbents (Fiorina 1981): since any incumbent prefers to be reelected, the voter's strategy will be taken into account when she selects a legislative effort level. Furthermore, the voter's strategy will be credible, in the sense that he will always be willing to use it when indifferent between candidates.

When the voter adopts a retrospective reelection strategy, he uses information relevant to the performance of the incumbent in determining his vote. This creates an incumbency effect in each election beyond the first: the voter's decision rule is nontrivially based on the identification of one of the candidates as the incumbent. But recall that the voter uses the strategy only when he is *indifferent* about which candidate takes office (if he has a strict preference for one candidate over the other, then he votes sincerely). In other words, an incumbency effect is generated endogenously through rational voter behavior and strategic candidate behavior, and not through any structural asymmetries between the candidates. Furthermore, we see how the electoral mechanism alone can provide a means by which rational voters can hold incumbents accountable, even when their legislative behavior is unobservable.

The next two sections of the essay are devoted to making the basic model and results discussed above precise. Subsequent sections offer some generalizations of the basic model, and discuss open questions.

Model

We consider a model in which there are two candidates, $j = 1,2$, competing for legislative office, and a single voter, v (the assumption of a single voter is unnecessary: later we extend the results to a wide class of finite and odd numbered electorates). There are two periods, each consisting of (1) the candidates' electoral decisions; (2) the voter's decision; (3) the successful candidate's legislative decision; and (4) a legislative outcome. Legislative outcomes are presumed to be elements of the real line, **R**. The voter is assumed to have a symmetric, strictly single-peaked utility, $u(\cdot)$, on outcomes, with ideal point $v > 0$.

At the start of each period $t = 1,2$, the two candidates simultaneously announce electoral platforms x_{t1}, x_{t2}, respectively, in $\mathbf{R}_+$ (see figure 1 for sequence of events). Given this pair of platforms, the voter elects one or other of the candidates to legislative office; call this candidate the *period t incumbent*. Once the incumbent is selected, he chooses an amount of effort $e_t \in [0,1]$ at cost $c(e_t) \in [0,1]$, where $c(\cdot)$ is discussed below. After e_t is chosen, Nature makes a draw from the distribution of a random variable, η. The legislative outcome from period t is then given by,

$$\lambda_t = e_t + \eta_t, \qquad (1)$$

where η_t is the period t realization of the *iid* random variable,

$$\eta \sim N(0,1). \qquad (2)$$

The assumption that effort moves the mean linearly is sufficient but not necessary for our results. Similarly, the disturbance term η does not

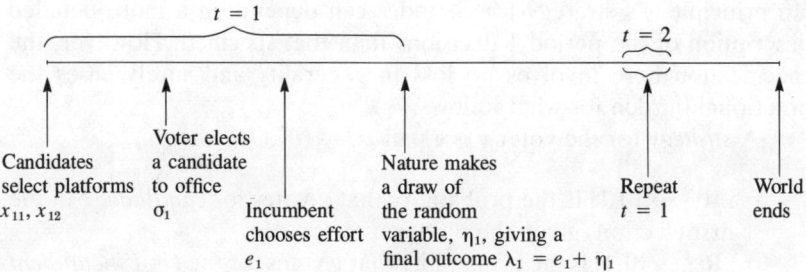

Fig. 1. The sequence of events

have to be distributed normally; any symmetric and strictly unimodal density will do. Finally, note that assuming effort can only move the expected outcome positively and restricting x_{tj} to $\mathbf{R}_+$ involves no loss of generality, because $v > 0$.

Thus the period t policy outcome λ_t is a normally distributed random variable with mean e_t and variance one (and we emphasize that the incumbent chooses effort prior to the realization of the random variable η). When $e_t = 0$, the expected policy outcome is zero: for expository purposes we refer to this outcome as the status quo. In a more general model, the "status quo" will be generated endogenously from strategic interaction between elected candidates from several districts. Here, we leave this implicit.

The period t incumbent's effort level e_t is assumed to be unobservable by the voter. But the voter—and the period t unsuccessful candidate—can observe the realized policy outcome λ_t. Further, expressions (1) and (2) imply that realized outcomes are structurally independent of electoral platforms. When the realization λ_t occurs the period ends.

In sum, there are two electoral decisions and two legislative decisions. A (pure) *strategy* for candidate $j = 1,2$ is a list $\tau_j = (x_{1j}, e_{1j}, x_{2j}^I, x_{2j}^C, e_{2j})$ where:

- $x_{1j} \in \mathbf{R}_+$ is j's period 1 electoral platform;
- $e_{1j}: \mathbf{R}_+ \to [0,1]$ is j's period 1 effort level, given x_{1j}, conditional on $j = I$ (incumbent) at $t = 1$;
- $x_{2j}^I: \mathbf{R}_+^2 \to \mathbf{R}_+$ is j's period 2 electoral platform, given x_{1j} and the realized period 1 legislative outcome, λ_1, conditional on $j = I$ at $t = 1$;
- $x_{2j}^C \in \mathbf{R}_+$ is j's period 2 electoral platform, conditional on $j \neq I$ at $t = 1$;
- $e_{2j}: \mathbf{R}_+ \to [0,1]$ is j's period 2 effort level, given x_{2j}, conditional on $j = I$ at $t = 2$.

(In principle, j's strategy for period 2 can depend on a more detailed description of the period 1 decisions than that specified. However, the specification here involves no loss in generality and surely eases the notational burden for what follows.)

A *strategy* for the voter v is a pair $\sigma = (\sigma_1, \sigma_2)$ where:

$\sigma_1: \mathbf{R}_+^2 \to [0,1]$ is the probability that v votes for *candidate 1* in the first election, given the platforms offered;

$\sigma_2: \mathbf{R}_+^5 \to [0,1]$ is the probability that v votes for the $t = 1$ *incumbent* in the second election, given the platforms offered in $t = 1,2$ and the de facto final policy outcome from the first legislative period λ_1.

Thus the voter is not restricted to choosing pure strategies. We assume no abstention, so that the probability v votes for candidate 2 in the first election is just $1 - \sigma_1$, etc.

Both candidates and the voter are rational and concerned to maximize their respective payoffs from the whole sequence. Without loss of any interesting generality, assume discount factors to be one. Given policy realizations λ_1 and λ_2, the voter's de facto payoff is simply $u(\lambda_1) + u(\lambda_2)$. Ex ante, therefore, v seeks to maximize:

$$U(\sigma \mid \tau_1, \tau_2) = \Sigma_t\, E[u(\lambda_t) \mid \tau_1, \tau_2, \sigma]. \tag{3}$$

Candidate $j = 1,2$ receives a gross payoff of $R \geq 1$ if he wins the period t election, and then, conditional on j becoming the period t incumbent, selects an effort level e_{tj} at cost $c(e_{tj}) \geq 0$ in trying to move the status quo. If j loses the period t election, he receives a period t payoff of zero. Consequently, candidates 1 and 2 wish to maximize, respectively:

$$\pi_1(\tau_1 \mid \sigma, \tau_2) = \sigma_1(x_1) \cdot \{R - c(e_{11}) + p_1 \cdot [R - c(e_{21})]\}$$

$$+ [1 - \sigma_1(x_1)] \cdot [1 - p_2] \cdot \{R - c(e_{21})\}$$

$$\pi_2(\tau_2 \mid \sigma, \tau_1) = [1 - \sigma_1(x_1)] \cdot \{R - c(e_{12}) + p_2 \cdot [R - c(e_{22})]\}$$

$$+ \sigma_1(x_1) \cdot [1 - p_1] \cdot \{R - c(e_{22})\}, \tag{4}$$

where p_j is the probability that candidate j gets elected in period 2, given j is the period 1 incumbent. Specifically,

$$p_1 = E[\sigma_2(X_1, x_{21}', x_{22}^C, \lambda_1) \mid e_{11}]$$

$$p_2 = E[\sigma_2(X_1, x_{21}^C, x_{22}', \lambda_1) \mid e_{12}]$$

where $X_1 = \{x_{11}, x_{12}\}$.

Notice that (4) describes the payoffs to a purely "private benefits of office"–oriented candidate: in particular, we do not assume that candidates are intrinsically interested in policy outcomes.

The cost of effort function is assumed to satisfy:

$c(0) = 0 < c(1) = 1$,

$\forall e \in (0,1)$: $c(e), c'(e) > 0$, $\lim_{e \to 0} c'(e) = 0$, and $\lim_{e \to 1} c'(e) = \infty$,

$\forall e \in (0,1)$: $c''(e) > 0$. (5)

Together (1), (2), and (5) imply that the candidates are entirely symmetric: there is nothing special about the abilities of one candidate over another to bring about various policy changes, and this is common knowledge.

Equilibrium

The model described above induces a sequential game in which the two candidates, the voter, and Nature are players. The equilibrium concept we use to solve the game is Subgame Perfect Nash: the candidates' and the voter's strategies must be mutually best responses on each subgame. To determine such an equilibrium $(\tau_1^*, \tau_2^*, \sigma^*)$, we construct strategies piecewise by solving the game "backwards," analyzing first the players' decisions in period 2.

The final decision by any agent in the game is the period 2 incumbent's choice of effort, e_{2j}. But period 2 is the final period and effort is costly. Hence, choosing $e_{2j}^* = 0$ unequivocally maximizes j's period 2 payoff, $j = 1,2$, for all period 2 electoral platforms. Consequently, because the policy realization λ_2 is independent of candidates' electoral platforms, and because the $t = 2$ incumbent will surely put in zero legislative effort, *the voter will be completely indifferent over which candidate takes office in period 2;* i.e., $\text{Eu}(\lambda_2)$ is a constant for all period 2 incumbent platforms. Therefore, the equilibrium second-period strategies for candidates are completely described by:

$(x_{2j}^{I*}, x_{2j}^{C*}, e_{2j}^*) = (x_j^*, y_j^*, 0)$ for any $x_j^*, y_j^* \in \mathbf{R}_+$, and $j = 1,2$. (6)

Now consider the voter's choice of second-period voting strategy. Recalling that his expected second-period payoff is a constant, the voter is necessarily indifferent over which candidate takes office in $t = 2$. So, in particular, v's choice of the $t = 2$ incumbent can, *in equilibrium*, be a function of historical data. The candidates, of course, are not indifferent as to who wins in period 2: the winner receives a $t = 2$ payoff of $R \geq 1$ and the loser gets nothing. Thus, if the voter's second-period voting rule is retrospective, then the $t = 1$ incumbent's effort choice will be influenced by this rule. Consequently, we can think of v as selecting a strategy pair (σ_1, σ_2) to maximize his first-period payoff, since his $t = 2$ payoff is already determined. Given (1), (2), and $u(\cdot)$ symmetric, this amounts to minimizing $|e_1^* - v|$. Hereafter, we confine attention to the following, retrospective, second-period voter decision rule. Let x be the period 1 electoral platform of the $t = 1$ incumbent, and let λ be the realized outcome in $t = 1$: at $t = 2$, these are historical data. Then:

$$\sigma_2^*(x, \lambda) = \begin{cases} 1 - k(x) \cdot (\lambda - x)^2, & \text{if } |\lambda - x| \leq k(x)^{-1/2} \\ 0, & \text{otherwise} \end{cases} \quad (7)$$

where $k(x) \geq 0$ for all platforms $x \in \mathbf{R}_+$, and the formal dependence of σ_2 on other arguments is ignored.

The reelection strategy says that the probability v votes for the $t = 1$ incumbent at $t = 2$ is dependent on how close the de facto first-period policy outcome is to the first-period electoral platform on which the incumbent was elected. Figure 2 illustrates (7).

For sufficiently wide disparities between the incumbent's $t = 1$ platform and the observed policy outcome, v votes for the challenger in period 2 with probability one. As the realized outcome approaches the incumbent's platform, the probability that v supports the current incumbent at $t = 2$ increases according to a quadratic, and equals one if outcome and platform coincide. The choice of a quadratic is motivated by its simplicity—it allows candidates to worry only about the mean and variance of outcomes in making their period 1 strategic decisions.

Apart from the specific functional form of (7), the key feature of the strategy is the selection of the function $k(x)$. Once candidates' *first-period* election positions are announced, the value of k for the second period is determined. The function $k(x)$ is part of the voter's strategy, and as such must be chosen optimally, given the strategies of candidates, etc. The derivation of $k(\cdot)$ is discussed momentarily. First we note that, given (7) with the schedule $k(x)$, the value of p_j—the probability that the $t = 1$ incumbent is returned to office in $t = 2$—can be explicitly computed. Letting $\Delta \equiv [x - k^{-1/2}, x + k^{-1/2}]$, p_j is given by:

$$p_j(x, e \mid \sigma_2^*(x, \lambda)) = [\Phi(x + k^{-1/2} - e) - \Phi(x - k^{-1/2} - e)]$$

$$\cdot \{1 - k(x) \cdot ((E[\lambda \mid \lambda \in \Delta; e] - x)^2 + \text{var}[\lambda \mid \lambda \in \Delta; e])\},$$

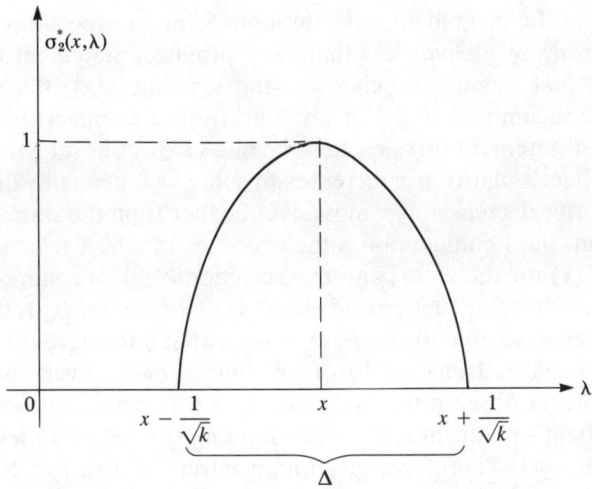

Fig. 2. $t=2$ voting strategy

where Φ is the *cdf* for the standardized normal distribution, and it is understood that $x = x_{1j}$, $e = e_{1j}$ when j is the period 1 incumbent.

Therefore, having been elected on platform x, the incumbent's optimal choice of e will depend on the voter's selection of k. Write this effort choice as $e^*(x,k)$. Specifically, $e^*(x,k)$ solves the following program:

$$\max_{e \in [0,1]} R \cdot [1 + p_j(x, e \mid \sigma_2^*(x, \lambda))] - c(e). \tag{8}$$

In the appendix to this essay we demonstrate that, so long as $c(\cdot)$ is sufficiently convex, $e^*(x,k)$ is a continuous function of x and (almost everywhere) of k. We also establish,

LEMMA.

(i) $\forall (x,k) \in (0,\infty)^2$, $e^*(x,k) \in (0,x)$; and $e^*(0,k) = 0$, $\forall k$.

(ii) $\forall x \in (0,\infty)$, $\exists\ \varepsilon(x) \in (0,x)$ such that:
$\forall e \in [0,\varepsilon(x)]$, $\exists k(x) \geq 0$ such that $e^*(x, k(x)) = e$;
and $e^*(x, k) > \varepsilon(x)$ for no k.

(iii) $\exists z > 0$ such that $\varepsilon'(x) > [\,=\,] < 0$ as $x < [\,=\,] > z$; and $\lim_{x \to \infty} \varepsilon(x) = 0$.

Since the incumbent's choice of effort level is the expected period 1 legislative policy outcome, statement (i) says that this expected outcome falls short of the incumbent's electoral platform; in expectation, elected candidates always deliver less than they promise. Statement (ii), however, says that by suitably choosing the schedule $k(x)$, the voter can induce the incumbent to select any one from a compact set of effort levels. And statement (iii) says that the measure of this set gets larger as the incumbent's platform x increases to some well-defined value $z > 0$, and thereafter decreases as x moves yet further from the status quo.

In sum, the Lemma implies the existence of a best selection of the schedule $k(x)$ for the voter, and this selection $k^*(\cdot)$, is common knowledge. When choosing first-period electoral platforms $\{x_{11}, x_{12}\}$, therefore, the candidates are able to compute exactly what effort level they will be induced to select if elected to office. Furthermore, even though the voter can never observe the incumbent's effort choice, given $k^*(\cdot)$ and the incumbent's platform x, the voter too knows what effort level solves the program (8). Therefore, given an arbitrary pair of $t = 1$ electoral platforms $\{x_{11}, x_{12}\}$, the voter's $t = 1$ strategy is simply:

$$\sigma_1^*(x_{11}, x_{12}) = 1 \ [1/2] \ 0 \Leftrightarrow \int u(\lambda) dF(\lambda \mid e^*(x_{11}, k^*(x_{11})))$$

$$> [\ =\ ] < \int u(\lambda) dF(\lambda \mid e^*(x_{12}, k^*(x_{12}))), \tag{9}$$

where F is the *cdf* for the normal distribution with mean e^* and variance one. In words, when not indifferent the voter votes sincerely relative to his expected first-period payoff, and flips a fair coin when he is indifferent—the voter's payoffs being computed on the basis of subsequent equilibrium behavior by candidates.

Given (7) and (9), we can finally solve for the candidates' choice of $t = 1$ electoral positions. (Strictly speaking, (7) and (9) are not quite enough: we have to specify what the voter does if only one candidate chooses to run for office in the first election, but both contest the second, etc. In the appendix to this essay we specify fully the voter's strategy under these circumstances: it is such that both candidates will choose to contest both elections in equilibrium.) Candidate 1 chooses:

$$x_{11}^* \in \mathrm{argmax}_{x \in \mathbf{R}_+} \ \pi_1((x, e^*(x, k^*(x)), x_1^*, y_1^*, 0) \mid \sigma^*, \tau_2^*). \tag{10}$$

Similarly, candidate 2 chooses:

$$x_{12}^* \in \mathrm{argmax}_{w \in \mathbf{R}_+} \ \pi_2((w, e^*(w, k^*(w)), x_2^*, y_2^*, 0) \mid \sigma^*, \tau_1^*). \tag{11}$$

By symmetry, if there is an equilibrium in candidate strategies $\{x_{11},x_{12}\}$—relative to the voter's strategy given by (7) and (9)—then there is one in which both candidates adopt the same $t = 1$ electoral platforms; i.e., $x_{11}^* = x_{12}^* = x^*$. In fact, we show that there is a unique equilibrium, so $x_{11}^* = x_{12}^* = x^*$ surely. We state this formally, along with the results obtained so far, in Propositions 1 and 2.

PROPOSITION 1. *The voting rules (7) and (9), for appropriately chosen $k(x) = k^*(x)$, are part of an equilibrium strategy, σ^*, for the voter. Furthermore, given the voter adopts (7) and (9), the candidates' equilibrium strategies relative to σ^* differ in at most period 2 electoral platforms. In particular,*

$$\tau_j^* = (x^*, e^*(x^*, k^*(x^*)), x_j^*, y_j^*, 0), j = 1, 2.$$

Proposition 1 says that both candidates, if elected in period 1, will choose the same effort level, $e^* = e^*(x^*,k^*(x^*))$, so that the (equilibrium) likelihood of the incumbent being reelected in period 2 is independent of the name of that incumbent; i.e., $p_j = p^* = E[\sigma_2^*(x^*,\lambda_1) \mid e^*], j = 1,2$.

From the Lemma and Proposition 1, we have:

PROPOSITION 2. *Define $z \in \mathbf{R}_{++}$ by $\varepsilon'(z) = 0$. Then there exists a unique $v^o \in (0,1)$ such that*

(i) $\forall v \in (0, v^o): z > x^* > v = e^*$;
(ii) $\forall v \geq v^o: x^* = z, v \geq e^*$ *with inequality strict for all $v > v^o$.*

Under the assumption of symmetric voter perferences, when $v = e^*$ the candidate equilibrium induced by the voter's strategy is a *first-best outcome* for the voter. That is, for $v \in [0,v^o]$ we lose no generality by constraining the voter to select a quadratic specification in (7). Also note that conditioning his vote-probability on the deviation of the outcome from the voter's ideal point v, rather than the incumbent's platform, could *not* induce such a first-best result. To see this, simply observe that $e^*(x,\cdot) < x$ for all platforms x: hence, $e^*(v,\cdot) < v$. When $v > v^o$, it is an open question whether or not the voter can improve on this outcome by adopting a different—non-quadratic—randomization device for the second-period election. This issue is discussed further in the concluding section.

Figures 3 and 4 illustrate Propositions 1 and 2: the diagrams are

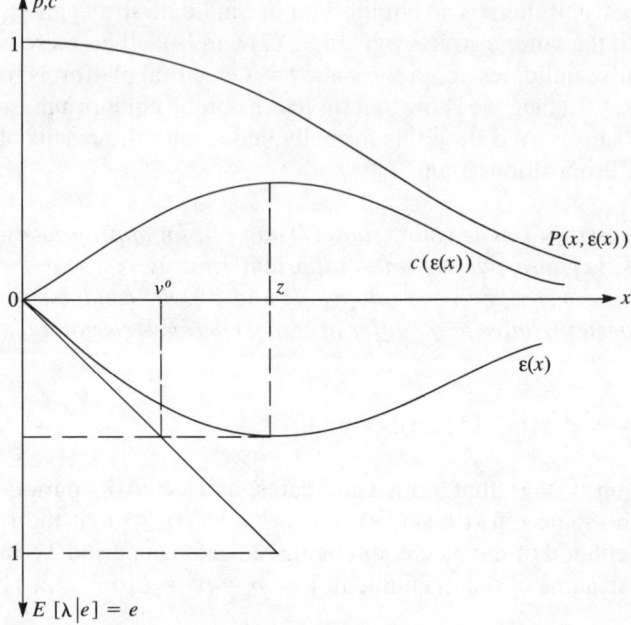

Fig. 3. The critical value, v^o

drawn assuming $R = 1$. In the lower quadrant of figure 3, the maximal level of effort, ε, the voter can induce by appropriately choosing k is graphed as a function of incumbent platform, x.

In the figure, effort is increasing in the downward direction. The upper quadrant describes the probability of incumbent reelection, p, and the costs of effort, c, as functions of incumbent platform when effort is set at $\varepsilon(x)$ for every x. The critical values v^o and z are easily read off from the diagram. Figure 4 reproduces figure 3, and superimposes the *equilibrium* values of induced effort choice, e^*, probability of incumbent reelection, p^*, and costs of effort, c^*, as functions of incumbent platform when the voter's ideal point is at $v < v^o$.

What is the equilibrium $t = 1$ electoral platform for the case illustrated? For simplicity, suppose both candidates adopt a common period 1 electoral platform at some $x < x^*$ (cf. fig. 4). Then the probability that candidate $j = 1, 2$ wins is $\frac{1}{2}$ and j's expected payoff is (from (4)),

$$\pi_j((x,\cdot)|\ \sigma^*, (x,\cdot)) = (\tfrac{1}{2})\cdot\{2R - c^*(\varepsilon(x))\} > 0.$$

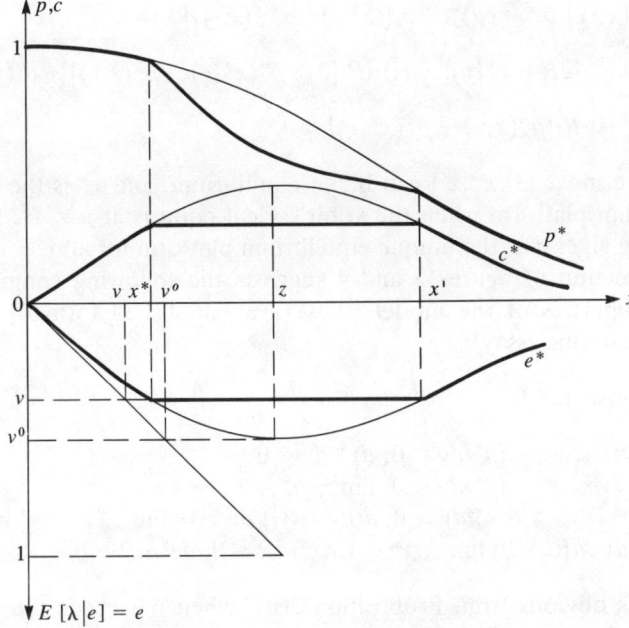

Fig. 4. $v < v^o$; equilibrium at x^*

Now suppose, say, candidate 2 remains at x, but candidate 1 adopts $x + \delta$, $x < x + \delta < x^*$. Then the voter's expected payoff from electing 1 strictly exceeds that from electing 2. Hence, candidate 1 wins with probability one and obtains an expected payoff of,

$$\pi_1((x+\delta,\cdot) \mid \sigma^*, (x,\cdot)) = R \cdot [1 + p^*(x+\delta, \varepsilon(x+\delta))]$$

$$- c^*(\varepsilon(x+\delta)).$$

And for sufficiently small δ, $\pi_1((x+\delta,\cdot) \mid \sigma^*, (x,\cdot)) > \pi_j((x,\cdot) \mid \sigma^*, (x,\cdot))$. So no $x < x^*$ can be an equilibrium. Similarly, no $x > x'$ can be an equilibrium. Let $x \in (x^*, x')$. For any such platform, the voter is capable of inducing more effort from the incumbent than the voter wants. Consequently, v will choose $k(x)$ for $x \in [x^*, x']$ to leave the incumbent's effort choice constant at $e^* = v$. Hence, v is totally indifferent over all platforms $x \in [x^*, x']$. The candidates, however, are not so indifferent. Suppose both candidates adopt some $x \in (x^*, x')$, and compare, say, candidate 1's payoff from this platform to that achieved by moving to x^*:

$$[\pi_1((x,\cdot) \mid \sigma^*, (x,\cdot)) - \pi_1((x^*,\cdot) \mid \sigma^*, (x,\cdot))]$$
$$= (\tfrac{1}{2}) \cdot \{2R - c^*(v)\} - (\tfrac{1}{2}) \cdot \{R \cdot [2 + p^*(x^*,v) - p^*(x,v)] - c^*(v)\}$$
$$= (\tfrac{1}{2}) \cdot R \cdot [p^*(x,v) - p^*(x^*,v)] < 0.$$

Therefore, no $x \in (x^*, x')$ can be an equilibrium, and x^* is the unique equilibrium platform when the voter's ideal point is at $v < v^o$. Similar reasoning gives z as the unique equilibrium platform for all $v \geq v^o$.

Inspection of figures 3 and 4 suggests the following comparative static properties of the model (these are established formally in the appendix to this essay):

PROPOSITION 3.

(i) $\forall v \geq v^o$: $dp^*/dv = 0$; $dx^*/dv = 0$.
(ii) $\forall v < v^o$: $dp^*/dv < 0$; $\lim_{v \to 0} p^* = 1$.
   $dx^*/dv > 0$; $d(|x^* - v|)/dv > 0$; $\lim_{v \to 0} |x^* - v| = 0$.
(iii) $dv^o/dR > 0$; $\lim_{R \to \infty} v^o = 1$; $dx^*/dR \leq 0$; $de^*/dR \geq 0$.

Part (i) is obvious from Proposition 2(ii): when v exceeds the critical value v^o, the probability of reelection and equilibrium first-period platform are independent of the voter's ideal point. Proposition 3(ii) says, first, that incumbency advantage becomes more pronounced as the pivotal voter's ideal point moves closer to the status quo position; in the limit, the incumbent is surely reelected. It is worth emphasizing that this result does not depend on any perceived or actual asymmetry in candidates' ability to deliver political benefits to the voter. Second, the discrepancy between the voter's ideal point and the equilibrium location of first-period electoral platforms is smaller the closer is v to the status quo.

Proposition 3(iii) claims that the location of the critical voter v^o increases with R. In other words, the more valuable the legislative office, the larger is the set of voters who can obtain a first-best equilibrium outcome with a quadratic reelection strategy. Correspondingly, for any v with a first-best outcome under $R < R'$, the equilibrium electoral platform under R' will be closer to v than under R, and the amount of effort that the voter can induce using the strategy σ^* for any platform ($<z$) is greater under R' than under R.

Extensions of the Model

In this section, we examine the robustness of the results with respect to three of the model's assumptions: (1) single voter, (2) two periods, and (3) symmetric candidates. Consider these in turn.

(1) Suppose the electorate consists of n voters, n odd, where all voters have symmetric and single-peaked preferences on **R**. Let the median voter's ideal point be $v > 0$, and let v^o be defined as in Proposition 2. In the appendix to this essay we prove,

PROPOSITION 4. *Suppose $v < v^o$. Then Propositions 1, 2, and 3 generalize to the n voter case: v randomizes as described above; all voters with ideal points less than v vote for the period 1 incumbent surely; and all voters with ideal points greater than v vote for the challenger surely.*

(2) As noted in the introduction, the key to the results is that the pivotal voter is indifferent across candidates in both elections. Suppose now that the candidates compete over T elections, $2 \leq T < \infty$. In this setting, the pivotal voter's maximand is the discounted present value of payoffs defined naturally from equation (3), and candidates' maximands are similarly generalized from equations (4). Assume a common discount factor, and extend strategies and the definition of equilibrium in the obvious fashion. Finally, we introduce an additional assumption: whenever the voter is indifferent between two candidates in *any* election, he votes for each with positive probability. (This perturbs Equation (7) above—replace 1 by $1 - \xi$ and replace 0 by $\xi, \xi > 0$ and arbitrarily small. Then taking ξ fixed leaves all results unchanged.)

PROPOSITION 5. *In any equilibrium to the T-period game, the pivotal voter will be indifferent between candidates in every election.*

The argument behind this claim is as follows. Suppose there exists a set of elections for which the voter strictly prefers one candidate over the other, and let t' be the maximal element of this set. Backwards induction implies $t' < T$. Without loss of generality, let the winning t' candidate be the (period $t' - 1$) incumbent. Strict voter preference at t' implies that the effort level the voter can induce from the incumbent in the t' legislative period is preferred to that he can induce from the challenger. This follows because indifference in elections subsequent to t' can only mean that both candidates will implement identical effort levels if elected; were this not the case, the voter would not be indifferent between candidates in election $t' + 1$, which contradicts the choice of t'. But because both candidates have positive probability of electoral success when the voter is indifferent, at least one candidate cannot be optimizing: either the challenger prefers to mimic the incumbent and have the same effort level induced, or conversely.

In view of Proposition 5, the logic supporting our conclusions for the two-period case extends to the T (finite)–period case. Although details of equilibrium behavior will surely differ when $T > 2$, the qualitative properties of electoral accountability and the incumbency effect are robust.

(3) One seemingly crucial feature of the model is the symmetry across candidates in their willingness and ability to influence the policy outcome in period 2: the first-period incumbent does not possess an advantage vis à vis the challenger due to her period 1 legislative experience. Suppose that this assumption is relaxed by introducing the following asymmetry: the cost of effort schedule in the second period is "more convex" for the incumbent, so the incumbent can provide any effort strictly between zero and one at a lower cost. In the two-period model analyzed above, this asymmetry clearly does not change the nature of the results because the period 2 incumbent, regardless of who it is, will provide zero effort. So extend the model to three periods: then it is no longer evident that the asymmetry is immaterial.

Specifically, let $c(\cdot)$ be the cost function defined in (5). Assume this describes the cost of effort of either candidate in her first legislative period; i.e, following her first electoral success. Now let $c_I(\cdot) = h(c(\cdot))$ be the cost function faced by a candidate in her second legislative period, where h is a convex transformation of $c(\cdot)$. As in the two-period case, both candidates will provide zero effort if elected in the final period, period 3, irrespective of their cost functions. Therefore, in the final election the voter can randomize as before. In the period 2 election, the voter is faced with the decision whether to reelect the period 1 incumbent with the associated cost advantage. In equilibrium, this decision will be based on his ability to induce effort from candidates in the second period with a suitable choice of a period 3 randomization scheme. The important feature here is that this scheme may differ according to which candidate held office in the first period. The relevant question, then, is whether the voter will in equilibrium be indifferent between candidates at the second period election.

PROPOSITION 6. *If $v < v^o$ and $c_I(\cdot)$ is a convex transformation of $c(\cdot)$, then in equilibrium the voter will be indifferent between candidates at each election, and can induce his most preferred effort level in legislative period 2.*

The claim essentially follows by definition of v^o. When $v < v^o$, there exists a platform for the challenger at the $t = 2$ electoral stage such that the voter, through suitably choosing a $t = 3$ voting strategy, can induce this candidate to select the voter's optimal effort level in legislative period 2. This is immediate from the two-period analysis presented above. Since c_I is a convex transformation of c, any effort level that can be induced from the challenger can a fortiori be induced from the incumbent. Therefore, the voter will be indifferent in the period 2 election, and hence can credibly randomize. This in turn allows the voter to select his period 2 voting strategy to influence the effort choice of the period 1 incumbent.

Notice that in the three-period model with candidate asymmetry, the equilibrium outcome is "socially inefficient": given a level of effort to be provided, the efficient solution has the lower cost candidate being the provider. But this solution can never be an equilibrium, since it is precisely the ability of the voter to reject an incumbent based on legislative performance that creates the incentives to exert positive effort.

Conclusion

In this essay, we have developed and analyzed a multiperiod model in which voters attempt to influence an incumbent's legislative decisions through a retrospective voting strategy. This strategy is a function of the platform announced by the incumbent and the final legislative policy outcome, where the latter is in part determined by the unobservable amount of costly effort the incumbent selects. The retrospective voting strategy is shown to be "credible"; in equilibrium the voter will be indifferent between voting for either candidate at each election and hence can randomize in his decision. In particular, it is optimal for the voter to base his decision at the current election on the difference between the platform of the previous period's incumbent and the legislative outcome.

The model illustrates how the electoral mechanism alone can be used to give representatives the incentive to expend costly, and unobservable, effort to promote the well being of their district's pivotal voter. It also offers an explanation of how the incumbency effect can emerge in equilibrium in an electoral model in which the incumbent and the challenger are identical in all respects. Together, these results suggest that the electoral accountability issue and the reason for the incumbency effect are intimately related. Finally, the use of a retrospective voting strategy provides a rationalization for why purely office-seeking candidates might act as if they had well-defined policy preferences in the legislature (Austen-Smith and Banks 1988; Banks 1987a): an incumbent's reelection chances decrease as the policy outcome moves away from her platform.

In the model, the "preferences" induced on the candidates by the pivotal voter are (essentially) quadratic (cf. (7)). And if the voter's ideal point v is less than some critical value, v^o, inducing quadratic "preferences" is unambiguously a first-best arrangement: the voter insures the incumbent will act entirely in the voter's interests (up to the final legislative period). When v exceeds v^o, the voter is unable to induce the incumbent to put in as much legislative effort as the voter would like by using a quadratic specification for his vote-lottery. Will an alternative randomization scheme improve the voter's payoff?

At present, the answer is: "Possibly, but only to a limited extent." To see this, note that if $v > 1$, then the voter's first-best outcome is to induce the incumbent to choose an effort level greater than one: but this is physically impossible. Therefore, there is no randomization scheme that can induce a first-best outcome for all ideal points of the pivotal voter. Similarly, so long as the cost of effort schedule is convex, there will always be a critical value v^o beyond which the first-best outcome is unavailable. The exact location of this critical value depends on the details of the cost function, the randomization scheme used by the pivotal voter, and the gross value of legislative office, R. However, for high enough R, use of the quadratic randomization scheme is as good as any other. In any event, the qualitative logic of the model and the results go through with other schemes.

A generalization of the model that would nontrivially alter the results would be to posit an asymmetry in *information* between candidates and voters. For example, if voters are uncertain of the value of office to each candidate, then, given a retrospective voting rule, candidates with different values will generally choose different effort levels. The pivotal voter wishes to elect the candidate who will provide his preferred effort level. This yields an adverse selection problem in which the ability of candidates to "signal" relevant information through their choice of electoral platform is attenuated. We leave this problem to future research.

APPENDIX

In the Appendix, we prove the Lemma and Propositions 1 through 4. Before proceeding, however, we fill in the missing parts of the voter's strategy, viz. what he or she does when some candidate(s) fails to offer a platform in some election(s).

Completion of the Voter's Strategy. First observe that, given σ_2^* both candidates would surely seek office in period $t = 2$. There is no cost to offering a platform, and there is payoff of $R \geq 1$ if successful and zero otherwise. Therefore, seeking office weakly dominates any other electoral strategy at $t = 2$ for both candidates. Moreover, because the voter is wholly indifferent about whether any or either candidate takes office in period 2, *any* period 2 voting rule for when neither of the candidates seeks office at $t = 2$ is credible and optimizing for the voter. And if only one candidate should seek such office, then voting for him with probability one is similarly equilibrium behavior. Now suppose only one candidate seeks office at $t = 1$ (and both run at $t = 2$), and consider the following strategy (conditional on this event) for the voter. At $t = 1$ elect the unopposed candidate; at $t = 2$, if indifferent between the candidates, for the $t = 1$ incumbent with probability one regardless of λ, x, and so forth, otherwise vote sincerely. Suppose that neither candidate seeks office at $t = 1$. Then the payoff to either candidate is at most R. But if one candidate runs at $t = 1$ and the other does not, then the $t = 1$ incumbent receives a total payoff of $2R$. This follows because, during the $t = 1$ legislative period, he can choose zero effort with impunity. In this instance, the candidate who failed to run at $t = 1$ receives a payoff of zero, while he or she can obtain a positive expected payoff by entering the first election. Therefore it is not an equilibrium for only one candidate to enter the first election. Hence, both candidates will contest both elections and the voter will be observed to employ the parts of his strategy given by (7) and (9). A fortiori, it cannot be equilibrium behavior for both candidates to fail to enter the first election; and we are done.

Some Useful Facts. From (1) and (2) and the realized policy outcome in period 1, λ, is a normally distributed random variable with mean e and variance 1 (where period subscripts are suppressed). Let $\Phi(\cdot)$ and $\phi(\cdot)$ denote the *cdf* and *pdf*, respectively, for the standardized normal distribution. Let ϕ be truncated to the left by A, and to the right by B ($B \geq A$); that is,

$$\phi(\lambda \mid e) > 0 \Leftrightarrow \lambda \in [A,B] \equiv \Delta.$$

Then we have (N. Johnson and S. Kotz 1970, chap. 13):

$$E[\lambda \mid \lambda \in \Delta] = e + [\phi(A - e) - \phi(B - e)] \cdot D,$$

$$D = [\Phi(B - e) - \Phi(A - e)]^{-1};$$

$$var[\lambda \mid \lambda \in \Delta] = 1 + [(A - e)\phi(A - e) - (B - e)\phi(B - e)] \cdot D$$

$$- \{[\phi(A - e) - \phi(B - e)] \cdot D\}^2.$$

Appropriately differentiating these expressions and using the fact that $\phi'(a) = -\phi(a)a$, yields, after some manipulation:

$\partial E[\lambda \mid \lambda \in \Delta]/\partial e = var[\lambda \mid \lambda \in \Delta]$

$\partial var[\lambda \mid \lambda \in \Delta]/\partial e > [=] < 0 \text{ as } e > [=] < [A + B]/2 \equiv x$

$\partial E[\lambda \mid \lambda \in \Delta]/\partial x = 1 - var[\lambda \mid \lambda \in \Delta]$

$\partial var[\lambda \mid \lambda \in \Delta]/\partial x = - \partial var[\lambda \mid \lambda \in \Delta]/\partial e.$

To save on notation, hereafter write $\hat{\lambda} = E[\lambda \mid \lambda \in \Delta]$, and $\widehat{var} = var[\lambda \mid \lambda \in \Delta]$.

Period 1 Incumbent's Choice of Effort. Fix the $t = 1$ incumbent's (hereafter, the incumbent) platform at some $x > 0$, and fix $k \in (0,\infty)$. The remaining cases are considered separately later on. Given he or she is elected on the platform x in period 1, the incumbent solves program (8). Substituting for p, this is,

$$\max_{e \in [0,1]} L \equiv R \cdot [1 + [\Phi(x + k^{-\frac{1}{2}} - e) - \Phi(x - k^{-\frac{1}{2}} - e)]$$

$$\cdot \{1 - k \cdot [(\hat{\lambda} - x)^2 + \widehat{var}]\}] - c(e). \tag{A.1}$$

There certainly exists a solution, e^*, to this program since L is continuous on $[0,1]$. Let $q = [\Phi(x + k^{-1/2} - e) - \Phi(x - k^{-1/2} - e)]$, and let $s = \{1 - k \cdot [(\hat{\lambda} - x)^2 + \widehat{var}]\}$. Then $p = q \cdot s$. Using subscripts to denote partial derivatives, we obtain:

$$L_e = R \cdot [q_e s + q s_e] - c' \tag{A.2}$$

$$L_{ee} = R \cdot [q_{ee} s + 2 q_e s_e + q s_{ee}] - c''. \tag{A.3}$$

By x,k positive and finite, Some Useful Facts (SUF), and assumption (5), L_e and L_{ee} are defined everywhere on $[0,1]$. Using SUF,

$$q_e = \phi(x - k^{-\frac{1}{2}} - e) - \phi(x + k^{-\frac{1}{2}} - e).$$

$$s_e = - k[2(\hat{\lambda} - x) \cdot \widehat{var} + \widehat{var}_e].$$

Let e^* be a solution to (A.1). Suppose $e^* \geq x$. Then $q_e \leq 0$ and $\hat{\lambda} \geq x$, so $s_e \leq 0$. But then $L_e < 0$. Hence, $e^* < x$; and, therefore, $\hat{\lambda} < x$. Suppose $e^* = 0$. Since $x, k > 0$ we have $q_e, s_e > 0$ at $e = 0$. But $\lim_{e \to 0} c'(e) = 0$ by assumption (5). Therefore, $L_e > 0$ at $e = 0$. Hence, $e^* > 0$. So, given $k > 0$ and finite, $e^* \in (0, x)$ for all $x \in (0, 1]$. By assumption (5), $\lim_{e \to 1} c'(e) = \infty$. Hence, given $k > 0$ and finite,

$e^* \in (0, \min\{1,x\})$ for all $x > 0$. (A.4)

Since e^* is interior for all x, k strictly positive and finite, $L_e = 0$ and $L_{ee} < 0$ at e^*. It is not hard to check that the function $p = q \cdot s$ is strictly quasi-concave in e for any x, k. In particular, for all strictly positive and finite values of k,

$$p_e > [=] < 0 \text{ as } e < [=] > x;$$

$$\exists e' < x \text{ such that } e \in [0,x] \Rightarrow p_{ee} > [=] < 0 \text{ as } e < [=] > e'. \quad (A.5)$$

So p is not concave everywhere (save for $k \in \{0, \infty\}$, when it is linear in e everywhere). Consequently, the maximand L is a sum of strictly quasi-concave functions and is thus not guaranteed to be quasi-concave. Therefore, for some pairs (x, k), there may exist multiple local maxima to the program (A.1). Indeed, for any $x > 0$, there exist k sufficiently large for which there are surely multiple local maxima. However, for c sufficiently convex, (i) the values of k for which this is true are such that $|\Delta| \approx 0$ but, in equilibrium, $|\Delta| > 0$; and (ii) the set of k-values for which there are multiple global maxima is negligible. So we assume c sufficiently convex to insure L is strictly quasi-concave for a sufficiently large set of pairs $\{(x, k)\}$; exactly what this set comprises is specified below. Then e^* is unique for any (x, k) in the set.

Comparative Static, $\partial e^*/\partial x$. Holding k fixed, consider an incremental change in platform, x. Differentiation of (A.2) at e^* gives,

$$L_{ee}\partial e^* + L_{ex}\partial x = 0. \quad (A.6)$$

By $L_{ee} < 0$ at e^*, $\partial e^*/\partial x > [=] < 0$ as $L_{ex} > [=] < 0$. Now,

$$L_{ex} = R \cdot [q_{ex}s + q_x s_e + q s_{ex}].$$

Computing these derivatives at e^*, and using SUF gives, $L_{ex} = -R \cdot [q_{ee}s + 2q_e s_e + q s_{ee}]$. Hence,

$$\partial e^*/\partial x > [=] < 0 \text{ as } p = q \cdot s \text{ is strictly concave [linear]}$$

convex at e^*. (A.7)

Voter's Choice of $k^*(\cdot)$. By assumption, the voter's preferences, u, are symmetric single-peaked on R. Therefore, since λ is distributed symmetrically and only the mean of λ is affected by the incumbent's choice of effort, the voter's payoff is unimodal in e with first-best at $e = v$. Hold $x > 0$ fixed, and consider the voter's optimizing selection of $k(x)$. Differentiation of (A.2) at e^* gives,

$$L_{ee}\partial e^* + L_{ek}\partial k = 0. \tag{A.8}$$

Since $L_{ee} < 0$ at e^*, $\partial e^*/\partial k > [=] < 0$ as $L_{ek} > [=] < 0$. By definition of $p = q \cdot s$,

$$[k = 0(\infty)] \Rightarrow [p = 0\,(1)], \text{ all } x.$$

By (A.1), $p \in \{0, 1\} \Rightarrow [e^* = 0]$. But L_e is continuously differentiable in $k \in (0, \infty)$, and $e^* > 0$ for all $(x, k) \in (0, \infty)^2$. Hence, there exists $k^*(x) \in (0, \infty)$ such that, at $e^* = e^*(x, k^*(x))$:

$$L_{ek} = \partial e^*/\partial k = 0; \text{ and } \partial^2 e^*/\partial k^2 =$$

$$-[L_{ee}L_{ekk} - L_{ek}L_{eek}] \cdot L_{ee}^{-2} = -L_{ekk}/L_{ee} < 0. \tag{A.9}$$

Moreover, by definition of q and s, for $x \in (0, \infty)$, $k^*(x)$ is unique; in particular, given uniqueness of the solution to (A.1), e^* is unimodal in k. We now introduce the following assumption, specifying the set of pairs $\{(x, k)\}$ for which the incumbent's optimizing choice of effort, $e^*(x, k)$, is surely unique.

Uniqueness assumption: $\forall x \geq 0$, L is strictly quasi-concave in e $\forall k \leq k^*(x)$. Hereafter, this assumption is left implicit. So, since (A.9) and $k = 0$ imply $e^* = 0$:

$$\forall x \in (0, \infty), \exists \varepsilon(x) \in (0, \min\{1, x\}) \text{ such that:}$$

$$\forall e \in [0, \varepsilon(x)], \exists k \text{ such that } e^*(x, k) = e. \tag{A.10}$$

Totally differentiating L_e gives,

$$L_{ee}de^* + L_{ex}dx + L_{ek}dk = 0.$$

Set $k = k^*(x)$ such that $e^*(x, k^*(x)) = \varepsilon(x)$. Then $L_{ek} = 0$ at every $x > 0$, and

$$d\varepsilon(x)/dx > [=] < 0 \text{ as } L_{ex} > [=] < 0 \text{ at } k^*(x).$$

By assumption, $\lim_{e \to 0} c'(e) = 0$. Moreover, by (A.5) and (A.7), $L_{ex} > 0$ at least in the neighborhood of x. Therefore, since $0 < e^* < x$ for all $x > 0$,

$$\exists z > 0 \text{ such that } d\varepsilon(x)/dx > [=] < 0 \text{ as } x < [=] > z. \tag{A.11}$$

Proof of Lemma. Let $k \in (0, \infty)$. From SUF, at $x = 0$, q_e, $s_e < 0$ for all $e > 0$. Hence,

$$e^*(0,k) = 0 \text{ for all } k \in (0,\infty).$$

Moreover, from the previous section, $k \in \{0, \infty\}$ implies $e^*(x, k) = 0$ for all x. With (A.4), (A.10) and (A.11), therefore, the Lemma is proved.

Lim $k^*(x)$ as x Goes to Zero. Since $e^*(0, k) = 0$ for all $k \in [0, \infty]$, the value of $p^* = q^* \cdot s^*$ is not well defined at $x = 0$. So consider $\lim_{x \to 0+} k^*(x)$; we show that this limit is zero, implying $p^* = 1$ at $x = 0$. By earlier reasoning, $e^* < x$ for all $x > 0$. So, by $v > 0$, for x positive and sufficiently small we have $e^*(x, k^*(x)) = \varepsilon(x)$, where $0 < k^* < \infty$. Then by (A.9),

$$L_{ek} = R \cdot [q_{ek}s + q_e s_k + q_k s_e + q s_{ek}] = 0, \tag{A.12}$$

at $e^*(x,k^*(x))$, for all $x > 0$ and small. Therefore,

$$L_{ekk}dk^* + L_{ekx}dk = 0 \tag{A.13}$$

at $e^*(x, k^*(x))$. By (A.9) and $L_{ee} < 0$ at e^*, $L_{ekk} < 0$. So $dk^*/dx > [=] < 0$ as $L_{ekx} > [=] < 0$. From (A.12),

$$s = -[(L_{ek} \cdot R^{-1}) - q_{ek}s] \cdot q_{ek}^{-1} \tag{A.14}$$

which is well-defined since

$$q_{ek} = \left(\frac{k^{-\frac{3}{2}}}{2}\right) \cdot [(x + k^{-\frac{1}{2}} - e) \cdot \phi(x + k^{-\frac{1}{2}} - e) - (x - k^{-\frac{1}{2}} - e)$$

$$\cdot \phi(x - k^{-\frac{1}{2}} - e)] \neq 0, \forall (x,k) \in (0,\infty)^2.$$

By the first-order condition for an interior maximum, $L_e = 0$ at e^*. Hence, from (A.2),

$$s = [c' - qs_e] \cdot q_e^{-1}. \tag{A.15}$$

Together, (A.14) and (A.15) imply,

$$L_{ek} = R \cdot L_e \cdot q_{ek} \cdot q_e^{-1}, \text{ at } e^*(x, k^*(x)). \tag{A.16}$$

Since x is parametric, we can differentiate (A.16) to give,

$$L_{ekx} = R \cdot L_{ex} \cdot q_{ek} \cdot q_e^{-1}. \tag{A.17}$$

From the argument for e^* being interior [(A.2) ff.], $R \cdot q_e^{-1} > 0$. Similarly, from the argument for $\varepsilon'(x) > 0\ \forall x < z$ [(A.10) ff.], $L_{ex} > 0$ for $x > 0$ sufficiently small. Now e^* interior and $k^*(x)$, $x > 0$ imply $(x + k^{*-1/2} - e^*) > 0$. Similarly, by the Implicit Function Theorem, e^* interior and $k^*(x)$, $x > 0$ imply $(x - k^{*-1/2} - e^*) \leq 0$ for x sufficiently small. Therefore $q_{ek} > 0$ for x sufficiently small. Hence, $L_{ekx} > 0$ for x sufficiently small, implying $\lim_{x \to 0+} k^*(x) < \infty$.

Substituting into the first-order condition, $L_e = 0$ for $x > 0$, gives:

$$[\phi(x - k^{*-\frac{1}{2}} - e^*) - \phi(x + k^{*-\frac{1}{2}} - e^*)] \cdot [1 - k^* \cdot [(\hat{\lambda} - x)^2 + \widehat{var}]$$
$$- [\Phi(x + k^{*-\frac{1}{2}} - e^*) - \Phi(x - k^{*-\frac{1}{2}} - e^*)] \cdot k^* \cdot [2(\hat{\lambda} - x) \cdot \widehat{var} + \widehat{var}_e]$$
$$= c'(e^*).$$

Thus,

$$k^*(x) = \{[\phi(x - k^{*-\frac{1}{2}} - e^*) - \phi(x + k^{*-\frac{1}{2}} - e^*)] - c'(e^*)\}$$
$$\times \{[\phi(x - k^{*-\frac{1}{2}} - e^*) - \phi(x + k^{*-\frac{1}{2}} - e^*)] \cdot [(\hat{\lambda} - x)^2 + \widehat{var}]$$
$$+ [\Phi(x + k^{*-\frac{1}{2}} - e^*) - \Phi(x - k^{*-\frac{1}{2}} - e^*)]$$
$$\times [2(\hat{\lambda} - x) \cdot \widehat{var} + \widehat{var}_e]\}^{-1}. \tag{A.18}$$

Since (A.18) holds at $e^*(x, k^*(x))$ for all $x > 0$, $\lim_{x \to 0+} k^*(x) = \lim_{x \to 0+} \text{RHS}(A.18)$. By assumption (5) and SUF, both the numerator and the denominator of RHS (A.18) go to zero as x goes to zero. By the earlier argument, $\lim_{x \to 0+} k^*(x) < \infty$. Hence, $\lim_{x \to 0+} \text{RHS}(A.18) < \infty$. Suppose $\lim_{x\to 0+} k^*(x) > 0$, and consider RHS(A.18). Writing $\alpha \equiv x - k^{*-1/2} - e^*$ and $\beta \equiv x + k^{*-1/2} - e^*$, we have

$$d[\text{NumeratorRHS(A.18)}]/dx = \phi'(\alpha) \cdot d\alpha/dx$$

$$- \phi'(\beta) \cdot d\beta/dx - c''(e^*)de^*/dx.$$

Recall $\lim_{x\to 0+} e^* = 0$ for all k; and $c''(0) > 0$ by assumption. Since $\lim_{e\to 0} c'(e) = 0$, $\lim_{x\to 0+} k^*(x) > 0$ implies $de^*/dx = 1$ at $e^* = x = 0$. Hence $\lim_{x\to 0+} c''(e^*)de^*/dx > 0$. Now,

$$[\phi'(\alpha) \cdot d\alpha/dx - \phi'(\beta) \cdot d\beta/dx]$$

$$= [1 - de^*/dx][\beta\phi(\beta) - \alpha\phi(\alpha)] - k^{*-\frac{3}{2}}dk^*/dx[\beta\phi(\beta) + \alpha\phi(\alpha)]/2.$$

$\text{Lim}_{x\to 0+}[1 - de^*/dx] = 0$, and (given $\lim_{x\to 0+} k^*(x) > 0$):

$$\lim_{x\to 0+}[\beta\phi(\beta) - \alpha\phi(\alpha)]$$

$$= \lim_{x\to 0+}[(x - e^*)(\phi(\beta) - \phi(\alpha)) + k^{*-\frac{1}{2}}(\phi(\beta) + \phi(\alpha))]$$

$$= 2k^*(0)^{-\frac{1}{2}}\phi(k^*(0)^{-\frac{1}{2}}) > 0;$$

$$\lim_{x\to 0+}[\beta\phi(\beta) + \alpha\phi(\alpha)]$$

$$= \lim_{x\to 0+}[(x - e^*)(\phi(\beta) + \phi(\alpha)) + k^{*-\frac{1}{2}}(\phi(\beta) - \phi(\alpha))]$$

$$= 0.$$

Hence, $\lim_{x\to 0+} d[\text{Numerator(A.18)}]/dx < 0$. Similarly, totally differentiating the denominator of RHS(A.18) with respect to x, taking limits and using SUF, we obtain:

$$\lim_{x\to 0+} d[\text{DenominatorRHS(A.18)}]/dx$$

$$= [\Phi(k^*(0)^{-\frac{1}{2}}) - \Phi(-k^*(0)^{-\frac{1}{2}})] \cdot \widehat{dvar}_e(k^*(0))/dx.$$

By supposition, $k^*(0) > 0$ so $[\cdot] > 0$, and by SUF,

$$\widehat{dvar}_e(k^*(0))/dx = -(\widehat{dvar}_e(k^*(0))/de) \cdot de^*/dx > 0 \text{ at } e^* = x = 0.$$

Hence $\lim_{x\to 0+} d[\text{DenominatorRHS(A.18)}]/dx > 0$. So by L'Hospital's Rule and the supposition that k^* is strictly positive in the limit, we have

$\lim_{x\to 0+}\text{RHS(A.18)} < 0$. But this contradicts $\lim_{x\to 0+} k^*(x) = \lim_{x\to 0+}\text{RHS(A.18)}$, establishing $\lim_{x\to 0+} k^*(x) = 0$ as required.

Proof of Propositions 1 and 2. With the exception of the candidates' choices of period 1 electoral platforms, all the claims of Propositions 1 and 2 are proven in the text and above. Define $v^o = \varepsilon^{-1}(z)$, where z is defined by $\varepsilon'(z) = 0$; by (A.11), v^o is unique. Let $v \geq v^o$. Then $k^*(x)$ will be chosen by the voter so that $e^*(x, k^*(x)) = \varepsilon(x)$ for all $x \geq 0$. It is now trivial to extend the discussion in the text following Proposition 2 to provide a proof for $x_j^* = z, j = 1,2$. Now suppose $v < v^o$. Define $x_v = \min\{x \mid \varepsilon^{-1}(x) = v\}$, and $y_v = \max\{x \mid \varepsilon^{-1}(x) = v\}$. Since $v < v^o$, (A.11) implies $x_v < z < y_v$. Then the voter chooses $k^*(x)$ so that:

$e^*(x, k^*(x)) = \varepsilon(x)$ for all $x \in [0, x_v)$;

$e^*(x, k^*(x)) = v$ for all $x \in [x_v, y_v] \equiv I(v)$;

$e^*(x, k^*(x)) = \varepsilon(x)$ for all $x > y_v$.

By (A.10), such a $k^*(\cdot)$ exists. Moreover, since e^* is unimodal in k for any x [see (A.9) ff.], for each $x \in (x_v, y_v)$ there exist exactly two values of k for which $e^*(x, k) = v$. In particular, there exist two continuous selections for $k^*(x)$ on $I(v)$. Because the voter is indifferent between these, we assume, without loss of generality, that v makes a fixed continuous selection for $k^*(\cdot)$. By an abuse of notation, let $p(x, k^*(x) \mid v)$ be the probability that the incumbent is reelected in period 2, conditional on first period platform x, and voter choice of $k^*(x)$ such that $e^*(x, k^*(x)) = v$. Then $p(x, k^*(x) \mid v)$ is continuous in x on $I(v)$. Once again, it is trivial to turn the discussion in the text following Proposition 2 into a proof for the claim:

$x_j^* \in \text{argmax}_{I(v)} p(x, k^*(x) \mid v), j = 1,2$; where $I(v) \equiv [x_v, y_v]$.

By definition of q and s, x_j^* is unique. Since $x_v > v$, it remains to show $x_j^* < z$. In fact, we show that $x_j^* \in [x_v, x(v))$, where $x(v) < z$, for any continuous selection of $k^*(x)$.

Differentiating $p(x, k^*(x) \mid v)$ with respect to x on $I(v)$ gives:

$$dp^*/dx = p_x + p_k \cdot dk^*/dx. \tag{A.19}$$

From SUF and $e^*(x, k^*(x)) = v$ for all x in $I(v)$, $p_x = -p_e = -c'(v) < 0 \,\forall x \in I(v)$. Consider p_k at any $x \in I(v)$. Clearly, $k = 0$ implies $p = 1$, and $\lim_{k\to\infty} p = 0$. Hence, $p_k < 0$ for small and for large k, and $p_{kk} > 0$ for sufficiently large k. Suppose $p_k > 0$ for some intermediate value of k. Then there exist k', k'' with $k' < k''$ such that $p_k(k') = p_k(k'') = 0$, and $p_{kk}(k') > 0$, $p_{kk}(k'') < 0$. But since σ_2^* is quadratic for $\lambda \in \Delta$, $\lambda \sim N(v, 1)$, and $v < x$ [by (A.4)], p_{kk} can change signs at most once $(-/+)$: contradiction. Therefore, $p_k < 0$ for all $k \in (0, \infty)$. So if $dk^*/dx > 0$, $x_j^* = x_v$ and we are done. Because $e^*(x, k^*(x)) = v \; \forall x \in (x_v, y_v)$, (A.2) at $e^* = v < \varepsilon(x)$ implies

$$dk^*/dx = -p_{ex}/p_{ek} = p_{ee}/p_{ek} \; \forall x \in (x_v, y_v), \qquad (A.20)$$

the last equality following from SUF. By (A.11), $d\varepsilon(x)/dx > [=] < 0$ as $p_{ee} < [=] > 0$, and, by definition of z, $p_{ee} < [=] 0$ as $x < [=] z$ when $e^* = \varepsilon(x)$. By assumption, k^* is a continuous selection. Hence, $p_{ee}(x, k^*(x) \mid v) < 0$ in a neighborhood of x_v. Moreover, since $v < \varepsilon(x)$, $\forall x \in (x_v, y_v)$,

$$0 \geq p_{ee}(x, k^* \mid e^*(x, k^*) = v) >$$

$$p_{ee}(x, k \mid e^*(x, k) = \varepsilon(x)) \; \forall x \in (x_v, z). \qquad (A.21)$$

Hence, there exists $x' \in (x_v, z)$ such that $p_{ee}(x', k^*(x') \mid v) = 0$. Therefore, by (A.19) and (A.20), for any selection of k^* on $I(v)$ there exists $x(v) \in (x_v, x')$ such that $dp^*/dx < 0$ at $x(v)$. Furthermore, by continuity of k^*, and $p_x = -c'(v)$ on $I(v)$, $dp^*/dx < 0 \; \forall x \geq x(v)$, $x \in I(v)$. This proves $x_j^* \in [x_v, x(v))$ as required.

Proof of Proposition 3. Part (i) is immediate from $x_j^* = z$ for all $v \geq v^o$. Consider part (ii). By statement (iii) of the Lemma, $v < v' \Rightarrow I(v) \supset I(v')$. Then, because $\varepsilon(x)$ is independent of v, $\forall x \geq 0$, (A.21) implies, $v < v' \Rightarrow x(v) < x(v')$. By earlier reasoning, $\lim_{x \to 0+} p(x, k^*(x) \mid e^*(x, k^*(x)) = 1$ for all v: hence, $\lim_{v \to 0+} p(x^*, k^*(x^*) \mid v) = 1$ for any selection of $k^*(\cdot)$. Part (ii) of the Proposition now follows.

Finally, inspection of (A.2) shows that for all (x, k), $e^*(x, k)$ is strictly increasing in R: this gives part (iii) of Proposition 3.

Proof of Proposition 4. Suppose v is the median voter's ideal point, with $0 < v < v^o$. Suppose all voters adopt second period voting strategies given by (7), with the parameters k indexed by voter ideal points, viz. k_i. Given many voters and no abstention, the probability of incumbent reelection is well approximated by total expected votes divided by the total number of voters, n (cf. Calvert 1986, 39–40). The period 1 incumbent's problem is then to choose effort e to maximize,

$$R \cdot [1 + \Sigma_i \{[\Phi(x + k_i^{-\frac{1}{2}} - e) - \Phi(x - k_i^{-\frac{1}{2}} - e)] \cdot \{1 - k_i \cdot [(\lambda - x)^2$$

$$+ \widehat{var}]\}\} \cdot n^{-1}] - c(e). \qquad (A.22)$$

Solving (A.22) yields the first-order condition,

$$R \cdot \Sigma_i [q_{ei} s_i + q_i s_{ei}] - n \cdot c' = 0. \tag{A.23}$$

Let e^* solve (A.22). Suppose in equilibrium that v is randomizing according to (7) with $k_v^* \in (0, \infty)$, and consider any voter i with ideal point $i > v$. By symmetric single-peaked preferences, i prefers some effort choice strictly greater than v. By supposition, $v < v^o$ and v is using a nondegenerate lottery. Therefore, $e^* = v$. If i uses any nondegenerate lottery to select the period 2 incumbent, then by (A.23) and given all other voters' decisions, there exists a variation in k_i which can induce a positive change in e^*. But this contradicts the supposition of being in equilibrium. Hence i must be using a degenerate lottery in any equilibrium in which v uses a nondegenerate lottery. Similarly, any $i < v$ must, in equilibrium, use an offsetting degenerate lottery for the second-period election. Finally, no equilibrium could involve v using a degenerate lottery, because in this event more than half of the electorate would be committed to voting surely for one candidate over the other, in which case the solution to (A.22) is zero effort: but $v > 0$, contradicting the optimality of v using a degenerate lottery. Proposition 4 follows.

Remark. The antecedent of Proposition 4 can be weakened somewhat. All we require is that there is no voter with an ideal point in $\{y \mid v^o < y < v\}$. When $v \leq v^o$, this is trivially satisfied since $\{\cdot\}$ is then empty. Whether or not the result holds when there is some ideal point in (v^o, v) is unclear.

International Relations

The Dynamics of Longer Brinkmanship Crises

Robert Powell

From the decline of the doctrine of massive retaliation through the doctrine of mutually assured destruction to the doctrine of limited nuclear options, the evolution of nuclear deterrence theory may be seen as a search for credibility. Can a threat to use nuclear weapons ever be sufficiently credible that a state may use such a threat to protect or further its national interests? Nuclear brinkmanship, at least conceptually, offered one solution to the problem of credibility. In a brinkmanship crisis, a state escalates by generating some risk that the crisis will "go out of control" and end in a general nuclear exchange. As continued escalation raises the risk of disaster, one state eventually finds the risk intolerably high and withdraws. In brinkmanship, crises become a competition in taking risks.

Recent work has used the notion of perfect or sequential equilibria in the context of games with incomplete information to model nuclear brinkmanship. In Nalebuff (1986), the states can vary the risk of disaster continuously from zero to one. The ladder of escalation in effect has a continuum of rungs. Nalebuff shows that as long as this risk may be varied continuously, the risk that will be generated in a crisis is independent of the structure of the system or process that creates the risk. It makes no difference if a state in order to escalate must generate high levels of risk early in a crisis or if it can delay creating grave risks until late in the crisis. The level of risk that is actually created will be the same. Powell (1987, 1988) assumes that a state must raise the risk of war incrementally if it decides to escalate. Here the ladder of escalation has discrete rungs. This work studies the effects of changes in the levels of the states' resolve, the degree of misperception, and the challenger's stake in the status quo on the dynamics of escalation and on crisis stability. The analysis of these changes, however, is confined to a case in which the length of a crisis is fixed exogenously and is, moreover, assumed to be very short. This essay extends that work. By modeling the lack of complete information somewhat differently and more simply, the length of a crisis may be treated as being endogenous and longer crises

---

This essay was assisted by a John M. Olin Research Fellowship.

may be examined. Indeed, because longer crises turn out to be more dangerous, the present formulation begins to make it possible to identify the factors that make for longer and therefore more dangerous crises.

This examination of crisis bargaining shows that changes in the states' levels of resolve affect the dynamics of escalation and crisis stability in complicated ways. The critical-risk model of crisis bargaining (Snyder and Diesing 1977, 48–52) suggests that a state will be less likely to escalate the greater the resolve of its adversary. In the model developed below, the challenger may be more, not less, likely to escalate throughout a crisis if it is facing a more resolute defender. Similarly, an increase in the challenger's resolve may make the defender more likely to escalate. Increasing levels of resolve may also make for longer crises and this may greatly reduce stability by increasing the probability of war. Détente and linkage politics are at least partially based on the assumption that an adversary will be less likely to dispute the status quo if it has a greater stake in the status quo (Litwak 1984, 89–96). Having a larger stake in the status quo generally does not make the challenger less likely to dispute the status quo. But it does tend to make the defender less likely to resist a challenge to the status quo. Accordingly, an increase in the challenger's stake makes crises more stable. As will be seen, incomplete information may also do much to enhance deterrence and crisis stability. Very small doubts may make a challenge to the status quo very unlikely. Yet, the analysis also suggests that stability is rather insensitive to wide variations in the size of these doubts.

The model is presented in the next section. The sequential equilibria are then described and discussed. There follows an examination of the roles of resolve, the challenger's stake in the status quo, and the effect of incomplete information on the dynamics of escalation.

The Model

In the doctrine of massive retaliation, the United States would launch a massive nuclear attack in response to a threat to any American national interest ranging from the most peripheral to the most vital. This doctrine was immediately criticized as being incredible as a means of protecting less important American interests. But as long as the United States remained relatively invulnerable to a Soviet nuclear attack, the doctrine was not criticized as being incredible if used to protect vital American interests.[1] Only as the United States became increasingly vulnerable to a Soviet attack did the credibility of massive retaliation as a way of protecting vital American interests become problematic.

---

1. See Kaufmann (1956) for the classic critique of massive retaliation.

Three decades later, the concerns about the credibility of massive retaliation may be expressed in terms of the notion of a perfect equilibrium. Loosely, the doctrine of massive retaliation was a Nash equilibrium. That is, the combination of an American strategy of retaliating massively to any challenge and a Soviet strategy of never challenging the United States constituted a Nash equilibrium. Given the American strategy of retaliating with a massive nuclear attack, it was better to live with the status quo than to challenge it. The Soviet Union had no incentive to deviate from its strategy. And, given the Soviet strategy of not challenging the status quo, the United States had no incentive to alter its strategy. Although these strategies constituted a Nash equilibrium, more important, they also formed a perfect equilibrium as long as the United States remained relatively invulnerable and vital American interests were at stake. In these circumstances, the cost of carrying out the threat to launch this attack was less than the cost of not implementing the threat and thus sacrificing a vital interest. The threat appeared credible and the doctrine of massive retaliation effective. But once the United States became vulnerable to a massive Soviet nuclear attack, the cost of carrying out the threat seemed greater than the cost of not doing so. This combination of strategies no longer seemed to be perfect. The doctrine of massive retaliation, even if only used in an attempt to protect vital American interests, appeared inherently incredible.

The inherent incredibility of massive retaliation confronted nuclear deterrence theory with a fundamental question. Could a sanction, such as a massive nuclear attack that was always too costly to be imposed deliberately, ever be used coercively? Could a state somehow use such a sanction to further its interests?

Schelling (1960) offered "the threat that leaves something to chance" and the analogy of brinkmanship to show how such a sanction could at least in principle be used coercively. In the brinkmanship analogy, two adversaries are tied together with a rope and standing near a brink. The rope insures that if one goes over the brink, so will the other. Going over the brink here is the analogue for a massive nuclear exchange. Because they are bound together, neither adversary can credibly threaten to push the other into the chasm intentionally. Neither can credibly threaten to launch a massive nuclear attack deliberately.

If the brink is a sharp edge so that it may be approached without any danger of unintentionally falling off, then the sanction of going over the brink cannot be used coercively. But if instead there is a curved slope leading to the chasm that becomes steeper and steeper as one nears the brink, then there is some risk of going over accidentally. There is some chance of the adversaries' falling into the abyss although no one wants to do so.

The possibility of losing control, of the sanction's being imposed without this being done deliberately, makes it possible to use the sanction coercively. During the confrontation, each of the adversaries may approach the brink. This generates larger and larger risks that someone will slip and tumble over the brink. As the adversaries near the chasm, then, assuming that they have not already accidentally gone over the brink, one of them will eventually find the risk too great and will submit to its adversary in order to stop it from moving yet closer to the brink.

Powell (1987, 1988) formalizes this analogy.[2] The same basic formulation will be used here although the lack of complete information will be modeled somewhat differently and more simply. The extensive form is illustrated in figure 1. The confrontation begins with a potential challenger, C, having to decide whether or not to challenge the status quo. If C does not challenge the status quo, the game ends with payoffs (q_C, q_D). If C does challenge the status quo, then the onus of escalation shifts to the defender, D.

D has three options. It can submit by playing Q. This leaves C with the payoff to prevailing, w_C, and gives D the payoff to submitting, s_D. D may also decide to launch a massive nuclear attack. This is assumed to bring a devastating nuclear reply from C. The game ends in disaster with payoffs (d_C, d_D). Prevailing is assumed to be better than the status quo which is better than losing which is better than ending in disaster. In terms of payoffs, this means $w_C > q_C > s_C > d_C$ and $w_D > q_D > s_D > d_D$. Finally, D may escalate the crisis by taking a step toward the brink. This generates a risk of disaster of δ. That is, the probability of the crisis going out of control and ending in a general nuclear exchange, albeit an accidental exchange, is δ.

D's step toward the brink is modeled by letting Nature, N, move immediately after D if D decides to escalate. Nature then plays disaster with probability δ and continues with probability $1 - \delta$. If there is a disaster, the game ends and the payoffs are (d_C, d_D). If Nature continues, then D's escalation has not triggered a disaster and the onus of escalation shifts back to C.

Now the challenger faces the same three options that just confronted D. Submission ends the game with (s_C, w_D). Attacking, as always, brings an attack in retaliation and ends the game with (d_C, d_D). C may also escalate by taking a step toward the brink. But to do so, C must generate a larger risk of disaster than D created when it escalated. Specifically, C must increase the risk in an increment of δ. That is, if C

---

2. See Nalebuff (1986) for a different formulation.

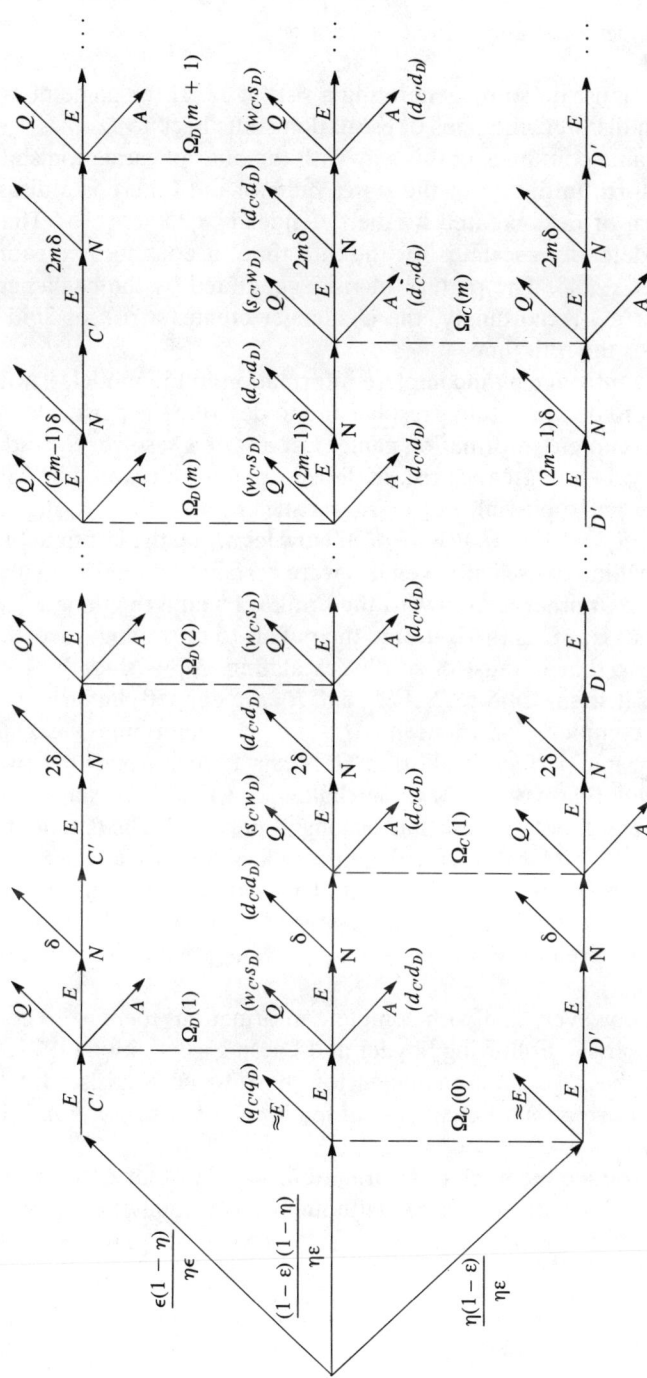

Fig. 1. Brinkmanship with incomplete information

escalates it must do so by generating a risk of 2δ. If the game does not now end in disaster, the onus of escalation shifts back to D.

The game continues in this way with the onus of escalation shifting back and forth until one of the states quits or until there is a disaster. The pattern of risks created by the defender is $\delta, 3\delta, 5\delta, \ldots$. That is, when the defender escalates for the mth time, it does so by creating a risk of $(2m - 1)\delta$. The pattern of risks generated by the challenger is $2\delta, 4\delta, 6\delta, \ldots$. Accordingly, the challenger creates a risk of $2m\delta$ if it escalates for the mth time.

Before introducing incomplete information in the model, it will be convenient to define a state's resolve and to describe the perfect equilibria of the complete-information game. Let a state's resolve, R_C and R_D, respectively, be the greatest risk of disaster that a state would be willing to run in order to prevail. For C, R_C satisfies $R_C d_C + (1 - R_C)w_C = s_C$. This leaves $R_C = (w_C - s_C)/(w_C - d_C)$. Now let M_C be the last time that C would be willing to escalate even if it were certain that after it escalates, after it takes another step toward the brink, D would then immediately submit. That is, M_C is the last time the payoff to prevailing is worth the inherent risk that C must create by escalating. M_C is thus the largest integer m satisfying $2m\delta < R_C$.[3] M_D and R_D are defined similarly.

With complete information, M_C and M_D determine the game's unique subgame perfect equilibrium. It is easy to see through backwards programming that if $M_C > M_D$, the challenger will always challenge the status quo and thereafter escalate as long as $m \leq M_C$.[4] The defender will always submit. If $M_D \geq M_C$, the defender will escalate as long as $m \leq M_D$ and the challenger will always submit. Thus with complete information, the state that is willing to take the last step prevails. In this sense, the state with the greatest effective resolve prevails when there is complete information.

Note, however, that with complete information, there is no escalation and no crisis. Following Snyder and Diesing's definition (1977, 13), there must be a resisted challenge for there to be a crisis. But with complete information, a challenge, if made, is never resisted and there are no crises.

To introduce incomplete information, suppose that C is uncertain about the type of its adversary. Although C is actually facing D, C is unsure if it is facing D or D'. D' is assumed to be wedded to a strategy

---

3. Throughout the essay, the focus will be on generic equilibria and so cases like $2m\delta = R_C$ will be ignored.
4. See Powell (1987) for the details of this derivation.

of always escalating. That is, D' will escalate until C stops escalating. Because D' always escalates, D' will be called the resolute defender.[5]

D' may be interpreted in two ways. First, because the game ends as soon as one state stops escalating, D' is in effect wedded to playing a strategy of tit-for-tat. In tit-for-tat, a state always does what its adversary just did, and, as in tit-for-tat, D' escalates if C just escalated. Of course, if C quits, then D', following its strategy of always escalating, would still escalate if it had the opportunity. D', therefore, is not strictly following tit-for-tat. But, this deviation is unimportant and makes no effective difference in the outcome of the game, for if C quits, the game ends before D' has another opportunity to escalate. Effectively, then, D' is wedded to playing tit-for-tat. Thus in deciding what to do, C is uncertain whether or not its adversary will play a strategy of tit-for-tat.[6] The second interpretation is based on the observation that D' is in some sense irrational. Because it is wedded to a strategy of always escalating, D' will escalate even if this entails creating a certainty of disaster. That is, D' will escalate even if doing so requires it to trigger a disaster with probability one. As will be seen, what drives escalation in this model is a state's attempt to maintain a reputation for being resolute. D, for example, wants to have a reputation for behaving like D'. That is, it is rational for D to seem to be irrational like D'. D in essence is employing what has been called the strategy of the rationality of the irrational (Kahn 1965, 57–58; Maxwell 1968) in that D rationally tries to appear to be to some extent irrational. In sum, modeling incomplete information by assuming that the resolute state is wedded to a strategy of always escalating illuminates the roles of both tit-for-tat and the strategy of the rationality of the irrational in brinkmanship bargaining.

The lack of complete information is two-sided. D will also be assumed to be uncertain of the type of its adversary. D does not know if it is facing C or C' where the resolute challenge, C', is wedded to a strategy of always escalating. The prior probability of facing D' is η and the prior probability of facing C' is ϵ both of which are assumed to be common knowledge.

Incomplete information is the force driving escalation in the model. If, for example, there was complete information, $M_C > M_D$, and C was facing D, then C would challenge the status quo and D would not resist.

---

5. Modeling incomplete information in this way is based on the approach taken in Kreps, Milgrom, Roberts, and Wilson (1982) in their study of the effects of incomplete information on cooperation in a finitely repeated Prisoner's Dilemma.

6. See Axelrod (1984) for a discussion of tit-for-tat as a bargaining strategy based on the results of computer simulations.

If, however, C was facing D', it would not escalate. But with incomplete information, C is unsure if it is facing D or D'. This gives D an incentive to develop and maintain a reputation for being like D', that is, for being resolute. For if D can sustain such a reputation, C may be less likely to challenge it. But to maintain this reputation, D must be willing to escalate if challenged, and, in the model, it is this willingness that drives escalation and creates crises.

The following notation will be convenient. Let the information set at which C must decide whether or not to escalate for the mth time be $\Omega_C(m)$, and let $\beta_C(m)$ be the conditional probability that C is facing D at $\Omega_C(m)$. (At $\Omega_C(0)$, C must decide whether or not to dispute the status quo.) Both $\Omega_D(m)$ and $\beta_D(m)$ are defined similarly. To describe the states' behavioral strategies, take $e_C(m)$ and $a_C(m)$ to denote, respectively, the probabilities that C will escalate and attack at $\Omega_C(m)$. Then the probability that C will submit is $1 - e_C(m) - a_C(m)$. The probabilities that D will escalate or attack at $\Omega_D(m)$ are, respectively, $e_D(m)$ and $a_D(m)$.

The Family of Sequential Crisis Equilibria

Much of the analysis will focus on the game's sequential crisis equilibria. A crisis equilibrium is an equilibrium in which there is a positive probability of a resisted challenge. That is, $e^*_C(0)e^*_D(1) > 0$ where an asterisk denotes an equilibrium strategy. Accordingly, a sequential crisis equilibrium is a sequential equilibrium (Kreps and Wilson 1982a) that is also a crisis equilibrium. These equlibria will be the center of attention for two reasons. First, unless the equilibrium is a crisis equilibrium, there is no crisis and no risk of war. The status quo may change, for the challenger may challenge the status quo and the defender may acquiesce in the change. But this change does not occur in the context of a crisis; there is no danger of war. The second reason for focusing on sequential crisis equilibria is that because they are sequential, these equilibria avoid the credibility problems on which the doctrine of massive retaliation foundered.

Proposition 1 specifies the complete set of sequential crisis equilibria for the incomplete-information game of brinkmanship. But before stating this proposition, note that no state will ever launch a general nuclear attack deliberately. That is, no state will ever play A in a sequential equilibrium. The reason for this is that a state can always do better than playing A by playing Q. Attacking brings C and D, respectively, d_C or d_D while quitting brings s_C or s_D. Thus in equilibrium $a^*_C(m) = a^*_D(m) = 0$ for all m. This in turn means that in order to describe the equilibrium strategies, only the probabilities of escalation $e^*_C(m)$ and $e^*_D(m)$ need to be determined. This leaves:

PROPOSITION 1: *If $\eta > \eta_1 = (w_C - q_C)/[(w_C - d_C)((1 - \delta)R_C + \delta)]$ then, generically there are no sequential crisis equilibria because C does not challenge the status quo. If $\eta < \eta_1$ but $\epsilon > \epsilon_1 = (R_D - \delta)/[(1 - \delta)([(1 - 2\delta)R_D + 2\delta]]$, there are again no sequential crisis equilibria, but this time D does not resist C's challenge. If $\eta < \eta_1$ and $\epsilon < \epsilon_1$, then there exists a generically unique family of sequential crisis equilibria. Each member of this family is indexed by $\overline{m} \geq 0$ and D's strategies for any $\overline{m}$ are given by:*

$$e^*_D(1) = \left(\frac{1}{1-\eta}\right)\left[\left(\frac{w_C - q_C}{w_C - d_C}\right)\frac{1}{(1-\delta)R_C + \delta} - \eta\right] = \frac{\eta_1 - \eta}{1 - \eta} \quad (1)$$

If $\overline{m} \geq 1$,

$$e^*_D(2) = \frac{R_C - 2\delta}{(1-2\delta)[(1-3\delta)R_C + 3\delta]}$$

$$- \left(\frac{\eta}{1-\eta}\right)\left[\frac{[1 - (1-2\delta)(1-3\delta)](1-R_C)}{(1-2\delta)[(1-3\delta)R_C + 3\delta]}\right]\frac{1}{e^*_D(1)} \quad (2)$$

If $\overline{m} \geq 2$, then for $2 \leq m \leq \overline{m}$,

$\times e^*_D(m+1) = 1$

$$- \left[\frac{[1 - (1-2m\delta)(1 - (2m+1)\delta)][R_C - 2(m-1)\delta]}{(1-m\delta)[1 - (1-(2m+1)\delta)\delta)(1-R_c)][1 - (1-2(m-1)\delta)(1-(2m-1)\delta)]}\right]$$

$$\times \frac{1 - e^*_D(m)}{e^*_D(m)} \quad (3)$$

And for $m > \overline{m} + 1$,

$$e^*_D(m) = 0$$

C's equilibrium strategies are given by:

$$e^*_C(0) = \frac{\epsilon}{1-\epsilon}\left[\frac{[1 - (1-\delta)(1-2\delta)](1-R_D)}{R_D - \delta - e^*_C(1)(1-\delta)[(1-2\delta)R_D + 2\delta]}\right] \quad (4)$$

For $1 \leq m \leq \overline{m}$,

$$e^*_C(m) = \left(1 + (1 - e^*_C(m+1))\right.$$
$$\left.\cdot \left[\frac{(1 - (2m+1)\delta)[1 - (1 - (2m+1)\delta)(1 - R_D)][1 - (1 - (2m-1)\delta)(1 - 2m\delta)]}{[1 - (1 - (2m+1)\delta)(1 - 2(m+1)\delta)][R_D - (2m-1)\delta]}\right]\right)^{-1} \quad (5)$$

And for $m > \overline{m}$,

$$e^*_C(m) = 0$$

Since all information sets are reached with positive probability, beliefs are simply given by Bayes' rule.

To complete the specification of the family, the range of $\overline{m}$ must be given. Use (1), (2), and (3) to generate a sequence of numbers and let $\overline{M}$ be the first integer for which $e^*_D(m) > 0$ for $0 \leq m \leq \overline{M} + 1$ and $e^*_D(\overline{M} + 2) \leq 0$. Now let $\overline{N}$ be the maximum value of $\overline{n}$ such that $e^*_C(0)$ generated by (4), (5), and the initial condition $e^*_C(\overline{n} + 1) = 0$ is positive. Then the range of $\overline{m}$ is $0 \leq \overline{m} \leq \min \{\overline{M}, \overline{N}\}$.

Proposition 1, which is derived in the appendix to this essay, formally describes the dynamics of escalation. Less formally, the confrontation begins with the potential challenger C believing that it is facing a resolute defender with probability η. If C is sufficiently confident that the defender is irresolute, then C challenges the status quo with probability $e^*_C(0)$.

A challenge shifts the onus of escalation to D and forces it to update its assessment of the likelihood of its facing a resolute challenger from ϵ to $1 - \beta_D(1)$. If, after this reassessment, D is sufficiently confident that it is facing an irresolute challenger, then D will resist the challenge. D escalates with probability $e^*_D(1)$ by taking a step that "leaves something to chance." That is, D by stepping toward the brink generates some autonomous risk that the states will lose collective control of the crisis and that it will end in disaster.

D's resistance shifts the onus of escalation back to C and forces it to revise its estimate of the probability that its adversary is resolute. If C is still sufficiently confident that its adversary is irresolute, it will meet D's resistance with escalation. C will escalate with probability $e^*_C(1)$ by generating a yet larger autonomous risk of disaster.

C's escalation shifts the onus back to D. The crisis continues in this way with the onus of escalation shifting back and forth until C or D quits

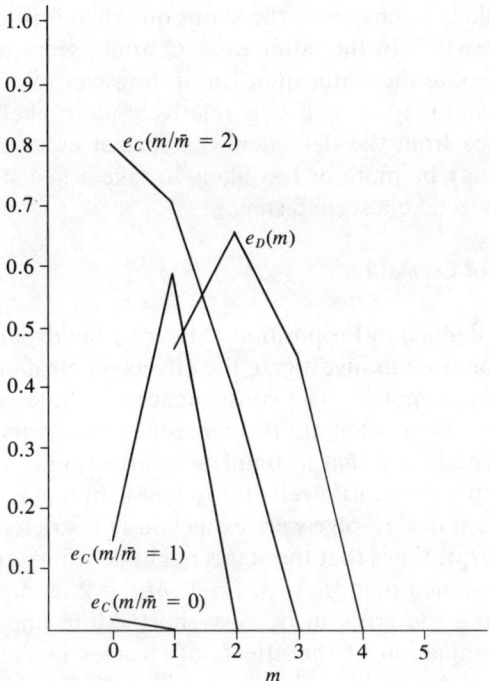

Fig. 2. The dynamics of escalation

or until the risk of disaster is realized and the crisis ends in the horror of a general nuclear exchange.

Figure 2 illustrates a family of equilibrium strategies. As the crisis unfolds and continued escalation entails generating larger and larger risks of disaster, each state becomes increasingly confident that it is facing a resolute adversary. Formally, the probabilities of facing a resolute adversary, $1 - \beta_C(m)$ and $1 - \beta_D(m)$, are increasing in m. That is, each state's reputation for being resolute grows stronger as the crisis continues.

After the first two steps toward the brink, the states become less and less likely to escalate. The appendix to this essay shows that as long as $e^*_C(m) > 0$, then $e^*_C(m)$ is decreasing in m for $m \geq 1$ and as long as $e^*_D(m) > 0$, then $e^*_D(m)$ is decreasing in m for $m \geq 2$. The beginning of a crisis is, however, more complex.

As (4) shows and figure 2 illustrates, $e^*_C(0)$ may be greater or less than $e^*_C(1)$ depending on the value of ϵ. The potential challenger may be more or less likely to challenge the status quo than it is to escalate if its challenge is resisted. In the latter case, C would seem to be relatively reluctant to dispute the status quo. But if, however reluctantly, C does challenge the status quo, then C is relatively more likely to meet any initial resistance from the defender with further escalation. Similarly, the defender may be more or less likely to take a first step toward the brink than it is to take a second step.

The Dynamics of Escalation

The strategies defined in Proposition 1 describe the dynamics of escalation and may be used to investigate the effects on escalation of changes in the model's parameters. The consequences of three changes will be considered here. First, what are the consequences of varying the state's levels of resolve? Recall that incomplete information is modeled somewhat more simply than in Powell (1987, 1988). In that work, however, the levels of the states' resolve were exogenously restricted in such a way that the number of times that the states might be willing to escalate was fixed. It was assumed that $M_C = M_D = 1$, $M_{D'} = 2$, and $M_{C'} \geq 2$. This restriction forced the crisis to be very short. More important, it precluded the examination of the effects of changes in the levels of the states' resolve that would make them willing to escalate a different number of times. The simpler treatment of incomplete information here results in a more tractable extensive form that facilitates the analysis of the game when the levels of resolve are arbitrary. The number of times that a state might escalate in a crisis becomes endogenous, and this permits the investigation of the effects of changes in levels of resolve that alter this number. The second set of consequences to be examined will be those due to changes in the value that the challenger places in the status quo. How do the equilibrium strategies vary as q_C varies? Third, what are the effects of incomplete information on deterrence?

Before examining these consequences, the length of a crisis should be defined. Note that in the $\overline{m}$th equilibrium, that is, in the $\overline{m}$th member of the family of equilibria, $e^*_C(m) > 0$ for all $m \leq \overline{m}$ and $e^*_D(m) > 0$ for all $m \leq \overline{m} + 1$. That is, C is willing to challenge the status quo, $e^*_C(0) > 0$, and then is willing to escalate $\overline{m}$ times. D is willing to escalate $\overline{m} + 1$ times. Thus, the maximum number of times that a state might generate some risk of disaster in this crisis is $2\overline{m} + 1$. This will be taken to be the length of a crisis. That is, the length of the crisis associated with the $\overline{m}$th equilibrium is $2\overline{m} + 1$.

Critical-risk models (e.g., Snyder and Diesing 1977, 48–52) suggest the greater an adversary's resolve, the less likely a state will be to escalate. The argument for this is the greater an adversary's resolve, the more likely it is to stand firm if a state escalates. Escalation is therefore more dangerous. Shying away from this greater danger, a state is less likely to escalate the more resolute its adversary. As has already been shown, this does not hold in the short crises examined in earlier work. The expressions for the game's sequential crisis equilibria reveal that the effects of a state's being more resolute are still more subtle and complex in longer crises.

As is apparent from the expressions in Proposition 1, a change in a state's level of resolve generally does not affect its own strategies but rather its adversary's strategies. Consider first the consequences of the defender's being more resolute. An increase in R_D makes C more, not less, likely to escalate.[7] C, however, may be less likely to challenge the status quo. Thus an increase in the defender's resolve may make the challenger simultaneously less likely to dispute the status quo but more likely to escalate throughout the rest of the crisis. Turning to the challenger's resolve, an increase in it may also make the defender more likely to escalate in an existing equilibrium.

Before considering the effects of changes in the levels of the states' resolve on stability, it will be useful to distinguish between crisis stability and situational stability. The former is a measure of stability given that there is a crisis. In particular, let P_W be the probability that the game will end in a general nuclear exchange given that there has been a resisted challenge. Then $P_W = \delta + (1 - \delta)e^*_D(2)[2\delta + (1 - 2\delta)e^*_C(2)[3\delta + (1 - 3\delta)e^*_D(3)[4\delta + \ldots]]]$ and crisis stability is given by $1 - P_W$. Situational stability does not assume that there has been a resisted challenge. Instead, the probability of war, S_W, is calculated from the point at which C is deciding whether or not to dispute the status quo. Accordingly, $S_W = e^*_C(0)e^*_D(1)P_W$ and situational stability is given by $1 - S_W$.

Because changes in the model's parameters often push $e^*_C(0)$ and $e^*_C(m)$ for $m \geq 1$ in opposite directions, it is technically important to distinguish between crisis and situational stability. More substantively, the distinction is also important as a means of correcting for a kind of sample bias. Historical investigation and case studies naturally focus on crises, for they are much easier to identify than situations that could have become crises but did not. This focus, however, introduces sample bias that may distort any conclusions drawn from the historical studies. Suppose, for example, that a certain policy has been found in a number

---

7. To establish this, differentiate (4.5) to show that for a fixed $e^*_C(m + 1)$, $e^*_C(m)$ is increasing in R_D. Then because $e^*_C(\overline{m} + 1) = 0$, an increase in R_D raises $e^*_C(\overline{m})$. But an increase in R_D coupled with a larger $e^*_C(\overline{m})$ unambiguously raises $e^*_C(\overline{m} - 1)$. Continuing in this way shows that $\partial e^*_C(m)/\partial R_D > 0$ for $1 \leq m \leq \overline{m}$.

of historical cases to reduce the probability of a crisis ending in war. Failing to take into account the possible sample bias may lead to the suggestion that a state should adopt this policy in order to enhance stability and reduce the probability of war. But suppose further that although this policy reduces the chances of war given that there is a crisis, this policy also increases the probability that there will be crises. The net effect of this policy may be to make war more, not less, likely. To allow for this possible bias, it is important to examine the effects of various changes on both crisis and situational stability.

Indeed, as just noted, an increase in R_D makes C more likely to escalate throughout the crisis. Thus, crisis stability must decline. But this change in the defender's resolve may make the challenger less likely to dispute the status quo and so reduce the probability that there will be a crisis. The net effect of this increase in R_D may be to enhance situational stability.[8] But an increase in R_D may not always enhance situational stability. For example, an increase in R_D may add new members to the family of sequential crisis equilibria.[9] These new crises are longer than any of the previously existing crises and may be more dangerous. Similarly, a larger R_C may also make for longer crises that are less stable.

The effects of changing the levels of resolve are subtle, complicated, and difficult to explain intuitively. (Indeed, it is difficult to determine which if any of these effects are artifacts of the model and ought not to be explained intuitively.) Although the model does not seem to offer an intuitive explanation of the precise effects on the dynamics of escalation of changes in the states' levels of resolve, the model does offer some intuitive insight into the competing influences that make these effects complicated. Consider the decision confronting the defender at a given stage of the crisis, say at the information set $\Omega_D(m_0)$. Now suppose that the defender's resolve is increased. In the new equilibrium associated with this higher level of resolve, D must still be indifferent between escalating and submitting at $\Omega_D(m_0)$, because $0 < e^*{}_D(m_0) < 1$. But with greater resolve, D will strictly prefer to escalate at this stage of the crisis if C's strategies are unchanged from the original equilibrium. Thus C's strategies must change in the new equilibrium so as to make D indifferent to escalating at this stage. Two types of change are possible. First, C may be more likely to escalate in the future. That is, C may be more likely to escalate at $\Omega_C(m)$ for $m > m_0$. This change does not affect the

---

8. More specifically, if $w_C = 1$, $q_C = 0$, $s_C = -1$, $d_C = -18.0476$, $\epsilon = .01$, $\eta = .01$, $\delta = .01$, and $\overline{m} = 2$, then if R_D rises from .075 to .085, P_W rises from .0460 to .0481 but S_W falls from .00344 to .00226.

9. That is, $\overline{N}$ may increase so that a larger $\overline{m}$ may satisfy the constraint that $\overline{m} \leq \min(\overline{M}, \overline{N})$.

strength of D's belief that it is facing C at $\Omega_D(m_0)$: $\beta_D(m_0)$ is unaffected. This change does, however, increase the expected cost to D of escalating at $\Omega_D(m_0)$ by making C less likely to submit in the future. This tends to restore D's indifference. In the second type of change, C may have been less likely to escalate before the crisis reached this stage. Formally, $e^*_C(m)$ for $m \leq m_0$ may be smaller in the new equilibrium than in the original. The effect of this change is that when D is deciding what to do at $\Omega_D(m_0)$, D is less confident that it is facing C and more confident it is facing C'. This reduces the expected value to D of escalation and also tends to make D indifferent. These are the influences on $e^*_C(m)$ that arise from the consideration of just one of D's information sets, $\Omega_D(m_0)$. But D has several information sets, and this creates opposing pressures on the $e^*_C(m)$. To make D less confident of facing C at D's information sets that follow, say, $\Omega_C(m_1)$, then $e^*_C(m_1)$ will tend to fall. But to reduce the expected return to D of escalating at its information sets that come before $\Omega_C(m_1)$, $e^*_C(m_1)$ will tend to rise. Intuition helps to identify the competing influences on $e^*_C(m)$; the precise balance struck between these opposing influences is specified in the equilibrium strategies described in Proposition 1.

The effects of a change in the challenger's stake in the status quo are less ambiguous than the effects of a change in the levels of resolve. Suppose that the challenger has a greater stake in the status quo. If a member of the family of sequential crisis equilibria exists after the increase in q_C, then the defender will be less likely to escalate throughout the crisis. To see this, note that as q_C rises, $e^*_D(1)$ decreases. Then (2) shows that this decrease in $e^*_D(1)$ reduces $e^*_D(2)$. Finally, (3) implies that as $e^*_D(m)$ falls, $e^*_D(m + 1)$ falls. Thus, the decrease in $e^*_D(2)$ reduces $e^*_D(3)$ which in turn reduces $e^*_D(4)$ which in turn reduces $e^*_D(5)$, and so on.

Previous work has shown that the belief that an adversary will be less likely to challenge the status quo if it has a greater stake in the status quo may not hold in short crises. The same is true of longer crises. In the model, having a greater stake in the status quo does not reduce the likelihood of a challenge in equilibria that exist both before and after the increase in q_C. The challenger's strategies are unaffected by its having a greater stake in the status quo. However, the increase in the challenger's stake in the status quo does reduce the likelihood of war. But it is the defender, not the challenger, who is less likely to escalate.

Table 1 illustrates the effects of the challenger's having different stakes in the status quo. The number at the top of each cell is the length of the longest crisis in the family of crises associated with that cell. A five, for example, means that in the longest crisis the maximum number of times that the states are willing to escalate by generating some risk of disaster is five. That is, there is some chance that the challenger will escalate twice and the defender three times. The number in the center of the cell is the probability that this longest crisis will end in a general nuclear exchange. Because in any family of equilibria the longer the crisis the more dangerous it is, the probability reported in any cell is therefore also the probability of the most dangerous crisis in the family ending in disaster. Finally, the number at the bottom of the cell is the probability that the situation will end in disaster. Reading across the rows of table 1 indicates that an increase in q_C enhances stability and may eliminate some equilibria. Note further that the probability of a challenge to the status quo will decrease only if the increase in the challenger's stake in the status quo eliminates some of the longer crises. Otherwise, as just noted, C's strategies are unaffected by the change in q_C. Generally, the challenger's having a greater stake in the status quo does not make it less likely to dispute the status quo.

Incomplete information plays an essential role in brinkmanship bargaining. Without it, there would be no bargaining: the state with the greatest effective resolve would escalate and its adversary would submit. Incomplete information may, however, greatly enhance deterrence by reducing the likelihood of a challenge. For example, C's effective resolve in all of the equilibria summarized in table 1 is greater than D's.

TABLE 1. The Length of a Crisis and the Probability of War

η	q_C				
	−.8	−.4	0	.4	.8
.1	5 .0457 .00423	5 .0454 .00376	5 .0427 .00175	3 .0298 .00011	*
.01	5 .0479 .00478	5 .0479 .00404	5 .0476 .00216	5 .0474 .00130	5 .0457 .00039
.001	5 .0481 .00450	5 .0481 .00407	5 .0481 .00226	5 .0480 .00135	5 .0479 .00046
.000001	5 .0481 .00452	5 .0481 .00407	5 .0481 .00317	5 .0481 .00226	5 .0481 .00045

Note: The length of the crisis and the probability of war are calculated for the case in which $R_D = .085$, $\epsilon = .01$, and $\delta = .01$, $w_C = 1$, $s_C = -1$, $d_C = -18.048$. The latter three values imply that $R_C = .105$.

*No sequential crisis equilibrium exists for these values.

The Dynamics of Longer Brinkmanship Crises

With complete information, C would always dispute the status quo and D would never resist. But with incomplete information, the probability of a challenge in any of these equilibria is never more than .11. Incomplete information about the resolve of the challenger in these examples does much to enhance deterrence. In other cases, however, incomplete information may not do much to improve deterrence. In the equilibrium associated with $\bar{m} = 2$ in figure 2, the probability of a challenge only falls .8. Incomplete information about the defender's resolve also affects the dynamics of escalation. The stronger the defender's initial reputation for being resolute, i.e., the larger η, the less likely D is to escalate throughout the crisis.

To examine the effects of incomplete information on escalation more formally, first note that ϵ, which is the probability of the challenger's being resolute, only affects $e^*_C(0)$. No other strategy is influenced by changes in ϵ. Observe further that given the value of $e^*_C(1)$ associated with the $\bar{m}$th equilibrium, equation (4) shows that the probability of a challenge can take on any value depending on the value of ϵ. The more confident the defender that the challenger is resolute, i.e., the greater ϵ, the easier it is for the challenger to play on the defender's fear of facing a resolute challenger and the more likely is a challenge.

To see that an increase in η makes the defender less likely to escalate throughout the crisis, differentiate (1) to show that $\partial e^*_D(1)/\partial \eta < 0$. Inspection of (2) then demonstrates that $e^*_D(2)$ will have decreased with the increase in η. Finally, (3) implies that if $e^*_D(2)$ declines so will $e^*_D(3)$ and if $e^*_D(3)$ falls so will $e^*_D(4)$, etc. Thus, the larger η and, therefore, the greater the defender's initial reputation for being resolute, the less likely the defender will be to escalate throughout the crisis.

The effects of incomplete information on the probability of war are mixed. The stronger the challenger's initial reputation for being resolute, i.e., the greater ϵ, the greater $e^*_C(0)$ and the more likely C is to challenge the status quo. This tends to make the situation less stable. But changes in ϵ only affect $e^*_C(0)$, and, therefore, the larger ϵ has no effect on the probability of a general nuclear exchange given that there has been a resisted challenge. This means that the increase in ϵ has no effect on crisis stability. If, however, the defender has a stronger initial reputation for being resolute, D is throughout the crisis less likely to escalate and this increases both situational and crisis stability. Table 1 illustrates the effects of increasing η with some numerical examples. Although the probability that the situation and crisis will end in war falls as η rises, the table suggests that once some uncertainty about the defender's resolve exists, variations in the degree of this uncertainty do not significantly affect the probability of war. In each column, the probability of the challenger's facing a resolute defender, η, varies from one chance in ten to one in a million. Yet, the probability of war hardly varies. Although deterrence is often said to be quite sensitive to the beliefs and perceptions of each state about its adversary, the model indicates that at least the probability of war is rather insensitive to a wide variation in beliefs about whether or not the defender is more resolute. Structural constraints more than beliefs about the defender's resolve seem to be more important determinates of the probability of war.

Conclusion

Earlier work on brinkmanship (e.g., Powell 1987, 1988) fixed the length of a crisis exogenously by placing restrictions on the states' levels of resolve. This essay extends the analysis to the case in which the levels of resolve are arbitrary. This makes the length of a crisis endogenous and permits the investigation of factors that affect the length of a crisis.

The results of this analysis are broadly consistent with those obtained in previous work. Changes in the levels of resolve continue to have a subtle and complicated effect on the dynamics of escalation and on crisis stability. An increase in the defender's resolve makes the challenger more likely to escalate, although it may also make it less likely actually to challenge the status quo. An increase in the challenger's stake in the status quo may or may not make the challenger less likely to dispute the status quo. In any case, an increase in the challenger's stake always leaves the defender less likely to resist a challenge by escalating and therefore always enhances stability. Incomplete information may also greatly enhance stability by reducing the probability of a challenge to the status quo. Yet despite these changes, the probability that a crisis will end in the disaster of a general nuclear exchange remains remarkably low. In table 1, for example, the maximum risk of a situation ending in war is less than three chances in a thousand. Brinkmanship appears to be very stable.

APPENDIX

This Appendix demonstrates Proposition 1. The demonstration is done in three steps. The first is to show that if a sequential crisis equilibrium exists, it must satisfy certain basic conditions. Then it will be shown that if a sequential crisis equilibrium satisfies these conditions, it must be of the form described in the proposition. Finally, ϵ and η will be restricted to ensure that a sequential crisis equilibrium actually exists.

The first step is to establish that if a sequential crisis equilibrium exists, then two conditions must hold. First, C must be indifferent between escalating and submitting at $\Omega_C(m)$ and $e^*_C(m) > 0$ for $0 \leq m \leq \bar{m}$ where $\bar{m}$ is some integer. Second, $e^*_C(m) = 0$ for $m > \bar{m}$. To see this, let $\bar{m}$ be the maximum integer m such that $e^*_C(m) > 0$. Clearly such an $\bar{m}$ exists, for in a sequential crisis equilibrium $e^*_C(0) > 0$. By construction, $e^*_C(m) = 0$ for $m > \bar{m}$, so it only remains to be shown that if a sequential crisis equilibrium exists then it satisfies the first condition. To do this, assume the contrary. That is, for some $m' \leq \bar{m}$, C must strictly prefer escalating at $\Omega_C(m')$, strictly prefer to submit, or be indifferent between them but with $e^*_C(m') = 0$. In both of the latter cases, $e^*_C(m') = 0$ and this leads to a contradiction. To reach this contradiction, note that $e^*_C(m') = 0$ implies $\beta_D(m' + 1) = 0$ and so $e^*_D(m' + 1) = 0$. But $e^*_D(m' + 1) = 0$ implies $\beta_C(m' + 1) = 0$ and then that $e^*_C(m' + 1) = 0$. Continuing in this way leaves $e^*_D(m) = 0$ for $m \geq m'$. In particular, $e^*_D(\bar{m}) = 0$ since $\bar{m} \geq m'$ and this is a contradiction.

Assuming that C strictly prefers escalating at $\Omega_C(m')$ also leads to a contradiction. Without loss of generality, let m' be the largest integer for which C strictly prefers to escalate at $\Omega_C(m')$, then

$$s_C < \beta_C(m')[2m'\delta d_C + (1 - 2m'\delta)[(1 - e^*_D(m' + 1))w_C + e^*_D(m' + 1)$$

$$[(2m' + 1)\delta d_C + (1 - (2m' + 1)\delta)s_C]]] + (1 - \beta_C(m'))$$

$$[2m'\delta d_C + (1 - 2m'\delta)[(2m' + 1)\delta d_C + (1 - (2m' + 1)\delta)s_C]].$$

Satisfying this inequality requires that $e^*_D(m' + 1) < 1$ and, therefore, implies that D's expected payoff at $\Omega_D(m' + 1)$ is s_D.

This and the fact that $e^*_C(m' + 1) = 1$ means that escalation at $\Omega_D(m')$ brings

$$[(2m' - 1)\delta d_D + (1 - (2m' - 1)\delta)[2m'\delta d_D + (1 - 2m'\delta)s_D].$$

This, however, is less than s_D which is what D can have if it submits at $\Omega_D(m')$. Thus, D's best reply at $\Omega_D(m')$ is $e^*_D(m') = 0$. But if $e^*_D(m') = 0$, then $\beta_C(m') = 0$ and C's best reply is $e^*_C(m') = 0$. This, however, contradicts the assumption that C strictly prefers to escalate at $\Omega_C(m')$.

In sum, if a sequential crisis equilibrium exists, then C is indifferent between escalating and submitting at $\Omega_C(m)$ and $e^*_C(m) > 0$ for $m \leq \bar{m}$ where $\bar{m}$ is some integer. If, moreover, $m > \bar{m}$ then $e^*_C(m) = 0$.

The second step is to demonstrate that if a sequential crisis equilibrium exists, then its strategies are defined by the expressions reported in

Models of Strategic Choice in Politics

Proposition 1. Suppose that C is indifferent to escalating or submitting at $\Omega_C(m)$ and $e^*_C(m) > 0$ for $m \leq \overline{m}$, then for $1 \leq m \leq \overline{m}$

$$s_C = \beta_C(m)(2m\delta d_C + (1 - 2m\delta)((1 - e_D(m+1))w_C + e_D(m+1)$$

$$[(2m+1)\delta d_C + (1 - (2m+1)\delta)s_C])) + (1 - \beta_C(m))$$

$$[2m\delta d_C + (1 - 2m\delta)[(2m+1)\delta d_C + (1 - (2m+1)\delta)s_C]]. \quad (A.1)$$

Simplification and substituting R_C for $(w_C - s_C)/(w_C - d_C)$ give

$$\frac{1}{\beta_C(m)} = (1 - 2m\delta)(1 - e_D(m+1)) \times$$

$$\left[\frac{R_C + (2m+1)\delta(1 - R_C)}{[1 - (1 - 2m\delta)(1 - (2m+1)\delta)](1 - R_C)} \right]. \quad (A.2)$$

But,

$$\beta_C(m) = (1 - \eta) \left[\prod_{i=1}^{m} e_D(i) \right] \left[\eta + (1 - \eta) \prod_{i=1}^{m} e_D(i) \right]^{-1}.$$

Substituting this expression into (A.2) yields

$$\prod_{i=1}^{m} e_D(i) = \frac{\eta}{1 - \eta} \times$$

$$\left[\frac{[1 - (1 - 2m\delta)(1 - (2m+1)\delta)](1 - R_C)}{R_C - 2m\delta - e_D(m+1)(1 - 2m\delta)[(2m+1)\delta + (1 - (2m+1)\delta)R_C]} \right]. \quad (A.3)$$

Reindexing this gives an expression for $\prod_{i=1}^{m-1} e_D(i)$ which holds for $2 \leq m \leq \overline{m} + 1$. Then dividing this into $\prod_{i=1}^{m} e_D(i)$ gives

$$e_D(m) = \left(\frac{[1 - (1 - 2m\delta)(1 - (2m+1)\delta)]}{[1 - (1 - 2(m-1)\delta)(1 - (2m-1)\delta)]} \right)$$

$$\times \left(\frac{[R_C - (2m-1)\delta - e_D(m)(1 - 2(m-1)\delta)[(2m-1)\delta + (1 - (2m-1)\delta)R_C]]}{[R_C - 2m\delta - e_D(m+1)(1 - 2m\delta)[(2m+1)\delta + (1 - (2m+1)\delta)R_C]]} \right).$$

Solving this equation for $e_D(m+1)$ leaves

$$e^*_D(m+1) = 1$$

$$-\left[\frac{[1-(1-2m\delta)(1-(2m+1)\delta)][R_C-2(m-1)\delta]}{(1-2m\delta)[1-(1-(2m+1)\delta)(1-R_C)][1-(1-2(m-1)\delta)(1-(2m-1)\delta)]}\right]$$

$$\times \frac{1-e_D(m)}{e_D(m)}. \tag{A.4}$$

for $2 \leq m \leq \overline{m}$.

C's indifference at $\Omega_C(0)$ also implies

$$q_C = (1-\eta)[(1-e_D(1))w_C + e_D(1)[\delta d_C + (1-\delta)s_C]] + \eta[\delta d_C + (1-\delta)s_C].$$

This leaves

$$e_D(1) = \left(\frac{1}{1-\eta}\right)\left[\left(\frac{w_C - q_C}{w_C - d_C}\right)\frac{1}{(1-\delta)R_C + \delta} - \eta\right]. \tag{A.5}$$

Equation (A.5) defines $e^*_D(1)$ and (A.4) links $e^*_D(2), \ldots, e^*_D(\overline{m}+1)$ recursively. Thus all that is needed to complete the specification of D's strategies is to provide an initial condition for the recursive relation. Evaluating (A.3) for $m = 1$ does this by defining $e^*_D(2)$ as a function of $e^*_D(1)$, leaving

$$e^*_D(2) = \frac{R_C - 2\delta}{(1-2\delta)[(1-3\delta)R_C + 3\delta]}$$

$$-\left(\frac{\eta}{1-\eta}\right)\left[\frac{[1-(1-2\delta)(1-3\delta)](1-R_C)}{(1-2\delta)[(1-3\delta)R_C + 3\delta]}\right]\frac{1}{e^*_D(1)}. \tag{A.6}$$

In sum, (A.5) defines $e^*_D(1)$, (A.6) then gives $e^*_D(2)$ and finally (A.4) determines $e^*_D(3), \ldots, e^*_D(\overline{m}+1)$. For $m > \overline{m} + 1$, $e^*_D(m) = 0$.

To determine C's strategies, recall that $e^*_C(0) = 0$ for $m > \overline{m}$. The expressions for $e^*_D(m)$ show that generically $1 > e^*_D(m) > 0$ for $1 \leq m \leq \overline{m} + 1$. Hence, D is indifferent between escalating and submitting at $\Omega_D(m)$ for $1 \leq m \leq \overline{m} + 1$. This implies

$$s_D = \beta_D(m)((2m - 1)\delta d_D + (1 - (2m - 1)\delta)((1 - e_C(m))w_D$$
$$+ e_C(m) [2m\delta d_D + (1 - 2m\delta)s_D])) + (1 - \beta_D(m))$$
$$[(2m - 1)\delta d_D + (1 - (2m - 1)\delta)[2m\delta d_D + (1 - 2m\delta)s_D]] \quad (A.7)$$

for $1 \leq m \leq \overline{m} + 1$. Letting $m = 1$ gives

$$e^*_C(0) = \frac{\epsilon}{1 - \epsilon}\left[\frac{[1 - (1 - \delta)(1 - 2\delta)](1 - R_D)}{R_D - \delta - e^*_C(1)(1 - \delta)[(1 - 2\delta)R_D + 2\delta]}\right]. \quad (A.8)$$

Solving (A.7) for $1 \leq m \leq \overline{m}$ in the same way that (A.1) was solved gives the following recursive relation for $e_C(1), \ldots, e_C(\overline{m} + 1)$:

$$e^*_C(m) = \left(1 + (1 - e^*_C(m + 1))\right.$$
$$\left.\times \left[\frac{(1 - (2m + 1)\delta)[1 - (1 - (2m + 1)\delta)(1 - R_D)][1 - (1 - (2m - 1)\delta)(1 - 2m\delta)]}{[1 - (1 - (2m + 1)\delta)(1 - 2(m + 1)\delta)][R_D - (2m - 1)\delta]}\right]\right)^{-1}. \quad (A.9)$$

But $e^*_C(\overline{m} + 1) = 0$. This in turn provides the needed initial condition so that (A.9) now defines $e^*_C(1), \ldots, e^*_C(\overline{m})$ and then determines $e^*_C(0)$ through (A.7). This completes the derivation of the challenger's and defender's strategies.

All that remains to be done is to restrict η and ϵ to ensure that a sequential crisis equilibrium actually exists. This amounts to choosing η and ϵ in a way that guarantees that the states' strategies are feasible. That is, the expressions for these strategies cannot, for example, require a state to escalate with a negative probability. Once the strategies have been shown to be feasible, then they will define the generically unique family of sequential crisis equilibria.

To obtain the restrictions on η, solve (A.5) for η subject to the condition that $0 < e^*_D(1) < 1$. Only the first inequality is binding, and it implies that

$$\eta < \eta_1 = \left(\frac{w_C - q_C}{w_C - d_C}\right)\frac{1}{(1 - \delta)R_C + \delta}.$$

There is also a second restriction on η. To specify it, solve (A.5) for $\eta/[(1 - \eta)e^*_D(1)]$, substitute this into (A.6), and then solve for η subject to the constraints that $0 < e^*_D(0) < 1$. Again only the first inequality is binding and satisfying it requires

$$\eta < \eta_2 = \eta_1\left[\frac{R_C - 2\delta}{[1 - (1 - 2\delta)(1 - 3\delta)](1 - R_C)}\right].$$

Note, moreover, that $\eta_2 < \eta_1$.

To ensure that $e^*_D(m)$ is feasible for $m \geq 2$, assume $\eta < \eta_2$. (If $\eta > \eta_2$ then $e^*_D(1)$ is not feasible and so the feasibility of $e^*_D(m)$ for $m \geq 2$ is no longer of any interest.) Suppose further that it can be established that $e^*_D(m)$ is decreasing in m as long as $m \geq 2$. Then let $\overline{M}$ be the largest integer m for which $e^*_D(m + 1) > 0$. Generically, $e^*_D(m + 2)$ will be less than zero and thus infeasible. If $\overline{M} = 0$, then $e^*_D(2) < 0$ and the feasibility of $e^*_D(m)$ for $m > 2$ is not of any interest. If, however, $\overline{M} > 0$ then $e^*_D(m)$ for $2 \leq m \leq \overline{M} + 1$ are feasible, for $e^*_D(2) > e^*_D(3) > \ldots > e^*_D(\overline{M} + 1) > 0 > e^*_D(\overline{M} + 2)$. In sum, if $\eta < \eta_1$ and $e^*_D(m)$ is decreasing in m, then $e^*_D(m + 1)$ is feasible for $0 \leq m \leq \overline{M}$.

To see that $e^*_D(m)$ for $m \leq 2$ is actually decreasing in m as long as $e^*_D(m) > 0$, solve (A.4) for $e^*_D(m)$ in terms of $e^*_D(m + 1)$, substitute this expression for $e^*_D(m)$ in $e^*_D(m) > e^*_D(m + 1)$, and solve this inequality for $e^*_D(m + 1)$. The result is that $e^*_D(m)$ is decreasing in m if $e^*_D(m + 1) < U_D(m)$ and $e^*_D(m + 1) > 0$ where

$$U_D(m) = \frac{[1-(1-2m\delta)(1-(2m+1)\delta)][R_C - 2(m-1)\delta]}{(1-2m\delta)[1-(1-(2m+1)\delta)(1-R_C)][1-(1-2(m-1)\delta)(1-(2m-1)\delta)]}$$

Now calculate $\overline{e}^*_D(m)$ where $\overline{e}^*_D(m)$ is the value of $e^*_D(m)$ defined by (A.4) and the initial condition $\overline{e}^*_D(2) = (R_C - 2\delta)/[(1 - 2\delta)[(1 - 3\delta)R_C + 3\delta]]$. This gives $\overline{e}^*_D(m + 1) = (R_C - 2m\delta)/[(1 - 2m\delta)[1 - (1 - (2m + 1)\delta)(1 - R_C)]]$. Comparing $\overline{e}^*_D(m + 1)$ and $U_D(m)$ gives $\overline{e}^*_D(m + 1) < U_D(m)$. But $\overline{e}^*_D(2)$, which is obtained by letting $\eta = 0$ in (A.5), is the least upper bound for $e^*_D(2)$. This and the fact that (A.4) shows that $\partial e^*_D(m + 1)/\partial e^*_D(m) > 0$ implies that $\overline{e}^*_D(3) > e^*_D(3)$. This then means that $\overline{e}^*_D(4) > e^*_D(4)$ and in general $\overline{e}^*_D(m + 1) > e^*_D(m + 1)$. Accordingly, $e^*_D(m + 1) < \overline{e}^*_D(m + 1) < U_D(m)$ and therefore $e^*_D(m)$ is decreasing in m.

In sum, if $\eta > \eta_1$, there are no sequential crisis equilibria. Equation (A.1) cannot be satisfied: η is too large and the payoff to not challenging the status quo at $\Omega_C(0)$ is always greater than the payoff to disputing the status quo. The probability that C is facing a resolute defender is too great and there is no challenge. If $\eta_2 < \eta < \eta_1$, then, assuming C's strategies to be feasible, $e^*_D(1)$ is given by (A.5) and $e^*_D(m) = 0$ for $m > 1$. If $\eta < \eta_2$, then (A.5) defines $e^*_D(1)$, (A.6) gives $e^*_D(2)$, and (A.4) yields $e^*_D(3), \ldots, e^*_D(\overline{m} + 1)$ where $\overline{m} \leq \overline{M}$.

To find the restrictions on ϵ that ensure that C's strategies are feasible, let $e^*_C(\overline{n} + 1) = 0$ be the initial condition and use (A.8) and (A.9) to determine $e^*_C(0), \ldots, e^*_C(\overline{n})$. Inspection of (A.9) shows that $1 > e^*_C(m) > 0$ for $1 \leq m \leq \overline{n}$. Thus only the feasibility of $e^*_C(0)$ is at issue. Constraining (A.7) to be between zero and one and then solving for $e^*_C(1)$ gives

$$e^*_C(1)_{\bar{n}} = \frac{R_D - \delta - \epsilon(1-\delta)[(1-2\delta)R_C + 2\delta]}{(1-\epsilon)(1-\delta)[(1-2\delta)R_C + 2\delta]}. \tag{A.10}$$

where the subscript of $e^*_C(1)$ indicates that $e^*_C(1)$ was obtained from the initial condition $e^*_C(\bar{n}+1) = 0$. Now assume that (A.10) is satisfied for some $\bar{n}$. Then if $\bar{n}' < \bar{n}$, $e^*_C(1)_{\bar{n}'}$, will also satisfy (A.10). This follows from the observation that (A.9) implies $\partial e^*_C(m)/\partial e^*_C(m+1) > 0$. Then because $e^*_C(\bar{n}'+1)_{\bar{n}} > e^*_C(\bar{n}'+1)_{\bar{n}'} = 0$, $e^*_C(\bar{n}')_{\bar{n}} > e^*_C(\bar{n}')_{\bar{n}'}$. This in turn gives $e^*_C(\bar{n}'-1)_{\bar{n}} > e^*_C(\bar{n}'-1)_{\bar{n}'}$ and in general $e^*_C(m)_{\bar{n}} > e^*_C(m)_{\bar{n}'}$. Letting $m = 1$ shows that $e^*_C(1)_{\bar{n}'}$ satisfies (A.10). Now let $\overline{N}$ be the maximum value of $\bar{n}$ for which $e^*_D(1)_{\bar{n}}$ satisfies (A.10). Then if $\overline{m} \leq \overline{N}$, all of C's strategies are feasible. Indeed, if $\overline{m} \leq \min(\overline{M}, \overline{N})$, then both C's and D's strategies are feasible.

To ensure that at least one sequential crisis equilibrium exists, $\overline{M}$ and $\overline{N}$ must be greater than or equal to zero. Taking $\eta < \eta_1$ makes $\overline{M} \geq 0$. To make sure that $\overline{N} \geq 0$, $e^*_C(1)_{\bar{n}=0}$ must satisfy (A.10). But the definition of $\bar{n}$ implies $e^*_C(\bar{n}+1) = 0$. So if $\bar{n} = 0$, $e^*_C(1) = 0$ must satisfy (A.10). Letting $e^*_C(1)_{\bar{n}} = 0$ and solving (A.10) for ϵ gives $\epsilon < \epsilon_1 = (R_D - \delta)/[(1-\delta)[(1-2\delta)R_D + 2\delta]$. If, therefore, $\eta < \eta_1$ and $\epsilon < \epsilon_1$, a family of sequential crisis equilibria exists, the members of which are indexed by $\overline{m}$ where $0 \leq \overline{m} \leq \min(\overline{M}, \overline{N})$.

Although the demonstration of Proposition 1 is now complete, it will be useful to show that $e^*_C(m)$ is also decreasing in m for $1 \leq m \leq \overline{m}$.

Use (A.9) to substitute for $e^*_C(m)$ in $e^*_C(m) > e^*_C(m+1)$ and solve for $e^*_C(m+1)$. The result is

$e^*_C(m+1) < U_C(m)$

$$= \frac{[1-(1-(2m+1)\delta)(1-2(m+1)\delta)][R_D-(2m-1)\delta]}{(1-(2m+1)\delta)[(1-2(m+1)\delta)R_D+2(m+1)\delta][1-(1-(2m-1)\delta)(1-2m\delta)]}.$$

That is, as long as $e^*_C(m) > 0$, $e^*_C(m+1) \geq 0$, and $U_C(m) > 0$, then $e^*_C(m) > e^*_C(m+1)$ if and only if $e^*_C(m+1) < U_C(m)$. Note moreover that if, as will be assumed, $R_C < 1 - 2\delta$, then, as long as $U_C(m) > 0$, $U_C(m)$ is decreasing in m. This means that if $e^*_C(\bar{k}+1) < U_C(\bar{k})$ for some $\bar{k}$, then $e^*_C(\bar{k}) < U_C(\bar{k}-1)$. This can be seen by assuming the contrary.

Assuming, that is, that $e^*_c(\bar{k}) \geq U_c(\bar{k} - 1)$ then $e^*_c(\bar{k} + 1) > e^*_c(\bar{k})$. This and the fact that $U_c(m)$ is decreasing implies $e^*_c(\bar{k} + 1) > e^*_c(\bar{k}) > U_c(\bar{k} - 1) > U_c(\bar{k})$. This contradicts the assumption that $e^*_c(\bar{k} + 1) < U_c(\bar{k})$. Thus, $e^*_c(\bar{k}) < U_c(\bar{k} - 1)$. Generalizing, $e^*_c(m + 1) < U_c(m)$ for $m \leq \bar{k}$. This then gives $e^*_c(m) > e^*_c(m + 1)$ for $2 \leq m \leq \bar{k}$. That is, $e^*_c(m)$ is decreasing from $e^*_c(2)$ to $e^*_c(\bar{k} + 1)$. To show that $e^*_c(m)$ is decreasing in m for $2 \leq m \leq \overline{m} + 1$, it will suffice to show that $e^*_c(\overline{m} + 1) < U_c(\overline{m})$. But the definition of $\overline{m}$ implies $e^*_c(\overline{m} + 1) = 0$. It need only be shown that $U_c(\overline{m}) > 0$. But, the definition of $U_c(m)$ shows $0 < e^*_c(\overline{m}) = U_c(\overline{m})/[1 + U_c(\overline{m})]$. Hence, $e^*_c(m)$ is decreasing in m from $e^*_c(2)$ to $e^*_c(\overline{m} + 1)$.

Uncertainty, Rational Learning, and Bargaining in the Cuban Missile Crisis

R. Harrison Wagner

The Cuban missile crisis was one of the most dramatic, and remains the best documented, of all the confrontations between the United States and the Soviet Union since the Second World War. It therefore figures prominently in debates about how to understand both deterrence and crisis bargaining. One important issue in such debates is the role of military threats, especially nuclear threats, in deterrence and military crises.[1] Another is how to assess the relative merits of rational-choice and psychological explanations of crisis behavior.[2]

Central to both debates is the role of misperception and learning in decision making. Until recently, however, there were no game-theoretic models of deterrence or crisis bargaining that incorporated these factors. The games usually employed to model military crises assume that all features of the situation are commonly known to the players. Any attempt to take misperception or learning into account therefore requires one to introduce cognitive psychology or learning theory into a game-theoretic model.[3]

Such informal adaptations of game theory have helped obscure the question of what theories of rational choice have to say about deterrence or crisis bargaining, since neither can be comprehended without an understanding of the effects of uncertainty. Thus when advocates of psychological approaches contend that the predictions of rational-choice models are inconsistent with the behavior of statesmen, it is not clear what predictions they have in mind.[4]

Psychological critics of rational-choice models are skeptical not only of the rationality assumption, but also of the use of deductive reasoning,

---

1. See, for example, the recent discussion in Betts (1987).
2. See, for example, Lebow (1981) and Jervis, Lebow, and Stein (1985).
3. The most important example of this is Snyder and Diesing (1977).
4. Contributors to a recent volume advocating various psychological approaches to the study of crisis behavior frequently contrast their explanations with the predictions of "rational" or "deductive" models, but no examples of these models are offered (Jervis, Lebow, and Stein, 1985). Perhaps one reason for this is that such models are only beginning to be developed.

which they believe to be incompatible with the study of historical cases. It is only through descriptive case studies, they claim, that one can "look at deterrence from the perspective of how statesmen actually make decisions. . ." (Jervis 1985, 6). Certainly many game-theoretic treatments of crises have been rather casual about the problem of modeling historical events. Rather than try to define the rules of a game that capture our best historical understanding of a crisis, scholars have used such simple, well-known games as Chicken as the focus of their analyses. This has lent credence to the contention of rational deterrence theory's critics that one must choose between deductive reasoning and historical case studies in studying deterrence and crisis bargaining.

The purpose of this paper is to present a game-theoretic model of the Cuban missile crisis. It combines rational-choice theory's use of deductive reasoning with the case study literature's emphasis on accurate description of historical events. Uncertainty, lack of common knowledge, and learning are all incorporated in this model. Thus it may help clarify some of the issues mentioned above.[5]

For example, Lebow (1981, 97) claims that the fact that Khrushchev failed to anticipate the American response to the Soviet missiles in Cuba is evidence of "wishful thinking" on Khrushchev's part, and thus counts in favor of psychological models, and against the relevance of models based on rational choice, in understanding deterrence and crisis bargaining. The analysis presented below, however, implies that once a small amount of uncertainty is admitted into a model, it may not be possible to get rid of it even under the best of circumstances, and fully rational behavior is consistent with a great deal of what seems, in retrospect, to be "misperception."

Another important issue in this literature is the relative importance of "commitments" and the "balance of interests" in determining the outcome of crises. An associated question concerns the relevance of Schelling's notion of "threats that leave something to chance" as a means of compelling a favorable outcome (Betts 1987, 10–16). The blockade in the Cuban missile crisis often plays an important role as an example in such discussions, where it is sometimes suggested either that it represented a commitment on the part of the United States, or that the

---

5. There are other recent models of crisis bargaining that incorporate the effects of uncertainty (Morrow 1985 and 1987b; Powell 1987 and 1988). To the best of my knowledge, however, there are no such models of a historical crisis. Since one of the lessons of the analysis of games in extensive form is that predicted behavior is highly sensitive to the exact form of the game, it is important that one make sure that any game forms used to support assertions about what takes place in crises not be too different from plausible models of historical examples of them.

risks that it entailed led to pressure on the Soviet Union to capitulate. The model presented below implies that neither of these interpretations is correct, and that the crucial role of the blockade in influencing the outcome was, paradoxically, to allow the Soviet Union to put pressure on the United States.

Discussions of military crises often implicitly assume that each participant must choose between standing firm and backing down. The Cuban missile crisis, however, ended with a compromise. There were other possible compromises, and the evidence now indicates that Kennedy was prepared to make further concessions in order to avoid military conflict over the missiles in Cuba. It seems plausible that the ability of statesmen to agree on compromise outcomes is important in determining whether a crisis will lead to war or peace. Bargaining over compromises, however, cannot be understood without taking uncertainty into account. Included in the model presented below is an analysis of the concession process in the Cuban missile crisis.

A Model of the Missile Crisis

The first step in constructing a model of the missile crisis is to specify the sequence of choices that were made, the alternatives among which each party had to choose at each choice opportunity, and the information each had, when choosing, about the choices made by the other. The crisis was begun by Khrushchev's decision to put missiles in Cuba. Let us assume, then, that the game was initiated by a simple choice by Khrushchev between two alternatives: either to place or not to place missiles in Cuba. Following Khrushchev's selection of the option of installing the missiles, it was Kennedy's turn to choose. Kennedy had a variety of distinguishable options, but for now it will be convenient to reduce them to just three: he could accept Soviet missiles in Cuba, he could attempt to remove them by military force, or he could attempt to induce the Soviets to remove them.

The only way to induce Khrushchev to remove the missiles was to threaten, if he did not remove them, to take some action that he would think was worse than removing them. Whatever action Kennedy might threaten to take, Khrushchev would have an opportunity to respond to it. Kennedy would then have an opportunity to respond to Khrushchev's response, and so forth. Similarly, Khrushchev would have an opportunity to respond to any initial effort by Kennedy to remove the missiles by force, Kennedy could then respond to Khrushchev's response, and so on.

A game with these properties is represented in figure 1, where

180   Models of Strategic Choice in Politics

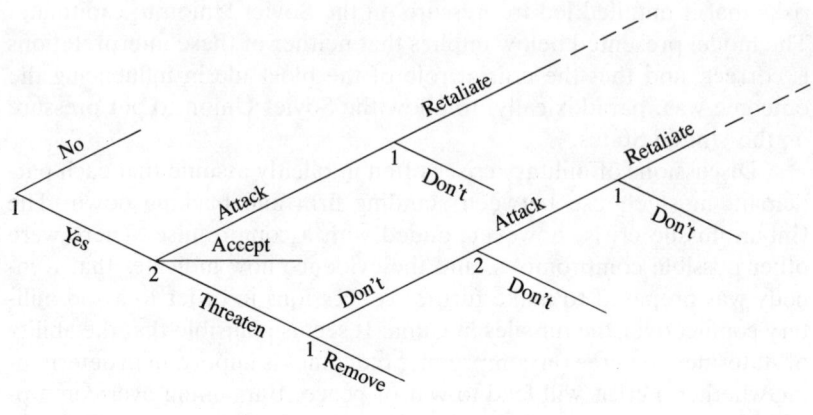

Fig. 1

Khrushchev is labeled Player 1 and Kennedy Player 2. The dotted lines after Player 1's two opportunities to retaliate indicate that if these options are chosen the game continues. To simplify the model it will be convenient initially to treat these portions of the game tree as separate subgames; their expected outcomes will then determine the payoffs for both players if Khrushchev chooses to retaliate.[6]

There are no independent choices in this game—in game-theoretic terminology, it is a game with perfect information. When the payoffs in such a game are common knowledge, it can be solved by backward induction. That is, starting at the end of the tree, one determines what choice each player would prefer, and then works backward until one reaches the beginning of the game. Suppose, for example, that the game ended with Player 2's execution of his threat. Then he would either prefer to execute it or not, and his choice, in accordance with this preference, would determine the payoff for Player 1 if Player 1 elected not to remove the missiles. Given that expected payoff, Player 1 would either prefer to remove them or not, and his choice would determine the payoff to Player 2 if Player 2 chose to issue the threat. Using this expected payoff and the expected payoffs from his other two alternatives, Player 2 could determine his most preferred response to Player 1's initial decision, which would in turn determine whether Player 1 should put the

---

6. In fact, all the end points of this tree lead to subgames of some larger game of which this is but a part. While we will have occasion to mention some possible implications of this fact, it will be convenient at the outset to treat the game defined by the solid lines in the figure as though it were self-contained, and led to final outcomes with definite (but not necessarily commonly known) payoffs to the two players.

missiles in Cuba or not. Of course, in figure 1 the game does not end with Player 2's execution of his threat, but a similar analysis of the retaliation subgame would enable Player 2 to determine what the expected outcome of that choice would be.

The game as actually played ended with Khrushchev's decision to remove the missiles in response to Kennedy's threat. Since it seems extremely unlikely that Khrushchev preferred this outcome to the one that would have resulted from an initial decision not to place the missiles in Cuba, he must not have anticipated it. Thus it seems likely that his expectations of Kennedy's behavior were altered by what happened during the crisis. One of the main problems in explaining Khrushchev's behavior is to understand how this could have occurred. And one of the main problems in evaluating Kennedy's conduct is to determine to what extent he can be given credit for it.

Before confronting these questions, let us notice some features of the game tree in figure 1. First, none of the specific, well-known alternatives considered by Kennedy and his advisers is represented there—the invasion, the air strike, the blockade, the approach to Castro, the secret approach to Khrushchev, etc., are all missing. There is no reason why they could not be represented, but the result of doing so would be not only to clutter up the figure, but also to obscure the fact that, whatever specific option Kennedy chose, it had to fall in one of the three categories represented in the figure. Thus a distinction between military and diplomatic options, for example, is irrelevant to understanding Kennedy's problem. The blockade, in spite of being a military measure, resembled a secret ultimatum more than an air strike, in that, if it had any bearing on getting the missiles out of Cuba, it was as a means of effectively communicating a threat.[7] And negotiations at the United Nations (UN), unless they effectively communicated a threat to Khrushchev, would have been merely a means of accepting the missiles in Cuba.

Second, some other important details of the crisis are also left out of figure 1. For example, however Kennedy chose to communicate his threat to Khrushchev, there was an opportunity for further communication between them before Kennedy had to decide, if Khrushchev rejected his demand, whether to execute his threat or not. And among the things that could have been communicated were possible compromise outcomes between the extreme possibilities of the Soviets removing the missiles without compensation, and the Americans simply accepting

---

7. The blockade may originally have been suggested as a way of accepting the missiles in Cuba, a point that I will return to later in the essay.

them. Moreover, once Kennedy had chosen the blockade, Khrushchev had to decide not only what to do about Kennedy's demand that he remove the missiles, but also how to respond to the blockade. And there was more than one way for him to respond. Each of the more specific options available to Kennedy and Khrushchev entailed a different set of payoffs associated with the endpoints of the game tree in figure 1, and/or a somewhat different micro-structure to the game.

There are some important explanatory questions about some of these features of the crisis that the existing literature has not treated clearly. One concerns the choice of the blockade over a secret ultimatum to Khrushchev—since they were really alternative means of doing the same thing, why was the blockade superior? Another concerns Khrushchev's response to the blockade. His actual response was to behave as though he planned to challenge it, while simultaneously accelerating construction of the missile sites. An alternative response would have been to offer immediately to respect the blockade and to stop all construction on the missile sites, in exchange for negotiations. This would have taken pressure off Kennedy for immediate action without in any way compromising the long-run Soviet missile program in Cuba. Why, then, did Khrushchev act so as to increase Kennedy's incentive to attack immediately?

Finally, the crisis ended, not with a Soviet capitulation, but with a compromise. There were other possible compromises. A hypothetical judgment by Khrushchev that Kennedy was, contrary to his initial belief, prepared to attack Cuba if the missiles were not removed is thus not enough to explain the outcome of the crisis. For at the end the question was not whether Kennedy was prepared to attack Cuba to get rid of Soviet missiles there, but whether Kennedy was prepared to attack Cuba in order to protect obsolete American missile sites in Europe—a different question entirely. What, then, explains Khrushchev's decision to accept the deal he did accept? To answer questions such as these, it will be necessary before we are through to encumber the diagram in figure 1 with some further details. First, however, it will be instructive to analyze this simplified representation of the missile crisis.

The Payoffs and Information Conditions

In order to determine rational play in this game it is necessary to specify the payoffs received by the players on reaching the various end points of the game tree, what information about the payoffs was commonly known, and what information was private knowledge. To do this we will first need to say something about the two retaliation subgames in figure

1.[8] In the literature on the missile crisis, there are two important issues associated with them. One concerns the role of the nuclear balance in influencing the outcome of the crisis, and the other concerns whether Kennedy was wise to decide not to take immediate military action against the missile sites.

The threat that lay behind the blockade was a military attack on Cuba. Given the balance of conventional forces in that area, the outcome of any conventional conflict was a foregone conclusion, and it is safe to assume that this assessment was shared by both Kennedy and Khrushchev. From this some have concluded that the nuclear balance played no role in the crisis. But this conclusion ignores the possible role that nuclear weapons might have played in one of the retaliation subgames. Kennedy and his advisers, for example, were very concerned about the possibility that an American attack on Cuba might be followed by a Soviet attack on Berlin, or on American missile sites in Turkey. Each of those actions would have required the United States to consider its response, and to each U.S. response the Soviets would have an opportunity to respond in turn. If at any point in such a sequence of moves the nuclear balance would have had an effect on the mutual expectations of Kennedy and Khrushchev, then it would also have had an effect on the Cuban missile crisis, through its influence on their expectations concerning the outcome of these subgames.[9]

The other issue is more pertinent to this essay. It concerns the relation between the payoffs to the United States from these two subgames. If the payoffs are identical, and Kennedy preferred to attack the missile sites rather than accept them, then there can be no question about his deciding first to try to induce Khrushchev to remove them. For the worst that could happen if he failed would be that he would then have to take direct military action; but if he succeeded, he would get rid of the missiles without any military costs. That is, any strategy including the "threaten" option dominates any strategy involving immediate military action. If, on the other hand, the payoff from the latter retaliation subgame is worse than the payoff from the former, then Kennedy no longer has a dominant strategy. In that case there is a risk involved in

---

8. With incomplete information, of course, it is technically incorrect to call extensions of this game *subgames*. Moreover, the figures are inadequate representations of the incomplete information versions of it. It should be clear from the text when I am referring to the complete and when to the incomplete information versions of the game, and nothing important is omitted by allowing the figures to do double duty for both.

9. This point has been well made by Trachtenberg (1985), and I will not pursue it further.

trying to induce Khrushchev to remove the missiles, and whether he should do so depends on the probability of his success.

Some, at least, of Kennedy's advisers strongly preferred early military action to later. There were at least three reasons for this. First, there was the advantage of surprise in attacking without warning. Second, attacking later would allow completion of the surface-to-air missile (SAM) sites protecting the Soviet missiles. And third, attacking later might allow the Soviets time to make more of the missiles operational.

To understand Khrushchev's decision to put the missiles in Cuba, one must examine these retaliation subgames from the Soviet point of view as well. If the expected value of retaliating was worse than the expected value of not retaliating, then the Soviets need not have retaliated. In that case the worst Khrushchev would have expected as a result of putting the missiles in Cuba was an American attack on Cuba; since he may have had doubts about the long-run prospects of Soviet gains in Latin America in any case, such an outcome would have been serious but not as devastating as it is sometimes portrayed (Dinerstein 1976).

Moreover, if Khrushchev anticipated that it was unlikely that Kennedy would attack without first trying to negotiate the missiles out, he could anticipate maintaining control over the ultimate outcome by judging the seriousness of Kennedy's response and replying accordingly. And even if Kennedy was prepared to attack rather than accept the missiles, he should have been willing to pay some price in order to avoid the costs of doing so. Thus Khrushchev could plausibly have anticipated as the most likely of the worst-case scenarios something similar to what actually happened.

Having said this much about the retaliation subgames, it will be convenient for the time being to ignore them, and treat any American military action as though it led to a final allocation of payoffs. If we eliminate the retaliation subgames from figure 1, only the threaten option leads to a subgame that must be analyzed, and it can end in only three ways: with the Soviets removing the missiles, with their refusing to do so followed by an American attack on Cuba, or with their refusing to do so followed by Kennedy's backing down from his threat.

It seems plausible to assume that it was common knowledge between Kennedy and Khrushchev that if Khrushchev expected Kennedy to attack Cuba, Khrushchev would prefer to remove the missiles voluntarily. Khrushchev, however, must have been uncertain whether Kennedy would choose to carry out his threat. Assume, then, that Khrushchev believed, when he decided to place missiles in Cuba, that there was some probability that Kennedy was prepared to take military action

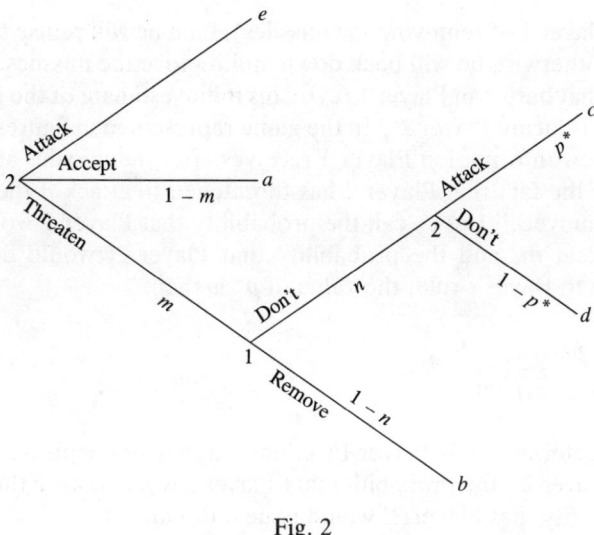

Fig. 2

to remove them and some probability that he was not. Khrushchev must not have believed at the outset that this probability was high enough that he would choose voluntarily to remove the missiles if Kennedy demanded it, since otherwise he would not have decided to put them in Cuba. Our problem, then, is to see how Kennedy's behavior in the course of the crisis might lead Khrushchev to revise this probability estimate. To do this, let us consider rational play in the subgame represented in figure 2.

The Threat Subgame

It is obvious from the figure that if Player 2 prefers c to d then he will carry out his threat and attack Cuba, but if he prefers d to c he will not. Let us call a player who prefers c to d Player $2'$, and a player with the opposite preference simply Player 2. Player 1's problem is to estimate the probability that he is facing a player of type $2'$. Let p be Player 1's initial estimate of the probability that he is facing Player $2'$ (on the basis of which he made his decision to place the missiles in Cuba), and p^* be his revised estimate of this probability (on the basis of which he must decide whether to remove the missiles or not). If, after the threat is made, Player 1 refuses to remove the missiles and he is facing Player 2, then the outcome will be d; if he is facing Player $2'$, on the other hand, the outcome will be c. Thus the expected value to Player 1 of refusing to remove the missiles is $p^*c_1 + (1 - p^*)d_1$. If this is greater than b_1 (the value to Player 1 of removing the missiles), then he will refuse Player 2's demand; otherwise he will back down and remove the missiles.[10]

On what basis can Player 1 revise his initial estimate of the probability that he is facing Player 2'? In the game represented in figures 1 and 2, the only new information Player 1 receives after the missiles are placed in Cuba is the fact that Player 2 has threatened to attack if the missiles are not removed.[11] Let us call the probability that Player 2 would issue such a threat m, and the probability that Player 2' would do so m'. According to Bayes's rule, the value of p^* is then:

$$\frac{pm'}{pm' + (1-p)m}. \tag{1}$$

Thus it is determined by Player 1's initial estimate of the probability that he faces Player 2', the probability that Player 2 would issue a threat, and the probability that Player 2' would issue a threat.

But Player 2, whichever type he is, will choose what to do on the same basis as Player 1, that is, he will select the alternative that has the highest expected value. In considering what this might be, let us begin by ignoring Player 2's option of an initial military attack (I will reintroduce this option shortly). If we do this, then, since Player 2' is assumed to prefer attacking Cuba to accepting the missiles, m' can be assumed to be one. The formula for p^* thus reduces to:

$$\frac{p}{p + (1-p)m}. \tag{2}$$

Note that if $m = 0$, then $p^* = 1$, whereas if $m = 1$, then $p^* = p$. That is, if Player 2 is expected never to issue a threat, then the fact that a threat has been issued is conclusive evidence that Player 1 is facing Player 2'. If Player 2 is certain to issue a threat, on the other hand, then the fact that a threat has been issued provides Player 1 with no new information, and his initial probability estimate is therefore unchanged.

Suppose, then, that Player 2 (the bluffer), knowing that he will accept the missiles if he has to, is indifferent between accepting the

---

10. Of course, whether Player 2 prefers to attack will be influenced by the probability he assigns to Player 1's subsequent retaliation. We know that Kennedy and his advisers believed that the probability of Soviet retaliation for an American attack on Cuba was significant. I will return to this aspect of the game later in the essay.

11. There were, of course, other cues that might have led Khrushchev to revise his estimate of what Kennedy was likely to do, but for the moment it will be convenient to focus on this one alone. This issue is discussed further below.

missiles immediately and accepting them after Player 1 has refused to comply. In that case Player 2 will certainly issue a threat, since he has nothing to lose by doing so: if Player 1 believes the threat then the missiles will be removed, and if not, Player 2 will be no worse off than if he had accepted the missiles immediately. But then $m = 1$, and therefore $p^* = p$.

Thus in order for Player 1 to learn anything about his opponent's true preferences from the fact that the opponent has issued a threat, he must know that Player 2 (as distinguished from 2') would rather accept the missiles immediately than issue a threat that he knew was going to fail; that is, Player 1 must know that Player 2 prefers a to d. Suppose, then, that Player 1's opponent is in fact Player 2'. How could such a player communicate to Player 1 that he should take his threat seriously?[12] We can now see that at a minimum he must choose a threat such that Player 1 knows that if it fails, someone who was bluffing would be worse off than if he had not issued a threat at all.

Even this, however, is not enough to remove all doubts from Player 1's mind. To see why, assume that Player 1 is in fact facing Player 2 and not 2'. What should Player 2 do in such circumstances? If he issues a threat that is costless to himself, it will not be believed. Should he then issue a threat that is sufficiently costly to himself that Player 1 will have no doubt that he would prefer to accept the missiles immediately if he was certain the threat would not work? If Player 1 expects Player 2 to issue such a threat, then it conveys no information to him and he will ignore it. But then the threat will not work, and therefore Player 2 would not want to issue it. If, on the other hand, Player 2 is expected not to issue such a threat, then if a threat is issued Player 1 will conclude he must be facing Player 2', and the threat will work. But then Player 2 would also want to issue such a threat.

In other words, it cannot be an equilibrium for a bluffer to issue such a threat with a probability of one, and it cannot be an equilibrium for him to issue such a threat with a probability of zero. Thus an equilibrium requires that Player 2 (as opposed to 2') issue a threat with some probability between zero and one. But this obviously requires that Player 2 be indifferent between issuing a threat and not issuing it (since otherwise he would want to choose one option or the other with a probability of one), and therefore that the probability with which Player 1 will back down (let us call this n) also be between zero and one.

Thus m determines p^*, which determines n, which in turn deter-

---

12. This is the subject of Jervis (1970), which is well worth a careful rereading in light of the recent literature on games with incomplete information.

mines m. The problem is to find equilibrium values of m and n (which are the result of the choices of Players 1 and 2), given their interdependence through p^*. This is an example of a sequential equilibrium.[13] A sequential equilibrium in this game requires that Players 1 and 2 randomize their choices, so that in equilibrium Player 2 is indifferent between accepting the missiles and issuing a threat, and Player 1 is indifferent between removing them and refusing to do so. Note that this implies that in equilibrium there is still some incentive for Player 2 to bluff, and thus even the fact that a costly threat has been issued is not enough to make Player 1 certain that he is facing Player 2' rather than Player 2.

Let us now consider the implications of these conclusions for rational play in the early stages of the game. First we must reintroduce Player 2's option of taking immediate military action against the missiles. By assumption, only Player 2' would elect such an option. If there is no cost to delaying military action, then the choice of threatening dominates immedate action. Otherwise, Player 2' must compare his payoff from immediate military action with the expected value of issuing a threat. Earlier we assumed that the probability that Player 2' would issue a threat (m') was one; now we can see that this must be modified to say that m' is either one or zero, depending on the expected value to Player 2' of issuing a threat. If m' is zero, then, for any positive value of m, p^* must also be zero. Thus if a threat is issued Player 1 will know for sure that the threatener is bluffing and ignore the threat. In that case, of course, no threat will be issued, and Player 2 will accept the missiles while Player 2' would take immediate military action.[14]

We now know that the expected value of issuing a threat to Player 2' is $nc_{2'} + (1 - n)b_{2'}$. If this value is greater than the payoff from immediate military action, Player 2' will elect to try to bargain the missiles out; otherwise he will take immediate military action. Note that n must be chosen to leave a bluffer indifferent between accepting the missiles and issuing a threat. Thus the larger the critical risk of a potential bluffer, the lower the expected value of bargaining to Player 2', and the more likely, therefore, that he will elect to take immediate action against the missile sites. In other words, the greater the incentive to bluff, the less likely Player 1 is to take a threat seriously, and hence the

---

13. See Kreps and Wilson (1982a). For a recent survey of applications of this concept to games with incomplete information, see Wilson (1985).

14. If the probabilities that Players 2 and 2' will issue a threat are both zero, then Bayes's rule is undefined if a threat is issued. The prediction that, if a threat is in fact made, this will not lead Player 1 to alter his estimate of p, thus requires the further assumption that neither type of Player 2 is more likely than the other to deviate from the equilibrium path.

less likely it is that Player 2' will be able to bargain the missiles out, even though he is really not bluffing.

We are now in a position to determine the payoff to Player 1 from deciding to put missiles in Cuba. If the value of an immediate attack for Player 2' is greater than the expected value of bargaining, then Player 1's expectation is $pe_1 + (1 - p)a_1$. Suppose, on the other hand, that the expected value of bargaining is known to be greater than the value of an immediate attack for Player 2'. Remember that, in equilibrium, if a threat is made Player 1 must be indifferent between removing the missiles and refusing to do so. This implies that the expected value to Player 1 of issuing a threat is equivalent to b_1. Remember as well that Player 2 may accept the missiles rather than issue a threat, while Player 2' will never do so. Thus Player 1's expectation in this case is $pb_1 + (1 - p)[mb_1 + (1 - m)a_1]$.

All of this may seem more complicated, and counter-intuitive, than it really is. The main effect of a game-theoretic interpretation of learning is to focus our attention on the problem of bluffing. Because there is nothing a nonbluffer can do that a bluffer would not have the ability and incentive to imitate, the recipient of a threat can never be completely convinced that the threatener is not bluffing. People who issue threats and mean them have an incentive to distinguish themselves from bluffers, but they cannot do so completely. Similarly, people who are threatened want to learn whether they should take the threat seriously, and therefore have an incentive to try to deter bluffing. But success in deterring bluffing is, after a point, counterproductive, since if the recipient of the threat is known to be confident that he has deterred bluffing, then that in itself constitutes an incentive to bluff. In equilibrium, therefore, neither a bluffer nor the recipient of a threat can know what to expect, and each is indifferent between backing down and standing firm.

I will return to the problem of providing an intuitive interpretation of this model in the context of the Cuban missile crisis. First, however, we must consider the effect of introducing the possibility of compromise outcomes.

Allowing More Moves

In order to allow Kennedy and Khrushchev to bargain over compromise outcomes, it will be necessary to add more moves to the game. Before doing that, it will be helpful to reconsider the move structure of the threat subgame without compromises. In figure 2, Player 2 has one opportunity to decide whether to issue a threat or not, and Player 1 has one opportunity to decide how to respond, after which Player 2 must either carry out his threat or back down. Suppose, however, that we

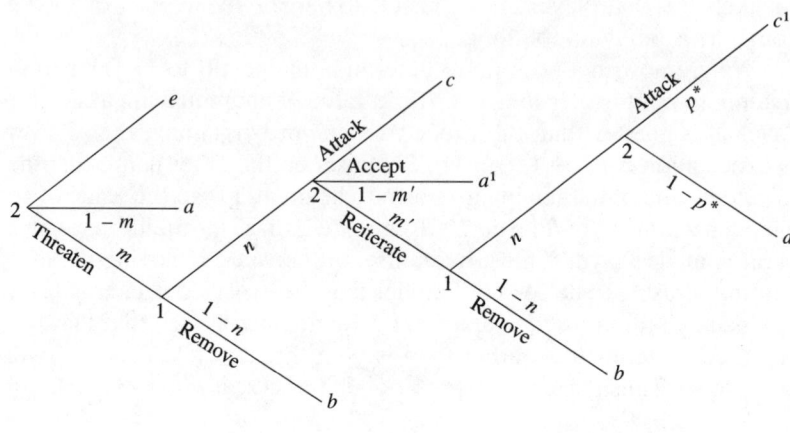

Fig. 3

allow Player 2 to respond to Player 1's refusal by reiterating his threat, after which Player 1 has an opportunity to reconsider his reply. There was nothing in the missile crisis, after all, that prevented this sort of exchange from occurring any number of times. Let us examine what effect this would have on the game.

In figure 3, Player 2 has been given a third alternative after Player 1 has refused to remove the missiles—he can now attack, back down, or reiterate his threat. If he chooses to repeat the threat, then Player 1 has another opportunity to reply and the original sequence of moves is followed. I will continue to assume that at every stage Player 2 would prefer, if he were sure that holding out would be unsuccessful, to concede immediately rather than hold out, and that the expected value of bargaining for Player 2' is always greater than the expected value of attacking immediately.

Note that the last three moves of this extended game are identical to the threat subgame examined above. Thus, with incomplete information, at Player 1's last move p^* must once again be such that Player 1 is indifferent between backing down and refusing to remove the missiles, and Player 2 (as opposed to 2') must be indifferent between backing down and reiterating his threat. On the other hand, there can again be no commonly known expectation that Player 2 will or will not issue a threat at his first opportunity to do so. Thus, as before, at each move Player 2 must randomize between accepting the missiles and threatening to remove them, and Player 1 must randomize between removing the missiles and refusing to do so. Moreover, at each opportunity to choose Player 1 must back down with the same probability.

But there is no reason why this game could not be further extended, with additional opportunities for Player 2 to reiterate his threat and for Player 1 to reconsider his response. Yet our analysis requires that there nonetheless be some final move at which Player 2 must choose between executing his threat and backing down. What could account for the fact that at some point Player 2 can no longer elect to extend the game by reiterating his threat? It is easiest to see why that might be true if there is an ongoing and increasing military penalty for postponing an attack. For then the expected value of continuing to bargain for Player $2'$ would eventually be less than the expected value of attacking immediately. The moment when this occurred would be the final move of the game.

If there is no cost to postponing military action, on the other hand, then someone threatening an attack is always subject to the temptation of postponing it in the hope of getting a better deal. For remember that at every move there is some probability that Player 1 will back down. This lessens the credibility of Player 2's threat, but it also makes it more difficult for Player 1 to interpret Player 2's behavior. I believe this fact has important implications for understanding the missile crisis, to which I will return later in the essay.

Bargaining Over Compromises

The simplest way to allow for possible compromises is to let Player 1, at his move in figure 2, suggest any alternative to Player 2's demand that he wants. Now, while Player 1 may still simply refuse to remove the missiles, he may instead suggest, for example, that American missiles be removed from Europe in exchange for the removal of Soviet missiles from Cuba. If Player 1 makes a counterproposal, Player 2 must, as before, choose between removing Soviet missiles from Cuba by force, and accepting Player 1's counterdemand. But the difference between the two outcomes is no longer, as in the original example, whether Soviet missiles are removed from Cuba or not. Now, no matter which choice Player 2 makes, the missiles will be removed. The question, rather, is which price Player 2 prefers to pay to have the missiles removed: military action against Cuba, or the removal of U.S. missiles from Europe.

Even if Player 2 would rather remove the missiles from Cuba by force than accept them, there is likely to be some concession he is prepared to make in order to have Player 1 remove them voluntarily, because then he can avoid the significant cost of military action. And since Player 2 must, in the end, simply decide which outcome he prefers,

Player 1 could, if all features of the game were common knowledge, make the largest demand that Player 2 would just barely prefer to removing the missiles by force, and expect Player 2 to accept it (Wagner 1982; Morrow 1985). With complete information, in other words, the Cuban missile crisis could be given the following interpretation: the change in Cuba's foreign policy resulting from the Cuban revolution gave the Soviet government the opportunity to put missiles in Cuba. In order to get the missiles removed the American government would have to pay some price, either as compensation to the Soviets for removing them, or as the result of taking direct military action against Cuba. Thus even if the American government was prepared to take military action to remove the missiles, if what it was willing to pay the Soviet government in order to avoid the cost of military action was enough to compensate the Soviets for any costs involved in installing the missiles and then removing them, then the Soviet government could collect that payment. If, on the other hand, the American government was not willing to bear the cost of military action to remove the missiles, then the missiles would stay in Cuba unless there was some alternative bargain that both governments preferred.

With incomplete information, on the other hand, the Soviets might miscalculate the payment the Americans were prepared to make. Thus they might agree to less than they could have demanded, or demand too much, leading the Americans to reject the Soviet demand and attack Cuba. Moreover, the latter possibility implies that, if there is a cost to postponing military action, the Americans might elect to forgo bargaining entirely and attack the missile sites instead.

The price Kennedy actually paid was a public pledge not to invade Cuba again, coupled, apparently, with a private assurance that U.S. missiles in Europe would, since they were obsolete, be removed. A public agreement to remove American missiles from Europe in exchange for the removal of the missiles from Cuba would have been politically more costly for Kennedy, and more beneficial for Khrushchev. In order to make the analysis manageable, let us distinguish between just two possible compromise outcomes: a simple no-invasion pledge in exchange for removal of the missiles, and a public exchange of U.S. missiles in Europe for Soviet missiles in Cuba.

Let us assume, then, that there are three types of preferences that Player 2 might have, instead of just two: (1) he might be prepared to accept the missiles rather than bear the costs of taking military action against them; (2) he might prefer to take military action rather than accept the missiles, but be willing to make a public trade of U.S. missiles in Europe for them; or (3) he might be willing to take military action against the missiles, and be willing to accept no more than a simple no-invasion pledge in order to avoid the costs of military action. Let us call players with these types of preferences Players 2, 2', and 2", respectively, and assume that Player 1 initially assigns some probability p to the possibility that he is confronting Player 2", q to the possibility that he is confronting Player 2', and $(1 - p - q)$ to the possibility that he is confronting Player 2. (As before, let us denote the revised versions of these probability estimates p^* and q^*.) We must also distinguish among three types of outcome d: acceptance of the missiles in Cuba, acceptance of the European missile deal, and acceptance of the no-invasion pledge. Let us call these outcomes d, d', and d'', respectively.

Assume, then, that if Player 1 elects not to remove the missiles he must decide which of these outcomes to demand instead. If a compromise demand is made, Player 2 must ultimately decide either to accept it or to attack Cuba. Before confronting that final choice, however, there is no reason why Player 2 should not also be able to make a counterproposal if Player 1 has offered an unacceptable compromise. A game incorporating such rules is depicted in figure 4. In this game Player 2 initially decides whether to attack, accept the missiles, or threaten to attack if the missiles are not removed. If a threat is made, Player 1 decides whether to remove the missiles, offer one of the two compromises, or refuse to remove them. If he offers d'', Player 2 will, by assumption, accept it. If he offers d', on the other hand, Player 2 must decide whether to reject the offer and attack, accept it, or offer a counterproposal d''. If Player 2 offers d'' as a counterproposal, then Player 1 must decide between accepting it or holding out for d'. If he decides to hold out, then Player 2 must finally decide between accepting d' and attacking Cuba.[15]

Note that the structure of the subgame beginning with Player 2's second move is identical to the threat subgame analyzed above. Now if Player 2 does not attack, he must choose between accepting Player 1's demand (in this case d') or making a counterdemand (in this case d''). If anyone but Player 2" makes such a demand he is bluffing, and would ultimately choose to accept d' rather than attack. But if a bluffer would prefer to accept Player 1's demand earlier rather than later, then, with incomplete information, the fact that a counterdemand is issued will lead Player 1 to revise again his estimate of p. This requires, as before,

---

15. To keep figure 4 as simple as possible, I have assumed that if Player 1 stands firm without offering compromise, Player 2 must either attack or back down. It would not change things if Player 2 is instead allowed to reiterate his demand or offer a compromise at that point, since in the absence of a compromise offer from Player 1, no information is transferred.

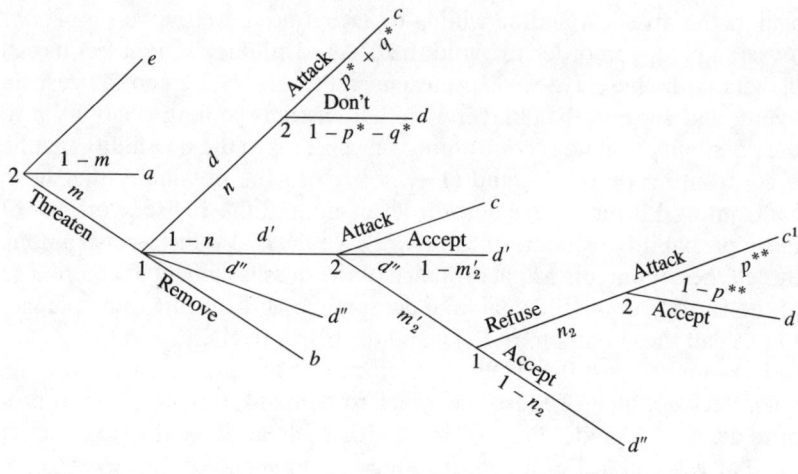

Fig. 4

that Player 1 randomize between accepting Player 2's counterdemand and holding out for his own. If we make the plausible assumption that the cost of bluffing is less for Player 2' than for Player 2, an equilibrium requires that Player 2 accept d', Player 2' randomize between accepting it and demanding d'' instead, and Player 2" make the counterdemand with a probability of one.[16]

Thus the value to Player 1 of the subgame that begins with his last move is equivalent to d''. At Player 1's first move, therefore, demanding d' dominates demanding d'', and Player 1 must choose between offering that compromise and simply refusing to remove the missiles. The fact that a threat has been issued, however, will lead Player 1 to revise his estimate of the probability that Player 2 will accept them (which is $1 - p - q$). Player 1 must therefore randomize between offering d' and refusing to remove the missiles, and Player 2, at his first move, must randomize between accepting them and demanding that they be removed. Players 2' and 2", however, must demand that they be removed with a probability of one. (A brief justification of these statements is presented in the appendix to this essay.)

Thus if Player 2 threatens to attack, Player 1 lowers his estimate of the probability that Player 2 will accept the missiles. If Player 2 subsequently also rejects Player 1's offer of a compromise, Player 1 is certain that Player 2 will not accept the missiles, and believes it is more likely

---

16. I continue to assume that, in equilibrium, the expected value of bargaining for Player 2" is greater than the value of attacking until the final move.

than he had initially thought that Player 2 will accept only the no-invasion pledge as a compromise. In the end, however, Player 1 is still not sure of this, and thus there is still some probability that he will hold out for the European missile deal.

If we allow a sequence of offers and counteroffers, then, Player 1 can gradually refine his initial estimate of the smallest compromise that his opponent is prepared to accept. But this is possible only as long as two conditions are met: (1) *there must be a penalty for postponing an attack,* so that beyond a certain point a player who is prepared to use force would prefer to do so rather than hold out for a better compromise; and (2) *a threatener who expects to concede must prefer to concede immediately,* rather than issue a threat, or renew it. That is, the threat itself must in some way be costly, and continue to be costly, so that a bluffer would not issue it or renew it unless the probability that it will work is high enough to justify the cost.

Remember that, at every move, even if Player 2 prefers accepting Player 1's demand to attacking, he will still be indifferent between accepting the demand and holding out for more, and there is some probability that he will hold out. Thus there is also some probability that Player 1 will make no concession. Therefore, even if we allow for the possibility of compromise settlements, and assume that Khrushchev, during the crisis, responded rationally to new information about Kennedy's true preferences, there was some irreducible probability that the crisis could have ended with an American attack on Cuba—unless, of course, Kennedy was bluffing from the beginning.

Game Theory and the Missile Crisis

One common interpretation of what happened in the missile crisis is that Kennedy's imposition of the blockade convinced Khrushchev to take seriously Kennedy's subsequent threat of military action against Cuba. The model I have constructed implies that for this to be true, the blockade must have been something that Kennedy would not have wanted to employ if he was bluffing and was certain that his bluff would not work. Thus it is interesting that early in the deliberation among Kennedy's advisers, McNamara seems to have defended the blockade as a way of accepting the missiles already in Cuba. He said:

> . . . I'll be quite frank. I don't think there *is* a military problem here. . . . it's just exactly *this* problem, that . . . if Cuba should possess a capacity to carry out offensive actions against the U.S., [we said] the U.S. would act. . . . this is a domestic, political problem. . . . we didn't say we'd go in and . . . kill them, we said we'd *act.* Well, how will we act?

McNamara's answer to that question was that the United States would institute a blockade to prevent further supply of offensive weapons to Cuba, and issue an announcement

> ... that we have located these offensive weapons; we're maintaining a constant surveillance over them; if there is ever any indication that they're to be launched ... we will respond not only against Cuba, but ... against the Soviet Union with a full nuclear strike. Now this alternative doesn't seem to be a very acceptable one, but wait until you work on the others.

To this Ball replied, "Yeah, well, as far as the American people are concerned, action means military action, period." McNamara then said, "Well, we have a blockade. Search and ... removal ... of offensive weapons entering Cuba."[17] McNamara's language suggests that the blockade might have been a way of satisfying the demand for military action without actually doing anything dangerous, thereby making it easier for President Kennedy to avoid taking direct action against Cuba. Thus it would have been a tactic that Kennedy, had he been bluffing, would have preferred to an initial acceptance of Soviet missiles in Cuba.

If so, then it could not have played the role attributed to the threat issued in the model developed above. The most plausible reason why it might have conveyed a different impression was given by Ball in response to McNamara. He said, "Now, one of the things we look at is whether ... the actual operation of a blockade ... isn't a greater involvement almost than a military action," to which McNamara responded, "Might well be, George." In other words, what made the blockade efficacious as a means of communicating a threat was the property for which it was most criticized, namely, that it entailed the risk of a military confrontation with the Soviet Union that was irrelevant to the main problem, which was getting the missiles out of Cuba.

But this property of the blockade was not inherent in it; rather it was the result of the behavior of the Soviet Union. If the Soviets had clearly announced from the beginning that they planned to respect the blockade, then there would have been little risk associated with it. And if they had simultaneously stopped all military construction in Cuba and asked for negotiations with the United States, they would not only have eliminated Kennedy's military risks, but also all pressure on him for immediate action. This, in fact, is what Kennedy demanded. The summary record of an ExCom meeting at 4:00 P.M. on October 27 reports that:

---

17. These quotations are taken from the transcript of audiotapes 28.2 and 28A.1, Presidential Recordings, Papers of John F. Kennedy, Presidential Papers, John F. Kennedy Presidential Library, Boston. President's Office Files, 45–48 (emphasis as in original).

The President asked whether we wanted to continue to say that we would talk only about the missiles in Cuba. He believed that for the next few hours we should emphasize our position that if the Russians will halt missile activity in Cuba we would be prepared to discuss NATO problems with the Russians. He felt that we would not be in a position to offer any trade for several days. He did feel that if we could succeed in freezing the situation in Cuba and rendering strategic missiles inoperable, then we would be in a position to negotiate with the Russians.

Mr. Bundy pointed out that there would be a serious reaction in NATO countries if we appeared to be trading withdrawal of missiles in Turkey for withdrawal of missiles from Cuba. The President responded that if we refuse to discuss such a trade and then take military action in Cuba, we would also be in a difficult position. (Trachtenberg 1985, 201)

Kennedy seems to have been interested in a trade; by rejecting his demand, Khrushchev may have missed an opportunity to deal.[18] Since accepting Kennedy's demand would not have had any immediate effect either on the missiles already in Cuba, or on the answer to the question of whether the Soviets would be allowed to keep them, an important question about Khrushchev's behavior is why he rejected it.

The answer to this question implied by the model presented earlier is that if Khrushchev had behaved differently he would have learned less about Kennedy's true preferences. If the blockade had entailed no risk of military conflict, then a bluffer would not have hesitated to use it. And if work on the missile sites had stopped, then even if Kennedy had been prepared to use force against them, he would have had no clear deadline for doing so, in which case his behavior in the meantime would have been harder to interpret.[19] Khrushchev's behavior, in other words, can be explained as a screening device.[20]

---

18. Recent revelations by Dean Rusk strengthen the impression that Kennedy was prepared to make a public trade of U.S. missiles in Europe for Soviet missiles in Cuba. See the *New York Times,* August 29, 1987, and the *New York Times Magazine,* August 30, 1987.

19. All accounts of the missile crisis that I have seen agree that Kennedy felt under some time pressure in deciding what to do, and that continued work on the missile sites contributed to that feeling. It is not entirely clear, however, what the nature of this contribution was. Acheson (1969) objected to the blockade because it would allow the Soviets time to complete the missile sites. Kennedy soon learned, however, that some of the medium range ballistic missile (MRBM) sites were already completed (Garthoff, 1987, 13). Perhaps the concern had to do with the intermediate range ballistic missiles (IRBM's), perhaps with the completion of the ancillary command structures and the arming of the missiles (Allison 1971, 224). Garthoff reports, however, that the issue was "how to bring the crisis to a head before the Soviet missiles already in Cuba became accepted as an element in the status quo" (Garthoff, 1987, 44).

20. Schelling (1966, 81–82), in discussing the blockade, suggests that one of its advantages was that it left the next move up to the Soviets. But this implies that if the

A Contest in Risk Taking?

This does not imply, however, that the blockade initiated, as Schelling (1966, 96) has suggested, a contest in risk taking. The question was not whether Kennedy or Khrushchev was prepared to take the greater risk, but rather whether Kennedy was prepared to take military action against Cuba. Only by exposing Kennedy to some prior risk could Khrushchev elicit information relevant to that question; the risks that Khrushchev ran were a necessary means of acquiring the information he needed.

The idea that crises are contests in risk taking is closely related to Schelling's concept of the "threat that leaves something to chance" (Schelling 1960, 187–203).[21] The "threat that leaves something to chance," however, assumes that there is some exogenous, autonomous risk that "things will get out of hand," and thus something bad will happen that is not the result of anyone's explicit decision (the image of two people fighting in a rowboat or on the edge of a cliff is often used to illustrate this idea). Crisis bargaining, interpreted in this way, involves the deliberate exposure of both adversaries to this autonomous risk. This provides one justification for the common contention that the side willing to accept the greater risk has the advantage in a crisis.[22]

In the model of the missile crisis offered above, however, uncertainty is not the result of some exogenous risk that chance will intervene and take things out of the hands of the parties to the crisis. It is, rather, the result of incomplete information about preferences.[23] And thus bargaining during the crisis was not a competition in risk taking, but a means by which information about Kennedy's preferences was transferred to Khrushchev.

One might object that Khrushchev was implicitly threatening to retaliate for any American military action, just as Kennedy was threatening to take such action, and therefore the risks to which both parties were exposed during the blockade were as relevant to enhancing the credibility of Khrushchev's threats as they were to enhancing the credibility of Kennedy's. Because I truncated the game after Kennedy's decision whether to take military action against Cuba, this possibility has not been discussed. Let us consider it now.

Soviets had not at first acted as though they planned to challenge the blockade, it would not have been much good as a way of communicating a threat. Thus Khrushchev *cooperated* with Kennedy in making the blockade an efficacious threat, perhaps because he had as much interest in learning what Kennedy might do as Kennedy had in teaching him.

21. See, for example, the discussion in Betts (1987).

22. See the discussion in Powell (1987 and 1988).

23. It is much more plausible that adversaries will be uncertain about each other's preferences than that they will literally lose all control over events—it is because these two sources of uncertainty are frequently confused that the implausibility of the latter idea is not often noticed.

Suppose that Kennedy, if he were certain that Khrushchev would retaliate for an American attack on the missile sites, would prefer instead to accept the missiles in Cuba. Suppose also that Kennedy was not certain that Khrushchev would retaliate. Let r be Kennedy's estimate of the probability that Khrushchev would retaliate. Then p, in our earlier discussion, is Khrushchev's estimate of the probability that Kennedy will prefer to attack anyway, given r.[24] But I have assumed that p was already low enough (and therefore r was high enough) that Khrushchev was willing to risk putting missiles in Cuba even if he was not prepared to retaliate for an American attack. Thus at the outset Khrushchev had no interest in enhancing the credibility of his threat of retaliation, and his decision to put missiles in Cuba conveyed no information about it.

If, however, Khrushchev was interested in learning more about Kennedy's true preferences (given r), then the probability with which he conceded to Kennedy's demands must still be exactly as defined above. For Khrushchev's behavior must provide Kennedy with the appropriate incentive not to bluff. If Khrushchev behaved in any other way, then p^* would, to be sure, be lower, but only because p could not be revised in light of Kennedy's behavior.

This feature of the model helps explain an aspect of Soviet behavior during the crisis that would otherwise be puzzling. If Khrushchev tried to compete with Kennedy in enhancing the credibility of his own threat of retaliation, it is hard to explain why the Soviets did not try to demonstrate their readiness to engage in a military confrontation with the United States. But apart from failing to turn around Soviet ships headed for Cuba and continuing construction on the missile sites, the Soviets maintained a low military profile throughout the crisis. As Betts says, the Soviets

> . . . neither prepared for a "fateful step" in response to the U.S. nuclear alert, nor undertook significant conventional military preparations in Europe. As Air Force General David Burchinal put it, Khrushchev never even put any bombers on alert: "We had a gun at his head and he didn't move a muscle." . . . The remarkable Soviet nonalert was equivalent to a threatened dog's rolling over belly-up.

This sort of behavior is hard to square with an effort on Khrushchev's part to enhance the credibility of a threat of retaliation. But it is consistent with the model presented above.[25]

---

24. More specifically, assume that Players 2 and 2' differ in the level of their critical risks. Then, given r, Player 2 is deterred from attacking but Player 2' is not.

25. One might object that Khrushchev was threatening to use force if the United States stopped a Soviet ship, and he had to be concerned about the credibility of this

On the other hand, Kennedy sought during the crisis not only to persuade Khrushchev that he would take military action against Cuba, but also that any Soviet retaliation for such action would be punished. Thus the nuclear balance may have had an influence on Khrushchev's ability, by his actions during the missile crisis, to enhance the credibility of his own threat of retaliation. A complete understanding of this aspect of Soviet behavior would therefore require an explicit model of the expected course of escalation.

Other Explanatory Issues

Our discussion is also relevant to explaining the choice of the blockade over a secret ultimatum, or other diplomatic initiatives, as a means of communicating a threat to Khrushchev. In explaining this choice it is sometimes suggested that no great power could accept an ultimatum (Allison 1971, 58–59). It is not clear why the sort of public challenge represented by the blockade should be more acceptable; arguably it would have been less costly for Khrushchev to have accepted privately the outcome he ultimately was compelled to accept publicly, and therefore he ought to have been more ready to do so. Diplomatic initiatives are also often said to have entailed a risk of delay while construction of the missile sites proceeded, or while the United States was exposed to pressure to trade U.S. missiles in Europe for Soviet missiles in Cuba. But the blockade was characterized by both these features as well.

There are two main differences between the blockade and secret diplomacy that seem more relevant to explaining Kennedy's choice. First, secret diplomacy entailed no immediate risks for Kennedy; thus any threat conveyed by that means was less credible. And second, secrecy prevented any announcement in advance of a U.S. attack against Cuba. The U.S. government used the time and publicity afforded by the blockade to publicize the existence of the missile sites, thereby reducing the political costs in Latin America that an American attack on Cuba would have entailed. This made the threat of such an attack more credible.

One should not understate the cost to Kennedy of bluffing in a secret ultimatum, however. Suppose Kennedy had threatened, if the missiles were not removed by a specific deadline, to attack the missile sites. If Khrushchev had refused and then Kennedy failed to carry out his threat, any future threat by Kennedy would have been much less

---

threat. But prior to the blockade Kennedy must have assigned some positive probability to the possibility that Khrushchev would challenge it. This was enough to constitute a penalty for bluffing. Khrushchev had only to behave initially in a way that would not lead Kennedy to revise this probability downward.

credible. Thus, like the blockade, issuing an ultimatum was not something that a bluffer would want to do if he were certain it would not work. Because the model presented here ignores the fact that this game was embedded in a larger, continuing game, it does not directly take into account this sort of effect.

Remember that n (the probability that Khrushchev will refuse to remove the missiles) is, in equilibrium, equal to the critical risk of a hypothetical bluffer. Thus the less the penalty for bluffing, the more likely it was that a threat would be ignored. In considering whether to bluff in an ultimatum, Kennedy would have had to balance the longer-run costs of being caught in deception against the immediate gains of success. By lying to Kennedy about the missile sites, Khrushchev and his representatives indicated that the prospect of immediate gain was, to them, more important than the future costs of such behavior. Since Khrushchev also was apparently unimpressed by Kennedy's earlier verbal warnings, Kennedy may have reasoned that Khrushchev expected him to behave similarly.[26]

Another limitation of my model is that it assumes that Khrushchev learned only from the choices Kennedy made among the alternatives represented in it. Obviously there were many other ways Khrushchev might have acquired relevant information, ranging from espionage to observation of Kennedy's body language in his television address. No matter what the source of information, however, Bayes's rule still would have applied. The crucial question, then, would still have been the relation between m and m' (the behavioral strategies of a bluffer and a nonbluffer, respectively). The assumption of the analysis offered above is that a bluffer could always mimic the behavior of a nonbluffer, and thus m could be any value a bluffer chose. In order for learning to occur, therefore, there had to be some cost to bluffing.

If Khrushchev believed that such mimicry was not possible, then learning would not have had a strategic component. For example, if Khrushchev had a spy among the members of the ExCom and was confident Kennedy did not suspect him, he might have believed that he had access to Kennedy's sincere thinking. Jervis (1970) calls evidence of this type an index, which he distinguishes from signals. Signals are, in effect, statements of intention, such as verbal threats. He says:

> Both the sender and the perceiver realize that signals can be as easily issued by a deceiver as by an honest actor. The costs of issuing deceptive signals, if

---

26. For an interesting discussion of the relation between Kennedy's behavior prior to the missile crisis and the problem of deterring Khrushchev from putting missiles in Cuba, see Etheredge (1985).

any, are deferred to the time when it is shown that the signals were misleading. (1970, 21)

But, as noted above, if the immediate benefits of deception are large relative to the future costs from its discovery, then signals will not be very credible. Thus it is important for the peaceful resolution of crises that signals and indices, in Jervis's terminology, not exhaust the possible means of communication.

Jervis writes that the blockade of Cuba "revealed an American willingness to run some risks in opposing the Soviet venture," and thus was "partly an index." But it was also

> ... a clear signal which could have been a bluff and did not involve any strong proof of American willingness to take the much higher risks which would have been necessary to secure American goals had Russia not retreated. (1970, 22)

The model presented above indicates how an action can be partly a signal and partly an index, and how a willingness to run some risks can influence an opponent's estimate of one's willingness to run greater ones.

One of the implications of this model, however, is that if deception is possible, then uncertainty cannot be eliminated. Thus, in equilibrium, Khrushchev is indifferent between accepting Kennedy's demand and rejecting it, and there is some probability that he will do either. If there was a penalty for postponing a military attack, therefore, there was some risk involved in choosing the blockade. Thus there was some set of utilities and subjective probability estimates that implied that Kennedy should have chosen to attack immediately, and some set that implied that the blockade was the proper choice. Because there was no way of determining which was correct, it was possible to disagree about what Kennedy should do, even if everyone agreed the missiles were important enough to warrant taking military action to get them out of Cuba. Moreover, the mere fact that the blockade worked does not in itself imply that it was the right choice.[27] Allison (1971, 62), in presenting a sketch of a "Model I" explanation of Kennedy's decision, concludes by saying, "Seen in this light, the blockade was the only real option." The model presented above implies that this could not be true. Thus the idea that rationality implies a single, optimal decision that all rational individuals will agree with is a myth, and the distinction between Model I and

---

27. For an example of the view that Kennedy made the wrong choice, even though it happened to work out well, see Acheson (1969).

Model III explanations offered by Allison is not as clear-cut as might at first appear.

Clearly there are alternative explanations of the choice of the blockade to the one implied by my model. If neither Kennedy's decision, nor the existence of disagreement among members of the ExCom, is sufficient evidence for choosing among them, what is? It would help to know how closely the model presented here paralleled Kennedy's thinking. He has been quoted as saying that "Khrushchev won't pay any attention to words. He has to see you move" (Jervis 1970, 23). He is also reported to have said that

> . . . we will get the Soviet strategic missiles out of Cuba only by invading Cuba or by trading. He doubted that the quarantine alone would produce a withdrawal of the weapons. (Trachtenberg, 1985, 195)

These remarks imply a rather clearer conception of the role of the blockade than Acheson's (1969) report that it was mainly a way of postponing hard choices. On the other hand, Kennedy at every turn seems to have tried to reduce the military risks entailed by the blockade, so that it is possible that without Khrushchev's belligerent behavior, and U.S. military actions that eluded Kennedy's control (such as the confrontations with Soviet submarines or the straying of a U-2 plane over the Soviet Union), the blockade would have been much less effective. Perhaps further archival research will give us a clearer picture of what Kennedy thought he was doing. If so, the model presented here may help us interpret what the documents have to say.

Concluding Comments

The concept of a sequential equilibrium provides a way of incorporating both incomplete information and learning into a game-theoretic model. One effect is to demonstrate that in the best of circumstances rational learning is more difficult than much of the psychological literature on crises suggests, and thus "misperception" may not be so easily attributed to faulty reasoning as at least some of this literature implies.[28]

Incorporating uncertainty also makes possible a game-theoretic analysis of bargaining. If bargainers had enough information to anticipate the outcome of crises, then crises would never occur, since the expected outcome could instead be accepted immediately. Crisis bargaining, like other forms of bargaining, can thus be best understood as a

---

28. See, for example, the discussion in Lebow (1981), especially chapter 4.

process by which adversaries acquire the information about each other that they need in order to know what outcome they should accept. The nature of this process depends on the structure of the situation.[29] It remains to be seen how typical of other military confrontations the bargaining process in the missile crisis was.

In order for bargainers to learn, bargaining must be costly, since otherwise they may be suspected of bluffing. The main source of uncertainty in the bargaining that took place during the missile crisis was Kennedy's willingness to take military action if the missiles were not removed. Thus the risk of conflict entailed by the blockade seems most plausibly understood, not as something that the Americans used to put pressure on the Soviets so that they would back down, but as something that allowed the Soviets to put pressure on the Americans so that Kennedy's threat of subsequent military action would seem more credible. And since the Soviets had good reason to want to know how seriously to take Kennedy's threats, this was something they were not averse to doing. Seen in this light, the missile crisis was not a competition in risk taking, but a strange sort of cooperation in the exchange of information.

APPENDIX

The problem is to show that in the incomplete information version of the game depicted in figure 4, there is a sequential equilibrium with the properties stated in the text. At his final move in this game, Player 2 must choose between accepting d' and attacking. Only a player of type $2''$ would choose to attack. The expected value to Player 1 of refusing d' is thus $p^{**}c^1 + (1 - p^{**})d'$. An equilibrium requires that this value be equal to the utility Player 1 assigns to d''.

If n_2 is the probability with which Player 1, at his last move, holds out for d', then the expected value of demanding d'' for both Player 2 and Player $2'$ is $n_2 d' + (1 - n_2)d''$. Since Players 2 and $2'$ differ in their evaluation of military costs, it is plausible to assume that the cost of bluffing is greater for Player 2 than for Player $2'$. Then Player 1 can choose n_2 so that Player $2'$ is indifferent between accepting d' immediately and demanding more, and Player 2 prefers to accept d' immediately. If Player 2 then accepts d' with a probability of one, and Player $2''$ demands d'' with a probability of one, Player $2'$ can randomize between

---

29. For models of other bargaining processes, see Roth (1985) and Binmore and Dasgupta (1987).

accepting d' and demanding d'', so that the resulting value of p^{**} leaves Player 1 indifferent between accepting d'' and holding out for d'.

This implies that the expected value to Player 1 of demanding d' at his first move is $(1 - p^* - q^*)d' + p^*d' + q^*[m_2'd'' + (1 - m_2')d']$. The expected value of holding out for the missiles, however, is $(p^* + q^*)c + (1 - p^* - q^*)d$. If Players 2' and 2'' both issue a threat with a probability of one, then Player 2 can randomize between accepting the missiles and issuing a threat so that the implied values of p^* and q^* are such that Player 1 is indifferent between holding out for the missiles and offering d' as a compromise. Player 1, on the other hand, must randomize between holding out for the missiles and offering a compromise so that Player 2 is indifferent between accepting them and demanding that they be removed. One can readily verify that these requirements imply unique values for m and n (the behavioral strategies of Players 2 and 1, respectively, at their opening moves of the game).

Bargaining in Repeated Crises: A Limited Information Model

James D. Morrow

International crises are not isolated events. The outcome of one crisis affects whether a second crisis occurs between the same nations. Some issues (e.g., Fashoda) are resolved by one crisis while other issues (e.g., Berlin) produce repeated crises. How do repeated crises differ from isolated crises? Empirical studies of repeated crises (e.g., Leng 1983; Diehl 1985) find that later crises in a set of repeated crises are more likely to lead to war than isolated crises.

Repeated crises create the possibility of reputation building (Kreps and Wilson 1982b); each side may draw lessons about its opponent's resolve from an earlier crisis. In the Munich crisis, for example, England destroyed its reputation for resolve in the eyes of the Germans by submitting to Hitler's demands. How can reputations arise in repeated crises?

Because reputations are inherently unobservable, formal models are a useful tool to analyze their origins and effects. Reputations require incomplete information; the parties must hold some private information about which the other side forms beliefs. One side's beliefs give the other side's reputation. By taking actions that influence the other side's beliefs, actors can build or destroy reputations. Any model of repeated crises that attempts to explain reputations must include incomplete information.

A model of repeated crises must also capture the dynamics of each individual crisis. The parties in a crisis exchange threats accompanied by offers to settle the dispute. Each side assesses the relative attractiveness of the current offer and a counteroffer when choosing their response to an offer. Crises end when either one side accepts the offer on the table or war breaks out. Modeling this strategic interaction requires a game theory model.

An earlier version of this paper was presented at the 1987 Annual Meeting of the American Political Science Association in Chicago, Illinois. I would like to thank Randy Calvert and Bob Powell for their comments on that earlier draft. This work was completed while the author was a National Fellow at the Hoover Institution, whose support I gratefully acknowledge.

Game theory models of crises must include at least three features to capture this process (cf. Wagner 1983). First, crisis bargaining is sequential; each side responds to the other's demands after learning of them and any threats attached to them. Second, the issue interests of the parties must be opposed, while they share an interest in avoiding war. Third, neither side should know for certain the outcome of a war before fighting begins, and the sides' expectations of the outcome of a war should differ. Each side's private information generates these different expectations and the possibility of reputations.

Elsewhere (Morrow, forthcoming), I have presented, solved, and discussed a model of crisis bargaining that includes the three features above. Each side has some private information about the state of their own military forces and an initial belief about the quality of their opponent's forces. Bargaining proceeds sequentially for two rounds before war begins. A sequential equilibrium of the model (Kreps and Wilson 1982a) illuminates the role of misperception in crises, how offers communicate resolve, and the importance of selection effects in the empirical study of crises.

This essay extends the previous model by adding the possibility of a second crisis. The outcome and the beliefs resulting from the first crisis create the initial conditions of the second. This model addresses the following questions: (1) How do repeated crises differ from isolated crises; (2) How do nations develop reputations for resolve; and (3) How should bargaining tactics change over a pair of crises?

The Isolated Crisis Model

The model of repeated crises is built by repeating the model of isolated crises in Morrow (forthcoming). This section presents that model and briefly discusses an equilibrium of it. The isolated crisis model reflects three conditions of crisis bargaining: sequential bargaining, conflicting interests on the issue at stake with a common interest in avoiding war, and uncertainty about the outcome of a war with the sides' expectations about war diverging.

Formally, there are three possible outcomes to the issue in dispute; 0—a victory for the defender, SQ—a moderate settlement at the status quo, and 1—a victory for the initiator. The status quo outcome is fixed at value SQ with $0 < SQ < 1$ and generally assumed to be close to ½. All offers in the isolated crisis model are restricted to one of these three values.

The game starts with three random draws, each resulting in either 0 or 1. If the sides cannot agree on a settlement by the last move of the game, the outcome of the three random draws will determine the outcome of the game (referred to as W in fig. 1). If two or three of the draws are 1, then 1 is the final outcome of an all-out war (i.e., $W = 1$). If none or one of the draws are 1, 0 is the final outcome if a war is fought to the bitter end. If the sides agree on a settlement, the offer accepted is the final outcome of the issue in dispute.

Two of the three draws produce the players' private information with each player seeing one draw. Nation i, the prospective initiator, sees a draw with probability λ for an outcome of 1 (probability $1 - \lambda$ for 0). The actual outcome of this draw is nation i's private information and will be referred to as I. Nation j will begin the game with a belief of λ that I equals 1. The higher λ is, the more likely that I equals 1, and so nation j's belief in the quality of nation i's forces increase with λ. Another draw has a probability of γ for an outcome of 1 ($1 - \gamma$ for an outcome of 0) and is seen only by nation j, the prospective target. The actual outcome of this draw will be referred to as J. Nation i will start the game with a belief of γ that J equals 1. Because draws of 0 improve nation j's chance of winning a war, nation i's belief in the quality of nation j's forces increases as γ decreases. The third draw, called L, has a ½ chance of an outcome of 1, and the result is kept secret from both sides at the start of the game.

Neither side can determine the outcome of a war before it begins because it can observe only one of the three draws. Each side does know γ and λ and their private information, so they can calculate their (subjective) probability of winning a war. Further, these initial estimates will differ (nation i's probability of victory after seeing its private information but before the bargaining starts is $\frac{1}{2}\gamma + \frac{1}{2}I$; nation j's probability for i winning is $\frac{1}{2}\lambda + \frac{1}{2}J$). If i has seen 1 or j seen 0 in its private draw, we will say that it possesses an advantage—its private information is favorable. Nation i is more likely to possess an advantage as λ increases, and nation j is more likely to possess an advantage as γ decreases.

The sequential bargaining game analyzed here structures the choices of the two sides (see fig. 1). One counteroffer by the defender follows the initial offer by the initiator before the initiator must choose between war and accepting the counteroffer. If war begins, the defender must choose between accepting an early settlement or continuing the war to the bitter end.

After the initial draw, the initiator, nation i, must decide whether or not to initiate a crisis. If nation i does not initiate a crisis, the status quo will continue. If i initiates a crisis, then it must submit an offer to nation j. This offer will be referred to as Ω_1 henceforth and like all offers in the game is restricted to the set of 0, SQ, and 1. If nation i does not make an offer at this move, no crisis has occurred.

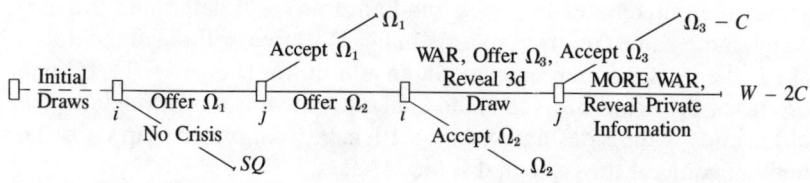

Fig. 1. A branch of the extensive game form of the model. Technically, this diagram should have four branches at each of the first three decision modes, one for accepting the previous offer and one for each of the three possible offers. The complete diagram of the game includes eight branches like the above repeated twice; each branch following from one of the eight possible initial draws; each repetition gives one stage of the game. For the first three moves in both crises, each player has two information sets, reflecting its ignorance of the other player's draw and the third draw. For the final move of either crisis, j has four information sets because j knows both its draw and the third draw. In the second crisis, each player has four information sets if the first crisis has gone to all-out war because both players' private information will have been revealed.

In the second move, nation j must respond to nation i's initial offer. It will update its beliefs about whether or not nation i possesses an advantage, call these new beliefs $\bar{\lambda}$. Nation j can accept Ω_1 or reject it and make a counteroffer, which will be referred to as Ω_2. Acceptance of Ω_1 terminates the crisis with an outcome equal to Ω_1.

A counteroffer of Ω_2 leads to a final chance to avoid war and its costs for nation i. Nation i's updated beliefs about whether or not j possesses an advantage will be given by $\bar{\gamma}$. If nation i accepts Ω_2, the crisis ends short of war with an outcome of Ω_2. If nation i rejects that offer, war will result, and each side must pay the costs of war, C_i for nation i and C_j for nation j. These costs are assumed to be small relative to the policy disagreement between i and j, specifically, $0 < C_i, C_j < 1/3$. Nation i will also make one final offer, Ω_3, if it rejects Ω_2. After Ω_3 is made, the third draw, L, is revealed to both sides, representing the information about the final outcome provided by the initial course of combat.

The final decision whether or not to continue the war rests in the hands of nation j. Once again, nation j will update its beliefs about nation i's forces, producing $\bar{\bar{\lambda}}$. Nation j can accept Ω_3, ending the war with each side paying costs once or it can continue the war. If nation j continues the war, each side pays the costs of war a second time, all private information is revealed, and the majority of the three draws determines the outcome.

Nation i prefers higher outcomes, deriving utility equal to the value of the outcome minus any costs of war. For example, if nation i offers 1 for Ω_3 and nation j accepts, i's utility for the outcome would be $1 - C_i$ (1 for the agreement minus C_i costs of war). Nation j prefers lower outcomes; deriving utility equal to the opposite of the outcome minus any costs of war. Continuing the above example, j's utility for the outcome would be $-1 - C_j$ (-1 for the agreement minus C_j costs of war). Both sides have identical interests because their values for the outcomes are exactly opposite. This restriction on model focuses the analysis on the effects of uncertainty about military capabilities.

This model captures three essential elements of crisis bargaining. First, the bargaining is sequential between the parties. Second, their interests are opposed; victory for one is defeat for the other. Still, they share an interest in avoiding the costs of war. Third, both sides possess some private information about the outcome of a war, but neither side knows for certain the outcome of a war before it begins.

Morrow (forthcoming) presents an equilibrium of this model that falls into four cases depending upon the initial beliefs of the two sides. Figure 2 presents the boundaries of the four cases as functions of the status quo and the costs of war. In the first case, nation i holds military preponderance over nation j; i is likely to possess an advantage and j is unlikely to possess an advantage. The costs of war determine how large this apparent military superiority must be; the higher j's costs and the lower i's costs, the less the edge required. Nation i will always initiate a crisis in Case 1. If j does possess an advantage, it will resist i's demands and offer a moderate settlement ($\Omega_2 = SQ$). If j does not possess an advantage, it will bluff by resisting some of the time and accept i's initial demands (Ω_1) the remainder of the time. Nation i will accept j's moderate offer short of war unless i possesses an advantage, in which case i will go to war some of the time. These crises are driven by i's probable military superiority; j will generally accept i's demands and if j does not, i will back off before war in most cases.

In the second case, nation i always initiates a crisis. Nation j's responses signal exactly whether or not j possesses an advantage; if j does not, it accepts i's demands; if j does, it resists and demands concessions beyond the status quo (i.e., $\Omega_2 = 0$). Nation i will reject j's demand and begin a war if it possesses an advantage. If i does not possess an advantage, it will generally grant j's demand for concessions. If war should break out, j will continue it unless the random draw is unfavorable to j. This case is also driven by i's expected military advantage, but i is not as likely to possess an advantage as in the first case. Consequently, j is willing to resist i's demands and make demands of its own if its own

212   Models of Strategic Choice in Politics

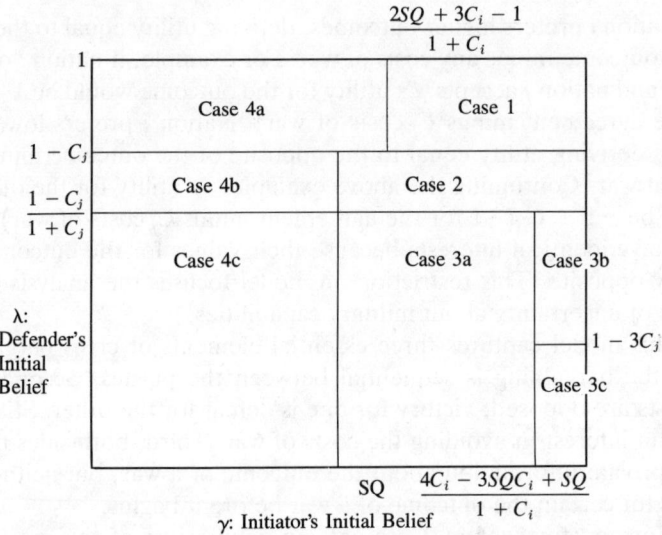

Probabilities of Crisis and War

Case	p(Crisis)	p(War)
1	1	$\frac{SQ(1+C_i)}{2(SQ+C_j)(1-SQ-C_i)}(1-\gamma)$
2	1	$\frac{1}{1-C_j}\lambda(1-\gamma)$
3a	$\frac{1+C_j}{1-C_j}\lambda$	$\frac{1-SQ}{1-C_j}\lambda$
3b	1	$\frac{1+C_i}{(1-3C_i)(1+3C_j)}(1-\gamma)(2-\lambda)$
3c	1	1
4a, 4b, 4c	0	0

Fig. 2. The probability of a crisis and war for isolated crises

forces are better than they appear (i.e., it holds an advantage). As a result of j's increased willingness to resist i's demands, war is more likely in this case than the first.

The third case covers situations where neither side believes the other has an advantage. Each side is confident in its position because it believes the other side is weak and will back down. They aggressively push their demands, hoping the other side will cave in. When either side possesses an advantage in this case, it will always refuse any compromise and press its demands. When a side does not possess an advantage, it will give in to the other side some of the time and bluff (i.e., press its demands) the rest of the time. Each side plays hard to force cheap concessions because they believe the other side does not possess an advantage. Only the likely weakness of both sides and the costs of war restrain the eruption of war.

The fourth case is the noncase; no crises occur under these conditions. Nation i never initiates a crisis because it cannot hope to gain. In cases 4a and 4b, both sides believe their opponent possesses an advantage, so both sides are happy to settle for the status quo. Deterrence holds because both sides understand and accept that the other's forces make winning a war chancy and that both sides are sufficiently confident in their forces that they are very likely to resist demands. Further, i is unwilling to start a crisis because j will never grant concessions to i in lieu of war. In Case 4c, j holds a superior military position on paper, and i will not challenge j because j will demand concessions to end the resulting crisis.

The Repeated Crises Model

The repeated crises model focuses on how the anticipation of a second crisis affects the sides' actions in the first. The isolated crisis model represents the second crisis with the first crisis given by a variation of it. The outcome of the first crisis determines the status quo position and the sides' initial beliefs in the second crisis. The importance of the outcome of the first crisis relative to the second is varied by changing the spread of the outcomes in the first crisis relative to the second. The structure of the bargaining in the second crisis is identical to the first except that the losing side in the first crisis initiates the second. Each side's payoff for the entire game is given by the sum of their payoffs from each of the two crises.

The outcome of the issue in dispute in the first crisis is restricted to one of three values; $1 - m$, victory for the initiator, SQ, the status quo, and m, victory for the defender. The value of m denotes the importance of the first crisis relative to the second. As the value of m grows, the importance of the first crisis decreases because the spread of possible outcomes decreases. M is assumed to fall between C_i and $SQ - C_j$ and generally be in the neighborhood of $(1 - SQ)/2$. When $m = (1 - SQ)/2$, the two crises are equally important. At that value, i will be indifferent between winning the first crisis with $1 - m$ holding as the outcome of the second and waiting for the second crisis to initiate and winning then (i.e., $2[1 - ((1 - SQ)/2] = SQ + 1)$. As the status quo is generally close to ½, the first crisis is more important than the second when $m < ¼$, and the second more important when $m > ¼$.

The outcome of the first crisis is the status quo for the second. However, the outcome of the second crisis is still restricted to 0, SQ, or 1. If the outcome of the first crisis is $1 - m$, then nation j becomes the initiator for the second crisis because it lost the first crisis. If the outcome of the first crisis is m or SQ, then nation i has the option of initiating the second crisis. Each side's beliefs at the end of the first crisis are carried over and define their initial beliefs for the second crisis; these beliefs will be denoted by γ' and λ' for nations i and j respectively. If j loses the first crisis, its beliefs are still denoted by λ' even though it initiates the second crisis. The third draw L, representing the random factors in war, are redrawn after the completion of the first crisis.

Summing the results for each separate crisis gives a side's total payoff for the two crises together. For example, if the first crisis ends in a victory for the initiator after one round of fighting and the second crisis ends in the original status quo before the war, nation i's payoff is $1 - m + SQ - C_i$ ($1 - m - C_i$ for the first crisis and SQ for the second).

The model allows us to analyze how bargaining in multiple crises differs from bargaining in an isolated crisis. The following three questions will be addressed with the model: First, under what conditions can repeated crises occur? Because bargaining transmits information, when will enough information be exchanged to resolve the conflict? Second, how do nations develop (or destroy) reputations for resolve from crisis to crisis? Third, how does bargaining behavior differ in repeated crises as opposed to isolated crises? By comparing bargaining and beliefs in the first and second stages of the model, we can analyze these differences.

Equilibrium Behavior in the Model

To solve the model, we find a sequential equilibrium (Kreps and Wilson 1982a) to the game. Equilibria consist of two elements, beliefs and strategies. Each side's beliefs give the probability the other side possesses an advantage at each node of the game, and the strategies specify the probability of playing each possible move for every node of the game tree. Beliefs are consistent with the strategies; both sides' initial beliefs are updated using Bayes's Law and the probabilities of observed moves in the equilibrium strategies. The strategies are optimal given the beliefs and the other player's strategy; neither player can improve its expected outcome by changing its stragegy.

Before presenting the equilibrium, we give seven different second crises for reference. These cases are drawn from Morrow (forthcoming), as any second crisis is just some case of that model. In some of these cases, the status quo point may be m or $1 - m$ and j may move first because of the outcome of the first crisis. If not noted at the start of a case, the status quo at the start of the second crisis is SQ and i has the first move.

Case 1.

$$\gamma' = \gamma > \frac{2SQ + 3C_i - 1}{1 + C_i} \quad \text{and} \quad \lambda' = \lambda > 1 - C_j.$$

First move: $\Omega_1 = 1$. Second move: $\bar{\lambda} = \lambda'$. If $J = 1$, accept Ω_1 with probability $[\gamma(1 + C_i) + 1 - 2SQ - 3C_i]/[2\gamma(1 - SQ - C_i)]$, otherwise, $\Omega_2 = SQ$. Third move: $\bar{\gamma} = [2SQ + 3C_i - 1]/[1 + C_i]$. If $I = 1$, $\Omega_3 = 1$ with probability $SQ/\lambda(SQ + C_j)$; otherwise accept Ω_2. Fourth move: $\bar{\bar{\lambda}} = 1$. Accept Ω_3 unless $J = L = 1$.

Case 2a.

$$\gamma' > SQ \quad \text{and} \quad \frac{1 - C_j}{1 + C_j} < \lambda' < 1 - C_j.$$

First move: If $I = 1$, $\Omega_1 = 1$; if $I = 0$, initiate with probability $[2(SQ - m) - \lambda SQ]/SQ(1 - \lambda)$. Second move: $\bar{\lambda} = \lambda SQ/2(SQ - m)$. If $J = 0$, $\Omega_2 = 0$; if $J = 1$, accept Ω_1. Third move: If $\Omega_2 = 0$, $\bar{\gamma} = 0$. If $I = 0$, accept Ω_2 with probability $[2(SQ - m) - \lambda(SQ + C_j)]/[2(SQ - m) - \lambda SQ]$; $\Omega_3 = 1$ otherwise. If $\Omega_2 = SQ$, $\bar{\gamma} = 1$. If $I = 0$, accept Ω_2 with probability $[2(SQ - m) - \lambda(SQ + C_j)]/[2(SQ - m) - \lambda SQ]$; $\Omega_3 = 1$ otherwise. Fourth move: $\bar{\bar{\lambda}} = 1 - C_j$. $L = 1$, accept Ω_3 with probability $4C_i/[1 + C_i]$; reject Ω_3 otherwise. If $\Omega_3 = SQ$, $\bar{\bar{\lambda}} = 0$. Reject Ω_3 unless $J = L = 1$.

Case 3d. $\gamma' = \gamma$ and $\lambda' = 0$. First move: i never initiates. Second move: $\bar{\lambda} = 0$. $\Omega_2 = SQ$. Third move: $\bar{\gamma} = \gamma$. Accept Ω_2. Fourth move: $\bar{\bar{\lambda}} = 0$. Accept Ω_3 only if $J = L = 1$.

Case 4a.

$$\gamma' < \frac{2SQ + 3C_i - 1}{1 + C_i} \quad \text{and} \quad \lambda' > 1 - C_j.$$

First move: i never initiates. Second move: $\bar{\lambda} = \lambda$. $\Omega_2 = SQ$. Third move: $\bar{\gamma} = \gamma$. Accept $\Omega_2 = SQ$; $\Omega_3 = 1$ otherwise. Fourth move: $\bar{\bar{\lambda}} = \lambda$. Accept Ω_3 unless $J = L = 0$.

Case 4c.

$$\gamma' < SQ \quad \text{and} \quad \lambda' < \frac{1 - C_j}{1 + C_j}.$$

First move: i never initiates. Second move: $\bar{\lambda} = \lambda$. If $J = 1$, $\Omega_2 = SQ$; if $J = 0$, $\Omega_2 = 0$. Third move: If $\Omega_2 = 0$, $\bar{\gamma} = 0$. If $I = 0$, accept Ω_2 with probability $[1 - \lambda - C_j]/[(1 - \lambda)(1 - C_j)]$; $\Omega_3 = 1$ otherwise. If $\Omega_2 = SQ$, $\bar{\gamma} = 1$. If $I = 0$, accept Ω_2 with probability $[1 - \lambda - C_j]/(1 - \lambda)(1 - C_j)$; $\Omega_3 = 1$ otherwise. Fourth move: $\bar{\lambda} = 1 - C_j$. If $J = 0$, accept Ω_3 with probability $4C_i/[1 + C_i]$ when $L = 0$. If $J = 1$, accept Ω_3 with probability $[2SQ + 3C_i - 1]/[1 + C_i]$ when $L = 1$. Reject Ω_3 otherwise.

Case 4d. $\gamma' = 1$, $\lambda' < m$, j has the first move, and $SQ = 1 - m$. First move: j never initiates. Second move: $\bar{\gamma} = 1$. $\Omega_2 = 1$. Third move: $\bar{\lambda} = \lambda$. Accept Ω_2. Fourth move: $\bar{\bar{\gamma}} = 1$. Accept Ω_3 only if $I = L = 0$.

Case 4e. $\gamma' = 0$, $\lambda' = 0$, and $SQ = m$. First move: i never initiates. Second move: $\bar{\lambda} = 0$. $\Omega_2 = 0$. Third move: $\bar{\gamma} = \gamma$. Accept Ω_2. Fourth move: $\bar{\bar{\lambda}} = 0$. Accept Ω_3 only if $J = L = 1$.

Now we present the equilibrium of the repeated crises model in all its gory detail. The equilibrium for the first crisis is given below. For all possible resolutions of the first crisis, the resulting second crisis is given by specifying the case above that corresponds to it. Cases are labeled by letters that correspond to the parallel cases in the isolated crisis game (i.e., cases A and 1 parallel each other). For those who do not wish to plow through the full equilibrium, an informal description of equilibrium behavior is given afterward.

PROPOSITION: *The following belief-strategy pairing is a sequential equilibrium of the repeated bargaining game:*[1]

Case A-1.

$$\gamma > \frac{2SQ + 3C_i - 2}{1 + C_i}, \quad \lambda > \frac{2 - 4m - C_j}{2 - 4m}, \quad \text{and} \quad m > \frac{C_i(2 - SQ)}{4SQ + 6C_i - 2}.$$

---

1. There are other sequential equilibria to this model. They generally involve bizarre beliefs off the equilibrium path. For example, nation i can force nation j to accept its initial offer by simply believing that if j does not accept it, they do not possess an advantage (i.e., $\bar{\gamma} = 0$). These beliefs allow i to escalate credibly, forcing j to accept the initial offer. In this model, we assume that neither side changes its beliefs when it observes an offer off the equilibrium path. They simply ignore defections and retain their prior beliefs about the opponent's type.

In the interest of preserving space, no proof of the equilibrium is provided. The cases follow from straightforward algebra similar to that given in the appendix of Morrow (forthcoming).

First Crisis: First move: $\Omega_1 = SQ$ (i.e., i does not initiate a crisis). Second move: $\bar{\lambda} = \lambda$. If $J = 1$, accept $\Omega_1 = 1 - m$; if $J = 0$, $\Omega_2 = m$. Third move: $\bar{\gamma} = 0$. $\Omega_3 = 1 - m$. Fourth move: $\bar{\lambda} = \lambda$. Accept Ω_3 unless $J = L = 0$. Second Crisis: If after the first move, $\gamma' = \gamma$ and $\lambda' = \lambda$; Case 1. If after second move, $\gamma' = 1$ and $\lambda' = \lambda$; Case 4d. If after fourth move, $\gamma' = 0$ and $\lambda' = \lambda$; Case 4a.

Case A-2.

$$\gamma > \frac{4SQ - 2 + 3C_i}{2 - 4m + C_i}, \; \lambda > \frac{2 - 4m - C_j}{2 - 4m}, \; \text{and} \; m < \frac{C_i(2 - SQ)}{4SQ + 6C_i - 2}.$$

First Crisis: First move: $\Omega_1 = 1 - m$. Second move: $\bar{\lambda} = \lambda$. If $J = 1$, accept Ω_1 with probability $[\gamma(2 - 4m + C_i) - 4 + 4m + 4SQ + 2C_i]/\gamma(4SQ - 2 + 3C_i)$; otherwise, $\Omega_2 = m$. Third move: $\bar{\gamma} = [4SQ - 2 + 3C_i]/[2 - 4m + C_i]$. Accept Ω_2 with probability $C_j/[2SQ - 2m + C_j]$, otherwise, $\Omega_3 = 1 - m$. Fourth move: $\bar{\lambda} = \lambda$. Accept Ω_3 unless $J = L = 0$. Second Crisis: If after second move, $\gamma' = 1$ and $\lambda' = \lambda$; Case 4d. If after third move, $\gamma' = [4SQ - 2 + 3C_i]/[2 - 4m + C_i]$ and $\lambda' = \lambda$; Case 4a. If after fourth move, $\gamma' = [4SQ - 2 + 3C_i]/[2 - 4m + C_i]$ and $\lambda' = \lambda$; Case 4a.

Case B-1.

$$\gamma > \frac{SQ - m}{1 - 2m}, \; \frac{2 - 4m - C_j}{2 - 4m + C_j} < \lambda < \frac{2 - 4m - C_j}{2 - 4m}, \; \text{and} \; m > \frac{1}{4}.$$

First Crisis: First move: $\Omega_1 = 1 - m$. Second move: $\bar{\lambda} = \lambda$. Accept Ω_1 if $J = 1$ with probability $[\gamma - SQ]/[\gamma(1 - SQ)]$; otherwise, $\Omega_2 = SQ$. Third move: $\bar{\gamma} = SQ$. Accept Ω_2. Fourth move: $\bar{\lambda} = \lambda$. Accept only if $J = L = 1$. Second Crisis: If after second move, $\gamma' = 1$ and $\lambda' = \lambda$; Case 4d. If after third move, $\gamma' = SQ$ and $\lambda' = \lambda$; Case 2a. If after fourth move, $\gamma' = 1$ and $\lambda' = \lambda$; Case 4d.

Case B-2.

$$\gamma > \frac{SQ - m}{1 - 2m}, \; \frac{2 - 4m - C_j}{2 - 4m + C_j} < \lambda < \frac{2 - 4m - C_j}{2 - 4m}, \; \text{and} \; m < \frac{1}{4}.$$

First Crisis: First move: $\Omega_1 = 1 - m$. Second move: $\bar{\lambda} = \lambda$. If $J = 1$, accept Ω_1, if $J = 0$, $\Omega_2 = m$. Third move: $\bar{\gamma} = 0$. If $I = 0$, accept Ω_2 with probability $[(1 - \lambda)(2 - 4m - C_j) - 3C_j\lambda]/(1 - \lambda)(2 - 4m - C_j)$; otherwise, $\Omega_3 = 1 - m$. If $\Omega_2 = SQ$, $\bar{\gamma} = 1$. If $I = 0$, accept Ω_2 with probability $[(1 - \lambda)(2 - 4m - C_j) - 3C_j\lambda]/(1 - \lambda)(2 - 4m - C_j)$;

otherwise, $\Omega_3 = 1 - m$. Fourth move: $\bar{\lambda} = [2 - 4m - C_j]/[2 - 4m]$. If $\Omega_2 = m$, $J = 0$, and $L = 1$, accept Ω_3 with probability $2C_i/[2 - 3C_i]$. If $\Omega_2 = SQ$, accept Ω_3 when $J \neq L$ with probability $[4SQ - 2 + 3C_i]/[2 - 4m + C_i]$. Second Crisis: If after second move, $\gamma' = 1$ and $\lambda' = \lambda$; Case 4d. If after third move, $\gamma' = 0$ and $\lambda' = 0$; Case 4e. If after fourth move, $\gamma' = 1$ and $\lambda' = \lambda$; Case 4d.

Case C-1.

$$\frac{SQ - m}{1 - 2m} < \gamma < \frac{2C_i(1 - m - SQ) + (SQ - m)(2 - 4m + C_i)}{(1 - 2m)(2 - 4m + C_i)}$$

and $\lambda < \dfrac{2 - 4m - C_j}{2 - 4m + C_j}$.

First Crisis: First move: If $I = 1$, $\Omega_1 = 1 - m$, if $I = 0$, $\Omega_1 = 1 - m$ with probability $2\lambda C_j/(1 - \lambda)(2 - 4m - C_j)$. Second move: $\bar{\lambda} = [2 - 4m - C_j]/[2 - 4m + C_j]$. If $J = 1$, accept Ω_1 with probability $[SQ - m]/\gamma(1 - 2m)$; otherwise $\Omega_2 = m$. Third move: $\bar{\gamma} = [\gamma(1 - 2m) - SQ + m]/[1 - m - SQ]$. If $I = 0$, accept Ω_2 with probability ½, otherwise, $\Omega_3 = 1 - m$. Fourth move: $\bar{\lambda} = [2 - 4m - C_j]/[2 - 4m]$. Accept Ω_3 if $J = 1$; if $J = 0$ and $L = 1$, accept Ω_3 with probability

$$\frac{2(2C_i(1 - m - SQ) - [\gamma(1 - 2m) - SQ + m][2 - 4m + C_i])}{(1 - \gamma)(1 - 2m)(2 - 4m + C_i)};$$

reject Ω_3 otherwise. Second Crisis: If after second move, $\gamma' = 1$ and $\lambda' = [2 - 4m - C_j]/[2 - 4m + C_j]$; Case 4d. If after third move, $\gamma' = [\gamma(1 - 2m) - SQ + m]/[1 - m - SQ]$ and $\lambda' = 0$; Case 4e. If after fourth move, $\gamma' \leq [\gamma(1 - 2m) - SQ + m]/[1 - m - SQ]$ and $\lambda' = [2 - 4m - C_j]/[2 - 4m]$; Case 4d.

Case C-2.

$$\frac{2C_i(1 - m - SQ) + (SQ - m)(2 - 4m + C_i)}{(1 - 2m)(2 - 4m + C_i)} < \gamma < \frac{4C_i}{2 - 4m + C_i}$$

and $\lambda < \dfrac{2 - 4m - C_j}{2 - 4m + C_j}$.

First Crisis: First move: If $I = 1$, $\Omega_1 = 1 - m$; if $I = 0$, $\Omega_1 = 1 - m$ with probability $2\lambda C_j/(1 - \lambda)(2 - 4m - C_j)$. Second move: $\bar{\lambda} = [2 - 4m - C_j]/$

$[2 - 4m + C_j]$. If $J = 1$, accept Ω_1 with probability $[SQ - m]/\gamma(1 - 2m)$; otherwise $\Omega_2 = m$. Third move: $\bar{\gamma} = [\gamma(1 - 2m) - SQ + m]/[1 - m - SQ]$. If $I = 0$, accept Ω_2 with probability ½, otherwise, $\Omega_3 = 1 - m$. Fourth move: $\bar{\lambda} = [2 - 4m - C_j]/[2 - 4m]$. Accept Ω_3 if $J = 1$; if $J = 0$ and $L = 1$, accept Ω_3 with probability

$$\frac{4C_i(1 - m - SQ) - [\gamma(1 - 2m) - SQ + m][2 - 4m + C_i]}{(\gamma[1 - 2m] - SQ + m)(2 - 4m + C_i)};$$

reject Ω_3 otherwise. Second Crisis: If after second move, $\gamma' = 1$ and $\lambda' = [2 - 4m - C_j]/[2 - 4m + C_j]$; Case 4d. If after third move, $\gamma' = [\gamma(1 - 2m) - SQ + m]/[1 - m - SQ]$ and $\lambda' = 0$; Case 4e. If after fourth move, $\gamma' \leq [\gamma(1 - 2m) - SQ + m]/[1 - m - SQ]$ and $\lambda' = [2 - 4m - C_j]/[2 - 4m]$; Case 4d.

Case C-3.

$$\gamma > \frac{4C_i}{2 - 4m + C_i} \quad \text{and} \quad \lambda < \frac{2 - 4m - 3C_j}{2 - 4m}.$$

First Crisis: First move: $\Omega_1 = 1 - m$. Second move: $\bar{\lambda} = \lambda$. $\Omega_2 = m$. Third move: $\bar{\gamma} = \gamma$. $\Omega_3 = 1 - m$. Fourth move: $\bar{\lambda} = \lambda$. Accept Ω_3 only if $J = L = 1$. Second Crisis: If after second move, $\gamma' = 1$ and $\lambda' = \lambda$; Case 4d. If after third move, $\gamma' = \gamma$ and $\lambda' = 0$; Case 4e. If after fourth move, $\gamma' = 1$ and $\lambda' = \lambda$; Case 4d.

Case C-4.

$$\gamma > \frac{4C_i}{2 - 4m + C_i} \quad \text{and} \quad \frac{2 - 4m - 3C_j}{2 - 4m} < \lambda < \frac{2 - 4m - C_j}{2 - 4m + C_j}.$$

First Crisis: First move: $\Omega_1 = 1 - m$. Second move: $\bar{\lambda} = \lambda$. If $J = 1$, accept Ω_1 with probability $[\gamma(2 - 4m + C_i) - 4C_i]/[\gamma(2 - 4m - 3C_i)]$; otherwise, $\Omega_2 = m$. Third move: $\bar{\gamma} = 4C_j/[2 - 4m + C_j]$. If $I = 0$, accept Ω_2 with probability $[3C_j - (1 - \lambda)(2 - 4m)]/(1 - \lambda)(2 - 4m + 3C_j)$; otherwise, $\Omega_3 = 1 - m$. Fourth move: $\bar{\lambda} = [\lambda(2 - 4m + 3C_j)]/[2(2 - \lambda)(1 - 2m)]$. Accept Ω_3 only if $J = L = 1$. Second Crisis: If after second move, $\gamma' = 1$ and $\lambda' = \lambda$; Case 4d. If after third move, $\gamma' = \gamma$ and $\lambda' = 0$; Case 4e. If after fourth move, $\gamma' = 1$ and $\lambda' = \lambda$; Case 4d.

Case D-1.

$$\gamma < \frac{4SQ - 2 + 3C_i}{2 - 4m + C_i} \left[\text{if } m < \frac{C_i(2 - SQ)}{4SQ + 6C_i - 2} \right]$$

$$\text{or } < \frac{2SQ + 3C_i - 2}{1 + C_i} \left[\text{if } m > \frac{C_i(2 - SQ)}{4SQ + 6C_i - 2} \right]$$

$$\text{and } \lambda > \frac{2 - 4m - C_j}{2 - 4m}.$$

First Crisis: First move: i never initiates. Second move: $\bar{\lambda} = \lambda$. $\Omega_2 = SQ$. Third move: $\bar{\gamma} = \gamma$. Accept Ω_3. Fourth move: Reject Ω_3 if $L = 0$; accept Ω_3 otherwise. Second Crisis: After the first, third, or fourth moves, $\gamma' = \gamma$ and $\lambda' = \lambda$; Case 4a.

Case D-2.

$$\gamma < \frac{SQ - m}{1 - 2m} \quad \text{and} \quad \frac{2 - 4m - C_j}{2 - 4m + C_j} < \lambda < \frac{2 - 4m - C_j}{2 - 4m}.$$

First Crisis: First move: i never initiates. Second move: $\bar{\lambda} = \lambda$. $\Omega_2 = SQ$. Third move: $\bar{\gamma} = \gamma$. Accept Ω_3. Fourth move: Accept Ω_3 if $J = L = 1$; reject Ω_3 otherwise. Second Crisis: After the first or third moves, $\gamma' = \gamma$ and $\lambda' = \lambda$; Case 4b. After the fourth move, $\gamma' = 1$ and $\lambda' = \lambda$; Case 4d.

Case D-3.

$$\gamma < \frac{SQ - m}{1 - 2m} \quad \text{and} \quad \lambda < \frac{2 - 4m - C_j}{2 - 4m + C_j}.$$

First Crisis: First move: i never initiates. Second move: $\bar{\lambda} = \lambda$. If $J = 0$, $\Omega_2 = m$; if $J = 1$, $\Omega_2 = SQ$. Third move: If $\Omega_2 = m$, $\bar{\gamma} = 0$. If $I = 0$, accept Ω_2 with probability $[2 - 4m - \lambda(2 - 4m + C_j)]/[(1 - \lambda)(2 - 4m)]$, $\Omega_3 = 1 - m$ otherwise. If $\Omega_2 = SQ$, $\bar{\gamma} = 1$. If $I = 0$, accept Ω_2 with probability $[2 - 4m - \lambda(2 - 4m + C_j)]/(1 - \lambda)(2 - 4m)$; $\Omega_3 = 1 - m$ otherwise. Fourth move: $\bar{\lambda} = [2 - 4m - C_j]/[2 - 4m]$. If $J = 0$, accept Ω_3 with probability $4C_i/[2 - 4m + C_i]$ when $L = 1$, reject Ω_3 otherwise. If $J = 1$, reject Ω_3 with probability $4(1 - SQ - C_i)/[2 - 4m + C_i]$ when $L = 0$, accept Ω_3 otherwise. Second Crisis: After first move, $\gamma' = \gamma$ and $\lambda' = \lambda$; Case 4c. After third move when $\Omega_2 = SQ$, $\gamma' = 1$ and $\lambda' = 0$; Case 3d. After third move when $\Omega_2 = m$, $\gamma' = 0$ and $\lambda' = 0$; Case 4e.

The equilibrium of the repeated crisis model falls into four general cases that roughly correspond to four cases in the isolated crisis model.

Figure 3 gives the location of each of these four cases as a function of the initial beliefs, the value of the status quo, and the costs of war. Each of these cases represents general families of crises based on the strategic situation the parties face.

The first case, labeled Case A, covers situations where nation i is very likely to hold an advantage and nation j is unlikely to hold an advantage. Case A falls into two possibilities based on the importance of the first crisis relative to the second. When the first crisis is more important than the second (Case A-2), the first crisis parallels Case 1 of the isolated crisis model. The initiator pushes for concessions which the target will generally grant. If the defender resists the demands of the initiator, the initiator will generally back off. If the initiator possesses an advantage, it will start a war.

However, if the second crisis is more important than the first (Case A-1), the initiator will simply wait for the second crisis. If the initiator were to start the first crisis, j is likely to grant its demands, preventing the initiator from demanding further concessions in the second, more crucial crisis. Consequently, all initiators ignore the initial opportunity to flex their military muscle and wait for the second crisis.

In the second case (cases B-1 and B-2), nation i is less likely to hold an advantage. The initiator still has a pronounced military advantage, but not as wide as in Case A. This case also falls into two subcases based on the relative importance of the two crises. If the first crisis is more important (Case B-2 where $m < \frac{1}{4}$), the first crisis will resolve the dispute as in Case A-2.

When the second crisis is more important than the first (Case B-1), nation i uses the first crisis as a probe of j's resolve. Sometimes defenders without advantages will submit in the first crisis here. Because the initiator no longer holds a vast military superiority over the defender, its value for the second crisis is less, so i is happy to test j's resolve in the first crisis even though j's submission freezes the outcome at $1 - m$. If nation j resists i's demands in the initial crisis, i will always back off and wait for the second crisis to renew its demands. If i does not hold an advantage, it will initiate the second crisis some of the time. Of course, if i possesses an advantage, it will always initiate the second crisis. The second crisis, when it occurs, is Case 2 in the isolated crisis model; if the defender holds an advantage, it is very likely to escalate to war.

The third case, cases C-1, C-2, C-3, and C-4, covers situations where each side believes the other does not hold an advantage. Each side will demand concessions in the hope that if the other side does not possess an advantage, it will back down. Then war is relatively likely in the first crisis here. However, a second crisis never occurs here because if one side grants the other's demands short of war, it signals to the other

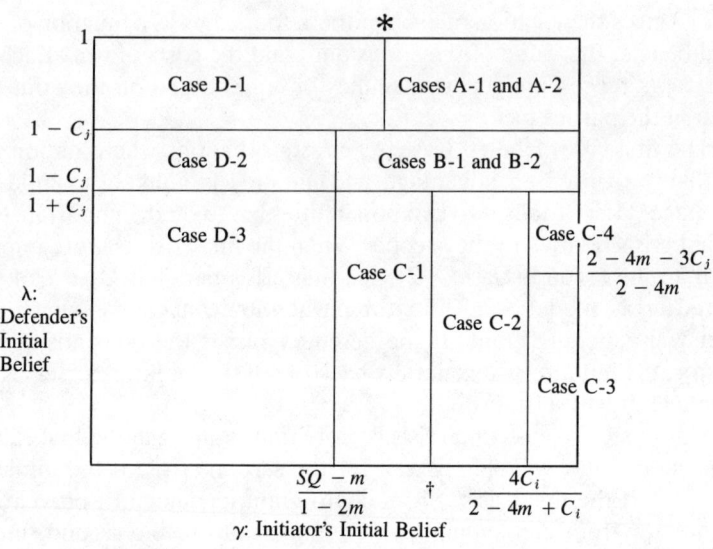

$* = \frac{2SQ+3C_i-1}{1+C_i}$ for Case A-1 and $\frac{4SQ-2+3C_i}{2-4m+C_i}$ for Case A-2

$\dagger = \frac{2C_i(1-m-SQ)+(SQ-m)(2-4m+C_i)}{(1-2m)(2-4m+C_j)}$

Probabilities of Crises and War

Case	p(1st crisis)	p(war | 1st crisis)	p(2d crisis)	p(war | 2d crisis)
A-1 (m > $\frac{C_i(2-SQ)}{4SQ+6C_i-2}$)	0	0	1	$\frac{SQ(1+C_i)(1-\gamma)}{2(SQ+C_i)(1-SQ-C}$
A-2 (m > $\frac{C_i(2-SQ)}{4SQ+6C_i-2}$)	1	$\frac{4(1-\gamma)(2-2m-2SQ-C_i)(SQ-m)}{\gamma(2SQ-2m+C_i)(4SQ-2+3C_i)}$	0	0
B-1 (m > $\frac{1}{4}$)	1	0	$\frac{2(SQ-m)}{SQ(1-SQ)}(1-\gamma)$	$\frac{1}{1-C_j}\lambda(1-\gamma)$
B-2 (m < $\frac{1}{4}$)	1	$\frac{2-4m+2C_j}{2-4m-C_j}\lambda(1-\gamma)$	0	0
C-1, C-2	$\frac{2-4m+C_j}{2-4m-C_j}\lambda$	$\frac{2(1-SQ-m)}{2-4m+C_j}$	0	0
C-3	1	1	0	0
C-4	1	$\frac{(1-\gamma)(2-\lambda)(2-4m)(2-4m+C_i)}{(2-4m+3C_j)(2-4m-3C_i)}$	0	0
D-1, D-2, D-3	0	0	0	0

Fig. 3. The probability of crises and war for repeated crises

that it does not possess an advantage. It cannot hope to regain any of its losses by renewing the conflict, so it does not. If neither backs down, war results and both sides learn each other's capabilities from combat.

The fourth case, cases D-1, D-2, and D-3, is a case of no crises. In cases D-1 and D-2, each side believes that the other possesses an advantage. Neither side will grant concessions then, so the motivation for initiating a crisis, the hope of gaining concessions short of war, is eliminated. These are cases of stable deterrence; each side knows the other will resist and that war is unlikely to provide victory. Case D-3 covers the situation where nation j is likely to hold an advantage and nation i unlikely. Nation i never starts a crisis because it never expects to gain by doing so.

Discussion

The first question the model is designed to address concerns when repeated crises can occur. Repeated crises occur in only Case B-1 of the model. The probability of a second crisis there is $2(SQ - m)(1 - \gamma)/SQ(1 - SQ)$. Repeated crises can occur in the model when the initiator is more likely to possess an advantage than not and the defender unlikely if the initial crisis is seen as less important than the second. Within that case, the probability of a second crisis rises as the initiator becomes less likely to hold an advantage. The decrease in the defender's beliefs that the initiator possesses an advantage encourages it to resist the initiator's initial demands more often.

Repeated crises are most likely when the initiator's forces appear to be stronger than the defender's forces but not overwhelmingly so. The probability the initiator will win a war before the draws are made, $\frac{1}{2}(\gamma + \lambda)$, measures the distribution of measurable capabilities between the two sides. This probability is the best judgment of an outside observer that the initiator would win a war and gives the balance of observable capabilities between the sides. The value of this probability depends on the boundaries of Case B, with the smallest values at the lower left corner of the case. Both boundaries decrease as m and C_j increase; when costs are high and the first crisis insignificant compared to the second, the probability of the initiator winning a war can drop as low as ½. Given that repeated crises are more likely as γ decreases (within Case B-1), the balance of observed capabilities in the set of repeated crises should tend to show the initiator with superior, but not overwhelmingly superior, forces.

Further, repeated crises require that both sides hold reservations about the quality of the other's forces. For example, there are cases with similar probabilities of victory in Case D-1 as those in Case B-1, but the former do not produce a first crisis, much less a second crisis. There both sides are convinced the other's forces are strong, leading the other side to resist any demand. In repeated crises, both sides must possess sufficient doubts about the other's forces to make them willing to test each other's resolve twice.

The critical factor in triggering repeated crises is a first crisis over a relatively minor issue. Repeated crises become more likely as m increases even though the probability of any given crisis recurring decreases as m increases (i.e., $[\partial p(\text{2nd crisis})]/\partial m < 0$). As m decreases, the set of crises that fall in Case B-1 expands, and this expansion of candidate repeated crises more than compensates for the decreased probability of each individual crisis recurring.[2]

The set of repeated crises then is very different from the set of isolated crises. Most of the cases in the model here produce isolated crises rather than repeated crises. The model predicts that repeated crises require the initiator to hold a military advantage over the defender and that the initial dispute be less important than the second. Furthermore, repeated crises should be more likely as the costs of war increase and as the status quo becomes more favorable to the initiator.

Turning to the second question, reputations can only rarely be built in the game, but they are easily destroyed. In some cases (cases D-1, D-2, and D-3), the defender already has a sufficiently strong reputation to deter the initiator, so it never has to develop its reputation. In the other situations, sides cannot really build a reputation in the game, but if they submit short of war in the first crisis, they lose all credibility in the second. In cases C-1, C-2, and C-4, whenever a side grants the other side's demands, it establishes that it does not possess an advantage. In the cases where a second crisis is possible, neither side is capable of building the reputation needed to deter the other. Only in Case A-2 can a side build a reputation that deters the other side by resisting the other's demands in the first crisis. A sufficient reputation for deterrence can also be built by the defender by fighting for one round in some cases.

Turning to the third question, how does bargaining unfold in repeated crises? There are two parts to this question; first, how do the parties change their bargaining from one crisis to another in repeated crises, and second, how does that bargaining differ from bargaining in

---

2. This calculation assumes that all combinations of initial beliefs are equally likely (i.e., γ and λ have uniform, independent distributions). It would not be true if, for example, initiators are very likely to hold advantages (γ likely to be close to 1). The calculation in the text is reasonable in the absence of any empirical evidence supporting a specific distribution.

isolated crises? When repeated crises occur in the model, the initiator backs off from its demands in the first crisis. In the second crisis, it will generally hold firm to its position, accepting the defender's counteroffer only if it does not possess an advantage. The defender must hold firm in the first crisis and will generally resist the initiator's demands in the second crisis as well. In the model then, the parties "harden" their bargaining strategies from the first crisis to the second. The initiator is restrained in the first crisis by its expectation of receiving concessions in the second crisis. When the possibility of a future crisis is removed in the second crisis, it demands concessions more vigorously. The defender, on the other hand, continues to hold firm in the second crisis because the ranks of those defenders who would like to back down (i.e., those that do not possess an advantage) have been thinned by the defenders who acquiesced to the initiator's demands in the first crisis. War is likely in the second crisis because each side is more likely to possess an advantage than the chance of the draw would lead us to expect. Both sides hold out for concessions from the other, and war is likely unless one side backs down.

The chance to gain concessions in the future makes bargaining in repeated crises different from bargaining in isolated crises. But comparing the model here to the isolated crisis model, there are few differences in the bargaining. The most important difference across the two models are the shifts in the boundaries of the cases introduced by the differential importance of the two crises. When the two crises are of roughly equal importance ($m \simeq \frac{1}{4}$), the boundaries of the cases across the models are almost equal. As the second crisis gains in importance relative to the first (i.e., m increases), cases A and B expand while Case C shrinks. These shifts are reflected in bargaining that is more moderate in the first crisis. As the first crisis gains in importance, both sides bargain harder, pushing their demands more aggressively in the first crisis. Otherwise, there is not much difference in how the sides bargain across the two models.

Because the first crisis generally solves the dispute, the possibility of a second crisis is generally irrelevant to how the parties bargain. When a second crisis is possible, the initiator will moderate its behavior in the first crisis in order to avoid war. The defender in turn will resist the initiator's demands more frequently in the first crisis. At the same time, the defender also moderates its behavior by not demanding concessions when it possesses an advantage (i.e., $\Omega_2 = SQ$ always). Repetition tends to moderate both sides' behavior, provided that a second crisis is a serious possibility.

How do the conclusions of the model compare to the historical record? Gochman and Maoz (1984) identify dyads of nations that frequently engaged in militarized disputes. Diehl (1985) defines an enduring rivalry as a dyad in which the two nations engage in three militarized disputes in fifteen years followed by at least one dispute every ten years thereafter. This definition captures the idea of two nations that face a fundamental policy disagreement, one serious enough to provoke multiple disputes between them. Each of these disputes can be thought of as a crisis in the model presented here.

According to the model, how should disputes in enduring rivalries differ from the typical dispute? First of all, they should be more likely to go to war because the cases of the model that are likely to produce multiple crises are also those that produce the greatest chance of war. However, these rivalries should flare into war only after several disputes because each side is restrained in the early disputes by the possibility of future disputes and the initial disputes generally address minor issues compared to the later disputes in the string. Diehl (1985) reports that fifteen of twenty-two enduring rivalries went to war at some point with twelve of the fifteen that went to war doing so late in the string of disputes.

Do nations increase the "hardness" of their bargaining from crisis to crisis as the model predicts? Leng has studied pattern of crisis bargaining behavior in a series of papers by coding the hostility of each side's actions and classifying their bargaining into several different strategies. One paper in particular (Leng 1983) provides evidence on bargaining in repeated crises by examining six sets of three crises between pairs of nations. This sample provides twelve second-stage crises, with twenty-four nations involved. Seventeen of those twenty-four nations escalated the average weekly hostility of their actions; four of the seven nations that decreased their average weekly hostility increased the coerciveness of their strategy. In only three cases out of twenty-four did a side both reduce the hostility of its actions and not escalate the coercion of its strategy. The historical record matches the general predictions of the model; repeated crises are more likely to escalate to war than isolated crises, and both sides will employ more coercive strategies and actions as a sequence of crises progresses.

Conclusion

This essay has presented a simple model of repeated crisis bargaining. The model demonstrates that the conditions that give rise to repeated crises are quite different from those underlying isolated crises. Repeated crises occur most frequently when the initiator holds a modest military advantage and the crises address increasingly important issues. Both sides have to believe that they can gain for a crisis to occur; for repeated crises to occur, those beliefs have to hold after the crucible of the first crisis. Crisis bargaining transmits information; repeated crises require that the parties cannot learn enough from the first crisis to deter the second. As Blainey (1973) argues, decisive war is a powerful cause of peace because then the sides know which side is stronger militarily.

In this model, crisis bargaining transmits sufficient information to prevent a second crisis most of the time. But many factors that might encourage the losing side to reopen a dispute are deliberately excluded from the model here. Between crises, sides can improve their military forces, in effect changing their private information. But if the quality of forces change between crises, what can the sides learn from the initial crisis? Reputations require not only private information, but also stable values of that private information. If a side's private information is constantly changing, it cannot develop a reputation, as the other side's beliefs will be based solely on its information about the changes between disputes. Similarly, a nation's reputation for resolve could be based on its willingness to bear the costs of war, its value for the status quo, or its willingness to take risks. But these values are not fixed over time, they change as the government of a nation changes.

This analysis suggests that the changes in a nation's resolve that lead it to reopen a dispute must also undermine any reputation it has built in a previous crisis. This observation may explain why empirical attempts to determine reputations for resolve have failed. Snyder and Diesing (1977, 187) report the following:

> What do our cases tell us about the actual importance of resolve reputation, or the related idea of the "interdependence of commitments," in the thinking and behavior of statesmen? Not a great deal, but something. What stands out is the discrepancy between the little evidence that statesmen *do* infer an opponent's resolve from his behavior and the massive evidence that decision makers *think* such inferences are made. (Italics in original)

The very existence of repeated crises undermines the idea of reputations for resolve, unless those reputations are extremely weak. If effective reputations for resolve could be developed, crises should not be repeated. But repeated crises are the perfect place to look for reputations in international politics; the opponents are the same across repeated interactions and the information gained from the first crisis directly relevant to the second crisis. If we must choose between the existence of reputations for resolve and the occurrence of repeated crises, we must choose the latter because they do occur. Further, the dynamics of repeated crisis can be explained without reputations, simply as the continued interaction of rational actors facing continued uncertainty in each other's resolve.

Stability in International Systems and the Costs of War

Emerson M. S. Niou and Peter C. Ordeshook

Beginning with Kaplan (1957) and Riker (1962), researchers have sought to reformulate in game-theoretic terms the explicit rationale of the realist view of balance of power politics in international affairs offered, for example, by Taylor (1954), Morgenthau (1948), Hass (1953), Claude (1962), and Waltz (1979). This view, although admitting the abstraction of supposing that nation-states act as unitary actors, is that of an international system in which stability (balance) emerges as the consequence of a "hidden hand" in otherwise anarchic systems. Using some simple lessons drawn from classical cooperative game theory, it is the theoretical basis of this hypothesis that subsequent research has sought to uncover. Kennedy's (1987) recent commentary on great power politics, though, offers this illustration of the sequential nature of strategy in international affairs, which serves as a critique of these earlier reformulations:

> The Russian general Kutusov, wishing to halt his army's west-ward advance in 1812, once the Grand Army had been driven from the homeland, may have spoken for more than himself when he doubted the wisdom of totally destroying Napoleon, since the "succession would not fall to Russia or to any other continental power, but to the power which already commands the sea, and whose domination would be intolerable." (P. 139)

There are two implications of this example. First, the games that nations play are sequential, and, second, the outcomes of initial plays can affect profoundly the strategic character of subsequent games. Thus, to see how this example affects our view of bargaining in international affairs, imagine three people whose initial wealth holdings are each zero and who use majority rule to divide $90. Viewed as a single-play game, this situation corresponds to a simple, constant-sum game without a core, and we can appeal to solution hypotheses such as the V-set, the bargaining set, and the competitive solution to predict that two players will coalesce to divide $90 evenly between themselves. Suppose, now, that we repeat this game an indefinite number of times, each time adding an additional $90 to the game. Although no game in the sequence has a core, the important feature of this scenario is that regardless of the current distribution of income, each person retains his one-third share of the "vote" in deciding how to divide the next $90. Thus, aside from the possibility of precluding multitrial agreements, we lose little by viewing each game in the sequence in isolation. Moreover, even if we allow the redistribution of all accumulated wealth at each stage, the players need not be concerned about the existence of future games in deciding how to play a current game. Although the outcome of any game in the sequence determines each person's relative wealth, it does not affect future strategic possibilities. We may witness wide swings in wealth as coalitions form and dissolve, but each person "remains in the game" as someone to be reckoned with in the next round.

This scenario is like the one Riker (1962) uses to argue that international politics are inherently unstable. In this case, an empty core for each game in the sequence or for the entire sequence means that, regardless of what coalition and payoff distribution is proposed, there exists some other coalition and distribution that the members of the new coalition can secure and that they unanimously prefer. Suppose, however, that we modify the situation to correspond to the second feature of the scenario that Kennedy describes. Specifically, although majority rule continues to be the decisive criterion, let each person's "voting weight" be endogenous and equal to the resources that he controls relative to all others. If this game is played once, then the players' strategic considerations are not much different from what we find in a single play of the game in our first scenario. Although voting weights are no longer equal, if there are only three players, if no player's weight is zero, and if no player already controls a majority share, then any two players can form a minimal winning coalition that expropriates all available resources. Now, however, repetition is significant to strategic imperatives in that current holdings play a critically important role. In particular, if any player secures a majority share, he controls all subsequent games. That is, the existence of future games affects one's thinking about the current game, so, by rendering voting weight endogenous rather than exogenous, the game becomes one of survival in which one or two players can be permanently "retired."

In summary, our two scenarios—the first with exogenous and equal voting weights and the other with endogenous weights—are equivalent if they are played once, but strategic considerations differ if the game is repeated. Thus, combining endogenous weights with repeated play yields a situation with strategic imperatives that differ significantly from the situations used previously to analyze international conflict. In the first scenario, even if everyone knows that the situation will be repeated, each can still concentrate on the current round. Long-term multitrial coalitions are no more stable than single trial agreements and, because a player retains his vote regardless of what coalitions form, agreements in the current round have no bearing on strategic possibilities in future rounds. Moreover, in the actual negotiation process, proposals in which one player receives a temporary advantage over all others can be part of the various offers, threats, and counterthreats. The second scenario is profoundly different, because participants must guard against agreements in which one person secures a majority of the wealth, so threats and counters in which one person allows another to secure a majority of resources are simply unbelievable. With exogenous weights I might agree to let you be the principal beneficiary of a decision to expropriate the resources from a third party. Although I prefer other outcomes, I may feel compelled to this outcome to forestall expropriation of my own resources. However, with endogenous voting weights measured by resources, such an agreement may only temporarily postpone my eventual elimination from the game. I will merely become your next victim if I permit you to secure a majority of the resources from the third player. Correspondingly, negotiation strategies and the attention participants pay to multiperiod consequences should be significantly different in the second scenario than in the first.

Thus, although the first scenario presents us with those instabilities we commonly associate with zero- or constant-sum cooperative games, the second scenario adds an additional consideration. Not only might we cycle indefinitely as we renegotiate the resources that each of us is to control, but there is also a potential instability in the number of viable participants. A player may be so weak—either because of initial inequities in the distribution of resources or because someone previously agreed to an outcome that was inappropriate to his welfare—that he may be incapable of securing his existence through negotiation and reallocation. So while the first scenario offers us a view of what we might term the "micro-instability" of shifting alliances and resources in constant-sum games, the second scenario adds the possibility of the "macro-instability" of the game's viable participants, and it is this macro-instability which is the focus of realist thinking.

Elsewhere, we offer an analysis of our second scenario with the specific objective of developing a model of balance of power politics that corresponds to the realist view of international affairs—specifically, of nation states that bargain to secure advantage in the overall distribution of some fixed supply of resources (Niou and Ordeshook 1986; Niou, Ordeshook, and Rose forthcoming). This bargaining may, of course, lead to the eventual elimination of countries, but systems in which we predict that no country will be eliminated are termed *system-stable,* and our primary objective is to establish necessary and sufficient conditions for system stability. System-stable systems, however, need not be *resource-stable.* Resource stability implies that no resource reallocations will occur—that the system's current distribution of wealth is in the core of the corresponding cooperative game. System stability does not imply resource stability, and thus our scenarios alert us to the possibility of observing systems which are macro-stable, but micro-unstable. Section I reviews the analysis that uncovers the necessary and sufficient conditions for each type of stability.

In recognition of the fact, however, that contemporary technology has the potential to drastically alter the strategic thinking of national leaders, and thus the operation of balance of power politics, this essay extends our previous analyses to take explicit account of the costs of war. Organski and Kugler (1980), for example, assert that "If nuclear weapons have influenced the rules of international politics inherited from prenuclear times, the influence has not operated in the expected direction: the weapons have not modified these rules, they have instead reinforced them" (217). The analysis that follows attempts to uncover the meaning of this generalization.

Letting wars be costly changes our analysis in important ways. It admits the possibility that certain strategies can destroy the resources that nations seek and it requires that we consider the possibility that the proportion of resources destroyed is a function of bargaining strategy and the relative resources (voting weight) of opposing coalitions. Section II describes the extensions of our model that accommodate war costs, and it introduces an important complication with which that analysis must contend. Specifically, if a system's resources are constant, then maximization of resource proportion and maximization of absolute resources are equivalent goals. However, if actions affect the total of resources, then these two objectives need not be equivalent, and this distinction may be important in the determination of strategy. For example, should we regard a nuclear conflict between the United States and the Soviet Union in which the United States emerges with a population of 25 million and a GNP of $100 billion, as compared to a Soviet Union with a population of 40 million and a GNP of $150 billion as a "victory" for the Soviets? And in the contemporary world economy, what are the implications of a policy in which the United States seeks to increase its per capita income while reducing its economic position relative to Japan and other trading partners, as against a policy that pays exclusive attention to economic control?

1. A Simple Balance of Power Model

We use the following notation: $S = \{1, 2, \ldots, n\}$ is the set of all countries; C, a subset of S, denotes a specific collection of countries in S; $\mathbf{r} = (r_1, r_2, \ldots, r_n)$ is an n-tuple of resources, where r_i denotes the resources controlled by country i ($r_i \geq 0$ for all i, and, for convenience, we let $r_1 \geq r_2 \geq \ldots \geq r_n$); R is the total resources controlled by all countries in S; $r(C)$ is the total resources controlled by the countries in C; $\mathbf{C}$ is a coalition structure that partitions S into exhaustive and disjoint subsets; E is the set of essential countries in S—the countries that are individually members of at least one minimal winning coalition—and $(S, \mathbf{r})$ is an outcome or a state of the world specifying the countries that constitute the system under consideration and the resources they control individually. To this notation we apply some assumptions common to cooperative games with transferable utility—resources are infinitely divisible and freely transferable among countries, and if $r(C) > r(C')$, then C can "defeat" C'. Also, we suppose that country i's utility is monotonically increasing with r_i, subject to certain constraints that we specify shortly.

This notation establishes a basis for describing a simple, n-person game in which each player's voting weight corresponds to the resources it controls, equating voting weight and utility. However, although we must accommodate the sequential nature of the situation, we do not proceed by formulating an extensive form or by modeling the situation as an infinitely repeated cooperative game. Instead, we develop a hypothesis about bargaining in the single-play version that takes the central strategic feature of repeated play into account, where that feature is the fact that no player or coalition should act to allow any other player to secure a majority of resources, since such a player can subsequently control the game and eliminate all others.

Before we develop such a solution hypothesis, we require two assumptions about strategic possibilities. First, although we initially assume that wars are costless, we suppose that, in lieu of taking resources directly from a country or a coalition that it outweighs, every country prefers to have resources ceded to it. Second, we assume that "third parties" can gain from conflict between other parties. This second assumption assures us that if one country is near-predominant—if the addition of any amount of resources to its total allows it to control the game—then no other sets of countries will threaten each other with conflict.

At this point we note that our treatment of bargaining, the definitions of threats, counterthreats, and the conditions for system stability that we offer parallel the development of the bargaining set. Bargaining set theory asks whether a particular distribution of payoffs, in conjunction with a specific coalition structure, is a reasonable prediction, which requires that every person have a counter to every threat—that everyone can "defend" his payoff. Although there are several variants of this set, the bargaining set is the collection of all such reasonable predictions. However, because we are concerned only with the notion of system stability and with the ability of countries to defend their sovereignty, which requires only that each country be assured of some positive amount of resources, we are less interested in the ability of countries to defend a specific resource distribution. Hence, we modify the definitions of threat and counterthreat to ask whether, given an initial distribution of resources, each country can ensure against having its resources set equal to zero.

Briefly, a threat is a "proposal" by one or more countries to reduce to zero the resources of one or more other countries that it outweighs. Thus, a threat, implicitly understood or explicitly made, is the ultimate aggressive action in that it is in effect a proposal to eliminate the threatened countries from the system or, depending on our interpretation of the circumstance $r_i = 0$, to exclude a country as a relevant power in the system. Formally, we define such a threat with the following four conditions.

THREAT. $(\mathbf{r}', \mathbf{C}')$ *is a threat by* C'_l *against* C'_k *with respect to* $(S, \mathbf{r})$, *the current status quo, if*

i. C'_l and $C'_k \in \mathbf{C}'$,
ii. $r(C'_l) > r(C'_k)$,
iii. $r'_i = 0$ for all $i \in C'_k$,
iv. $r'_j > r_j$ for all $j \in C'_l$

and $(\mathbf{r}', \mathbf{C}')$ is a threat against i if $i \in C'_k$.

Surveying this definition, condition (i) requires that C'_l and C'_k both be disjoint coalitions in the coalition structure $\mathbf{C}'$, whereas (ii) corresponds to the presumption that countries will threaten others only if they anticipate the possibility of victory; hence, the requirement that the resources of C'_l exceed the resources of C'_k. Condition (iii) requires that a threat is a proposal to eliminate attacked countries. Finally, (iv) states that the members of C'_l will coalesce to threaten others only if, individually, each anticipates some immediate gain in terms of increased resources from such an act. The threat, in other words, must be profitable for all participating countries.

Clearly, only preponderant or near-preponderant countries—countries that control half or more of the resources in a system—are immune to threats. Thus, system stability prevails only if all countries also possess counterthreats—threats against one or more countries party to the original threat or a proposal that induces some of those countries into joining a new coalition.

COUNTERTHREAT. *The threat* $(\mathbf{r}'',\mathbf{C}'')$ *is a counterthreat to* $(\mathbf{r}',\mathbf{C}')$ *by* $K \subseteq C'_k \cap C''_m$ *if*

i. *either* $C'_l \subseteq C''_h$ *or* $C'_l \cap C''_m \neq \emptyset$, *where* C''_m *and* $C''_h \in \mathbf{C}''$,
ii. $(\mathbf{r}'',\mathbf{C}'')$ *is a threat to* C''_h *by* C''_m,
iii. $r''_i > r'_i$ *for all* $i \in C''_m$ *and* $r''_i \geq r_i$ *for all* $i \in K$ *if* $C''_h \neq \emptyset$.

A counterthreat by K, then, is, according to (i) and (ii), a proposal in which K is in both C'_k (the coalition that is being threatened) and C''_m (the coalition that is formulating the counter) which either threatens all the members of C'_l (the originally threatening coalition) or which coopts one or more members of C'_l. In addition, condition (iii) requires that all countries in the counter coalition, C''_m, prefer the counter to the original threat.

Notice now that condition (iii) is the feature of counterthreats that differs from the notion of a counter offered in bargaining set theory. Because bargaining set theory asks whether a particular distribution is "stable," those making the counter to some threat must prefer the counter to the original proposal. Here, however, we allow two types of counterthreats. First, one or more countries can transfer resources directly to another so as to render that country near-predominant (in which case C''_h is empty). Although such a counter reduces the threatened players' resources below what that player enjoys in the original resource distribution, if successful, our earlier assumptions imply that the counter "freezes" the system and thereby secures their continued existence. This change in the definition of a counter is warranted, then, by the fact that we are merely interested in whether countries can counter to ensure their existence and not in whether they can defend some particular payoff. The second type of counter allows one or more of the threatened countries to formulate an alternative threat directed at members of the originally threatening coalition. In this instance, we require that members of the new threat who were targets of the old threat defend, as in the bargaining set, their original payoffs. Otherwise, the possibility is left open that such players can have their resources "whittled away" to zero in repeated play.

Counterthreats are available to nearly all players for the game we are presently considering. Yet, for a smaller country, say i, counters may require the assistance of others and we must be certain that these other countries have an incentive to join i. Thus, we require the additional refinement, which we call a viable counterthreat.

VIABLE COUNTERTHREAT. *The counterthreat* $(\mathbf{r}'',\mathbf{C}'')$ *is viable for* $i \in K$ *if there exists no* $C_o \subseteq C''_m - \{i\}$ *such that* C_o *has a threat,* $(\mathbf{r}_o,\mathbf{C}_o)$, *against* C''_h *or* $C''_h + \{i\}$, *with* $r_{oj} > r''_j$ *for all* $j \in C_o$.

Hence, a counterthreat is viable for a threatened member of C'_k if i's coalition partners in the counter have some incentive to coalesce with i in the sense that whenever they exclude i (to form $C''_m - \{i\}$, or some subset if they also exclude others in addition to i), they cannot formulate a counterthreat that they all prefer to the counter they can form by including i in their coalition.

The hypothesis we offer now about the properties of outcomes to our game is: *Country i will not be eliminated if and only if it has a viable counterthreat to every threat.* Implicit in this idea, of course, is the supposition that if i is vulnerable—if there exists some threat that i cannot counter—then, from our implicit adoption of the common knowledge assumption, all other participants will take advantage of the situation to eliminate i. Thus, $(S,\mathbf{r})$ is system-stable if and only if, for all i in S and for every threat against i, i has a viable counterthreat. Assuming, finally, that preferences accommodate the assumption that countries prefer receiving resources as the consequence of a transfer as part of a viable counterthreat rather than as a consequence of an uncountered threat, and that no country will join in a threat or counter that permits third parties—countries that are not members of threatening or counterthreatening coalitions—to become predominant, we show in our earlier research that $(S,\mathbf{r})$ *is system-stable if and only if every member of S is essential—if and only if every member of S is a member of some minimal winning coalition.*

Although this result is derived using the perspectives of traditional cooperative game theory, we can see the possibility of its derivation from a noncooperative formulation. Suppose j, chosen randomly from those players who wish to make a threat, threatens i, and that we give a randomly chosen threatened player, say i again, the opportunity to formulate a counter. Suppose next that all players, using weighted voting in accordance with the status quo distribution, choose between the threat and the counter. If the threat prevails, it becomes the new status quo, whereas if the counter is chosen, a randomly selected partner of i can introduce a modification of the counter that excludes i. If this modification gains majority approval it becomes the status quo. Since the decision to threaten, the form of a counter, the choice between threat and counter, and the decision about whether to modify the counter are conditioned on what follows if that decision prevails, the relevant question concerns the incentives of i's partners in the counter. Notice that if every player can "buy" stability by rendering someone near-predominant, then any such counter is necessarily successful since choosing to be near-predominant is a dominant action. Formulating such a counter is dominant for i, moreover, if i is "sufficiently" risk averse with respect to other options (e.g., has a lexicographic preference for survival). Hence, to take the more difficult case, suppose no country can buy stability, and in particular, consider $\mathbf{r} = (60,60,60,60,60)$. Let the threat be $\mathbf{r}' = (75,75,75,75,0)$ and the counter be $\mathbf{r}'' = (0,0,120,120,60)$. If 3 and 4 choose the counter, which gives them more than the threat and which they cannot implement without 5's cooperation, 1 and 2's threat is not part of a subgame perfect equilibrium. That 5 can offer a counter that makes its coalition partners better off than in the original threat without yielding subgames in which its resources are eventually reduced to zero is guaranteed by the definition of a viable counter and by the fact that i is essential. Of course, neither $\mathbf{r}'$ nor $\mathbf{r}''$ terminate the game—once 1 and 2 or 5 is eliminated, a new round of bargaining begins—but for this situation at least, circumstances are symmetric for 3 and 4 (membership in winning coalitions, and the like) so 3 and 4 might reasonably be assumed to prefer the counter to the threat. Knowing, then, that a threat by $\{1,2,3,4\}$ can result in a counter that eliminates 1 and 2, 1 and 2 would not participate in the threat if both are "sufficiently" risk averse and the threat to eliminate 5 cannot be part of a subgame perfect equilibrium. It is the refinement of this argument that provides a rationale for our bargaining assumptions and for our conclusion about the necessary and sufficient conditions for system-stability.

Our conclusion that the necessary and sufficient conditions for system stability is that all $i \in S$ are essential establishes the possibility of a "balance of power" in otherwise anarchic international systems. Of perhaps equal importance is the fact that if any or all members of the set of countries that are not essential are eliminated, then, regardless of how the resources of those countries are reallocated, all members of E remain essential. Thus, a country should be unconcerned about the attempts of other countries to absorb the resources of inessential countries unless, for reasons exogenous to the present analysis (e.g., differential rates of internal resource growth among the essential countries), such an absorption is part of a strategy by the absorbing country to become predominant. This result also establishes an appropriate characteristic function representation of any portion of play of the game among essential countries. Letting **r** be a vector that denotes the initial distribution, and **r**′ a distribution that prevails from negotiation, suppose that all countries are essential—that inessential countries have been eliminated and their resources reallocated to yield **r**. Now let C be a winning coalition ($r(C) > R/2$), and let ϵ be a small positive number, which we use to bound coalitional values away from but arbitrarily close to zero. (Although an essential country cannot have its resources set equal to zero so that it is eliminated, a country may find it necessary to cede some of its resources to others so as to ensure its continued, albeit limited, existence. The amount ϵ represents the amount of resources that it would subsequently control in such an eventuality.) Then the characteristic function of a system-stable game becomes:

$$v(C) = r(C) + (R/2 - \max [r_i]) \text{ if } r(S - C) >$$

$$R/2 - \max [r_i], \text{ otherwise } v(C) = R - \varepsilon;$$

$$v(S - C) = r(S - C) - (R/2 - \max [r_i]) \text{ if } r(S - C) >$$

$$R/2 - \max [r_i], \text{ otherwise } v(S - C) = \varepsilon; \text{ and}$$

$$v(S) = R.$$

where "max" is taken over all $i \in C$. If a coalition C is blocking—if $r(C) = R/2$—then $v(C) = r(C)$. Roughly, then, the value of a winning coalition is the sum of the resources of its members, plus whatever resources must be ceded to its largest member in order to render that member near-predominant. The value of a losing coalition equals the summed resources of its members, minus the minimum resources required to render someone outside of the coalition near-predominant.

Two facts emerge from this representation. First, the corresponding (constant-sum) cooperative game has a core if and only if $r_i = R/2$ for some i. Thus, in general, system-stable systems are resource-unstable. Second, if we apply solution hypotheses such as the main simple V-set (or, equivalently, the strong bargaining set or the competitive solution), no essential country will become inessential. Thus, if the assumed threat and counterthreat process assures a country its sovereignty in the next period, it assures it in all subsequent periods.

2. War Costs and Goals

The sole accommodation of the costs of conflict that the preceding analysis allows is the assumption that countries prefer receiving resources as the consequence of a transfer as part of a viable counterthreat rather than as a consequence of an uncountered threat. Such an assumption, however, seems less tenable in a nuclear age, as against an age in which conflict might deplete human resources but not the material substratum upon which economies and national power are based. Suppose, then, that if C threatens and subsequently absorbs C', its resources become $f(r(C),r(C'),\alpha) \leq r(C) + r(C')$, and the net resource gain that C realizes is,

$$g(r(C),r(C'),\alpha) = f(r(C),r(C'),\alpha) - r(C) \leq r(C') \tag{1}$$

where α is merely some parameter that we use later to measure the severity of war costs. We have in mind a function f such that g is continuously differentiable in its arguments, $g < 0$ if $r(C) < r(C')$, $\partial g/\partial \alpha < 0$ and $\partial g/\partial r(C) > 0$. For example, then, we could illustrate expression (1) thus:

$$g(r(C),r(C'),\alpha) = (r(C) + r(C'))[1 - \alpha r(C')/r(C)] - r(C) \tag{2}$$

where α is constrained by $0 \leq \alpha \leq r(C)/r(C')$. Notice that if $r(C) + r(C') = R$, then the right side of expression (2) becomes $r(C') - \alpha R r(C')/r(C)$.

To illustrate expression (2) and the properties that we believe g ought to satisfy, consider $(S,\mathbf{r}) = (\{1,2,3,4\},(120,80,60,40))$. Using (2), notice first that $g(r(2,3,4),r_1,2/3) < 0$, $g(r(1,3,4),r_2,2/3) = 7.27$, $g(r(1,2,4),r_3,2/3) = 10$, and $g(r(1,2,3),r_4,2/3) = 9.23$. Hence, the most profitable threat is not against the largest or the smallest country, but against country 3, thereby illustrating that although larger threatening coalitions gain a larger percentage of an adversary's resources with expression (2), there is less to be gained with a smaller adversary, and that, depending on the value of α, attacking a coalition with greater resources may result in smaller gains.

The particular complication that war costs introduce, however, is not the specification of the properties of f or g, but rather the appropriate specification of utility as it relates to resources. Traditional realist thinking about balance of power, of course, is predicated on the assumption that national leaders maximize "power." Although power is related to national resources in some inexactly specified way, its important feature is that it is a relative concept and, thus, it implies that nation-states maximize relative resources. Fortunately, if the total resources in the system are constant, maximization of resources and share of resources are synonymous objectives, but if war costs deplete resources, then these two formulations of goals are no longer equivalent. We are left, then, with two alternative assumptions about preference. Specifically, subject to the condition that they remain essential: (A1) Utility is monotonically increasing in absolute resources; or (A2) Utility is monotonically increasing in relative resources.

In choosing between these two assumptions, the realist view, as expressed by the following quotation from Waltz (1979, 105), argues for A1: "When faced with the possibility of cooperating for mutual gains, states that feel insecure must ask how that gain will be divided. They are compelled to ask not 'Will both of us gain?' but 'Who will gain more?' If an expected gain is to be divided, say, in the ratio of two to one, one state may use its disproportionate gain to implement a policy intended to damage or destroy the other." On the other hand, there seems little doubt that decision makers are concerned with the absolute welfare of their countries, and many recoil at the idea that a nuclear conflict can yield winners and losers. These two assumptions, then, highlight the possibility of alternative formulations in which decision makers perceive a tradeoff between absolute and relative resources. In an extreme form, though, these tradeoffs can be expressed as lexicographic preferences in which: (A3) Subject to the constraint that relative resources do not decrease, utility is monotonically increasing with absolute resources; and (A4) Subject to the constraint that absolute resources do not decrease, utility is increasing with relative resources. Assumption A3 is equivalent to A1 if the system's resources cannot grow, but A4 introduces some complexities we cannot consider here. And, of course, all of these assumptions are equivalent if the total resources in the system are constant. By focusing on A1 and A2, though, we can show how alternative formulations of preference change the conditions for system and resource stability.

Before proceeding, however, we must consider two issues associated with contemporary technology and nuclear weapons. The first issue is whether our formulation of the costs of war accommodates the realities of nuclear technology, and the second concerns the treatment of the concept of sovereignty. The intuition behind a formulation such as expression (2) is that, regardless of a war's destruction, the material substratum upon which a country's resources are predicated—its population, natural resources, geographic position—remain essentially intact. One possibility, of course, is that modern technology has merely increased the parameter α in expression (2) from values near 0 to values near $r(C)/r(C')$—perhaps identically to $r(C)/r(C')$. This view corresponds to Waltz's (1979, 180–81) argument that "Nuclear weapons do not equalize the power of nations because they do not change the economic bases of a nation's power. Nuclear capabilities reinforce a condition that would exist in their absence." It is arguably the case, though, that nuclear weapons open the possibility that any nation or coalition possessing them is blocking and capable of the destruction of an opponent. Nuclear weapons may not be an additive or transitive resource in the sense that additional nuclear capability confers some advantage over an adversary who is also armed with such weapons: if i can eliminate j, then i can eliminate j regardless of what additional resources are added to j; moreover j can eliminate i as well. This alternative view implies that the sole contexts in which our analysis is relevant is either a world disarmed of such weapons or a world in which no one would use them, unless otherwise threatened with elimination.

Since the first possibility is a mere utopia, we suppose that deterrence works—that each state with such weapons has an infrangible guarantee of sovereignty, so threats to eliminate such a country are unbelievable, thereby precluding any extreme form of system instability. This fact might seem to augur well for balance of power politics, but we must once again emphasize that system stability does not imply resource stability, so the viability of the nuclear threat does not inhibit countries from vying with each other for control over global resources. In fact, resource instability here is doubly dangerous, since it implies a continual process of threat and counterthreat in which errors in judgment may be supremely costly. Moreover, if sovereignty for all states possessing such weapons is guaranteed, then there is no constraint that acts to prevent countries from seeking and successfully securing over half the resources, and the resource instability that prevails looks more like the one that Riker (1962) describes than the one we deduce.

Such an argument would seem to imply that the deterrence provided by nuclear weapons would lead national leaders to fear only miscalculation, but such an inference relies on too narrow an interpretation of the concept of sovereignty. Sovereignty comes in many different forms, and it was probably of small consolation to the Romanovs to know that, both before and after World War I, Russia approximated Waltz's (1979, 96) requirement that it be able to decide "for itself how it will cope with its internal and external problems." Indeed, this example compels us, in the context of the effective deterrence scenario, to treat sovereignty as applying to regimes rather than to states.

If we keep in mind that it is merely a convenient abstraction to suppose that collectivities such as states have an existence that is independent of those who lead them, then the idea of regime survival provides a more theoretically justifiable basis for asserting the relevance of our analysis to contemporary circumstances. And, once we make this adjustment in terminology, we see little reason for supposing that nuclear weapons provide regimes with an infrangible guarantee of survival or that, in an era of effective nuclear deterrence, regimes necessarily maximize absolute as against relative power in international affairs. Waltz's requirement for sovereignty and our transformation of this concept's meaning, nevertheless, reveals a potential confusion between sovereignty and resources. Is the United States less sovereign today than a decade ago when it relied less on foreign investment for maintenance of employment and on Tokyo for maintaining the stability of the dollar's relative value, or should we treat current trends in the world economy "merely" as an erosion of U.S. resources? Such issues bring into question our sharp distinction between essential and inessential countries, and the methodologies that ought to be used to apply our analysis in contemporary affairs.

Admittedly, our analysis is built on a sequence of distinctions that imperfectly characterize international politics, but we now see an international competition in which territorial sovereignty seems to take a back seat at times to sovereignty based on economic control. The concept of economic control or economic power in a complex world market economy is, of course, no easier to operationalize than any classical notion of power, and thus the nuclear threat in combination of contemporary economic realities forces us to consider the possibility that we may have to adjust our assumption about national goals—that, however measured or defined, the maximization of power or economic control no longer summarizes a viable hypothesis about objectives. Thus, the reformulation of balance of power in terms of alternative specifications of goals is an integral part of rendering that model germane to contemporary circumstances.

3. System Stability with War Costs

Although the proof that only essential countries possess viable counters to every threat is offered elsewhere (Niou and Ordeshook 1986; Niou, Ordeshook, and Rose forthcoming), the principles that underlie it are straightforward. Each country knows that everyone else will oppose it if it formulates a threat that renders it predominant, and therefore the best outcome it can secure is control of precisely half of the system's resources. The condition that S equals E guarantees that every country possesses, either individually or in combination with some others, enough resources to render someone near predominant or, enough resources to formulate a counterthreat that is advantageous to all participants. Provided that countries continue to be concerned solely with maximization of proportion of resources, this argument does not depend on the assumption that wars are costless. That is,

Stability in International Systems and the Costs of War 243

REMARK 1. $S = E$ is necessary and sufficient for system stability even if war costs deplete the resources of countries in accordance with expression (1), provided that all countries, conditional on maintaining their sovereignty, maximize their proportion of resources.

Suppose all countries can form viable counterthreats by transferring resources. The same must be true if wars are costly since that cost is irrelevant to the transfer. Now suppose that all countries are essential but that some cannot individually buy stability, and, in particular, suppose that the target, C', of a threat made by C hasn't enough resources to buy stability. Notice that we can suppose that $C = S - C'$, because, even if C does not explicitly include all of $S - C'$, the members of $S - C' - C$ are implicitly parties to the threat—with the destruction of any of the resources of C', the players' shares will increase. And because every $i \in C'$ is essential, it must be the case that some $K \subseteq C'$, $i \in K$, can form a winning coalition smaller than or equal in weight to $S - C'$. So even if resources are destroyed to a greater or lesser degree in the counter than in the threat, the counter affords the partners of K a greater proportion of resources than they can secure in the threat, and for $i \in K$, $r''_i > r_i$. Finally, if C' is inessential, its "coalition partners" can always increase their proportion by dropping C' from the counter—even, perhaps, adding C' to a counterthreat's target—in which case C' cannot form a viable counter.

We might have conjectured that war costs would make system stability more pervasive—that such costs would render otherwise inessential countries essential—but this intuition has in mind decision makers who maximize absolute level of resources rather than proportion, or who perceive a tradeoff between relative and absolute resource. Suppose, then, that conditional on maintaining their sovereignty, countries maximize absolute level. If all countries are not merely essential but can individually "buy" stability with a resource transfer to the largest threatening country, then the system remains system-stable since, as before, all countries can "freeze" the system with such a transfer. What changes here, however, are the conditions under which stability can be bought and this, in turn, establishes that war costs are not necessarily stabilizing. Recalling that a system is resource-stable (has a nonempty core) when countries maximize resource proportion if and only if there exists some $i \in S$ such that $r_i = R/2$, suppose we use the formulation of war costs offered by expression (2) and that $\alpha = 2/3$. If $\mathbf{r} = (120, 100, 80)$, then, when countries maximize proportion, 3 can formulate a viable counter and "buy" stability by ceding 30 units to 1, but now 1 can secure all of 3's resources and 2 knows that it will not be threatened by 1 since such a threat is not profitable to 1. Thus, 3 cannot "buy" stability nor will 2 have an incentive to join 3 in a counterthreat should 1 threaten 3. Thus, 3 is inessential.

More generally, i is predominant if $g(r_i, r(S - \{i\}), \alpha) > 0$. Since we assume that g is positive only if $r_i > R/2$, this condition assures us that i has the means to threaten $S - \{i\}$, and the members of $S - \{i\}$, by coalescing, cannot negate i's motivation to formulate such a threat. Similarly, a near-predominant country satisfies $g(r_i, r(S - \{i\}), \alpha) = 0$ and $g(r_i + \in, r(S - \{i\}) - \varepsilon, \alpha) > 0$, where the equality assures us that $r_i \geq r(S - \{i\})$, but that i has no incentive to threaten the remaining members of S. The inequality assures us that this incentive reappears if any small positive amount of resources are added to i. Restated for the special case of expression (2), some simple algebra establishes that

REMARK 2. *Assuming that gains are given by expression (2), and that, conditional on remaining essential, countries maximize absolute resources, $(S, \mathbf{r})$ is resource-stable if and only if (1) for no C such that $r(C) > R/2$, is it the case that $r(S - C) \leq (1 - \alpha)R$, or (2) there is an $i \in S$ which is near-predominant, which requires that $r_i = \alpha R$ whenever $\alpha > 1/2$, and $r_i = R/2$ otherwise.*

We should not interpret our three-country example to mean, however, that war costs necessarily destabilize otherwise stable systems. The system $(\{1,2\},(200,100))$ is system-stable whenever $\alpha \geq 2/3$, since a threat by 1 against 2 leaves 1 with fewer than 200 units of resources. This simple example, then, in combination with our earlier discussion of the system $(\{1,2,3\},(120,100,80))$ reveals that the requirements for system stability can be altered dramatically if we introduce war costs and if we suppose that decision makers maximize absolute resource levels.

Turning, then, to the issue of system stability, notice first that $(S, \mathbf{r})$ is system-stable if (1) no coalition prossesses a threat, or (2) if C'_1 threatens C'_2, then every i in C'_2 has a viable counterthreat. Because the formulation of conditions (1) and (2) change when absolute resources are maximized, we offer the following remark as an extended statement of them (letting lower-case c's and k denote the number of members of a coalition):

REMARK 3: *If, conditional on remaining essential, countries maximize absolute resources, $(S, \mathbf{r})$ is system-stable if and only if (1) $g(r(C), R - r(C), \alpha) < 0$ for all C, $r(C) > R/2$, or, if $(\mathbf{r}', C')$ is a threat by C'_1 against C'_2, with $i \in C'_2$, then either (2a) there exists a $j \in S - C'_2$ such* that C'_2 can render j near-predominant, or (2b) there exists a C''_1 such that $i \in K = C'_2 \cap C''_1$, with

$$g(r(C'_1), r(C'_2), \alpha)/c'_1 < g(r(C''_1), r(C''_2), \alpha)/[c''_1 - k],$$

$$g(r(C''_1 - \{i\}), r(C''_2 + \{i\}), \alpha) < g(r(C''_1), r(C''_2), \alpha).$$

Condition (1) is irrelevant if war costs are zero, but it is important if war costs are high. Our statement of this condition follows from the fact that, since we assume that g increases, ceteris paribus, as $r(C)$ increases, if $C'_1 + X$ has no threat against $S - C'_1 - X$, then C has no threat against $S - C'_1$. The second condition differentiates between two types of counterthreat—a counter in which one or more members of the threatened coalition can "buy" stability (can render some country in S near-predominant), and a counter in which some subset of C'_2, say K, formulates a viable threat against C'_1. In the context of countries that maximize absolute resource levels, we say that $i \in K$ possesses a counter of this second type if, first, the per capita gain to the members of the countering coalition, C''_1 exceed the per capita gain to C'_1. Notice that we exclude K from the calculation of per capita gain since K is in the originally threatened coalition and, therefore, it need not share in any gains realized by the counter. The second inequality of condition (2b) requires, as before, that $C''_1 - \{i\}$ does not possess a viable counter against C'_1 or $C'_1 + \{i\}$. By expression (1), if $C''_1 - \{i\}$ does not possess a viable counter, then proper subsets of $C''_1 - \{i\}$ do not possess viable counters either. Notice that if we merely decrease the counterthreatening coalition by excluding i without augmenting the target of the counter accordingly, then gains are necessarily smaller for this alternative counter than for the counter with i. Thus, we include i in the target of the alternative counter. Also, this inequality should be stated in per capita terms, but the denominator of the first term—the size of $(C''_1 - \{i\}) - (K - \{i\})$—equals the denominator of the second term—the size of $C''_1 - K$.

4. Special Cases and Examples

Remark 3, although necessary for formalizing the influence of war costs when decision makers maximize absolute resource levels, is little more than a restatement of the definition of a viable counterobjection. As such it fails to tell us whether war costs, in conjunction with the goal of maximizing absolute resources, increases or decreases the likelihood of system stability. Unfortunately, there is no simple relationship between system stability and such costs. To see, for example, that there is no monotonic relationship, consider the system $(\{1,2,3,4\},(90,90,90,30))$, and suppose that war costs are governed by expression (2). If $\alpha = 0$, then total resources are constant and our previous analysis applies, so country 4 is inessential. Similarly, if $\alpha = 2/3$, then 4 continues to be inessential. If $\{1,2,3\}$ threatens 4, it can realize a net gain of 23.3, and 4 has no viable counter—4 hasn't enough resources to "buy" stability, and even a counterthreat of $\{2,3,4\}$ against 1 fails to yield a positive gain so that 4 can't attract 2 and 3 away from $\{1,2,3\}$. However, if $\alpha = 1/2$, then 4 is essential. Hence, $\{1,2,3\}$'s threat against 4 yields 13.3 whereas a counter by $\{2,3,4\}$ against 1 yields 20, so 4 can counter the most potent threat against it. That this system is system-stable follows from Remark 2, which establishes that countries with 90 units of resources can "buy" stability by rendering someone near-predominant. Alternatively, if, say, $\{2,3,4\}$ threatens 1, its per capita gain is $20/3 = 6.7$ whereas if 1 counters with $\{1,2\}$ against $\{3,4\}$, the gain to 2 with 1 excluding himself from any share, is 20, which is sufficient to attract 2 to the counter. Thus, as α increases from 0, $(\{1,2,3,4\},(90,90,90,30))$ moves from being system-unstable, to being stable, and then to being unstable once again.

The preceding example illustrates the difficulty that war costs and absolute resource maximization occasion with regards to establishing generalizations. However, if we limit ourselves to two-country and three-country systems, we can offer an analysis based on expression (2) which casts some light on the impact of war costs on stability. First, it is evident that two-country systems are system-stable only if costs are sufficiently great that neither country can threaten the other. Thus, following immediately from Remark 2;

REMARK 4. *Assuming that gains are given by expression (2), and that, conditional on remaining essential, countries maximize absolute resources, $(\{1,2\},\mathbf{r})$ is system- and resource-stable if and only if $r_1 \leq \alpha R$ for $\alpha \geq 1/2$, and $r_1 = R/2$ otherwise.*

Thus, since a two-country system is system-stable when countries maximize relative resources if and only if $r_1 = R/2$, war costs and absolute resource maximization increase the likelihood of system stability in such systems.

Some care should be exercised in using this result as a mechanism for explaining the apparent stability of bipolar relations characterizing international politics after World War II despite the considerable resource advantage enjoyed by the United States and its allies over the communist block. For Remark 4 to be relevant, we must suppose that countries maximize absolute resources and not proportion. And indeed, it was perhaps the rationality of the argument that 300 million dead was a defeat for both sides, regardless of who suffered the fewest casualties, which averted a preemptive strike by either side.

Matters are considerably different and more complicated if we turn to three-country systems. Keeping in mind our convention that $r_1 \geq r_2 \geq r_3$,

REMARK 5: *Assuming that gains are given by expression (2) and that, conditional on remaining essential, countries maximize absolute resources, $(\{1,2,3\},\mathbf{r})$ is system-stable if and only if (1) country 1 is not predominant, and (2) either $\alpha \leq 1/2$, or $\alpha > 1/2$ and either $r_1 + r_2 \leq \alpha R$ or $r_1 + r_3 > \alpha R$.*

To establish sufficiency, notice that if no country is predominant, then, from Remark 2, $r_1 \leq \alpha R$ when $\alpha > 1/2$ and $r_1 \leq R/2$ when $\alpha \leq 1/2$. When $\alpha \leq 1/2$, if $r_1 = R/2$, then 1 is near-predominant and the system is system-stable. If $r_1 < R/2$, then, since $r_1 + r_2 > R/2$ and $r_1 + r_3 > R/2$, countries 2 or 3 can render 1 near-predominant. If $\alpha > 1/2$, then, by Remark 2, if $r_1 = \alpha R$, 1 is near-predominant so the system is system-stable. If $r_1 < \alpha R$ and $r_1 + r_2 \leq \alpha R$, then, from expression (2), $g(r(1,2),r_3,\alpha) \leq 0$, and no coalition can gain from any threat. If $r_1 < \alpha R$ and $r_1 + r_3 > \alpha R$, then since $r_2 \geq r_3$, $r_1 + r_2 > \alpha R$ and, by Remark 2, countries 2 or 3 can render country 1 near-predominant. To establish necessity, suppose (1) but not (2) is satisfied, in which case there must be an unstable system when $\alpha \leq 1/2$ or when $r_1 + r_2 > \alpha R$, $r_1 + r_3 \leq \alpha R$, and $\alpha > 1/2$. If $\alpha \leq 1/2$, the system is system-unstable if $r_1 + r_2 \leq R/2$ or $r_1 + r_3 \leq R/2$, which is impossible since this requires that r_3 or r_2 exceed $R/2$, in violation of the assumption that there is no predominant country. In the second case, substitution into expression (2) shows that $\{1,2\}$ can form a threat. However, country 3 has no counter—it hasn't enough resources to render country 1 near-predominant, nor can 3 form a counter-threat with 1 against country 2 or with 2 against 1 since $g(r(2,3),r_1,\alpha) \leq g(r(1,3),r_2,\alpha) \leq 0$.

To see the implications of this remark, figure 1 portrays the simplex defined by $r_1 + r_2 + r_3 = R$, and shows as shaded those distributions that are system-stable whenever $\alpha \leq 1/2$ and as hatched those distributions that are system-stable when $\alpha = 2/3$. Figure 2 shows an intermediate case of $\alpha = 3/5$ and figure 3 shows an extreme case of $\alpha = 4/5$. Looking first at figure 1, notice that rather than increasing or decreasing the likelihood of system stability in any simple way, war costs render some systems stable and others unstable. Because war costs allow the largest country to be even larger before becoming predominant, the region of stable systems expands toward the vertices of the simplex. However, this

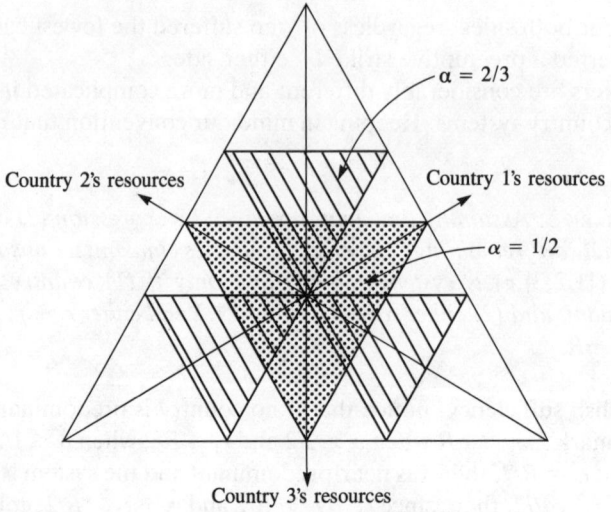

Fig. 1

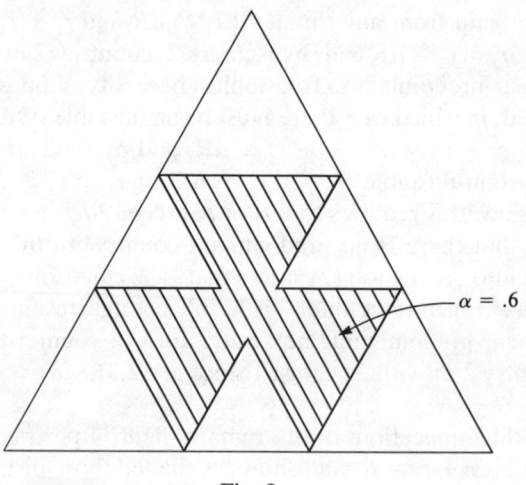

Fig. 2

cost renders it more difficult for smaller countries to "buy" stability, so the regions in which one small country confronts two large adversaries become unstable. As costs increase beyond $\alpha = 2/3$, the region of system-stable systems is portrayed by four triangles (see fig. 3). The

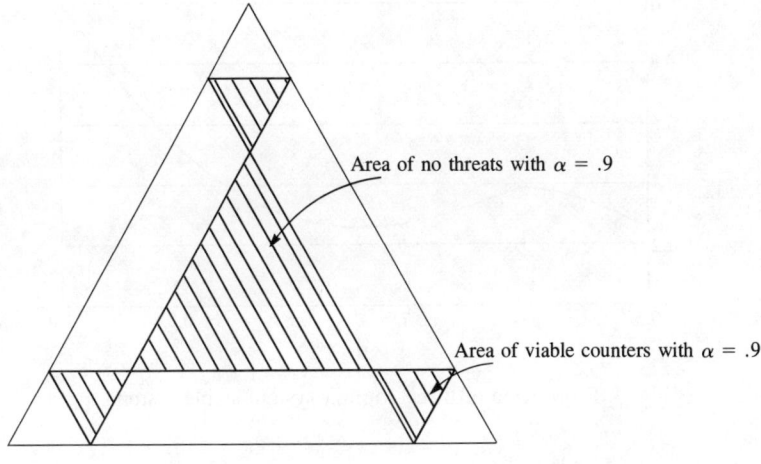

Fig. 3

interior triangle corresponds to those systems that are stable because no country can mount a worthwhile threat—such systems are, of course, both system- and resource-stable—whereas the three smaller triangles correspond to systems in which the smallest country can either buy stability or formulate a viable counter.

These figures bear directly on the balance of power literature. First, any presumption that war costs *necessarily* render systems more stable—that "The more potentially destructive a war seemed to be, the less the probability of its occurring, and vice versa" (Gilpin 1981, 216)—has in mind the stability that arises because no threat is worthwhile. This is a natural presumption if no distinction is made between resource stability and system stability, but the presumed effect does not arise if costs are sufficiently low ($\alpha < 2/3$), and it fails to consider the fact that increasing costs can make it more difficult for smaller countries to formulate counterthreats. Figure 4 graphs against α the percentage of three-country systems that are system-stable, and although we see that this percentage is maximized as α increases to 1, we also find a local maximum near $\alpha = .6$ as a consequence of the declining utility of counterthreats to smaller countries for larger values of α. Thus, perhaps it is the intuitive understanding of the declining value of counterthreats that yields Gilpin's qualification that ". . . an effective system of deterrence . . . also makes the world that much safer for limited wars and the calculated exploitation of nuclear threats" (216).

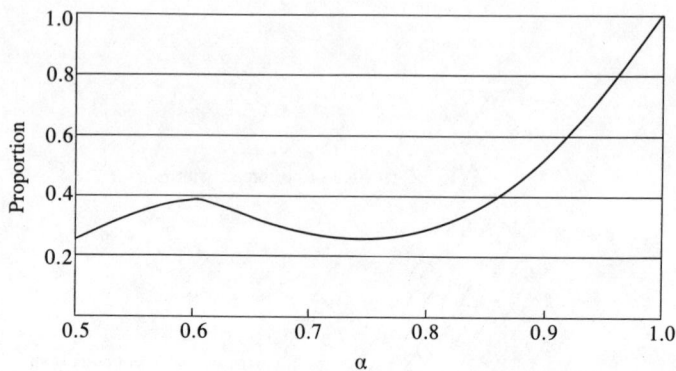

Fig. 4. Proportion of three-country system-stable systems

Second, points near each simplex's center are generally stable and a precisely uniform distribution is always system-stable. This pattern does not mean that stability requires that "there must be several actors of relatively equal power" (Jervis 1986, 60), but stability is less sensitive to costs when the distribution is uniform. Those in the realist school who argue, then, that uniform resource distributions are more conducive of stability are both right and wrong—they are wrong if countries maximize relative resources, since all three-country systems are then system-stable (provided no country has more than $R/2$ resources), but they are right if countries maximize absolute resources since it is only a uniform distribution that is system-stable for all costs.

Finally, our analysis bears on the question of the relative stability of bipolar and multipolar systems, and in particular, on Waltz's (1979) argument that bipolar systems are more stable. Again, the issue concerns the objectives of decision makers and the magnitude of costs. If decision makers are concerned with maximizing relative advantage, then, regardless of costs, we must deem three-country systems more stable since the only two-country system which is system-stable is one in which countries are evenly matched. On the other hand, if decision makers are concerned with maximizing absolute resources, then our conclusions depend on the parameter α. If $\alpha \leq 1/2$, then the same conditions for stability apply as before. But if $\alpha > 1/2$, then our conclusion is more ambiguous. Although the set of two-country systems that are system-stable increases as α increases, the set of three-country systems that are similarly stable changes according to the complex pattern illustrated by figures 1 through 3.

5. Conclusions

Because our analysis ends with special cases, we cannot preclude the possibility that there exist patterns that hold for more general formulations of war costs. Nevertheless, our analysis does show that hypotheses about the effects of the costs of war must take more into account than merely magnitude—they must also consider the dual nature of stability and the alternative goals that national leaders pursue. If leaders pursue the maximization of relative advantage, then such costs have little effect on the requirements for system and resource stability. On the other hand, if maximization of absolute resources better characterizes goals, then although such costs increase the likelihood of resource stability, they affect system stability in complex ways. This complexity arises because, although costs make it more difficult for coalitions to formulate believable threats, they also make it more difficult for countries to defend their sovereignty with viable counters.

It is interesting, of course, to speculate on the conditions under which policy would be dictated by one goal as against the other. To the extent that regime survival depends on domestic political factors and, in particular, on the satisfaction of traditionally defined economic needs, then maximization of absolute resources seems especially relevant, whereas if policy is dictated solely by issues of national sovereignty, then relative resource maximization is more germane. And if domestic and international politics exert independent influences on goals, then any complete analysis must consider tradeoffs between goals or the possibility of systems in which some decision makers act on the basis of one goal and others act on the basis of another. Consideration of such possibilities, of course, would complicate further the picture of the consequences of costs that we have drawn here.

The Road to War Is Strewn with Peaceful Intentions

Bruce Bueno de Mesquita and David Lalman

> And it's hard to find true equilibrium when you're looking at each other down the muzzle of a gun.
>
> —Jethro Tull, 1987 (ASCAP)

Nations in crisis manage sometimes to resolve their differences without resort to arms. Yet other seemingly comparable crises result in violence. The identification of factors that distinguish peacefully settled disputes from those that escalate to bloodshed is a central concern of scholars of international conflict. Empirical and theoretical analyses draw attention to such elements as the resolve or the motivations of competing parties; the national capabilities and networks of alignments of disputants; the past experiences and "war weariness" of antagonists; the domestic political pressures; and the need for scapegoats confronting decision makers as possible explanations for conflict escalation.

Much research and discussion on the causes of war focuses on the importance of perceptions in heightening or dampening the prospects that nations will resort to force to settle their disputes. Indeed, there has been a recent convergence of opinion among scholars, regardless of their epistemological or methodological orientation, that misperception is a necessary condition for the escalation of disputes into warfare. Several recent game theoretic analyses, for instance, lend credence to John Stoessinger's well-known claim that "on the eve of each war, at least one nation misperceives another's power" (Stoessinger 1974, 229). Yet, we demonstrate here in the context of a game theoretic structure that war can be an equilibrium outcome even under the assumption of complete

---

We gratefully acknowledge the helpful assistance of David Austen-Smith, Fay Booker, Barry Nalebuff, Barry O'Neill, Piotr Swistak, and the Hoover Institution in preparing this essay. This research was supported by a grant generously awarded by the United States Institute of Peace. The opinions, findings, and conclusions or recommendations expressed in this publication are those of the authors and do not necessarily reflect the views of the United States Institute of Peace.

information and even when war is a strictly less desirable outcome than negotiations. Furthermore, we believe this result and several others follow from a decision-making model that captures the sequence of decisions in a crisis and is empirically testable.

Assumptions and Definitions

We model the evolution of international conflict as an extensive form game of sequential decisions (Kreps and Wilson 1982*a;* Brito and Intriligator 1985; Cho and Kreps 1987; Morrow 1987; Powell 1987). National decisions whether to negotiate or to use force are assumed to be made by a single decision maker seeking the best course of action. We assume that international crises, the focus of our study, arise out of conflicts of interest between two nations, A and B.[1] Our game begins when two nations find themselves in a confrontation involving their own national interests. Each side has demanded a different resolution to their differences, and at least one issue remains unresolved. Demands may involve anything of value to the state, whether it be territory, trading rights, human rights policy, and so forth. In short, demands may concern any alteration of the behavior or policies of the antagonist state. The sequence of strategic choices employed by A and B lead to the terminal outcomes of our game, each of which is an observable event. In as much as our concern is with the escalation of disputes from conflicts of interest to violent confrontations, the game terminates with five possible outcomes: negotiations, war initiated by A, war initiated by B, military intervention by A, and military intervention by B. The outcomes do not specify who the ultimate winner or loser might be, rather they identify the form of conflict resolution.

Figure 1 depicts the paths that adversaries A and B can traverse in arriving at the five terminal events of our game. Nations A and B each associate a value with the event represented at each terminal node.

Nation A moves first. A elects either to use force (denoted F_A) or not to use force ($\tilde{F}_A$). B, moving second, possesses analogous choices. If both A and B forgo the use of force ($\tilde{F}_A$, $\tilde{F}_B$), then nations A and B are said to engage in negotiations with one another without resorting to violence. If both A and B elect the strategy of using force then a war is said to ensue. If A initially chooses to fight and B makes the same strategic choice (F_A, F_B), then the war is initiated by A and denoted as

---

1. We do not assume a two-nation world, however. Rather, we assume that the members of any pair of nations have already factored into their calculations the expected behavior of all other states (Altfeld and Bueno de Mesquita 1979).

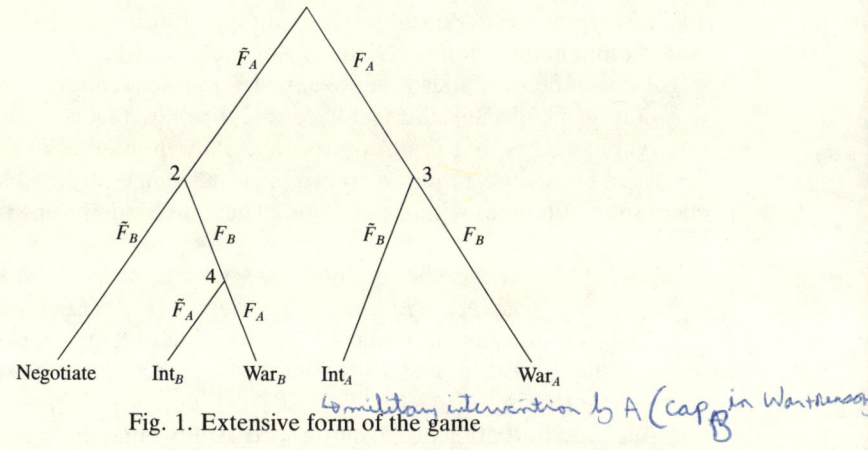

Fig. 1. Extensive form of the game

War$_A$. If A initially selects not to use force, and B then uses force, A has the opportunity to capitulate to B's demands by again foregoing its option to use force ($\tilde{F}_A, F_B, \tilde{F}_A$). We call such an event a military intervention by B and denote it as Int$_B$. Alternatively, A can respond with force to B's attack ($\tilde{F}_A, F_B, F_A$). Such a sequence of choices leads to a war initiated by B, denoted as War$_B$. Finally, A may initially use force and B may respond by not using force ($F_A, \tilde{F}_B$), resulting in a military intervention by A (Int$_A$).

Although the game structure is quite simple, it captures the sequence of events surrounding international conflict. Frequently, research on international conflict focuses on war and peace as if they are mutually exclusive and exhaustive events (Singer, Bremer, and Stuckey 1972; Blainey 1973; Bueno de Mesquita 1978; Organski and Kugler 1980). That our various pairings of strategies in this model lead to mutually exclusive events is clear. Also evident from the strategy paths we have delineated is that war and peace do not exhaust the set of possible outcomes. By characterizing the outcomes according to strategic choices we are able to exhaust the set of possible conflict events (Lalman 1988). Not only are the initiators of military interventions identified by using a sequential approach, but the initiators of wars as well. Recently, researchers have drawn distinctions between peace, asymmetries in the use of force, and the joint application of violence (Siverson and Tennefoss 1982; Bueno de Mesquita 1981; Bueno de Mesquita and Lalman 1986; Gochman and Leng 1983; Lalman 1988), but, unlike the game described here, they have overlooked the important implications of the sequence leading to these events. The sequence frequently dictates whether violence can or cannot be averted (Brams and Kilgour 1987; Morrow 1987; Powell 1987; Brito and Intriligator 1985). Games with simultaneous moves (Niou, Ordeshook, and Rose, forthcoming) might mask the subtleties that are exposed in a sequential process.

Our game design allows for terminal nodes that are empirically observable events that seem to arise naturally in international politics. Six assumptions are required to establish the range of possible preferences over outcomes within our game. These six assumptions are:

A1. Players (i, j) choose the strategy with the greatest expected utility: $E(U^i_F) > E(U^i_{\tilde{F}})$ implies F and $E(U^i_{\tilde{F}}) > E(U^i_F)$ implies $\tilde{F}$.
A2. The initiator of a military intervention obtains gains with certainty: Int_i implies $P_i = 1$ and $P_j = 0$, where P is the probability of gaining.
A3. The probability of a nation successfully obtaining gains is unaffected by whether the conflict is resolved through negotiations, through a war it initiated, or through a war initiated by its antagonist: P_i given $\text{War}_A = P_i$ given $\text{War}_B = P_i$ given Negotiate.
A4. $C_t > C_{t'}$ and $C_t > C_f$, where C_f is the cost of using force. C_t is the cost of being the target of the use of force when that force is applied directly on one's own territory. $C_{t'}$ is the cost associated with being the target of force applied on territory other than one's own.
A5. All cost terms are positive: $C_f > 0$, $C_t > 0$, $C_t' > 0$.
A6. The utility from gains are greater than the utility from losses: $G > L > 0$.

Assumption A1 stipulates that nations are led by rational, expected utility maximizing leaders.[2] Assumptions A2 and A3 are concerned with the probability of success given alternative mixes of strategies for A and B. If either decision maker selects a strategy of force, the adversary has the option to defend itself. We assume that a decision not to defend oneself in the face of a forceful challenge is a decision to accept defeat (A2). This means that if the opponent does not retaliate with force, the challenger using force obtains with certainty whatever benefits were

---

2. This need not imply a single decision maker forms foreign policy. Rather we have in mind that whatever the internal political process by which policy preferences become revealed, national policy follows directly from the ordering emerging from that internal process.

sought. For all events other than interventions, the gains and losses are not determinate but are probabilistic. The ultimate outcomes of wars, like negotiations, are risky prospects. Therefore, nations A and B select their strategies on the basis of estimated values for these events. We assume that the probability of a desirable outcome for A (or B) is invariant across the events negotiation, war by A and war by B (A3).

Assumption A3 may appear controversial. In making this argument we assume that negotiations take place in the face of a tacit or explicit threat to use force. Our notion is that the expectation of realizing gains through negotiations is equivalent to the likelihood that one would realize the same gains by resorting to violence. Setting the prospects of gains equal makes negotiations always more attractive than warfare, because negotiations avoid the high costs incurred in fighting. We relax this assumption and allow war to be preferred to negotiation in another study (Bueno de Mesquita and Lalman 1988).

The advantage normally associated with initiation is captured by the assumption that $C_{t'} < C_t$ (A4). A main advantage to the initiator of a conflict is the enhanced ability to select the venue of fighting. The costs to a nation of being engaged in combat on its own territory are greater than the costs incurred when combat takes place on someone else's territory. Our rationale is that combat on someone else's territory involves controllable losses; the number of combatants and the amount of military matériel committed to the fight are at the discretion of the nation's political leadership. On the other hand, fighting on one's own territory usually involves losses of civilian lives and nonmilitary property in addition to military losses, and these costs are not so easily controlled unless one capitulates.

A4 also recognizes that losses arise in relation to decisions to use force. Such costs (C_f) are presumed to be primarily political in nature. They entail domestic political opposition to using force in order to achieve policy goals. For instance, demonstrations in the streets and/or the fear of electoral defeat were political costs for American policy makers associated with the Vietnam War during the late 1960s and early 1970s. Politicians must take account of these costs just as surely as they must be attentive to the expenditure of lives and national wealth. The very need to resort to force suggests a political failure by the national leadership. The inability to settle international disputes through the much less costly approach of negotiating might reflect poor diplomacy.

The strategies available to nations A and B are the means by which they can realize gains or losses. Except for strategic combinations that eventuate in a military intervention, gains and losses are, as noted earlier, probabilistic so that decision makers must choose across lotteries.

Table 1 gives the values associated with each event described at the terminal nodes of figure 1.

These lotteries, together with our assumptions, imply restrictions on the order in which alternative outcomes will be preferred. To demonstrate the effect of our assumptions on the relative valuations, we focus on the lotteries for decision maker A. B's feasible preferences on outcomes are analogous. It is evident that the initial use of force can be superior or inferior to not using force initially if A believes B will not use force. Thus, the value of Int_A can be greater than, less than, or equal to the value of Negotiate. If $(1 - P_A)(G - L) > C_f$ then force is preferred. If $(1 - P_A)(G - L) < C_f$ then A prefers not to use force.

By A2, A4, and A5 the expected utility for A given Int_A is greater than the expected utility given Int_B. By A2, A3, and A4, $\text{Int}_A > \text{War}_A$ or War_B.

Assumptions A2, A3, and A5 are sufficient to establish that $\text{Int}_B <$ Negotiate for A. A's expected utility from Int_B, however, can be less than, greater than, or equal to A's expected utility from War_A or War_B. This may seem surprising at first blush as B's intervention against A insures defeat for A, meaning that A will realize the worst outcome, L, for sure. War, on the other hand, gives A some chance (A3) of success. However, rearrangement of the War_B lottery and the Int_B calculation for A reveals that $\text{Int}_B > \text{War}_B$ if $C_f > P_A(G - L)$. This inequality, indeed, may be a critical element in understanding war termination. With regard to Int_B and War_A we see that A prefers certain defeat by B over a prospect of victory in war if $C_f + C_{t'} - C_t > P_A(G - L)$. Although A4 stipulates that $C_t > C_f$, $C_{t'}$, we have not assumed that C_t is larger than $C_f + C_{t'}$. Thus, capitulation is preferred if the costs of waging war are anticipated to be unacceptably high.

Assumptions A3 and A5 establish that negotiation is strictly preferred to waging either type of war in our game. Thus, we assume away war mongers who value war for its own sake. Instead, we recognize that it is preferable to obtain a given end at as low a cost as possible. And,

TABLE 1. Expected Utilities Associated with Each Possible Outcome

	A's Expected Utility	B's Expected Utility
Negotiate	$P_A G + (1 - P_A)L$	$P_B G + (1 - P)L$
Int_B	$L - C_t$	$G - C_f$
War_B	$P_A G + (1 - P_A)L - C_f - C_t$	$P_B G + (1 - P_B)L - C_f - C_{t'}$
Int_A	$G - C_f$	$L - C_t$
War_A	$P_A G + (1 - P_A)L - C_f - C_{t'}$	$P_B G + (1 - P_B)L - C_f - C_t$

finally A3 and A4 postulate that *A* prefers to initiate a war rather than waiting for *B* to initiate it.

In an earlier study (Bueno de Mesquita and Lalman 1988), each player had 20 admissible orderings of preferences over the five outcome events, yielding 400 possible combinations. Here we have added A3 and A4, thereby reducing the set of feasible pairs of orderings from 20×20 to 6×6. Table 2 displays the admissible orderings for *A* and *B*.

It is instructive to note that only two events in table 2 can occupy the status of being most preferred. Nations either most prefer to negotiate or to use force in a situation where the adversary will capitulate. These two top preferences seem consistent with the informal division of nations into Doves (negotiate > intervene) and Hawks (intervene > negotiate). Which type a nation is depends upon the size of C_f, the costs in domestic political opposition to the use of force. Nations are defined as Hawks if $(1 - P_A)(G - L) > C_f$. Doves are characterized by the fact that $(1 - P_A)(G - L) < C_f$. Where domestic opposition to the use of force is politically inconsequential, hawkishness is more likely and, conversely, where the use of force can be made politically costly, dovish policies are more likely to follow. Knowing the value of C_f, then, can be invaluable for an opponent trying to estimate a nation's likely response to alternative strategies. Although knowledge of the magnitude of an opponent's C_f term can profoundly influence the equilibrium in the game, this knowledge is not sufficient to discern differences within the two categories, Hawk and Dove. As table 2 reminds us, our game contains three distinct varieties of hawks and three distinct varieties of doves. In this article we ignore ties between expected utility payoffs for a player, thereby restricting our analysis to cases of strict differences in expectations across outcomes.

TABLE 2. Possible Preference Orderings on the Outcomes of the Game

For *A*	For *B*
Hawk	**Hawk**
Int_A > Negotiate > War_A > War_B > Int_B	Int_B > Negotiate > War_B > War_A > Int_A
Int_A > Negotiate > War_A > Int_B > War_B	Int_B > Negotiate > War_B > Int_A > War_A
Int_A > Negotiate > Int_B > War_A > War_B	Int_B > Negotiate > Int_A > War_B > War_A
Dove	**Dove**
Negotiate > Int_A > War_A > War_B > Int_B	Negotiate > Int_B > War_B > War_A > Int_A
Negotiate > Int_A > War_A > Int_B > War_B	Negotiate > Int_B > War_B > Int_A > War_A
Negotiate > Int_A > Int_B > War_A > War_B	Negotiate > Int_B > Int_A > War_B > War_A

The Game under Differing Information Conditions, Doves vs. Hawks

Our objective here is to investigate how in equilibrium preferences over force strategies enhance or diminish opportunities for peace. We begin by developing our logic in the case of complete information. First we assume that whether a nation is a Hawk or a Dove (and the precise sort of Hawk or Dove that it is) is known to both players. Then we relax this assumption, examining the effect of incomplete information about players' types on the equilibrium obtained. The game is solved on the basis of subgame perfect equilibria. This is equivalent to a backward induction up the game tree.

We begin by proving that when two Doves, with common knowledge about each other's type, confront each other in a dispute, the equilibrium outcome is always negotiation. This is an important benchmark from which to begin.

PROPOSITION 1. *With common knowledge of types, Doves with a conflict of interest always negotiate.*

Proof: We begin with B's response to an offer by A to negotiate, $\bar{F}_A$. B, a Dove, by definition prefers negotiation to all other outcomes. B recognizes that any outcome that could follow from its use of force is inferior to negotiation. Therefore, if A does not use force, B will also not use force, leading to negotiation. It only remains to determine that A will offer to negotiate on the first move. A, fully aware that Dove B will agree to negotiate, compares this outcome to the outcomes that follow from A's use of force. A, also a Dove, prefers to negotiate over either Int_A or War_A, and therefore chooses the no use of force option.

We should not, however, infer from proposition 1 that decision makers with complete information would never wage war even though negotiations are always preferred to waging war in our game. The conclusion that incomplete information is a necessary condition for war enjoys widespread acceptance among students of international conflict. Blainey, for instance, argues that "wars can only occur when two nations decide that they can gain more by fighting than by negotiating" (Blainey 1973, 159). As noted earlier, Stoessinger (1974) contends that misperception is required for war to ensue. The views of Blainey and Stoessinger are reinforced by some recent results in game theoretic examinations of war and peace decisions. Niou, Ordeshook, and Rose (forthcoming, chap. 2, 29) report, for instance, that "we can easily imagine circumstances in which countries are not merely uncertain about the resources of others, but uncertain also about what others believe about their capabilities. . . . [A] thesis which our analysis supports is that such uncertainty is a necessary condition for war." Powell (1987) and Lalman (1988) reach similar conclusions about the need for uncertainty or misperception to produce war. In our game structure, however, we show that neither uncertainty nor misperception (Jervis 1976), is necessary for war. This result is of importance because, while it clearly does not obviate the equilibria found by others in other games, it does disprove the *general* claim that war cannot arise under complete information conditions.

PROPOSITION 2: *War can occur even when the leaders of two nations know that they can gain more by negotiating than by fighting.*

Proof. Suppose A is a Dove with the following feasible preference ordering:

$$\text{Negotiate} > \text{Int}_A > \text{War}_A > \text{Int}_B > \text{War}_B$$

and that B is a Hawk whose preference ordering is:

$$\text{Int}_B > \text{Negotiate} > \text{War}_B > \text{War}_A > \text{Int}_A.$$

We begin the backward induction at the subgame that branches out from node 3 in figure 1. If node 3 is reached, so that A has already selected F_A over $\tilde{F}_A$ at node 1, B chooses F_B over $\tilde{F}_B$ because the preference ordering for B indicates that $\text{War}_A > \text{Int}_A$. Next we show that A will fight at node 1 and node 3 will be reached. At node 4, A would choose $\tilde{F}_A$ over F_A, because $\text{Int}_B > \text{War}_B$. At node 2, B's choice is between $\tilde{F}_B$ and F_B: $\tilde{F}_B$ implies Negotiate, and F_B implies Int_B. Since B prefers Int_B to Negotiate, B would choose to use force at node 2. Summarizing A's decision at node 1, A, knowing B's preferences, compares $\tilde{F}_A$ to F_A. F_A implies War_A because B will fight at node 3. As demonstrated above, $\tilde{F}_A$ implies Int_B. A's choice is reduced to A's preference for War_A over Int_B. A fights at node 1, B follows by fighting at node 3, and the equilibrium is War_A.

Nation A, a Dove in this example, is highly desirous of negotiating, but is willing to use force if necessary. This Dove certainly is not a pacifist but a realist who wishes to avoid violence if possible. A is the sort of Dove who will act preemptively if negotiations seem unproductive rather than yield the first-strike advantage to the adversary. The Hawk (nation B) is also a realist, neither so bellicose as to wish to fight at any cost (Morgenthau 1973), nor fearful of using force to obtain its ends. This Hawk is most eager to exploit the opponent's desire to negotiate, but will negotiate rather than bear the heavy costs of full-fledged war.

This example clarifies some important features of war. Doves, as we can see, are not immune from waging war, nor is the world safe from war even when neither initial belligerent particularly desires to engage in that action. And we see in this example that negotiation is Pareto superior to the equilibrium outcome, War_A. It is possible for nations to find themselves at war even though both belligerents would be better off negotiating and each *knows* it. Since we used the assumption of complete information to arrive at this equilibrium, it is not possible that the failure to arrive at an equilibrium of negotiation was dependent on any misperceptions by either actor. This is to be compared with the seemingly intuitive claim that "wars can only occur when two nations decide that they can gain more by fighting than by negotiating" (Blainey 1973, 159).

Since, as we have shown, war is never the most desired event for players in the game we have structured, it seems paradoxical that nations can fail to negotiate their differences away when they realize that doing so would be beneficial. Such apparent paradoxes are well known within the context of the Prisoner's Dilemma. The difficulty facing nations A and B here, as in the Prisoner's Dilemma, is one of trust. A can leave the opportunity for negotiations open only by risking that B will exploit A's cooperative behavior. Since B does not have to commit itself to a course of action until *after* A has done so, B is greatly advantaged if A has a trusting nature. A's fear of a worse outcome, then, precludes negotiations.

How might A or B reorient their interactions to escape the dilemma? Clearly, each national leader has an incentive to do better if possible. The problem is whether other outcomes with higher payoffs are reachable. In order to obtain a greater payoff at least one of the nations must accept the risk of a strategy that appears to the adversary to be out of equilibrium with his/her type. That such behavior could occur is to be expected if we adopt the more realistic view that information about the preferences of other policy makers is incomplete. With incomplete information, national leaders may build reputations or exploit uncertainties about their true expectations and their strategic choices, thereby steering their opponents toward more desirable outcomes. What beliefs are required to support negotiations in the face of a crisis?

The conditions for negotiation to be the equilibrium outcome are:

$$\pi^A(\text{War}_A) + (1 - \pi^A)(\text{Int}_A) < (1 - \mu^A)(\text{Negotiate}) +$$

$$\mu^A \max\{\text{Int}_B, \text{War}_B\} \qquad (1)$$

$$\pi^B(\text{War}_B) + (1 - \pi^B)(\text{Int}_B) < \text{Negotiate} \qquad (2)$$

where π^A is A's belief that B prefers War_A to Int_A, π^B is B's belief that A prefers War_B to Int_B and μ^A is the probability with which A believes that B believes A prefers War_B to Int_B. Thus, expression (1) indicates that A chooses not to use force if A believes the lottery including negotiation is superior to the lottery involving its use of force. Expression (2) indicates that B chooses not to use force, given expression (1), if negotiation is superior to the lottery of outcomes that arises if B elects to use force. Expressions (1) and (2) imply proposition 3:

PROPOSITION 3: *To insure that crises are resolved through negotiations each adversary must be sufficiently confident that if it were to initiate the use of force, the rival would retaliate with force rather than capitulate.*

Proof. Substituting the lotteries associated with the terminal nodes and solving for π^A and π^B (A's and B's levels of confidence, respectively, that the rival would retaliate with the use of force), expressions (1) and (2) are rewritten as:

$$\pi^A > [(1 - P_A)(G - L) - (1 - \mu^A)C_f + \mu^A(C_t)]/$$

$$[(1 - P_A)(G - L) + C_{t'}] \text{ if War}_B > \text{Int}_B \text{ by } A \text{ or}$$

$$\pi^A > [(1 - P_A)(G - L) - C_f + \mu^A (P_A(G - L) + C_t)]/$$

$$[(1 - P_A)(G - L) + C_{t'}] \text{ if Int}_B > \text{War}_B \text{ by } A \qquad (1')$$

$$\pi^B > [(1 - P_B)(G - L) - C_f]/[(1 - P_B)(G - L) + C_{t'}]. \qquad (2')$$

In this game negotiations are always preferred to war (see table 2) and may or may not be preferred to a successful intervention. For all A and B, the denominators of (1') and (2') are strictly positive. For doves (those that prefer negotiating to intervening) the numerator in expression (2') is negative, yielding a negative value for the right-hand side of the expression. Thus, if B is a dove, any belief about retaliation is sufficient to satisfy expression (2′).

Hawks prefer to intervene over negotiating but prefer to negotiate rather than face a war that follows from the adversary's retaliation. The initial use of force creates the risk of facing a retaliatory strike. Therefore, for a sufficiently high degree of belief that retaliation will follow the use of force, (expressions (1′) and (2′)), the choice to negotiate dominates initiating the use of force.

Proposition 3 is instructive. It reinforces the well-known claim of Vegetius that those who desire peace should prepare for war. Reliance on the good will of others is not sufficient for peace, but *convincing* demonstrations of preparedness are. Thus, mutual reputations for preparedness to retaliate against aggression can insure peace even between the most hawkish adversaries. Paradoxically, failure to build a war-readiness reputation, or the belief that one has failed in such reputation building, can lead one to initiate war.

Proposition 3 shows that only three conditions are required to insure negotiations. These are:

a) A believes B will retaliate if A uses force;
b) B believes A will retaliate if B uses force; and
c) A believes that B is persuaded of A's willingness to retaliate with force.

What happens in a crisis as these conditions are relaxed?

If A does not expect B to retaliate and A is a hawk, then for A, using force dominates offering to negotiate. Of course, if A is mistaken in its expectation that B will not retaliate, the mistaken belief will lead to war and away from negotiations. Similarly, should Hawk B anticipate that A will capitulate to its use of force, then B will not offer to negotiate, but will use force instead. If B is mistaken in its expectation that A would not retaliate, then again war, rather than negotiations, will ensue. Thus far we can see that a willingness to retaliate coupled with a failure to persuade the adversary of one's intention to strike back can result in war when otherwise negotiations would have taken place.

Even if A and B are sufficiently persuaded of the rival's willingness to retaliate, war can follow, as suggested by condition (c) above. A may be convinced of B's willingness to fight back but fear that B is not adequately convinced of A's own resolve to retaliate. In such a case, as in the example used to prove proposition (2), A dare not forego the advantages of striking first on the chance that B would negotiate. Thus, the violation of any of the conditions sufficient to insure negotiations can result in war. Nations wishing to negotiate conflicts of interest rather than fight over them must not fail to be convincing in their willingness to use force.

War, as the equilibrium outcome of the game, arises when

$$\pi^A(\text{War}_A) + (1 - \pi^A)(\text{Int}_A) > (1 - \mu^A)(\text{Negotiate}) +$$
$$\mu^A \max\{\text{Int}_B, \text{War}_B\} \quad (3)$$

and

$$\text{War}_A > \text{Int}_A \text{ for } B \quad (4)$$

or

$$\pi^A(\text{War}_A) + (1 - \pi^A)(\text{Int}_A) < (1 - \mu^A)(\text{Negotiate}) +$$
$$\mu^A \max\{\text{Int}_B, \text{War}_B\} \quad (5)$$

$$\pi^B(\text{War}_B) + (1 - \pi^B)(\text{Int}_B) > \text{Negotiate} \quad (6)$$

and

$$\text{War}_B > \text{Int}_B \text{ for } A. \quad (7)$$

Expressions (3) and (4) yield War_A as the equilibrium outcome, while (5), (6), and (7) result in War_B as the equilibrium outcome. Conditions (5), (6), and (7) highlight the similarity between the conditions sufficient for yielding negotiations and conditions sufficient for war. Condition (5) is identical to condition (1) used in proving proposition (3). Condition (6) reverses the inequality sign from condition (1). What circumstances can lead to this reversal of signs?

Given our initial assumptions, we found that B strictly prefers negotiation and Int_B to War_B. A, similarly, must prefer negotiation to War_B and to Int_B. What is indeterminate is A's willingness to retaliate if attacked by B. If B is a Hawk, then the more confident B is that A will *not* retaliate, the more desirable is the lottery involving the use of force relative to negotiating for B. Thus, A's failure to persuade B that A would retaliate opens the possibility for war. Indeed, if A believes it has failed to convince B of its resolve to fight back, then the inequality in expression (3) favors A's preemptive use of force, leading to a war initiated by A. Negotiations, then, can break down, leading to war if the belief that the adversary will retaliate is reduced enough to reverse the inequality in expression (3). The risk that A will initiate a war rises if A's willingness to defend itself in war is suspect.

According to the logic of our game, deterrence is sufficient, though not necessary, to insure that crises are resolved peacefully. Mutual belief in the dovishness of one's rival, if correct, always yields negotiations. But, if faith in the dovishness of one's adversary is misplaced, war or surrender are real dangers for those who are not prepared to use force. Fear of the retaliatory potential of one's opponents alone, regardless of hawkishness or dovishness, can insure peaceful crisis resolution at minimal risk. To err on the side of preparedness to retaliate cannot, according to the logic of this game, lead to war. As Henry Kissinger has noted, "In the final reckoning weakness has invariably tempted aggression and impotence brings abdication of policy in its train" (1979, 195).

Conclusion

We have set out a game in extensive form in which national leaders make choices over the use of force. We have stipulated the necessary and sufficient conditions for crisis resolution through negotiations. We have also shown conditions that precipitate war. Interestingly, these conditions appear to be only slightly different from the circumstances sufficient for negotiations. Claims for peace through deterrence are reinforced by our analysis.

Dove-like intentions are inadequate to insure peace, even when both rivals are Doves, although dovishness together with complete information is sufficient for peace. Hawkish intentions also are not sufficient to preclude the peaceful resolution of disputes, and this is true even under conditions of complete information. Indeed, a convincing willingness to meet force with force is sufficient to insure that crises are resolved through negotiations. Good intentions do not preclude war just as surely as hostile intentions do not insure violence. Even a world made up only of Doves could be a very dangerous place.

Legislative Processes

Reciprocity among Self-Interested Actors: Uncertainty, Asymmetry, and Distribution

Randall L. Calvert

Reciprocity is a behavioral pattern in which each of two actors repeatedly bears a short-run cost to provide a benefit to the other, provided the other does the same. Since this pattern is a basic element of social cooperation generally (Blau 1964; Gouldner 1960; Homans 1961; Malinowski 1932), it is no surprise to find that nearly any kind of ongoing political interaction features reciprocity. Matthews (1960) and Fenno (1966) document the importance of a reciprocity norm in the political lives of members of Congress, perhaps the concept's best-known application in political science. Reciprocity may underlie other important legislative norms, when they exist, such as committee autonomy, deference to experts, or party loyalties. Legislators refer to the keeping of informal accounts of favors granted and received in such concrete terms as "political capital" or "political IOUs." Obviously reciprocity is a basic fact of legislative life, and an important lubricant in the strategic give and take among individual legislators. The concept applies with similar importance to fields ranging from bureaucratic politics (Heclo 1977, chaps. 5 and 6) to international relations (Keohane 1984, esp. 126–30).

Axelrod (1981, 1984) has offered the repeated, two-player Prisoner's Dilemma game as a model of reciprocity, citing in particular Matthews's (1960) work on the U.S. Senate. His approach captures several important aspects of reciprocity, in particular the myopic temptation to withhold one's contribution and the central role of repeated interaction. The model demonstrates that reciprocity depends on the relation between discounting of future payoffs and the costs and benefits of cooperative behavior. In particular, Axelrod is able to characterize

---

The first versions of this paper were written while the author was postdoctoral fellow in political economy at the Graduate School of Industrial Administration at Carnegie-Mellon University. Thanks are due to GSIA for their generous support. The author is also grateful for helpful comments at earlier stages from: Robert Axelrod; Kenneth Shepsle; Michael MacKuen; and seminar participants in GSIA, the Graduate School of Business at Stanford University, and the departments of political science at Ohio State University, the University of Rochester, and Washington University.

conditions on these parameters under which a cooperative strategy can be maintained in equilibrium.

The present essay has two general purposes. One is to introduce key features of real-life reciprocity relations not represented in the Axelrod model, and to understand how reciprocity depends on these features. The first feature is uncertainty. I grant you a favor today in the hope that at some future time I will be able to ask and receive a favor of you. However, neither of us can be sure when that will happen. If we discount future payoffs, then the "repayment" for the favor has uncertain value to me, and the "cost" of your obligation is uncertain to you. For such situations, the analysis presented below examines the nature of stable reciprocity arrangements and the conditions under which they can be maintained.

A second key feature introduced here is that reciprocity relationships may involve important forms of asymmetry. I may ask frequent favors of you, while you can benefit only rarely by a favor from me. The benefit I receive from you may be only slightly greater than the cost I bear on your behalf, while your costs are trivial and your benefits great. Such asymmetries are especially likely to occur in interaction between actors of different status, such as a legislative leader and a rank-and-file member. The analysis below takes these features into account as well.

The other purpose of this essay is to examine the extent to which available gains from cooperation are achieved and how these gains are distributed. Even if the costs, benefits, and frequencies for two actors are identical, it is possible for reciprocal behavior to be lopsided. I may expect you to do everything I ask, while I only occasionally provide you benefits in return. Using the analysis developed here, it will be possible to examine when various distributions of the gains from reciprocity can be achieved in equilibrium. In particular, we will see that bargaining over the gains is likely to lead to a particular form of symmetrical reciprocity, even if the frequencies and payoffs are asymmetrical.

The essay proceeds as follows. The first section below presents notation and describes the reciprocity game. The next section examines the patterns of behavior under which players could achieve the full gains from reciprocity. Then the analysis turns to the question of equilibrium behavior: when will rational actors be able to carry out the required patterns of behavior? An examination of the distribution of the gains follows. The final section summarizes and concludes.

The Model

The reciprocity game consists of infinite repetition of a two-player constituent game G. The game G proceeds as follows.

Stage 1. Nature moves first, selecting at random whether each player will have the opportunity to "receive a favor" from the other. Each player i is selected with probability p_i and each player's selection is independent of the other's. Thus one, both, or neither player may be able to receive a favor on a given turn.

Stage 2. Both players learn the result of Stage 1. If player j has the opportunity to receive, the other player i now chooses a *level of effort* $q_i \in [0,1]$ to devote to providing the favor. If both players can receive, they make this decision simultaneously.

Stage 3. If player i exerted effort q_i, then player j (the other player) receives a benefit $q_i b_j$ and player i bears a cost of $q_i c_i$. Throughout we assume b_i and c_i positive.

Payoffs in the reciprocity game are the benefits and costs summed over all iterations of G, discounted by a factor $w \in (0,1)$ for each iteration. In particular, if each player i provides a level of effort q_i in every iteration at which a favor is available to the other player j, then player i's expected payoff is

$$\sum_{t=1}^{\infty} w^{t-1}(q_j p_i b_i - q_i p_j c_i) = \frac{q_j p_i b_i - q_i p_j c_i}{1 - w}. \tag{1}$$

If a player sets $q_i = 0$, we will say he *refuses* the favor; if $q_i = 1$, we say that he *grants* it. We call each repetition of G a *turn* or *iteration* of the reciprocity game. Since a favor may not be available on every turn, we distinguish the turns on which Player i can receive a favor as *opportunities*.

A player's *strategy* in the reciprocity game consists of a description of how much effort the player will devote to providing favors in every possible situation that can arise in the game. To be precise, let $N^T = (n_1, n_2, \ldots, n_T)$ be the sequence of selections by nature on turns up to and including iteration T; for each t, $n_t \in \{\phi, \{1\}, \{2\}, \{1,2\}\}$. Let $F_1^T = (k_1, k_2, \ldots, k_{r(N^T)})$ be the subsequence of iterations in $(1, 2, \ldots, T)$ on which a favor was available to player 1 (that is, the iterations $t \leq T$ for which $1 \in n_t$), and $F_2^T = (j_1, j_2, \ldots, j_{s(N^T)})$ those on which a favor was available to player 2. Let $Q_1^T(N^T) = (q_{j_1}, q_{j_2}, \ldots, q_{j_{s(N^T)}})$ be the levels of effort exerted by Player 1 on all relevant turns up to and including T; similarly $Q_2^T(N^T) = (q_{k_1}, q_{k_2}, \ldots, q_{k_{r(N^T)}})$. Then, if $i \in n_{T+1}$, the effort of player $j \neq i$ on turn $T + 1$ is given by a function σ_j^{T+1}:

$$q_j^{T+1} = \sigma_j^{T+1}(N^T, Q_1^T, Q_2^T).$$

Player j's strategy σ_j consists of the set of functions $\{\sigma_j^t\}_{t=1}^{\infty}$.

It is important in what follows to distinguish strategies from *outcomes*. An outcome is a sequence of moves that actually occurs in a play of the reciprocity game, and is determined by the players' strategies σ_i and the infinite sequence N of moves by Nature. Thus a player's expected payoff from the reciprocity game is the expectation of the player's payoff from each possible outcome of the game, given the probability distrubution over outcomes induced by p_1, p_2, σ_1, and σ_2. We write this payoff as $U_i(\sigma_1, \sigma_2; p_1, p_2)$, or, when unambiguous, just $U_i(\sigma_1, \sigma_2)$.

A particularly useful way of writing this payoff function is as follows. Let $q_i^t(N)$ be the effort levels devoted by player i on turn t under (σ_1, σ_2) given the first $t - 1$ elements of the sequence N of moves by nature. Then

$$U_i(\sigma_1, \sigma_2) = E \sum_{t=1}^{\infty} w^{t-1} [q_j^t(N) b_i - q_i^t(N) c_i] \ , \tag{2}$$

where the expectation is taken with respect to the distribution over values of N generated by the probabilities p_1 and p_2.

The reciprocity game would be a standard iterated Prisoner's Dilemma provided $b_1 = b_2$, $c_1 = c_2$, and $p_1 = p_2 = 1$, and provided that the defining conditions for the Prisoner's Dilemma are satisfied by G (Axelrod 1981):

$$-c_i < 0 < b_i - c_i < b_i$$

and

$$\frac{b_i - c_i}{2} < b_i - c_i \ .$$

The reciprocity game thus incorporates several features important in real-life reciprocity relations but missing from the iterated Prisoner's Dilemma. First, a player who performs a favor does not know precisely when there will be an opportunity for the recipient to repay in kind. Second, the frequency p_1 with which player 1 has a favor to ask of player 2 may differ from the frequency with which player 2 can benefit from the help of player 1. Third, the relative values of the benefit of receiving and the cost of granting a favor may differ between the players. Finally, in any opportunity to provide a favor, a player may perform with varying degrees of diligence.[1] These differences suggest two reasons why the outcomes of the reciprocity game generally may differ from those of the iterated Prisoner's Dilemma: there may be no single obvious analogy to the Tit-for-Tat strategy around which the players can coordinate their cooperation; and there are several ways in which a player could provide partial cooperation, in either the long or short run.

After examining in the next section what sorts of strategies are necessary in order to realize the full gains from cooperation, we will proceed to analyze rational behavior in the reciprocity game with special attention to the possibility of incomplete cooperation in the outcomes.

Efficiency

Through reciprocity, each player can gain a higher expected payoff than he would get if each repetition of G were played myopically. A strategy pair is *efficient* if these gains are fully realized: that is, given the expected payoff of player 1, player 2 receives the maximum possible payoff, and vice versa.[2] In this section we examine what efficiency requires of strategies in the reciprocity game. It turns out that full reciprocity, in which each player always grants all favors, is always efficient. We provide conditions under which partial reciprocity is efficient as well. Then in the next section we determine the extent to which reciprocity and efficiency are possible in equilibrium.

Formally, we will say that a strategy pair (σ_1, σ_2) is *efficient* if no change in strategies by either or both players could increase one player's expected payoff without decreasing the other's:

$$U_i(\sigma'_1, \sigma'_2) > U_i(\sigma_1, \sigma_2) \Rightarrow U_j(\sigma'_1, \sigma'_2) < U_j(\sigma_1, \sigma_2) \text{ for all } \sigma'_1$$

and $\sigma'_2, i \neq j$.

The first lemma gives a condition under which the players *cannot* achieve mutual gains by granting each other favors.

LEMMA 1. *If $c_1/b_1 \geq b_2/c_2$, then the strategy pair in which both players refuse all favors is efficient.*

---

1. The continuous scale of effort is included both for realism and to afford an extra avenue for asymmetric reciprocity. Despite the availability of such asymmetric outcomes, neither efficiency nor bargaining need lead the players to use them, as we will see.
2. Note that we ignore for the moment any possible incentive problems. This is "first best" efficiency.

Proof. If both players refuse all favors, the expected payoff to each player is zero. We prove that no alternative strategy pair yields a Pareto improvement. Suppose that, for each infinite sequence N of moves by Nature, each player i were to devote positive effort $q_i^t(N)$ for each t in some subsequence of iterations, and for all other t, $q_i^t(N) = 0$. Let

$$h_i(N) = \sum_{t=1}^{\infty} q_i^t(N) \, w^{t-1}.$$

Now either $Eh_2(N)/Eh_1(N) < c_1/b_1$ or $Eh_2(N)/Eh_1(N) > b_2/c_2$ or all three ratios are equal (expectations are taken with respect to the probability distribution induced by p_1 and p_2 on the sequences N of moves by Nature). In the first case,

$$Eh_2(N)b_1 - Eh_1(N)c_1 < 0,$$

that is,

$$E\left[\sum_{t=1}^{\infty} w^{t-1}[q_2^t(N)\,b_1 - q_1^t(N)\,c_1]\right] < 0.$$

But from (2) this is exactly player 1's expected payoff from the alternative sequences of moves q_i^t. In the second case, similarly,

$$Eh_1(N)b_2 - Eh_2(N)c_2 < 0,$$

so player 2's expected payoff would be negative. Finally, in the third case both players receive 0. Thus for no pattern of positive favor-doing by the players can either player receive a positive payoff without the other receiving a negative payoff. Q.E.D.

Using a similar method of proof, the second lemma gives a condition under which a Pareto improvement is available.

LEMMA 2. *Suppose that $c_1/b_1 < b_2/c_2$. Let (σ_1, σ_2) be a strategy pair such that for each player there is set of sequences of moves by Nature, occurring with positive probability, on which that player does not grant all available favors. Then (σ_1, σ_2) is not efficient.*

Proof. For $i = 1, 2$, let $\mathcal{N}_i$ be the set of sequences of Nature's moves on which player i sometimes sets $q_i < 1$. For each $N \in \mathcal{N}_i$, let $F_i(N)$ be a finite subsequence of turns on which $q_i < 1$. Let f_1 and f_2 be functions of N such that $f_i(N) < 1 - \sigma_i^t(N^t, Q_1^t, Q_2^t)$ for all $t \in F_i(N)$, and such that

$$\frac{c_1}{b_1} < \frac{f_2(N)}{f_1(N)} < \frac{b_2}{c_2}.$$

Existence of such f_i is guaranteed by the finiteness of the $F_i(N)$ and the assumption $c_1/b_1 < b_2/c_2$. Now for each $N \in \mathcal{N}_i$, on each turn $t \in F_i(N)$, increase player i's effort by adding $f_i(N)$ to the effort level called for by σ_i. Player 1's utility gain from this change under each sequence N is $f_2(N)b_1 - f_1(N)c_1$, which is positive since $c_1/b_1 < f_2(N)/f_1(N)$, and thus player 1's overall gain in expected utility is positive. Likewise player 2 realizes a positive utility gain. Thus the change is a Pareto improvement. Q.E.D.

Lemmas 1 and 2 help prove the main proposition on efficiency. It states that, whenever the trading of favors is desirable at all, efficiency is achieved only when at least one player grants all available favors. In other words, arrangements in which the players match their efforts, such as by rewarding each favor with exactly one favor, or maintaining "balanced accounts" by matching totals of benefits provided or effort expended, will inevitably fail to realize some of the available gains from reciprocity. For efficiency, at least one player must be willing to grant every available favor regardless of his own lack of opportunities to receive favors.

PROPOSITION 1. *Suppose refusal of all favors is inefficient. Then a strategy pair is efficient if and only if at least one of the players grants every available favor (except perhaps on a set of sequences of Nature's moves having probability zero).*

Proof. Lemma 1 explains the role of the initial assumption. Necessity follows directly from Lemma 2. For sufficiency, we need to show that no Pareto improvement is available. Suppose that for each sequence N of Nature's moves and each iteration t, each player i changes his original strategy so that the levels of effort are increased by $r_i^t(N)$ (which may be positive, negative, or zero). Let

$$h_i(N) = \sum_{t=1}^{\infty} w^{t-1} r_i^t(N).$$

Assume that player 1 was previously granting all favors. Then $r_1^t(N)$ must be nonpositive for all N and all t, so $Eh_1(N) \leq 0$. If player 1 gains from the changes in strategies, $E[b_1 h_2(N) - c_1 h_1(N)] > 0$. But then $Eh_2(N)/Eh_1(N) < c_1/b_1 < b_2/c_2$, so $E[b_2 h_1(N) - c_2 h_2(N)] < 0$ and player 2 is a loser. On the other hand, suppose player 2 gains from the change. Since $h_1(N) \leq 0$ necessarily, for player 2 to gain it must be that $h_2(N) \leq 0$ also, so $E[b_2 h_1(N) - c_2 h_2(N)] > 0$ implies $Eh_1(N)/Eh_2(N) < c_2/b_2 < b_1/c_1$, and player 1 is a loser. Q.E.D.

Of course, such a strategy pair need not be individually rational, that is, need not give each player a payoff at least as great as what he could guarantee himself without the assistance of the other player, namely zero. If one player always grants while the other always refuses, the result is efficient, but the granting player receives a negative payoff.

A strategy pair exhibits *full reciprocity* if, for every sequence of moves by Nature, both players grant every available favor. The following proposition demonstrates conditions under which full reciprocity is both efficient and individually rational for each player.

PROPOSITION 2. *Suppose $c_1/b_1 < p_1/p_2 < b_2/c_2$. Then any strategy pair yielding full reciprocity is efficient, and gives each player a positive payoff.*

Proof. By Proposition 1, full reciprocity is efficient since both players always grant. To show individual rationality, note that player 1's expected payoff from full rationality is $b_1 p_1 - c_1 p_2$ per turn, which by the assumption is positive. Similarly player 2's expected payoff per turn is $b_2 p_2 - c_2 p_1 > 0$. Q.E.D.

Proposition 2 demonstrates that the underlying reciprocity game need not be particularly symmetrical for a symmetrical outcome such as full reciprocity to be efficient.

In the next section we examine whether such efficient outcomes can be achieved by rational players, that is, whether equilibrium strategies can yield the required pattern of favor-granting to achieve efficiency. After that, we turn to the question of distribution—how lopsidedly can the gains from reciprocity be distributed while maintaining both efficiency and equilibrium?

Full Reciprocity in Equilibrium

For the players to achieve full reciprocity, they must use strategies that counteract the temptation for each player to occasionally refuse a favor and avoid the associated cost. If this is possible, we will say that full reciprocity is "implementable," that is, achievable through equilibrium strategies. As Abreu (1986) points out, if there is any way to enforce a given pattern of cooperation, it can be done by making the "punishment" for deviating from it as severe as possible. In the reciprocity game, the worst thing a player can do to his opponent is to deny all future favors, holding the opponent's payoff down to at most zero. So consider the following strategy.[3]

Permanent Retaliation (σ_{PR}). If the opponent has granted every available favor in the past, then grant (set $q_i = 1$); if the opponent has ever failed to grant, then refuse (set $q_i = 0$).

This corresponds to the classic "grim" strategy for enforcing cooperation in the repeated Prisoner's Dilemma game (Friedman 1971). Intuitively, it is clear that σ_{PR} will succeed in enforcing full reciprocity provided that the discount factor is not too small, the frequency of receiving favors is large enough, and the frequency of giving favors is small enough, all relative to costs and benefits. The following result makes this precise.

PROPOSITION 3. *Full reciprocity can be implemented if and only if*

$$\frac{c_1}{b_1} \leq \frac{wp_1}{1 - w(1 - p_2)} \quad \text{and} \quad \frac{c_2}{b_2} \leq \frac{wp_2}{1 - w(1 - p_1)}. \tag{3}$$

Proof. Since full reciprocity can be implemented if and only if it can be done through permanent retaliation, it suffices to show that (σ_{PR}, σ_{PR}) is an equilibrium strategy pair. Since a one-time deviation from always granting incurs eternal noncooperation, the only deviation from σ_{PR} that could ever pay off would be to switch all at once and permanently to always refusing favors. It pays player 1 to avoid such a deviation only if, on a turn in which a favor is available to player 2, the gain from doing so is nonpositive:

$$c_1 - \frac{w}{1 - w}(p_1 b_1 - p_2 c_1) \leq 0.$$

The first term is the gain, relative to σ_{PR}, from refusing on the current turn, and the second term is the foregone benefit from continued full

---

3. Notice that neither the following strategy, nor the ones given below, yield subgame perfect equilibria, since it would not be rational to punish an opponent who uses the same strategy except for a refusal on one isolated move. This could easily be remedied by including punishments for failing to punish, and so on at every "level" of punishment. Since the strategies as stated have the virtue of simplicity, we proceed to ignore this problem; but obviously the corresponding subgame perfect strategies yield the same results.

reciprocity on the next and succeeding turns. Algebraic manipulation yields the first condition in (3); a similar argument for player 2 yields the second condition. Q.E.D.

Condition (3) is important for what it tells us about how the various parameters constrain reciprocity, and for its implications about the bounds placed on c_i/b_i in (3) as the other parameters go toward extreme values. As w approaches 1, the bound for player i approaches p_i/p_j; thus (3) becomes simply an individual rationality criterion, $c_i/b_i \leq p_i/p_j$, identical to the condition in Proposition 2. As p_1 and p_2 approach 1 together, the bound approaches w; for cooperation in the repeated Prisoner's Dilemma, then, we would need $c_i/b_i \leq w$ (cf. the condition in Axelrod 1981). Finally if p_1 is large, say $1 - \epsilon$, and p_2 is small, say ϵ, then as $\epsilon \to 0$ the bounds approach $c_1/b_1 \leq w/(1 - w)$ and $c_2/b_2 \leq (1 - w)/w$. Thus if player 2 seldom gets to ask a favor but player 1 does so frequently, and if discounting is not too severe (w near 1), then c_2/b_2 must be tiny for full reciprocity to be possible. However, c_1/b_1 could be quite large since $w/(1 - w)$ is large; even if c_1 is much greater than b_1, then, the high frequency of favors received makes reciprocity worthwhile for player 1.

Since permanent retaliation seems rather severe a punishment to use in a more complex environment than the two-player, full-information setting modeled here, it is interesting to examine a less harsh punishment scheme. The following is one possible analogy to the Tit-for-Tat strategy of the repeated Prisoner's Dilemma:

Tit-for-Tat (σ_{TFT}). If the opponent set $q_j < 1$ at the last opportunity, then set $q_i = 0$; otherwise set $q_i = 1$.

This differs from the Prisoner's Dilemma Tit-for-Tat in that, here, a failure to grant may incur a long string of punishments or none at all, depending on when the refuser next has an opportunity to grant another favor (and thus "apologize"). The present Tit-for-Tat has the following interesting property:

PROPOSITION 4. *(σ_{TFT}, σ_{TFT}) is an equilibrium strategy pair if and only if (σ_{PR}, σ_{PR}) is also.*

Proof. Suppose player 2 uses Tit-for-Tat. We must examine three kinds of possible deviation for player 1. First, for player 1 to deviate by switching to permanent refusal, condition (3) would have to fail. Thus if Permanent Retaliation is an equilibrium, such deviations from Tit-for-Tat are unprofitable, and vice versa.

A second type of deviation is as follows: refuse the currently available favor; after refusing every available favor for a total of t iterations, grant the next favor available, and continue with σ_{TFT} (beginning with another grant) thereafter. The gain from such a deviation can be computed as follows. In the first period, player 1 saves the cost of providing a favor, c_1, with certainty. In the next $t - 1$ iterations, player 1 loses the favors that would otherwise have been done and saves the cost of the favors that he would otherwise have granted, for a discounted expected gain of

$$\sum_{s=2}^{t} w^{s-1}(p_1 b_1 - p_2 c_1) \quad \text{or} \quad \frac{w(1 - w^{t-1})}{1 - w}(b_1 p_1 - c_1 p_2).$$

At that point player 1 begins looking for the first opportunity to perform a favor for player 2. With probability p_2 this opportunity occurs immediately; player 1 performs a favor, does not receive one if available, and the players return thereafter to granting all favors. The expected payoff loss (undiscounted) compared with the original strategies from this event would be $p_2 p_1 b_1$. With probability $1 - p_2$, however, no favor is available to player 2 and player 1 cannot "apologize" yet; player 1 still foregoes any favor available to him, losing an expected $p_1 b_1$, and the game proceeds to the next iteration, where the whole situation is repeated. The discounted expected loss from this situation in which player 1 begins, $t + 1$ periods in the future, to look for an opportunity to "apologize" is thus

$$w^t \{ p_2 p_1 b_1 + (1 - p_2)(p_1 b_1 + w \{ p_2 p_1 b_1 + (1 - p_2)(p_1 b_1 + w \{ \ldots$$

$$= w^t \sum_{s=0}^{\infty} (1-p_2)^s w^s [p_2 p_1 b_1 + (1-p_2) p_1 b_1]$$

$$= w^t \sum_{s=0}^{\infty} (1-p_2)^s w^s p_1 b_1 = w^t \frac{p_1 b_1}{1 - w(1 - p_2)}.$$

The total gain from this deviation, then, is

$$c_1 - \frac{w(1 - w^{t-1})}{1 - w}(b_1 p_1 - c_1 p_2) - w^t \frac{p_1 b_1}{1 - w(1 - p_2)}.$$

By (3) the middle term, the intervening period of mutual refusal, is never profitable for player 1, so the only possible deviation of this type is one in which $t = 1$, that is, player 1 skips one favor for player 2 and then immediately attempts to return to reciprocity. This kind of deviation is profitable if and only if its gain is nonpositive:

$$c_1 - w\frac{p_1 b_1}{1 - w(1 - p_2)} \leq 0, \text{ or}$$

$$\frac{c_1}{b_1} \leq \frac{w p_1}{1 - w(1 - p_2)}, \tag{4}$$

exactly as in condition (3). A similar argument holds for player 2.

A similar calculation can be applied to a variant on this kind of deviation, in which player 1 maintains mutual refusal for a given number of *refusals* rather than for a given number of periods. Again, the intervening period of mutual refusal is unprofitable, and condition (4) applies.

A final form of deviation would be to repeat the latter type several times. If condition (3) holds, each of these episodes of refusal will be unprofitable; if condition (3) fails, each will be profitable. Thus the conditions for $(\sigma_{TFT}, \sigma_{TFT})$ to be an equilibrium are exactly the same as those in Proposition 3. Q.E.D.

Thus reciprocity, or any other pattern of behavior, is implementable only if implementable by Tit-for-Tat; we need not worry about the realism of Permanent Retaliation since it is never required.[4] Note that this would also be true of the repeated Prisoner's Dilemma if its payoffs could be expressed as appropriate sums of b_i and $-c_i$. The payoffs in Axelrod (1981, 1984) cannot be expressed in this way, and Axelrod proves accordingly (indirectly; see 1981, theorem 2) that for some parameter values Permanent Retaliation will yield a cooperative equilibrium and Tit-for-Tat will not.

Partial Reciprocity

There are two sets of circumstances in which the players in the reciprocity game might reach some cooperative agreement that falls short of full reciprocity. First, if condition (3) fails, so that reciprocity cannot be maintained in equilibrium, it might still be possible to find an equilibrium in which the players realize "gains from trade" in doing some

---

4. From the methods of proof used here, it is readily apparent that several other retaliation schemes are equivalent to Permanent Retaliation and Tit-for-Tat in their ability to enforce cooperation. These include: (1) retaliating for n opportunities after every defection; (2) retaliating for n iterations after every defection; and (3) behaving as in Tit-for-Tat but resuming cooperative behavior only after receiving a string of n "apologies" rather than just one.

favors, or in providing less than full effort. Second, even if condition (3) is satisfied, the players might arrive at some reciprocity arrangement other than full reciprocity. (In the next section we will model one such process of equilibrium selection by appending a "preplay" bargaining phase to the reciprocity game.) We will refer to outcomes in which one or both players expend some, but not full, effort on their opponents' behalf as "partial reciprocity."

Under partial reciprocity, the players could in principle vary their levels of effort from one turn to the next, depending on random devices or the entire history of previous turns. For simplicity, however, we confine attention to outcomes in which each player uses a constant level of effort $\bar{q}_i$ during cooperative periods, and perhaps a different level (here, $q_i = 0$) in retaliation for the opponent's deviations. The task of this section is to identify conditions on $\bar{q}_1$ and $\bar{q}_2$ that are required for equilibrium. We explore variations of the strategies σ_{PR} and σ_{TFT}, and identify the condition for efficient partial reciprocity equilibrium.

In order to discuss equilibrium strategies, we need to broaden our definitions of the repeated game strategies used in the previous section. For enforcing a partial reciprocity pattern, the strongest punishment is again a variant of Permanent Retaliation:

Permanent Retaliation with $\bar{q}_1$ and $\bar{q}_2$ ($\sigma_{PR}(\bar{q}_1,\bar{q}_2)$). If the opponent j has ever given effort less than $\bar{q}_j$ then i sets $q_i = 0$; otherwise i sets $q_i = \bar{q}_i$.

Using this strategy we can prove the following.

PROPOSITION 5. *Effort levels $\bar{q}_1$ and $\bar{q}_2$ are implementable if and only if*

$$\frac{c_2(1 - w + wp_1)}{wp_2b_2} \leq \frac{\bar{q}_1}{\bar{q}_2} \leq \frac{wp_1b_1}{c_1(1 - w + wp_2)}. \tag{5}$$

Proof. Suppose both players use the strategy $\sigma_{PR}(\bar{q}_1, \bar{q}_2)$. As in Proposition 3, equilibrium requires

$$w\frac{\bar{q}_2p_1b_1 - \bar{q}_1p_2c_1}{1 - w} \geq \bar{q}_1c_1$$

to keep player 1 from deviating. (Notice that player 1 has no incentive to give more effort than $\bar{q}_1$, and that there is never any point in deviating by giving any positive effort less than $\bar{q}_1$.) Algebraic manipulation gives

$$\frac{\bar{q}_1}{\bar{q}_2} \leq \frac{wp_1b_1}{c_1(1 - w + wp_2)},$$

and a similar argument applied to player 2 gives the condition

$$\frac{\bar{q}_1}{\bar{q}_2} \geq \frac{c_2(1 - w + wp_1)}{wp_2 b_2}.$$

If defection from $(\bar{q}_1, \bar{q}_2)$ cannot be prevented using permanent retaliation, it cannot be prevented under any other strategy either; thus the indicated conditions are necessary for any equilibrium with positive effort. If the conditions hold, then $(\bar{q}_1, \bar{q}_2)$ can always be implemented using permanent retaliation, so the conditions are sufficient as well. Q.E.D.

Since Proposition 5 also applies if $\bar{q}_1 = \bar{q}_2 = 1$, we have the following general condition for cooperative equilibrium:

COROLLARY 1. *Reciprocity is implementable only if*

$$\frac{wp_1 b_1}{c_1(1 - w + wp_2)} \geq \frac{c_2(1 - w + wp_1)}{wp_2 b_2}. \tag{6}$$

If (6) holds, at least partial reciprocity is implementable.

Proof. Manipulation of (5).

Notice that condition (3), the necessary and sufficient condition for full reciprocity equilibrium, is sufficient for condition (6). Condition (6) compares a function of all player 1's parameters with the same function of all player 2's parameters to determine whether any $\bar{q}_1$ and $\bar{q}_2$ can be maintained in equilibrium other than $\bar{q}_1 = \bar{q}_2 = 0$. With proper translation, all our interpretations of (3) apply to (6): note especially the independence of p_1 and p_2 and the limiting role of w.

Using expression (5) it is easy to see how partial reciprocity could be implementable when full reciprocity is not. Formally, full reciprocity requires that $q_1 = q_2 = 1$ satisfy (5); but it may be that the right- and left-hand sides of (5) are both less than 1 or both greater than 1, with the inequality still satisfied. Under such circumstances, achieving cooperation in equilibrium *requires* partial reciprocity, because condition (3) fails. Substantively, this happens if the asymmetries in the game are too great: b_1/c_1 too small, c_2/b_2 too large, or p_1 or p_2 too small. The point at which too large or too small is reached is partly determined by the discount factor w. The smaller w is, the less asymmetry is tolerable for full reciprocity.

It is also easy to see the conditions under which efficiency can be achieved.

COROLLARY 2. *If full or partial reciprocity is implementable then efficiency is implementable.*

Proof. Condition (6) implies that condition (5) holds for some q_1 and q_2. Obviously we can choose these so that max$\{q_1, q_2\} = 1$ and $0 < q_i \leq 1$. The result then follows from Proposition 2. Q.E.D.

Finally, with an appropriate extension of Tit for Tat, we can prove the analogue of Proposition 4. Define the strategy

Tit for Tat with $\bar{q}_1$ and $\bar{q}_2$ ($\sigma_{TFT}(\bar{q}_1, \bar{q}_2)$). If the opponent j gave effort $q_j \geq \bar{q}_j$ on the last opportunity, i uses $q_i = \bar{q}_i$; otherwise set $q_i = 0$.

COROLLARY 3. *Partial equilibrium can be achieved in equilibrium using $\sigma_{TFT}(\bar{q}_1, \bar{q}_2)$ if and only if it can be achieved using $\sigma_{PR}(\bar{q}_1, \bar{q}_2)$.*

Proof. Proceed just as in Proposition 4, inserting $\bar{q}_1$ and $\bar{q}_2$ where appropriate.

The results thus far are summarized by the diagrams in figure 1. Figure 1a shows the feasible combinations of q_1 and q_2 (those inside the square) and the implementable combinations (those between the two diagonal rays). The two rays are loci satisfying the two weak inequalities in (5) with equality. As long as (6) holds, they will be oriented as shown, and everything in between them satisfies (5). The upper right corner of the square is the full reciprocity outcome; it lies between the two rays as shown if the conditions in (3) and (6) are satisfied. Figure 1b translates figure 1a into the space of discounted expected payoffs u_i to the two players (notice that the northwest corner in figure 1a becomes the southeast corner in figure 1b). The kinked line is the set of efficient outcomes, and the kink itself is the full reciprocity outcome. The smaller c_2/b_1 and c_1/b_2 are, the more "square" the feasible set in payoff space is. The more asymmetric the game is, that is the more p_1 and p_2 differ, or c_1/b_1 and c_2/b_2 differ, the more skewed the feasible set is.

Preplay Bargaining and Distribution

If partial reciprocity is implementable, then it is almost certainly implementable with a wide range of values of q_1 and q_2. In other words, there are multiple equilibrium outcomes. The model developed thus far gives us no way to distinguish among these outcomes for predictive purposes. However, it is possible to address the question in two ways. First, we imagine a preplay bargaining process in which the players negotiate over how to divide the available gains from reciprocity, that is, negotiate over

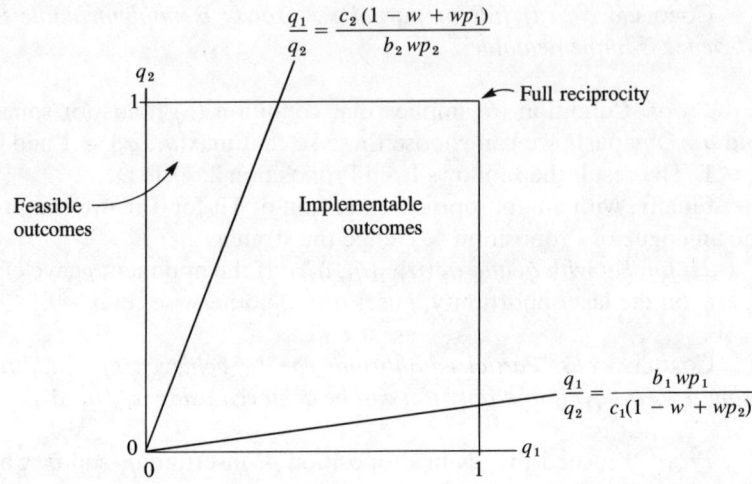

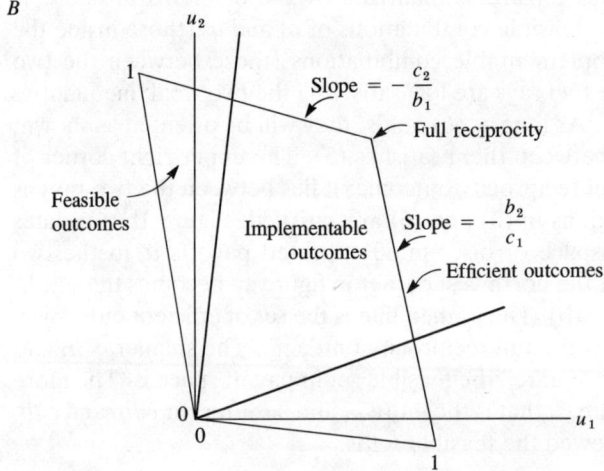

Fig. 1. *A*) Outcomes in effort space. *B*) Outcomes in utility space

the values q_1 and q_2 to implement. If they choose values compatible with equilibrium, their agreement will be self-enforcing. We may then examine the distributional consequences of such an agreement.

Second, for several interesting possible distributions of the gains, it is possible to derive conditions under which such a distribution is implementable. Two "fair" distribution schemes, one based on equality of effort and the other on equality of payoffs, can be shown to differ in general from full reciprocity. At the other extreme, distributions in which one player "exploits" the other could be implemented, with the game's parameters determining how little the exploited player can receive and still be better off cooperating than not cooperating.

Preplay Bargaining

Imagine that, before the actual play of the reciprocity game, the players engage in a negotiation process such as that modeled by Rubinstein (1982). The object of bargaining, ultimately, is to divide the payoffs that will be generated in the subsequent reciprocity game. If we let the first proposer in this negotiation be chosen by a coin flip and look at the players' ex ante expected payoffs, or if we imagine that the time between proposals is insignificant, then the unique subgame perfect equilibrium to this bargaining stage results in a distribution determined by the Nash Bargaining Solution (NBS) (Nash 1950; Rubinstein 1982). We therefore employ the NBS in the subsequent analysis. The NBS is the payoff pair (u_1, u_2) that maximizes the product $u_1 u_2$ over the feasible set. Among other things, the NBS must be individually rational for each player, and must be efficient.

Any division of the gains agreed upon in the negotiation stage must then be achieved through the appropriate partial reciprocity scheme. It is rational for the players to carry out such an agreement if and only if the resulting partial reciprocity outcome is implementable, as provided in Proposition 5. Thus the set of distributions over which the players bargain is exactly the set of "implementable" payoff pairs depicted in figure 1b. The resulting Nash bargaining problem is shown in figure 2, where contour curves of $u_1 u_2$ are superimposed on the bargaining set. In terms of the Rubinstein model, the players negotiate over the Pareto frontier of this implementable set.

The important conclusion from this two-stage model of reciprocity leaps out of figure 2: because of the prominent corner in the feasible set, any reciprocity game in which the players' parameters are at all similar is likely to yield *full reciprocity* as the outcome of bargaining. This is formalized as follows:

PROPOSITION 6. *Full reciprocity is the Nash Bargaining Solution if and only if (3) is satisfied and*

$$\frac{2b_2 c_1}{b_1 b_2 + c_1 c_2} \leq \frac{p_1}{p_2} \leq \frac{b_1 b_2 + c_1 c_2}{2 b_1 c_2}. \tag{7}$$

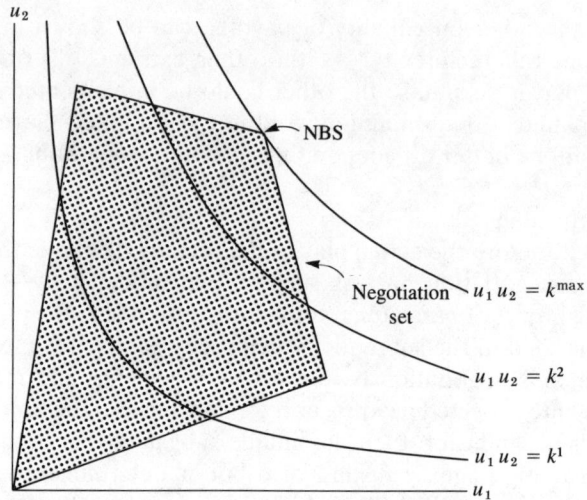

Fig. 2. The bargaining problem

Proof. Condition (3) ensures that full reciprocity is feasible. Let $\bar{P}(q_1, q_2)$ be the product of the payoffs:

$$\bar{P}(q_1, q_2) = \frac{q_2 p_1 b_1 - q_1 p_2 c_1}{1 - w} \frac{q_1 p_2 b_2 - q_2 p_1 c_2}{1 - w}.$$

Since the denominators do not involve q_i, we can solve for the NBS by maximizing the product of the numerators, $P(q_1, q_2)$. By Proposition 1, efficiency, and therefore the NBS, requires that at least one player devote maximum effort. Therefore we fix $q_2 = 1$, and demonstrate that $P(q_1, 1)$ is maximized at $q_1 = 1$. The relevant derivatives of P are

$$\frac{\partial P}{\partial q_1} = p_1 p_2 q_2 (b_1 b_2 + c_1 c_2) - 2 p_2^2 q_1 b_2 c_1 \tag{8}$$

$$\frac{\partial^2 P}{\partial q_1^2} = -2 p_2^2 c_1 b_2.$$

If (8) is zero, then, a maximum occurs at $q_1 = 1$, as required. If (8) is positive, then $q_1 = 1$ gives a constrained maximum. Otherwise $P(1, 1)$ is not a maximum at all. Setting (8) greater than or equal to zero, putting $q_2 = 1$, and rearranging gives the left-hand inequality in (7). A similar

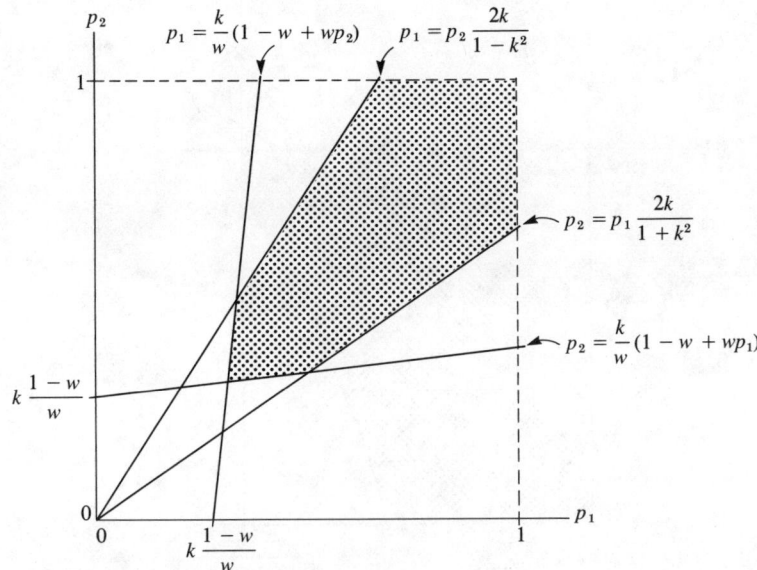

Fig. 3. Values of p_1 and p_2 for which the NBS is full reciprocity, with $c_1/b_1 = c_2/b_2 = k < 1$.

argument holding $q_1 = 1$ and maximizing over q_2 gives the left-hand inequality. Q.E.D.

To get an idea of how forgiving of asymmetry these bounds are, it is convenient to express (7) in terms of the ratios $k_i \equiv c_i/b_i$, and consider the situation when $k_1 = k_2 = k$. Then (7) becomes

$$\frac{2k}{1+k^2} \leq \frac{p_1}{p_2} \leq \frac{1+k}{2k}. \tag{9}$$

Figure 3 shows the resulting set of combinations of p_1 and p_2 for which full reciprocity is the NBS, that is, for which (3) and (9) hold. Notice that as k increases, all the constraints become more severe; on the graph in figure 3, all move *into* the shaded area. The rays converging to the origin, representing (9), close up, and the other lines, corresponding to (3), slide toward higher values of the respective p_i. The latter constraints also become steeper, so that feasibility becomes a more important constraint relative to the NBS criterion (9). Decreases in w have exactly the same effect on (3), but no effect on (9). Thus higher costs or more

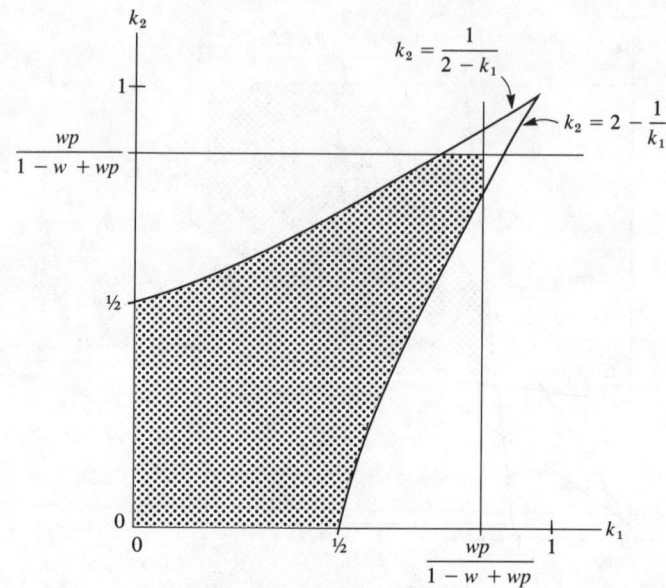

Fig. 4. Values of $k_1 = c_1/b_1$ and $k_2 = c_2/b_2$ for which the NBS is full reciprocity, with $p_1 = p_2 = p$

discounting reduces the set of (p_1, p_2) pairs for which the NBS is full reciprocity.

Similarly, we can fix $p_1 = p_2$ to get an idea of the combinations of k_1 and k_2 that yield full reciprocity as the NBS. From (7) with $p_1 = p_2$, the NBS requires $2 - 1/k_1 \leq k_2 \leq 1/(2 - k_1)$. This constraint is shown by the two curves in figure 4. From condition (3), feasibility requires $k_i \leq wp/(1 - w + wp)$ for $i = 1, 2$, shown as the horizontal and vertical lines in figure 4. The shaded area indicates the (k_1, k_2) values yielding full reciprocity. Note that decreases in w or p move the constraints corresponding to (3) toward the origin, decreasing the size of the set. Increases in p move the constraints out toward $k_i = 1$, enlarging the set.

To summarize, a considerable amount of asymmetry between the values of the p_i, c_i, and b_i will lead the negotiating players to agree upon a self-enforcing plan of full reciprocity. It should be noted that the NBS itself, among cooperative bargaining solutions, is not critical for this conclusion. Any bargaining solution that is reasonably symmetrical and that maximizes some function increasing in both u_1 and u_2 will exhibit the same kind of robustness of full reciprocity, due to the angular shape of the set of feasible payoff values. And for any such solution method, lower costs, higher benefits, or higher values of p_1, p_2, or w will sharpen this angular shape and strengthen this conclusion.

Equal Distribution Schemes

Another possible outcome of preplay negotiation would be for the players to agree on some equal division of the gains from reciprocity. Indeed, some sociologists have identified reciprocity norms with norms of justice or fairness (see the discussion by Chadwick-Jones 1976, 242–61). If costs and benefits are assumed to be transferable or interpersonally comparable, the players might agree to choose q_1 and q_2 to equalize net discounted expected payoffs from the game. If not, fair distribution might call for the players to devote equal amounts of total effort to providing favors. We connect each of these schemes with the conditions for existence of cooperative equilibrium.

If p_1 and p_2 differ, the players can restore equality of effort by setting $q_1 p_2 = q_2 p_1$. Such an arrangement is possible provided that p_1 and p_2 satisfy condition (3) for partial reciprocity equilibrium. This gives the following corollary to Proposition 5 and Corollary 2:

COROLLARY 4. *Efficient partial reciprocity can be implemented by setting the players' expected efforts equal if and only if condition (3) holds.*

This is illustrated in figure 5, which superimposes the equal-effort solution on the graphs from figure 1. The set of outcomes where $q_1 p_2 = q_2 p_1$ is just a ray in the graph of q_1 and q_2 (fig. 5a), having slope p_2/p_1. Its translation to the space of utility outcomes (fig. 5b) is also a ray. The efficient solution occurs where the ray crosses the kinked line, the set of efficient outcomes.

In the case of transferable utility, expected payoffs could be equalized by setting q_1 and q_2 so that $q_2 p_1 b_1 - q_1 p_2 c_1 = q_1 p_2 b_2 - q_2 p_1 c_2$, that is,

$$\frac{q_1}{q_2} = \frac{p_1 \, b_1 + c_2}{p_2 \, b_2 + c_1}.$$

As before, we can state the following condition for this to be implementable:

COROLLARY 5. *Efficient partial reciprocity can be implemented by setting the players' expected payoffs equal, if and only if*

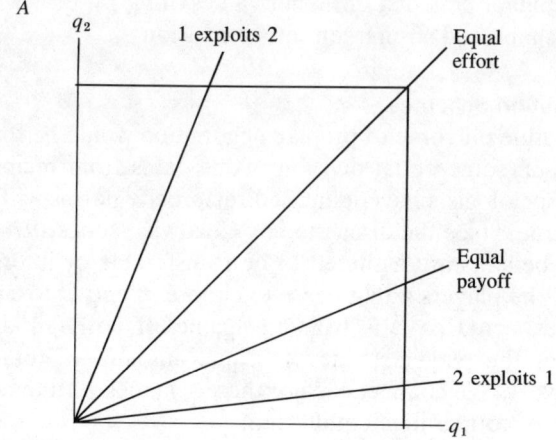

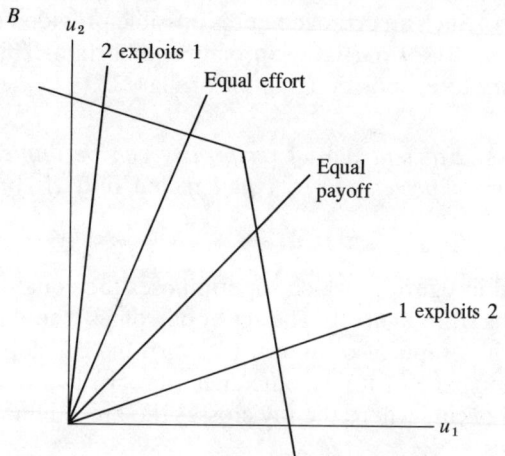

Fig. 5. Distribution schemes

$$\frac{c_1}{b_1}\frac{b_1 + c_2}{b_2 + c_1} \leq \frac{wp_2}{1 - w + wp_2} \quad \text{and} \quad \frac{c_2}{b_2}\frac{b_2 + c_1}{b_1 + c_2} \leq \frac{wp_1}{1 - w + wp_1}.$$

Figure 5 also illustrates the equal-payoff outcomes. They too lie on a ray in each diagram. Again, if any such solution is available, then an efficient one is. Corollaries 4 and 5 amount to conditions for the rays to lie within the wedge-shaped area defined in Proposition 5.

Exploitation

The opposite of equal distribution would be a maximally unequal distribution, in which one player receives just enough benefits to keep him engaging in reciprocity, and the other player receives the rest. As can be seen from the proof of Proposition 5, this minimum payoff occurs (assuming player 2 is the exploited party) when

$$-q_2c_2 + w\frac{q_1p_2b_2 - q_2p_1c_2}{1 - w} = 0,$$

that is, $q_1/q_2 = c_2(1 - w + wp_1)/wp_2b_2$. If player 2's payoff can be pushed down to this level in equilibrium, we might say that player 1 can "fully exploit" player 2. Notice that player 2's payoff is *positive:*

$$\frac{q_1p_2b_2 - q_2p_1c_2}{1 - w} = \frac{q_2c_2}{w} > 0.$$

If it were any smaller, the uncertainties of receiving his small benefits in the near future would cause him to deviate from reciprocity, even if player 1 threatens Permanent Retaliation.

In terms of figure 1, full exploitation occurs when the constraint for equilibrium is satisfied with equality; the outcome lies on one of the inside rays in each diagram. It is obvious that exploitation equilibrium is possible if any equilibrium is possible, and that exploitation can always be achieved together with efficiency.

It is apparent from the foregoing that for some parameter values the NBS, the equal-payoffs outcome, or the equal-effort outcome could coincide with an exploitation outcome. This would require highly asymmetric values of the parameters, so that even a fairly large effort on the part of player 1 (the "exploiting" player) is just barely sufficient to entice player 2 into reciprocity. Generally, this requires low values of p_2, b_2, and c_1 relative to p_1, b_1, and c_2. For example, according to Proposition 5, equal efforts would coincide with exploitation of player 2 if the parameter values satisfy

$$\frac{q_1}{q_2} = 1 = \frac{c_2(1 - w + wp_1)}{wp_2}.$$

In such cases, exploitation and fairness would coincide, contrary to the usual meaning of "exploitation." Such a situation is better described simply by noting that the asymmetries in payoffs or probabilities make it difficult for the players to reach certain types of agreements.[5]

Conclusion

This essay has analyzed a reciprocity game incorporating asymmetries in payoffs, irregular and nonsimultaneous moves, and multiple methods for implementing asymmetric patterns of cooperation.

On the surface, it is not clear what reciprocity ought to look like in such a game. Reciprocity could consist of providing full benefits to the other player whenever possible; on the other hand, it could involve trading favors one-for-one, or more generally, not allowing the balance of benefits provided over any period to lean too far in either player's favor. The analysis here clears up this ambiguity in several ways. Efficiency requires that at least one player provide full benefits at every opportunity. One-for-one favor trading is inefficient. Furthermore, such keeping of accounts is not necessary in order to enforce reciprocity: if any reciprocity is achievable at all, it can be achieved by a strategy analogous to Tit-for-Tat, which requires only that the players remember and act on what happened "last time."

Given that gains can be achieved through reciprocity, there remains the question of how they are to be distributed. This question inheres in the repeated Prisoner's Dilemma as well, but there the use of symmetric games and the prominence of symmetric equilibria such as Tit-for-Tat has deflected attention from the distribution issue. In the present game, if the players have differing payoffs (differing b_i/c_i) and differing frequencies of available favors, there may be no obvious or "focal" distribution (Schelling 1960). The analysis above derives (1) the conditions under which various fair distribution schemes are possible, and what they look like, and (2) the extent to which "exploitive" distributions are possible. In addition, we have seen that under any sort of preplay negotiation over the distribution of gains, moderate asymmetries in the parameters will wash out and bargaining will lead to full reciprocity. This result may also be interpreted as an indication that full reciprocity is a "focal" outcome even when the players are not identical.

The asymmetric distributions considered here suggest that lopsided reciprocity arrangements might underlie various political interactions

---

5. Gouldner (1960, 165–67) also discusses exploitation in connection with reciprocity. There, however, exploitation is precisely the absence of reciprocity in the presence of unequal "power." Reciprocity norms supposedly curb socially harmful exploitation. This is not the kind of exploitation treated in the present study; here, exploitation is simply an unequal, though still two-sided, reciprocity.

involving unequal partners. Political leadership, legislative apprenticeship norms, patron-client relations, and hegemonic international regimes all have the property that one party seems to do a disproportionate share of the giving in return for a smaller share of the taking. Yet the disadvantaged party often continues voluntarily in the relationship. The reciprocity model demonstrates how the parameters of the game can be used to determine the extent to which such unbalanced exchange is possible, and can be used to predict how exogenous changes will affect such relationships.

Finally, several important features of reciprocity are omitted from the present model and could provide further insight. One simple point is that the players in this model never have to *ask* favors—the favors just become available. Especially if information is incomplete, the asking itself may become an important signal. Conversely, "punishment" might come in response to a player's asking of too many favors as well as to his providing too few.

A more complicated addition to the model would be incomplete information about opponents' payoffs, perhaps varying across iterations. It may then be that full reciprocity is not efficient, since it may sometimes require a favor whose cost outweighs all future gains from reciprocity. Indeed, it is likely to become impossible to achieve efficiency in the sense used in this essay, so that a notion of second-best efficiency would have to provide the benchmark. Such phenomena as reputation building and communication, important in real life social and political interaction, may take on key roles in reciprocity behavior in an enriched model of this sort.

Collective Choice without Procedural Commitment

Thomas W. Gilligan and Keith Krehbiel

I. Introduction

The ability of a collective choice organization to choose the procedures that govern its decision making is a fundamental right of many political institutions. Invariably, an organization's menu of procedural choices contains rules that constrain members' rights to amend proposals. Recent advances in formal political theory have contributed to an understanding of the comparative consequences of rules.[1] However, models in which rules are actually chosen by the members of the organization who subsequently may be constrained are almost nonexistent.

A similarly salient characteristic of modern collective choice institutions is their reliance on specialized committees to study the consequences of alternative courses of collective action and issue reports and proposals to the parent organization. Indeed, a well-established committee system is often regarded as a hallmark of an "institutionalized" political organization (Polsby 1968). Furthermore, the committees on whom the parent organization relies for information are almost always composed of members who possess policy expertise that exceeds that of other members (Cooper 1970). But, although specialization is widely regarded as a defining characteristic of a rationally structured organization, only a few theoretical papers have analyzed and interpreted informational asymmetries in collective choice institutions.[2]

Organizations in which rules are endogenous and that utilize specialized committees include legislatures, labor unions, corporate boards of directors, and academic departments. From a distributional perspective, the choice of self-restricting rules is puzzling since they often permit a proposer (e.g., committee, labor leader, CEO, or departmental chair) to obtain benefits at the expense of the pivotal voter and, thus, decisive coalition in the larger group. While some steps have been taken recently

---

1. See, for example, works by Romer and Rosenthal (1978, 1979), Denzau and Mackay (1983), Baron and Ferejohn (1987), and Gilligan and Krehbiel (forthcoming).

2. See Austen-Smith and Riker (1987), Banks (1987*b*, 1988), and Gilligan and Krehbiel (1987, 1988, forthcoming).

to solve puzzles posed by endogenous restrictive rules,[3] such efforts assume that the collective choice organization is committed to a given procedure prior to the proposing process. That is, the presumption invariably has been that all actors in the parent organization and its specialized committee know with certainty *beforehand* which procedure will be used for considering the committee's proposal. Clearly, this assumption is inconsistent with the formal rules and behavior in many collective choice institutions. In legislatures, for example, a rules committee may decide not to propose a restrictive rule *after* seeing the standing committee's bill, or a majority may defeat a proposed rule. In a corporate board (or faculty) meeting, a maverick executive (assistant professor) may challenge the presumption of take-it-or-leave-it proposals and set forth an amendment counter to the proposer's preferences but nevertheless preferred by a decisive coalition. Or, an electorate (or labor union) may vote down a referendum (contract) proposal, knowing that the schools (plant) will not close permanently and that defeat of the current proposal may result in a subsequent, preferable one. Any of these scenarios gives rise to the possibility that commitment to a given amendment procedure may be difficult.

The corresponding objective of this essay is to answer the following question. What are the incentives for a decisive coalition of a collective choice organization to employ restrictive rules when considering a proposal of a committee whose members are asymmetrically informed about the consequence of policy, but when commitment to any particular rule is infeasible?

Several unique properties of collective choice without commitment are identified by analyzing a model whose original form presumed procedural commitment. A two-person noncooperative game under incomplete information reflects the strategic interaction between a decisive coalition in a parent organization and its committee of policy specialists. Section II introduces the exact structure of the game. Section III characterizes and interprets the equilibrium of the game and identifies the distributional and informational properties of collective choice without procedural commitment. Section IV contains comparative statics results and compares the properties of the game to earlier results for an otherwise identical game with procedural commitment. These results have implications for predicting rule assignments in actual majority institutions, particularly when compared to the earlier model with procedural commitment. Section V elaborates on the implications of the model, and section VI summarizes.

---

3. See Gilligan and Krehbiel (1987) and Banks (1988).

II. The Model

We consider a two-person game in which a specialized committee of an organization and the organization's pivotal voter make a sequence of decisions culminating in a policy, $P \in R$, from the real number line. The relationship between any policy and its consequence or outcome is stochastic and given by $X = P + \omega$, where X is the policy outcome and ω is a random variable that lies within the interval $0 \leq \omega \leq \overline{\omega} < \infty$ and is distributed according to the strictly increasing frequency distribution $F(\omega)$ with corresponding density $f(\omega)$.

Detailed defenses for this characterization are given elsewhere (Gilligan and Krehbiel 1987, 1988, forthcoming). Aside from the more general characterization of ω and the absence of procedural commitment, the only difference between this model and our earlier one is semantic. The embodiment of the parent body in the player called the *pivot* (in previous models, the *floor* or the *legislature*) is meant to stress the general applicability of the model to nonlegislative institutions and/or to institutions that employ decision rules other than simple majority rule. Due to the assumption regarding the policy space, the last-stage actor may be thought of as the pivotal voter on the policy dimension in question. In other words, the members of the parent organization may not have homogeneous preferences, and the pivotal individual may not be the median voter if, say, the parent body employs a super-majority voting rule.

Individual actors are assumed to maximize their expected utility. Utility is given, in part, by the negative of the squared deviation of the consequence of the policy from the actor's ideal point. Thus, both actors are risk-averse. For simplicity and without loss of generality, we assume that the pivot's ideal point equals zero, $x_v = 0$, while the committee's ideal point is nonnegative, $x_c \geq 0$. Thus, for any given value of ω, the committee always weakly prefers a larger policy than the pivot.

The committee is assumed to incur a constant cost equal to c if its proposed bill, B, is considered under an open rule. An open rule, of course, means that the bill may be amended at a later stage. The motivation for this assumption about open-rule costs is simply that, even aside from policy consequences, committees may suffer from a perceived loss of control over policy in their jurisdictions if and when their proposals are targets of amendments by nonspecialist members of the parent organization. In the House of Representatives, for example, the inability to employ restrictive rules to "manage uncertainty" (Bach and Smith 1988) often distresses standing committees, presumably, in part, because they

TABLE 1. Structure of the Game

Stage	Player	Action	Parameters	Strategies
0	Nature	Fixes set Φ of feasible rules and tells both players.	$\Phi = \{\Phi^{open}, \Phi^{closed}\}$	—
		Fixes value of ω and tells only the committee.	$\omega \in [0,\bar{\omega}]$	—
1	Committee	Proposes bill, B	$b:[0,\bar{\omega}] \to R$	$B = b(\omega)$
2	Pivot	Updates beliefs, M	$\mu: R \times [0,\bar{\omega}] \to [0,1]$	$M = \mu(\omega|B)$
3	Pivot	Selects rule assignment probability, Π	$\pi: R \to [0,1]$	$\Pi = \pi(B)$
4	Nature	Randomly assigns rule given Π	$\Phi^i \in \Phi$	—
5	Pivot	Chooses policy, P	$p: R \times \Phi \to R$	$P = p(B, \Phi^i)$

are less able to engage in "credit claiming" upon final passage of legislation (Mayhew 1974b).

Collective choice is represented as a sequence of actions which is summarized in table 1. In addition to actors' preferences, the exogenous features of the model include the set of feasible rules, the random variable in the mapping from policies to outcomes, and the committee's informational advantage. Two pure types of amendment procedures or rules may be employed. These are given by the set $\Phi \equiv \{\Phi^{open}, \Phi^{closed}\}$. The open rule does not limit the ability of the pivot to alter the proposal made by the committee. The closed rule, however, constrains the pivot's choice to one between the committee proposal and the exogenous status quo, given by p_o. While these two amendment procedures do not exhaust the set of possible rules that may be utilized to consider a committee's proposal, they are analytically tractable opposites on the procedural spectrum which yield several insights.[4]

The asymmetric distribution of information about the consequence of policy also plays a key role in the analysis. This, too, is determined prior to the commencement of the game. Contrary to most multistage models of collective decision making, we assume that the committee possesses specialized knowledge within its policy domain. In the parlance of game theory, the committee has "private information" or is "asymmetrically informed" about the consequences of policy. This is characterized as a nonstrategic actor, nature, permitting only the committee to know the value of the random variable ω. In contrast, the pivot knows only that $\omega \in [0,\bar{\omega}]$ and is distributed by $F(\omega)$. From these exogenous features, the decision making occurs in five stages.

---

4. See Gilligan and Krehbiel (forthcoming) for a comparative analysis of open and closed rules with modified rules, which lie between the endpoints of the spectrum.

In stage 1 the committee initiates the collective choice process by recommending a bill B for the pivot's consideration. The committee is not permitted to circumvent collective choice by refusing to report a bill, that is, there is no "gatekeeping" power in the model.[5] Formally, the committee's *proposal strategy* is a function $b:[0,\overline{\omega}] \to R$ where $B = b(\omega)$ is the proposal of a committee whose private information is ω. The remaining strategic actions are taken by the pivot.

In stage 2 the pivot observes the committee's proposal but not its private information. He then forms a *belief M* about the value(s) of ω that may have generated B. Let $\mu(\omega|B)$ be the probability that the pivot assigns to the event that the private information is ω when the committee proposes B.

In stage 3, based on his beliefs, the pivot chooses a probability distribution over the two alternative amendment procedures. This is the pivot's *procedural strategy*. Formally, it is a function $\pi:R \to [0,1]$ where $\Pi = \pi(B)$ is the probability that the pivot will choose a closed rule given the committee's bill B.

In stage 4, nature randomly selects a value of either 0 or 1 which determines the actual choice of the rule. The probability distribution governing this selection is given by the pivot's procedural strategy. Although it may seem artificial, this characterization has several natural analogues. For example, in some academic departments, members may not know what procedures are operable on any given day. In Congress, legislators cannot perfectly anticipate rule proposing by the rules committees or rule selection by floor majorities. Thus, the possibility of random assignment in which the pivot determines probabilities of alternative rules is a reasonable means of representing this uncertainty.

In stage 5, the pivot chooses a policy consistent with the randomly assigned procedure. The pivot's *policy strategy* is a function $p:R \times \Phi \to R$ where $P = p(B,\Phi^i)$, for $i \in \{open, closed\}$, is the policy chosen by the pivot given the committee's proposal and the amendment procedure.

Within this framework, we employ a refinement of sequential equilibrium to analyze the game developed above.[6] The equilibrium satisfies the best response property commonly found in games of complete information. The equilibrium also requires that each player, according to Bayes's Rule, incorporate information and beliefs about the game into

---

5. Were such an assumption to be made, it would be tantamount to exogenously imposing a restrictive procedure, since such power may restrict absolutely the parent organization's right to engage in collective choice. This point is developed in further detail in Krehbiel (1987).

6. See Kreps and Wilson (1982a) for a general definition of sequential equilibrium.

its optimal strategy. In addition, it is common for signaling games to have multiple sequential equilibria resulting from alternative specifications of the beliefs the uninformed player entertains to signals that do not arise in equilibrium. The refinement of "universal divinity" is applied to limit these beliefs and narrow the set of equilibria (Banks and Sobel 1987). In this model, universal divinity requires that the pivot assign positive probability only to those committee types "most likely" to deviate from the equilibrium proposal strategy. The pivot's response to committee proposals that are inconsistent with the equilibrium proposal strategy is differentially harmful to the committee based on its private information. Universal divinity requires that the pivot believe that committee proposals that are inconsistent with the equilibrium proposal strategy are made by committees whose private information together with the pivot's response is least punitive relative to the equilibrium beliefs and strategies of the pivot.

DEFINITION. A universally divine sequential equilibrium to the game is a set of strategies $b^*(\omega)$, $\pi^*(B)$ and $P^*(B,\Phi^i)$ and beliefs $\mu^*(\omega|B)$ where

(a) $b^*(\omega)$ maximizes $EU_c(B,\omega;\pi^*(B),p^*(B,\Phi^i))\ \forall\ \omega \in [0,\overline{\omega}]$,
(b) $\pi^*(B)$ maximizes $EU_v(\Pi,B;\mu^*(\omega|B),p^*(B,\Phi^i))\ \forall\ B \in R$,
(c) $p^*(B,\Phi^i)$ maximizes $EU_v(P,B,\Phi^i;\mu^*(\omega|B))\ \forall\ B \in R$ and $\Phi^i \in \Phi$, and
(d) whenever $b^{*-1}(B) \neq \emptyset$, $\mu^*(\omega|B)$ is derived via Bayes's Rule as defined by $b^*(\omega)$ and $f(\omega)$, and
(e) whenever $b^{*-1}(B) = \emptyset$, $\mu^*(\omega|B) > 0$ only for ω that are "most likely" to deviate from the equilibrium.

Conditions (a), (b), and (c) fulfill the *best response* criterion while (d) and (e) identify the way in which the committee's private information is transmitted, or not transmitted, in equilibrium.

A common standard for comparing results has been the *distributional consequences* of various forms of collective choice. Some research contains models in which restrictive amendment procedures yield outcomes that are clearly inimical to the interests of a decisive coalition in the parent organization. An inextricably linked but rarely raised puzzle is why this distributionally disadvantaged decisive coalition would adopt procedures that appear to limit its influence over the policy choice. The structure of the game without procedural commitment sheds light on this puzzle of endogeneity of rules because it uniquely incorporates choice of rules by the decisive coalition[7] in whose strategic calculus the distributional consequences of alternative rules play a part.

A second unique determinant in the pivot's procedural strategy lies in the *informational consequences* of the alternative procedures which typically have been ignored in the literature. Recall that both players in the game are risk-averse and therefore jointly derive benefits from the elimination of uncertainty prior to the final policy choice apart from the comparative distributional consequences of alternative rules. When the pivot can infer the precise value of ω from the committee's proposal strategy and its procedural strategy, a *fully revealing* or *separating* equilibrium is said to obtain. The policy choice of the pivot in a separating equilibrium is made under perfect certainty about the consequences of the policy and no loss in expected utility results. When the pivot cannot associate a unique ω with each B, a *pooling* equilibrium results. That is, a range or pool of ω is consistent with the proposal strategy $B = b(\omega)$. In a pooling equilibrium, the policy choice of the pivot is accompanied by uncertainty about the consequences of the selected policy and losses in expected utility. Thus, the informational consequence of alternative amendment procedures is also an important determinant of the pivot's procedural strategy.

III. The Equilibrium

PROPOSITION: *The set* $\{b^*(\omega), \pi^*(B), p^*(B,\Phi^i), \mu^*(\omega|B)\}$ *is the unique universally divine sequential equilibrium of the game when*

$$b^*(\omega) = \{ -\omega \text{ for all } \omega \in [0,\overline{\omega}]$$

$$\pi^*(B) = \begin{cases} exp\{-2x_c(\overline{\omega} + B)/c\} \text{ for all } B \in [-\overline{\omega},0] \text{ otherwise} \\ 0 \end{cases}$$

$$p^*(B,\Phi^i) = \begin{cases} B & \text{for all } B \in [-\overline{\omega},0] \\ -\overline{\omega} & \text{otherwise} \end{cases}$$

$$\mu^*(\omega|B) = \begin{cases} 1 & \text{if } \omega = b^{*-1}(B) \text{ and } B \in [-\overline{\omega},0] \\ 1 & \text{if } \omega = \overline{\omega} \text{ and } B \notin [-\overline{\omega},0] \\ 0 & \text{otherwise.} \end{cases}$$

Proof. See the appendix to this essay.

Figure 1 graphs $b^*(\omega)$, $\pi^*(B)$, and X where the possible values of

---

7. In our earlier paper, the choice of procedure was endogenous and the choice was made by the "floor" actor, presumed to represent a decisive (majority) coalition. However, in that model the chooser of the rule was able to commit credibly to its subsequent deployment.

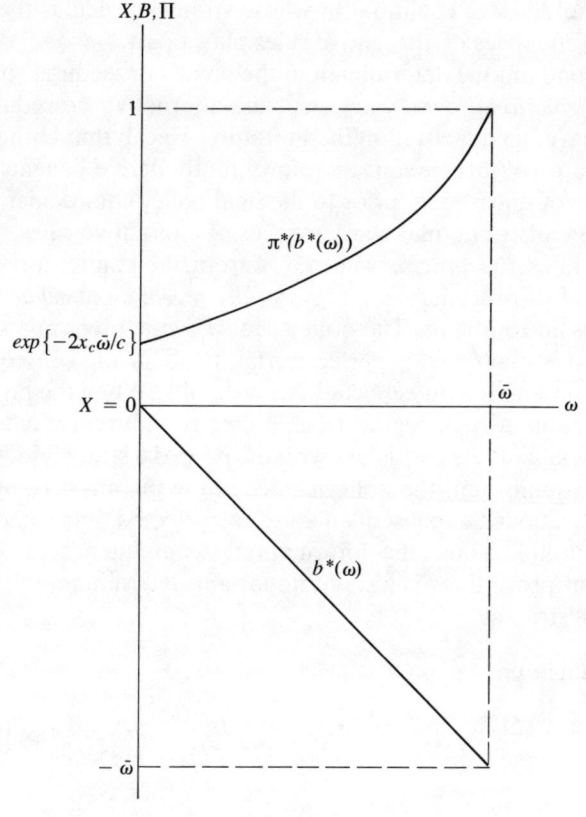

Fig. 1

the committee's private information appear on the horizontal axis and the committee's proposal and pivot's procedural strategies as well as the outcome are plotted on the vertical axis. The figure illuminates the behavioral dynamics of the game. To begin, nature exogenously selects and reveals to the committee a value ω, a point on the horizontal axis. The committee's equilibrium proposal strategy, $b^*(\omega)$, maps this value into a proposal B. Since $b^*(\omega)$ is strictly monotone decreasing, the pivot is able to infer the value ω from the committee's proposal; $\omega = b^{*-1}(B)$. Given its belief, the pivot's procedural strategy, $\pi^*(B)$, determines the probability distribution governing nature's rule assignment. Regardless of the rule assigned, the outcome is always at the pivot's ideal point, $X = 0$.

To develop some of the logic underlying the equilibrium, we examine the implications of the supposition that the equilibrium is separating and, accordingly, consider the pivot's and committee's strategies. We then show that given the resulting strategies the supposition is true.

If the equilibrium is separating, then the pivot will always insure that his ideal outcome obtains whenever he is able to amend the committee's proposal. That is, he will exploit the open rule to get exactly the outcome that yields his maximum utility. Formally, a separating equilibrium means that the pivot infers the committee's information from B. Let $\omega = b^{*-1}(B)$ represent the inference drawn by the pivot. He then chooses the policy $p^*(B, \Phi^{open}) = -\omega$ which necessarily yields the outcome $X = 0 = x_v$, his ideal point.

Having established that the optimal policy under an open rule yields the pivot's ideal point, we can identify a condition under which the pivot will assign positive probability to use of a closed rule, that is, a necessary condition for $\pi^*(B) > 0$. The condition is simply that the committee propose a bill that yields the pivot's ideal point, i.e., $B = -\omega$. This is because given a $B \neq -\omega$, the pivot, who by assumption knows ω, knows also that acceptance of the policy under the closed rule cannot yield his ideal point. Thus, by setting $\Pi = 0$ the pivot could guarantee himself the opportunity to amend the bill under an open rule so that the policy outcome would lie at his ideal point.

The formal argument that establishes this claim is straightforward. Note that whenever the equilibrium is separating, the pivot's expected utility is given by

$$EU_v(\Pi, B; \mu^*(\omega|B), p^*(B, \Phi^i)) = -\Pi(B + \omega)^2, \qquad (3.1)$$

where $\omega = b^{*-1}(B)$. Differentiating (3.1) with respect to Π yields $-(B + \omega)^2$. If this term is negative, which it is if $B \neq -\omega$, $\pi^*(B) = 0$. Thus, a necessary condition for a separating equilibrium in which a closed rule is applied with any probability is

$$b^*(\omega) = -\omega. \qquad (3.2)$$

From (3.2) it follows that in any separating equilibrium, the (weakly) optimal policy choice under a closed rule is to adopt the committee's bill, that is, $p^*(B, \Phi^{closed}) = B$.

Now we must also show that $b^*(\omega) = -\omega$ is optimal for the committee. First note that if a closed rule is to be applied with any nonzero probability, then it is (weakly) optimal for the committee to propose a bill that the pivot prefers to the status quo (even if the bill is the status quo itself). If the committee did not do this, the pivot, knowing ω, would simply set $\Pi = 0$ and proceed under the open rule to select his ideal point inducing policy. Thus, the committee's expected utility is given by

$$EU_c(B,\omega;\pi^*(B),p^*(B,\Phi^i)) = -\pi^*(B)(x_c - B - \omega)^2$$

$$- (1 - \pi^*(B))(x_c^2 + c). \tag{3.3}$$

Differentiating (3.3) with respect to B, equating the result to zero, and combining the resulting expression with (3.2) yields

$$\pi^{*'}(B)c + 2x_c\pi^*(B) = 0. \tag{3.4}$$

Equation (3.4) is a first-order, linear differential equation that $\pi^*(B)$ must solve. It has a generalized solution of $\pi(B) = \lambda exp\{-2x_cB/c\}$. A specific solution can be found by recognizing that for $B = -\bar{\omega}$, $\pi^*(B) = 1$. Since $B = -\bar{\omega}$ is the smallest possible committee proposal consistent with $\omega \in [0,\bar{\omega}]$ that yields the pivot's ideal point, *and* since the committee has a strategic incentive to shift the policy outcome in a positive direction, the pivot's optimal strategy is to accept this proposal with certainty. Thus, $\pi^*(-\bar{\omega}) = 1$. This expression yields a specific solution to (3.4) and the equilibrium procedural strategy

$$\pi^*(B) = exp\{-2x_c(\bar{\omega} + B)/c\}. \tag{3.5}$$

Inspection of (3.5) confirms that $\pi^*(-\bar{\omega}) = 1$ while $\pi^*(B)$ achieves its smallest value for $B = 0$.

Finally, since $b^*(\omega)$ is strictly monotone decreasing, the pivot is able to invert the committee's proposal strategy and infer ω. Thus, the equilibrium is separating and the premise used for this construction obtains.

It is easy to confirm that the out-of-equilibrium beliefs specified in the proposition are universally divine. Given that $\pi^*(B) = 0$ and $p^*(B,\Phi^{open}) = -\bar{\omega}$ for any $B \notin [-\bar{\omega},0]$, what realization of ω would be "most likely" to cause the committee to deviate from its equilibrium proposal strategy? That is, which committee type would lose the least by proposing some $B \notin [-\bar{\omega},0]$? In equilibrium, the expected utility of the committee is given by $-[1 - \pi^*(b^*(\omega))]c - x_c^2$, the probability of an open rule times c and the distributional loss resulting from $X = 0$. For some out-of-equilibrium proposal, the committee's expected utility is $-c - (x_c + \bar{\omega} - \omega)^2$, the loss resulting from the certain application of the open rule minus the distributional loss given $P = -\bar{\omega}$ and ω. We show in the appendix to this essay that the difference between the in-equilibrium and out-of-equilibrium expected utilities of the committee is minimized when $\omega = \bar{\omega}$. That is, the committee type $\bar{\omega}$ is most likely to deviate from the equilibrium proposal strategy. Thus, the out-of-equilibrium belief that $\mu^*(\bar{\omega}|B) = 1$ for $B \notin [-\bar{\omega},0]$ is universally divine.

Inspection of equation (3.4) reveals the behavioral tension implicit in the equilibrium. The committee prefers to shift policy outcomes toward its ideal point, which is greater than the pivot's. It also wishes to avoid the open rule. Since $\pi^*(B)$ is strictly monotonically decreasing, larger committee proposals are met with an increasing likelihood of an open rule. Indeed, the equilibrium procedural strategy balances precisely the expected benefits the committee realizes from shifting the outcome slightly toward its ideal point, $2x_c\pi^*(B)$, and the expected costs it incurs from making a larger proposal, $\pi^{*\prime}(B)c$. The pivot uses the credible threat of an open rule to counter the strategic incentives of the committee to move the outcome of policy closer to the committee's ideal point.

Three characteristics of the equilibrium accentuate several differences between this model and previous, similar models. First, all committees with private information have some likelihood of receiving a closed rule and some likelihood of receiving an open rule for consideration of their proposals. That is, in the absence of procedural commitment, an optimal process of rule assignment is one in which the rule chooser strategically deploys uncertainty rather than, for example, setting some criterion that a committee's proposal must meet in order to "earn" a restrictive rule. The optimal probability distribution for the use of a closed rule does, however, depend on the bill reported by the committee. That is, the pivot's refusal to use a pure procedural strategy does not imply that he ignores the committee's proposal when determining the probabilities for rule assignment. In particular, the probability that a closed rule is used diminishes as the committee's proposal becomes larger. Loosely, this means that the greater is the appearance that the committee is being selfish by attempting to gain distributionally at the expense of the pivot, the higher is the probability that the final policy choice will be made under an open rule.

Second, regardless of its private information, the committee reports a bill which, if adopted, yields the pivot's ideal point. The adoption of the pivot-yielding policy may result from either the application of the closed rule and the choice $P = B$ or under an open rule with $P = -b^{*-1}(B) = B$. Two surprising implications arise from this characteristic. The distributional consequences of the two amendment procedures are identical. That is, the final outcome of the game is the same regardless of the rule that is employed. This differs from games of incomplete information with procedural commitment and from complete-information games. Similarly, the status quo has no bearing on the outcome even when a closed rule is used. This follows trivially from the fact that the outcome of the game is always at the pivot's ideal point and also differs from previous results.[8]

Third, the pivot is always able to infer precisely the committee's private information ω from the bill B and thus becomes perfectly informed about the consequences of policy prior to choosing the rule. Consequently, the informational properties of the two rules are identical, and the expected utility of both the pivot and the committee is independent of procedural choice. This result also differs from models with procedural commitment that suggest that closed rules enhance the informational efficiency of collective decision making.[9] Furthermore, neither actor suffers any loss in expected utility due to risk-aversion and the incomplete transmission of the committee's information. That is, the pivot's choice is fully informed in that all of the committee's information is implicitly contained in its policy strategy. This result, too, stands in contrast to the findings of models with procedural commitment, in which losses due to the incomplete transmission of the committee's information occur even under restrictive amendment procedures.

IV. Comparative Statics

The consistent pattern of differences between collective choice without procedural commitment and prior models suggests that further progress in the study of endogenous institutional arrangements requires precise empirical implications of the competing models. We therefore examine the comparative statics of the equilibrium and, in particular, the pivot's optimal procedural stragegy $\pi^*(B)$. These in turn reveal several positive implications of the model.

COROLLARY 1: *$\pi^*(B)$ is strictly decreasing in x_c for all $B \in (-\overline{\omega}, 0]$.*

Ceteris paribus, the probability that a closed rule is applied to a committee's proposal diminishes as the ideal policy outcome of the pivot and the committee diverge. The intuition is contained in equation (3.4). The incentive for the committee to report a "large bill" (which attempts to yield a policy outcome closer to the committee's ideal point) is given

---

8. See, for example, Romer and Rosenthal (1978), Denzau and Mackay (1983), and Banks (1987*b*).

9. Gilligan and Krehbiel (1987, forthcoming) and Banks (1988).

by $2x_c\pi^*(B)$. This expression is increasing in x_c, which represents the divergence of the committee's from the pivot's ideal point. In equilibrium, the pivot counters this incentive by reducing the probability of a closed rule Π, or, in other words, by increasing the likelihood of deploying its credible open rule threat. This response reduces the gains from a larger bill, $2x_c\pi^*(B)$, and increases the committee's expected procedural costs by the amount $\pi^{*\prime}(B)c$. Indeed, in equilibrium, the pivot's procedural strategy leaves the committee indifferent between $B = -\omega$ and a slightly higher bill that would shift the outcome towards x_c. Thus, the empirical implication is that preference-outlying or high-demand committees should be recipients of closed rules less frequently than moderate committees or committees that more closely approximate microcosms of the parent organization.

COROLLARY 2: $\pi^*(B)$ *is strictly increasing in c for all* $B \in (-\bar{\omega},0]$.

Ceteris paribus, the probability of assignment of a closed rule is greater the larger are the costs the committee bears under an open rule. Recall that the threat of an open rule is credible largely due to the costliness of the procedure to the committee in terms of, for example, the resulting perceptions that the committee is not effectively managing affairs within the parent organization and/or is not a recipient of deference. The larger are these costs, the more effective is the threat of an open rule in controlling the incentive of the committee to shift the policy outcome to its ideal point. This can be seen again in equation (3.4) where the increase in the expected procedural costs to the committee are $-\pi^{*\prime}(B)c$, which are increasing in c. Here the empirical implication is, roughly, that the higher is the value to committee members of being perceived as "in control" within the parent organization, and thus the larger of the costs associated with the open rule (since such rules undermine the perception of control), the more frequent will be applications of the closed rules to its proposals.

The final corollary requires some motivation. The relationship between policies and their consequences may be more predictable in some environments than in others. Some policies' consequences, such as those pertaining to the development or diffusion of technology, may be subject to extreme "shocks" because they are implemented in highly uncertain, complex, and changing environments. Other policies, such as those bearing on ordinary personal income taxation, are repeatedly implemented in stable environments and thus their consequences are relatively certain. The random variable of our model quantifies the uncertainty or riskiness that characterizes a particular policy environment.

Suppose that the stochastic part of the relationship between policies and their consequences is given by z instead of ω where $z = \omega + s$. Let $k(s|\omega)$ be the conditional probability function of s, and $\int sk(s|\omega)ds = 0$, so that z and ω have the same mean, but z is "more noisy." That is, z is simply ω with some additional, uncorrelated variation added. Then z is said to be more "risky" or "uncertain" than ω. Equivalently, consider two alternative distribution functions for ω, $G(\omega)$, and $H(\omega)$ with corresponding densities $g(\omega)$ and $h(\omega)$ such that $\int_0^{\bar{\omega}} \omega g(\omega)d\omega = \int_0^{\bar{\omega}} \omega h(\omega)d\omega$. Thus, the mean of ω is the same under both distribution functions. However, assume that $g(\omega)$ has "fatter tails" than does $h(\omega)$; one density function is obtained through a mean-preserving spread of the other. The random variable ω is said to be more risky or uncertain when distributed by $G(\omega)$ than by $H(\omega)$.[10] Corollary 3 follows from this construction.

COROLLARY 3. *The ex ante expected probability of a closed rule, $\int_0^{\bar{\omega}} \pi^*(b^*(\omega))f(\omega)d\omega$, is strictly increasing in the riskiness or uncertainty of ω.*

Ceteris paribus, the probability that the committee's proposal is considered under a closed rule is greater the more uncertainty there is in the committee's jurisdiction. This result can be seen through inspection of figure 1 (and a simple proof is contained in the appendix to this essay). Notice that the equilibrium probability of a closed rule, $\pi^*(b^*(\omega))$, is strictly increasing and convex in ω. Recall that "increasing risk" can be thought of as shifting more of the density of ω toward the boundaries 0 and $\bar{\omega}$ while preserving the mean of ω. The part of the density shifted toward 0 is more likely to receive an open rule, but at a decreasing rate. The equal portion of $f(\omega)$ moved toward $\bar{\omega}$ is more likely to generate a closed rule, but at an increasing rate. The overall effect of this mean-preserving spread is to increase the likelihood that a closed rule is applied to the committee's proposal. Empirically, then, we would expect that committees whose jurisdictions are complex or uncertain to be granted restrictive rules with greater frequency than committees whose jurisdictions are characterized by relatively precise expectations about the relationship between policies and outcomes.

V. Discussion

Analysis of the game of procedural choice without commitment raises a variety of additional concerns that touch on technical, normative, com-

---

10. Rothschild and Stiglitz (1970).

parative, and empirical topics. Elaboration on these yields a deeper understanding of procedural commitment in politics.

First, several of the assumptions of the model are unnecessary for the proposition and corollaries. The particular form of the pivot and committee utility functions and, indeed, even the fact that actors are risk-averse, are not required and are specified only to facilitate comparison with similar models contained in other papers.[11] Surprisingly, it is not even necessary that the committee is the player who wishes to avoid the open rule. An alternative characterization is that the pivot prefers to avoid open rules for reasons of organizational efficiency or individual opportunity costs. Under this assumption, the committee (expectationally) extracts the value the pivot associates with conducting its business under a closed rule. And the pivot, by threatening an open rule under which he will choose an ideal policy with certainty, can insure that the committee extracts nothing more. In other words, all that is required is that either the committee or the pivot have a marginal preference for closed over open rules, apart from their comparative policy consequences. Although some normative notions of the intrinsic value of "open" or "democratic" decision making may be regarded as inconsistent with such assumptions, several positive arguments support them. Chief of these are (from the committee's perspective) the commonly cited value of credit-claiming and (from the parent organization's perspective) the desire to reduce demands imposed by cumbersome processes within the larger organization, thereby increasing opportunities to engage in more rewarding activities, such as committee work and constituency service.[12]

In spite of the rather astounding informational properties of collective choice without procedural commitment, the institutional arrangement analyzed in this paper is *not* Pareto optimal. Because the policy outcome is always at the pivot's ideal point it may appear to be Pareto optimal, since it is impossible to adopt a policy that would make the committee better off without harming the pivot. However, due to the probabilistic application of rules, the expected utility of the committee is inevitably reduced from what it would be under certain application of procedures. The reduction in the committee's expected utility is given by the committee's cost of an open rule times the expectation that the open rule is applied, $c[1 - \int_0^{\bar{\omega}} \pi^*(b(\omega))f(\omega)d\omega]$. This cost could be avoided if the pivot could credibly commit to the use a closed

---

11. The form of the committee's utility function affects the specific solution to $\pi^*(B)$, but not its general form.

12. Concise and compelling statements of these features of congressional decision making can be found in Mayhew (1974b) and Fiorina (1974).

rule for all committee proposals. However, when such a commitment can be made, it is no longer optimal for the committee to report bills that yield the pivot's ideal point. Indeed, collective choice with commitment to a closed rule results in a shift in the expected outcome to the *committee's* ideal point. Thus, within the context of this model, it is difficult to see why a decisive coalition that is institutionally capable of making commitments to employ restrictive rules would want to exercise such capabilities.

There is, however, a potentially important consideration that this model omits: the need for the parent organization to induce its members to become policy specialists within their committees' jurisdictions. The game without commitment simply asserts that committees have this expertise. And ironically it reveals that one of the chief costs of collective choice without procedural commitment results from the ability of the pivot to obtain his ideal outcome with certainty. In previous research, we showed how commitment to a restrictive amendment procedure shifts the expected outcome from the pivot's to the committee's ideal point and thereby encourages the committee to specialize. This distributional shift along with informational superiority of the closed rule in the commitment setting act as inducements for the committee's information gathering activities. In this model of collective choice without procedural commitment, however, the pivot cannot compensate the committee for the costs the committee bears to acquire expertise.

This comparison reveals what appears to be a fundamental trade-off in the design of collective choice institutions. The principal benefit of collective choice with commitment is the ability of the organization to exploit procedural endogeneity to induce specialization; its principal drawback, however, is an inevitable informational loss. The principal benefit of collective choice without commitment is the ability to eradicate informational losses; its principal drawback, however, is the absence of a specified mechanism that induces committees to acquire the information that would increase the benefits to all members of the organization.

VI. Conclusion

An empirical question naturally emerges from existing theories of procedural choice. Is a model with or without procedural commitment a better representation of collective choice under incomplete information? A generally correct answer may not exist insofar as different collective choice institutions employ significantly different methods of procedural choice. The U.S. Congress, for example, illustrates the diversity of mechanisms of procedural choice within a single organization. The Senate relies primarily on unanimous consent agreements to determine when and under what conditions proposals will be considered. Since objection by a single senator effectively vetoes the procedure in question, the choice of rules in the Senate may be regarded as quite unpredictable. Likewise, procedural commitment may be regarded as difficult in the Senate. In contrast, the House frequently employs special rules which are proposed by the Rules Committee and submitted to the entire House for a simple majority approval. If the majority party is large or can command the votes of its members, and if majority leaders make promises to committees regarding the treatment of their proposals, then procedural commitment seems possible. An analogous interpretation is readily available with respect to the House's often-used procedure of suspending the rules whereby a two-thirds majority can implement an enormous range of unamendable motions with a single vote. Such comparisons suggest that the presence or absence of procedural commitment in real institutions is more a matter of degree than a dichotomy. If so, then validity of models of procedural choice with or without commitment is likely to vary across collective choice organizations. Fortunately, the results in this and related essays illustrate that empirical examination of the frequency of application of restrictive rules in different collective choice environments is possible.

APPENDIX

Proof of the Proposition

We show (1) that the set $\{b^*(\omega), \pi^*(B), p^*(B,\Phi^i), \mu^*(\omega|B)\}$ is a separating equilibrium of the game, (2) that this set is the *only* separating equilibrium, and (3) that pooling or partial-pooling equilibria do not exist.

1. Existence of Separating Equilibrium. To prove that $\{b^*(\omega), \pi^*(B), p^*(B,\Phi^i), \mu^*(\omega|B)\}$ is a separating equilibrium to the game, we must show that:

(a) given $\pi^*(B)$ and $p^*(B,\Phi^i)$, $b^*(\omega)$ maximizes the committee's expected utility,
(b) given $\mu^*(\omega|B)$ and $p^*(B,\Phi^i)$, $\pi^*(B)$ maximizes the pivot's expected utility,
(c) given $b^*(\omega), \mu^*(\omega|B)$ and Φ^i, $p^*(B,\Phi^i)$ maximizes the pivot's expected utility,
(d) $\mu^*(\omega|b^*(\omega)) = 1 \ \forall \ B \in [-\overline{\omega}, 0]$, and
(e) $\mu^*(\overline{\omega}|B) = 1 \ \forall \ B \notin [-\overline{\omega}, 0]$.

(a) Recall that the committee's expected utility is $EU_c(B,\omega;\pi^*(B),p^*(B,\Phi^i)) = -\pi^*(B)(x_c - B - \omega)^2 - (1 - \pi^*(B))(x_c^2 + c)$. Proposals $B \notin [-\overline{\omega},0]$ are dominated by $B = -\overline{\omega}$ since the same outcome is achieved in both cases but the costs of the open rule are avoided with certainty in the later case. Thus, $b^*(\omega) \in [-\overline{\omega},0]$ for all $\omega \in [0,\overline{\omega}]$. Differentiating $EU_c(B,\omega;\pi^*(B),p^*(B,\Phi^i))$ with respect to B, setting $z(B) = -2x_c(\overline{\omega} + B)/c$, and equating to zero yields $(B + \omega)exp\{z(B)\}[x_c(B + w - 2x_c) - c]/c = 0$ which, given $d^2EU_c(b^*(\omega),\omega;\pi^*(B),p^*(B,\Phi^i))/dB^2 = -exp\{z(b^*(\omega))\}[2x_c^2 + c]/c < 0$, yields $b^*(\omega) = -\omega$ as the unique global maximum.

(b) For $B \in [-\overline{\omega},0]$, $\mu^*(\omega|B) = 1$ if and only if $B = b^*(\omega)$. That is, $b^{*-1}(b)$ exists and is unique, and $EU_f(\Pi,B;\mu^*(\omega|B),p^*(B,\Phi^i)) = 0$, which is independent of Π since the equilibrium policy strategy is to adopt the bill, regardless of the rule. Therefore $\pi^*(B)$ is (non-uniquely) optimal for $B \in [-\overline{\omega},0]$. For $B < -\overline{\omega}$ and $B > 0$, $\mu^*(\overline{\omega}|B) = 1$ and $EU_f(\Pi,B;\mu^*(\omega|B),p^*(B,\Phi^i)) = -\Pi(B + \overline{\omega})^2$. Since $B + \overline{\omega} > 0$ for $B > 0$ and $B + \overline{\omega} < 0$ for $B < -\overline{\omega}$, $\pi^*(B) = 0$ is optimal in both cases.

(c) For $B \in [-\overline{\omega},0]$, $\mu^*(\omega|B) = 1$ if and only if $B = b^*(\omega)$. If $\Phi = \Phi^{open}$, $P = B$ is optimal since this yields the pivot's ideal point given its beliefs. If $\Phi = \Phi^{closed}$, $P = B$ is again optimal since $B = b^*(\omega) = -\omega$ and this bill, too, yields the pivot's ideal point. For $B \notin [-\overline{\omega},0]$, $\mu^*(\overline{\omega}|B) = 1$, $\pi^*(B) = 0$, and $P = -\overline{\omega}$ is optimal.

(d) Substitution of $b^*(\omega)$ into $\mu^*(\omega|B)$ establishes consistency $\forall B \in [-\overline{\omega},0]$.

(e) For $B \notin [-\overline{\omega},0]$, $\pi^*(B) = 0$ and $p^*(B,\Phi^i) = -\overline{\omega}$. The expected utility of a committee with information ω playing its equilibrium proposal strategy is given by $EU_c(IN) = -[1 - \pi^*(b^*(\omega))]c - x_c^2$. The expected utility of this committee proposing some $B \notin [-\overline{\omega},0]$ is $EU_c(OUT) = -c - (x_c + \overline{\omega} - \omega)^2$. Let $\Delta \equiv EU_c(IN) - EU_c(OUT)$. Then $d\Delta/d\omega = 2x_c exp\{-2x_c(\overline{\omega} + B)/c\} - 2(x_c + \overline{\omega} - \omega)$, which is minimized at $\omega = \overline{\omega}$ since $d^2\Delta/d\omega^2 = 4x_c^2 exp\{-2x_c(\overline{\omega} + B)/c\}/c + 2 > 0$. Thus, the committee type $\omega = \overline{\omega}$ would lose the least by deviating from the equilibrium proposal strategy.

2. *Uniqueness of the Separating Equilibrium.* To illustrate that the set $\{b^*(\omega),\pi^*(B),p^*(B,\Phi^i),\mu^*(\omega|B)\}$ is the unique separating equilibrium to the game, it is sufficient to show that:

(a) $\pi^*(B)$ is continuous and strictly decreasing and
(b) given (a), $\pi^*(B)$ is unique.

(a) A necessary condition for a separating equilibrium is that $\pi^*(B)$ is strictly decreasing in B. Suppose (to the contrary) that $\pi^*(B)$ is constant or strictly increasing over some range $[B',B'']$. Then all relevant committee types would propose B'' since this proposal increases the likelihood of obtaining a policy outcome nearer its ideal point while maximizing the probability of receiving a closed rule. Thus, if $\pi^*(B)$ is not strictly decreasing, a separating equilibrium cannot obtain. It also must be the case that $\pi^*(B)$ is continuous. Given the previous argument, any jump discontinuities must be downward. However, for any such discontinuity at a particular proposal B' such that $B' = b^*(\omega')$, a committee with private information of ω' would strictly prefer a proposal $B' - \epsilon$ for sufficiently small ϵ. Thus, if $\pi^*(B)$ is not continuous, a separating equilibrium cannot obtain.

(b) The function $\pi^*(B)$ is continuous in B, so $EU_c(\cdot)$ is differentiable. Differentiating $EU_c(B,\omega;\pi^*(B),p^*(B,\Phi^i))$ with respect to B and equating to zero yields $\pi'^*(B)c + 2x_c\pi^*(B) = 0$, a first-order linear differential equation. This equation has a general solution of the form $\pi(B) = \lambda exp\{-2x_cB/c\}$ where λ is determined by some additional information about the value of $\pi^*(B)$ at a boundary. A natural candidate arises in $\pi^*(-\overline{\omega}) = 1$. The pivot knows that the committee has an incentive to cause it to infer that ω is smaller than it actually is, i.e., to induce policies yielding outcomes larger than the pivot would like. A proposal equal to $-\overline{\omega}$ has no potential for an outcome greater than $x_v = 0$, the pivot's ideal point. The committee has no interest in inducing an outcome smaller than x_v since $x_c \geq 0$. Thus, the proposal $B = -\overline{\omega}$ should be adopted with certainty. Given $\pi^*(-\omega) = 1$, a specific solution of $\pi^*(B) = exp\{-2x_c(\overline{\omega} + B)/c\}$ is obtained. Notice once again that $\pi^*(B)$ is continuous and strictly decreasing in B. Thus, the equilibrium identified above is unique.

3. *Nonexistence of Pooling Equilibria.* Suppose there is an equilibrium in which $b^*(\omega) = -E(\omega)$, the unconditional expectation of ω under $f(\omega)$, for all $\omega \in [0,\overline{\omega}], \pi^*(B) = 1$ for $B \leq -E(\omega)$ and small enough otherwise, and $\mu^*(\omega|B) = f(\omega)$ for $B = -E(\omega)$. This pure pooling equilibrium is only possible if (a) $-E(\omega) + \overline{\omega} \leq x_c$, so that no committee type has an incentive to propose $B < -E(\omega)$, and (b) out-of-equilibrium beliefs consistent with the refinement of universal divinity can be found to support the equilibrium. However, it can be shown that even if (a) holds, no supporting beliefs that are universally divine exist. Let $[1 - \theta(\omega;B)]$ be the probability of an open rule that leaves a committee of type ω indifferent between $B = -E(\omega)$, the equilibrium proposal, and some $B > -E(\omega)$. Recall that the committee has an incentive to shift the adopted policy in a positive direction. Then $-(x_c + E(\omega) - \omega)^2 = -\theta(\omega;B)(x_c - B - \omega)^2 - (1 - \theta(\omega;B))(x_c + E(\omega) - \omega)^2 - (1 - \theta(\omega;B))c$, or $\theta(\omega;B) = c/[(x_c + E(\omega) - \omega)^2 - (x_c - B - \omega)^2 + c]$ and

$\theta'(\omega;B) = 2c(E(\omega) + B)/[(x_c + E(\omega) - \omega)^2 - (x_c - B - \omega)^2 + c]^2 > 0$. Since $[1 - \theta'(\omega;B)] < 0$, the type $\omega = 0$ is the most likely to deviate from the equilibrium proposal strategy. Intuitively, it is easy to see that committee types with large realizations of ω are benefited under this pooling equilibrium since the policy outcome is closer to their ideal point. By continuity, the committee type who is hurt the most in the pooling equilibrium is $\omega = 0$ and, therefore, the most likely to deviate from the equilibrium strategy. The refinement of universal divinity requires that whenever $B > -E(\omega), \mu^*(0|B) = 1$. For $B = 0 > -E(\omega)$, the best response of the pivot is to accept the committee's proposal with probability one. Since the committee of type $\omega = 0$ moves the outcome closer to its ideal point with $B = 0$, this proposal will be made. Thus, the pure pooling equilibrium identified above does not survive the refinement. Similar arguments can be made to preclude partial pooling equilibria as well.

Proof of Corollary 3

Consider two additional random variables, z and s, such that z has the same distribution as $\omega + s$ and $\int sk(s|\omega)ds = 0$ where $k(s|\omega)$ is the conditional probability function of s given ω. Given the strict convexity of $\pi^*(\cdot)$ in ω and Jensen's inequality, $\int \pi^*(\omega + s)k(s|\omega)ds > \pi^*(\omega + \int sk(s|\omega)ds) = \pi^*(\omega)$ for every ω. Taking expectations with respect to ω, $\int_0^{\bar{\omega}} \int \pi^*(\omega + s)k(s|\omega)f(\omega)ds\,d\omega > \int_0^{\bar{\omega}} \pi^*(\omega)f(\omega)d\omega$. The expectation of observing a closed rule is greater the more risky is the ex ante uncertainty of the committee's private information.

Condorcet Consistent Binary Agendas under Incomplete Information

Joon Pyo Jung

1. Introduction

Understanding the impact of voting procedures and agendas on the outcomes of collective decision problems under majority rule is evidently important. And for the class of agendas based on the amendment procedure under complete information, the structure of the voting process as well as the influence of the agenda setter over the voting outcome are now fairly well understood. Four results best summarize the central findings of the research with respect to the agendas based on the *amendment procedure,* where two alternatives are put to a vote, the winner (under majority voting) being paired with a new alternative, the winner of that then being paired with a new alternative, and so on until one alternative is chosen. Let X stand for the set of all alternatives in an agenda based on the amendment procedure. Assume that the number of voters is odd and that all voters have strict preferences. Then these results are as follows. First, only an alternative in the uncovered set of X and therefore the Condorcet winner,[1] if it exists, can be the final outcome if all voters are strategic, that is, "sophisticated" in the sense of Farquharson (1969), and McKelvey and Niemi (1978)—if all voters foresee the future consequences of their actions and vote throughout the agenda in accordance with appropriate strategies that maximize their benefits (Miller 1980; and see Banks 1985, for additional restrictions).

I am grateful to David Austen-Smith, Jeffrey Banks, and William Riker for their numerous comments and encouragements. In addition, a short talk with Peter Ordeshook was helpful in preventing some mistakes at the initial stage of the development of this paper. The responsibility for any errors is entirely mine.

1. We say that *a beats b* if more voters prefer *a* to *b* than prefer *b* to *a*. We say that *a covers b in X* if and only if *a* beats *b* and beats everything in X that *b* beats. The set of alternatives not covered by any other alternatives in X is called the *uncovered set* of X. The uncovered set of X is a subset of the *top cycle* of X, the smallest set of alternatives not beaten by any other alternatives in X outside of the set, and both the uncovered set and the top cycle of X will collapse into a single alternative if there exists an alternative called the *Condorcet winner* that beats everything in X.

Second, if all voters are strategic, any agenda based on the amendment procedure is equivalent to some two-stage agenda in the sense that if an alternative, a, can be reached via some agenda based on the amendment procedure from the status quo, b, then a can be reached from b in one or two votes (Miller 1980; Shepsle and Weingast 1984). Third, if all voters are sincere—if all voters vote at each stage for the most preferred of the two alternatives being considered, than any alternative in the top cycle can be the final outcome via some agenda based on the amendment procedure (Miller 1980). Finally, with spatial preferences and sincere voting, any point in the entire space, if there is no Condorcet winner, can be the outcome of some agenda based on the amendment procedure (McKelvey 1979). Since in the "usual" multidimensional spatial context, the absence of the Condorcet winner is the rule rather than the exception (Cohen and Matthews 1979; McKelvey 1976, 1979; Plott 1967; Schofield 1983, 1984), an agenda setter, if he can control the set of feasible alternatives as well as the order of voting, has almost a dictatorial power over the outcome.

However, all the above findings are more or less based on the assumption of complete information with exogenously determined agendas under the amendment procedure. Considering that the amendment procedure is not the only voting procedure employed by voting bodies such as Congress, that the actual process by which outcomes are arrived at encompasses numerous stages prior to the final voting stage, and that voters are not in general completely informed about each other's preferences, the general applicability of the above findings to the analysis of actual voting bodies such as Contress is quite limited.

Recently, efforts have been made to look at what happens when agendas are not of the amendment procedure type (e.g., Ordeshook and Schwartz 1987), when agendas are not set monopolistically (e.g., Banks and Gasmi 1987; Baron and Ferejohn 1987; McKelvey 1986) or when there is incomplete information (e.g., Austen-Smith and Riker 1987; Enelow and Hinich 1983; Ordeshook and Palfrey 1988).[2]

Following Ordeshook and Palfrey (1988), this essay explores some implications of incomplete information with exogenously determined agendas based on some multistage binary procedures, of which the amendment procedure is a special type.

The assumption that voters are completely informed about each

---

2. The sources of incomplete information or uncertainty are numerous. For example, Austen-Smith and Riker (1987) address the problems of uncertainty regarding the consequences of alternative policies. Enelow and Hinich (1983) deal with uncertainty about the linkage between present alternatives and future decisions. But the main concern in this essay is that of Ordeshook and Palfrey (1988).

other's preferences, though analytically convenient, is highly unrealistic. In real world situations, voters in a committee may not possess full information about each other's preferences simply because information is costly or because some kinds of informations are intrinsically hard to acquire. Moreover, it is likely that some people, a chairman of a committee, for example, possess more information than other members of the committee.

With complete information, McKelvey and Niemi (1978), Moulin (1979), and Gretlein (1983) show how "working backwards up" the extensive form representation of a voting procedure produces an outcome that corresponds to a (perfect) Nash equilibrium of voting strategies, and the previously stated results about strategic voting in the amendment procedure are based on this "backward induction" argument. With incomplete information, however, these results do not in general hold, since it is no longer possible to work backwards up the extensive form representation of a voting procedure to calculate the "sophisticated equivalent" at each node; voters can not, in advance, tell for sure which alternative beats which. Through some very carefully selected examples, Ordeshook and Palfrey (1988) show that, if information is incomplete, even a Condorcet winner (more precisely, an almost certain Condorcet winner) need not be selected and that the "two-step reduction" theorem is not always applicable.

The examples of Ordeshook and Palfrey (1988) are provocative, suggesting that the results of complete information models are extremely sensitive to the informational assumption. However, all of their examples include preferences which are not single-peaked—an important class of preferences for political analysis.

In this essay, I analyze agendas with incomplete information in an environment where all voters are known to have single-peaked preferences over a one-dimensional issue space. Single-peakedness requires that the set of alternatives can be arranged on a line such that the utility curve of everyone is unimodal—either always downward sloping, or always upward sloping, or sloping upward to a particular point and then sloping downward. I show that the inferences drawn from the examples of Ordeshook and Palfrey (1988) about agendas with incomplete information, in general, still hold in this environment of single-peaked preferences. In general, even with single-peaked preferences, the analysis of agendas with incomplete information requires considerably more effort than with complete information in that it is necessary to model how voters learn the preferences of other voters. With complete information, voters' beliefs about the preferences of others do not change as the voting process goes on; voters possess the whole truth about the preferences of other voters before the voting process begins. But with incomplete information, beliefs about preferences can change as the voting proceeds and voting behavior in the process reveals information. Results in early stages of voting can be used by voters to convey information (or misinformation) that affects the decisions of voters in later stages of voting. In this respect, even nonbinding votes such as straw polls, by revealing some information, can critically affect the final outcomes (for an example, see Ordeshook and Palfrey 1988). One more difficulty with the analysis of agendas with incomplete information is that usually a multiplicity of equilibria are possible, and there is no evident way in the presence of multiple equilibria to make predictions about how voters would choose to play. With complete information, the backward induction guarantees a unique equilibrium. But with incomplete information, a great many equilibria may exist as the examples in Ordeshook and Palfrey (1988) show. But with some particular structures on the agenda, it turns out that the information that all voters have single-peaked preferences is sufficient for voters to arrive at a unique equilibrium and the equilibrium outcome is the Condorcet winner (which always exists given single-peaked preferences [Black 1958]).

The essay is organized as follows: section 2 contains notations, definitions, and assumptions for the subsequent analysis. Section 3 offers some examples illustrating how the equilibrium concept developed in section 2 can be applied to concrete cases. These examples provide some hints about how to construct agendas with a unique equilibrium. Section 4 shows the main finding: there exist agendas such that sincere voting by all voters at each stage of voting results in a unique equilibrium, and the associated equilibrium outcome is the Condorcet winner. In addition, it shows how to construct agendas where the Condorcet winner emerges as the outcome with minimum number of ballots to be planned in a binary agenda to reach one definite outcome. Section 5 contains some concluding remarks and provides an interpretation of the results in terms of "implementation theory."

2. Basic Model

Let $X = \{x_1, x_2, \ldots, x_m\}$ be a given finite set of alternatives over the one-dimensional issue space R, where $x_1 < x_2 < \ldots < x_m$. Let N be the set of voters, $|N| = 2n + 1$, where n is any natural number. Each voter $i \in N$ is known to have single-peaked preferences over R. Assume that each voter has strict preferences over X and let xP_iy denote "x is strictly preferred to y by i." Throughout this essay, I assume that each voter has a cardinal utility function over X, although the main results in this essay depend only on the ordinal nature of the preferences. A voter's *type* is given by his preferences over X. Since preferences are single-peaked and X has m alternatives, there exist 2^{m-1} possible types. Each voter is assumed to know his own utility function (and therefore, his own type) and the common prior probability distribution over the 2^{m-1} possible types.[3]

The committee, N, must select some alternative from X. The decision-making mechanism is simple majority voting over an agenda based on a multistage binary procedure. An agenda is said to be based on the *binary procedure* if at every stage of the voting a voter can either vote in favor of one set of outcomes in X or in favor of some other set of outcomes in X. The purpose of such an agenda is to eliminate alternatives until one alternative in X remains as the final outcome. I represent such an agenda as a binary tree:

DEFINITION. An *agenda* on X is a complete specification of a finite binary tree T such that (1) every element of X occupies some terminal branch of T, (2) every terminal branch is occupied by only one element in X, and (3) every branch of T is occupied by some nonempty subsets of X consisting of the elements of X reachable from that branch.

Condition (1) states that every alternative in X can be the final outcome via some path in T. Condition (2) guarantees that only one alternative is chosen as the final outcome. Condition (3) differs from the usual definition others make for agendas based on the amendment procedure (e.g., Shepsle and Weingast 1984) in that in the above definition each branch is occupied by all the alternatives in X reachable from that branch, whereas in the usual definition for agendas based on the amendment procedure each branch is occupied by only one alternative in X. Condition (3), however, does not differ from the usual definition in identifying sincere voting for agendas based on the amendment procedure, as the following definition shows.

DEFINITION. *Sincere voting* of voter i at each decision node is voting for the branch that has the alternative that has the highest ranking in i's preference ordering over the alternatives remaining after eliminating common elements. Correspondingly, *insincere voting* is voting for the other branch.[4]

For agendas based on the amendment procedure, only one alternative remains for each branch if we eliminate alternatives occupying both branches. Thus, the above definition of sincere voting corresponds to

---
3. For the purpose of this essay, it is not necessary to assume "common knowledge." The main results in this essay are valid even if voters have asymmetric subjective information about other voters' preferences.

4. Both sincere and insincere voting can be the result of strategic behavior of voter i.

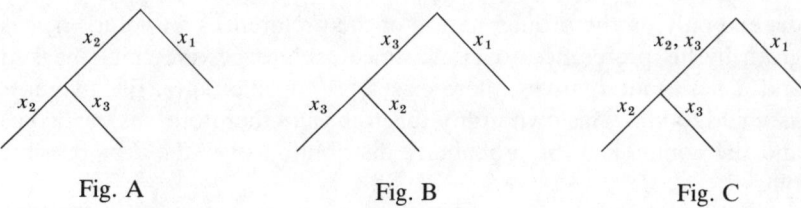

Fig. A   Fig. B   Fig. C

the usual definition others make for agendas based on the amendment procedure.[5] However, for agendas based on nonamendment procedures, sincere strategy derived from the above definition may differ from sincere strategy derived from the definition such as that of Ordeshook and Schwartz (1987), which characterizes binary agendas by the fact that each stage of voting is between two alternatives. For example, the following three specifications of trees are all based on the *successive procedure* where an alternative is introduced first and voted up or down under majority rule; if voted up, it is the outcome; otherwise, another alternative is introduced and voted up or down; and so forth. If the first $m - 1$ alternatives are voted down, the one remaining alternative is the outcome (Farquharson 1969; Miller 1977).[6]

According to the definition of Ordeshook and Schwartz (1987), figures A and B express two different agendas depending on whether x_2 or x_3 plays the role of the status quo. In my definition, however, figures A and B are equivalent to each other and both are expressed as figure C. Similarly, sincere voting of voter i at the first stage of voting for whom, for example, $x_2 P_i x_1 P_i x_3$ holds, according to the definition of Ordeshook and Schwartz, is voting for the left-hand branch (x_2) in figure A and voting for the right-hand branch (x_1) in figure B, whereas it is, according to my definition, voting for the left-hand branch (x_2, x_3) in figure C.

In a binary voting tree T, at any given decision node, the branches emanating from that node can be indexed by L or R. I will sometimes call branch L the left-hand branch and branch R the right-hand branch. A noninitial node in T can be identified in terms of the history of the branches that are taken to get to it. Thus, a noninitial node d is identi-

---

5. The definition of "sophisticated" or "strategic" voting with complete information will be equivalent to the usual definition (eg., McKelvey and Niemi 1978), since working backwards up the tree requires only the specification of alternatives occupying each terminal branch.

6. The definition of sincere strategy under the successive procedure here is the same as that of Farquharson (1969) or Miller (1977). What I call "agendas based on the successive procedure," Ordeshook and Schwartz (1987) refer to as "nonrepetitive sequential-elimination agendas." For another possible definition of sincere strategy under successive procedure, see Riker (1982a, 73).

fied by a p-tuple $d = (d_1, d_2, \ldots, d_p)$, where d_1 is the first branch that is taken, d_2 is the second, etc. The variable p is called as the *order of node d* and represents the number of branches that must be traversed to get to the node d. The maximum order of nodes in a given tree T is referred to as the *length of the agenda* and represents the number of branches that are taken to reach the terminal node that is farthest from the initial node of T.

The game proceeds as follows: at each decision node, a voter votes either L or R and the branch that gets *more than n* votes wins and the next stage of voting is held between the two branches at the decision node where the winning branch leads. Letting $|T|$ denote the number of decision nodes in the binary tree T, each voter has $2^{|T|}$ (pure) strategies available to him, where a strategy is a $|T|$-tuple of Ls and Rs. I assume that all voters are expected utility maximizers and that the payoffs are dependent only on the final outcome.

I now define the equilibrium concept. With incomplete information, unlike with complete information, beliefs about the preferences of others are not fixed: after the results of a particular ballot are revealed, voters might change these beliefs. Consequently, an equilibrium concept should explicitly deal with beliefs. The relevant equilibrium concept is therefore *strategic voting equilibrium* (Ordeshook and Palfrey 1988). Briefly, a strategic voting equilibrium (SVE) is a sequential equilibrium applied to the reduced game where reduction of the original game is done by sequentially eliminating dominated strategies; at each voting stage in the reduced game, each voter's strategy maximizes his expected final payoff, conditional on his beliefs over the distribution of types at that stage, and beliefs are consistent with Bayes's rule where applicable. Since the main results in this essay depend only on the dominance reduction argument, I leave the concept sequential equilibrium imprecise (for further discussion of the concept of the sequential equilibrium, see Kreps and Wilson 1982*a*).

3. Examples with three alternatives

In this section, I provide two examples with three alternatives. The first example is based on the amendment procedure and the second example is based on the successive procedure. These examples clarify the preceeding definitions and show how the concept of the SVE is applied to concrete cases. In addition, they provide some clue as to how to construct multistage binary agendas that produce the Condorcet winner as the unique equilibrium outcome. Suppose that the set of alternatives is $\{A, B, C\}$ where $A < B < C$ and the number of voters $|N| = 2n + 1$. Given single-peaked strict preferences, only four possible types of preference orderings can exist:

Type 1: $A\ B\ C$
Type 2: $B\ A\ C$
Type 3: $B\ C\ A$
Type 4: $C\ B\ A$

where, for example, $A\ B\ C$ denotes AP_iBP_iC.

Let the common prior probability that any voter has Type j preferences be p_j ($p_1 + p_2 + p_3 + p_4 = 1$), and let n_j be the number of Type j voters each voter thinks exist without counting himself ($n_1 + n_2 + n_3 + n_4 = 2n$). Given the probability terms, each voter calculates the probability that there are $k1$ Type 1, $k2$ Type 2, $k3$ Type 3, and $k4 = 2n - k1 - k2 - k3$ Type 4 voters among the $2n$ voters in the committee by the following multinomial formula:

$$Pr[n_1 = k1,\ n_2 = k2,\ n_3 = k3,\ n_4 = k4] = \{(2n)!/k1!k2!k3!k4!\}$$

$$p_1^{k1} p_2^{k2} p_3^{k3} p_4^{k4}.$$

Next, I assume that each voter i has a well-defined Von Neumann–Morgenstern utility function such that the utility of first, middle, and last ranked alternative is 1, $0 < v_i < 1$, and 0 respectively.

EXAMPLE 1: The first example is based on the amendment procedure. Figure 1(a) depicts the agenda "A vs B, the winner against C," and figure 1(b) is the agenda "A vs C, the winner against B." I do not describe another possible agenda "C vs B, the winner against A," since results from this agenda can be obtained by appropriately renaming the alternatives and types in figure 1(a).

In figure 1, numbers attached to a branch mean that those types of voters have dominant strategies of voting for that branch.

In reducing the original game by eliminating dominated strategies, Farquharson's theorem on "straightforwardness" plays an important role (Farquharson 1956; 1969, 31).[7] A *straightforward strategy* is unconditionally best or dominates all other strategies. A binary division (weakly) *separates* a voter's preference ordering if his least preferred alternative in one subset is at least as good as his most preferred

---

[7]. I owe this observation to an anonymous reviewer, who also suggested a revision of the proof of Theorem 2 more in line with Farquharson's concepts than the one in section 4.

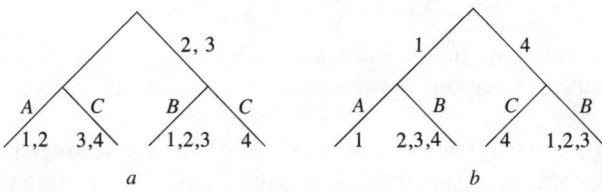

Fig. 1

alternative in the other subset. Then Farquharson's theorem says: a procedure is *straightforward* for a voter if and only if *every* division of it separates his preference ordering. Farquharson also says that a straightforward strategy is always sincere, but a sincere strategy is not necessarily straightforward. Thus if a voter has a straightforward strategy, then this voter has a dominant strategy of being sincere throughout the agenda. But even if a voter does not have a straightforward strategy, if his preference ordering is separated by a particular division, he has at that division a dominant strategy of voting sincerely. For "if he chose a subset whose least desirable member is as desirable as any member of the other subset, then he cannot regret his choice, whatever outcome is actually selected, for no other choice could have resulted in a preferable outcome" (Farquharson 1969, 32). For example, all Type 3 voters in figure 1(a) and all Type 1 and Type 4 voters in figure 1(b) have straightforward strategies of voting sincerely; every division of the tree separates the preferences orderings of these voters. Because a binary division with only two alternatives necessarily separates all preference orderings, everyone votes sincerely at the last stage of voting in figure 1(a) and in figure 1(b). Thus applying Farquharson's theorem on straightforwardness and related arguments in reducing the original games leaves us with greatly simplified games.

In figure 1(b), no further reduction is possible. In figure 1(a), however, another reduction is possible. Type 2 voters in figure 1(a) have (iterated) dominant strategies of voting sincerely at the first stage of voting because any lottery between B and C is preferred to any lottery between A and C; the utility of B is 1 and that of A is less than 1 for Type 2 voters and the probability of B being the outcome in the right-hand subgame if it is reached is greater than the probability of A being the outcome in the left-hand subgame if it is reached, since in the right-hand subgame Type 1, 2 and 3 voters vote for B whereas in the left-hand subgame only Type 1 and Type 2 voters vote for A.

To these reduced games generated by eliminating dominated strategies from the original games, I now apply the sequential equilibrium concept. I check only whether everyone being sincere can be a sequential equilibrium in the reduced games, and therefore an SVE in the original games, since the Condorcet winner will be the outcome if everyone is sincere.

In figure 1(b), it can be easily checked that any strategies of Type 2 and 3 voters at the first stage can be part of equilibrium strategies: given Types 1 and 4 vote sincerely at the first stage of voting and all voters vote sincerely at the last stage of voting, the only case in which A (respectively C) can be the final outcome is the case in which the number of Type 1 (Type 4) voters is greater than n. B wins in all other cases where neither Type 1 voters alone nor Type 4 voters alone constitute a majority, *regardless of the strategies of Type 2 and 3 voters*. Thus, the Condorcet winner will necessarily be the outcome in any SVE given the agenda with 3 alternatives depicted in figure 1(b).

I now check whether the agenda in figure 1(a) can result in an SVE with everyone voting sincerely. To establish that it is possible, it has to be shown that no one has any incentive to be insincere given his belief that everyone else is sincere. Since Type 2 and 3 voters have dominant strategies of voting sincerely, all that has to be checked is whether any Type 1 or 4 voters have any incentive to be insincere. Consider a Type 1 voter, say voter j with utility v_j for B, who believes that everyone else is sincere. Given his belief about the strategies of other voters, his expected utility $EU(L)$ from voting sincerely (a vote for the left-hand branch) equals:

(The probability that A wins given his strategy and belief about the strategies of other voters) (The utility of A) + (The probability that C in the left-hand subgame wins given his strategy and belief about the strategies of other voters) (The utility of C) + (The probability that B wins given his strategy and belief about the strategies of other voters) (The utility of B) + (The probability that C in the right-hand subgame wins given his strategy and belief about the strategies of other voters) (The utility of C)

$= Pr[n_1 \geq n \ \& \ n_1 + n_2 \geq n] \cdot 1 \ + \ Pr[n_1 \geq n \ \& \ n_3 + n_4 \geq n + 1] \cdot 0$

$+ \ Pr[n_2 + n_3 + n_4 \geq n + 1 \ \& \ n_1 + n_2 + n_3 \geq n] \cdot v_j$

$+ \ Pr[n_2 + n_3 + n_4 \geq n + 1 \ \& \ n_4 \geq n + 1] \cdot 0.$[8]

---

8. For example, given his belief (Type 1 voters vote for the left-hand branch and all others vote for the right-hand branch in the first ballot, and all voters including himself are sincere in the second ballot) and his strategy (a vote for the right-hand branch in the first ballot and a sincere vote in the second ballot), A can be the final outcome only if the number of Type 1 voters *excluding himself* is more than or equal to n in the first ballot and the number of Type 1 (again not counting himself) and 2 voters together is more than or

The expected utility EU(R) for j from voting insincerely (a vote for the right-hand branch) equals:

$$Pr[n_1 \geq n + 1 \ \& \ n_1 + n_2 \geq n] \cdot 1 + Pr[n_1 \geq n + 1$$

$$\& \ n_3 + n_4 \geq n + 1] \cdot 0 + Pr[n_2 + n_3 + n_4 \geq n \ \& \ n_1 + n_2 + n_3 \geq n] \cdot v_j$$

$$+ Pr[n_2 + n_3 + n_4 \geq n \ \& \ n_4 \geq n + 1] \cdot 0.$$

He can be sincere at the first stage of voting if $EU(L) - EU(R) \geq 0$. It can be easily checked that

$$EU(L) - EU(R) = Pr[n_1 \geq n \ \& \ n_1 + n_2 \geq n] \cdot 1 - Pr[n_1 \geq n + 1$$

$$\& \ n_1 + n_2 \geq n] \cdot 1 + Pr[n_2 + n_3 + n_4 \geq n + 1$$

$$\& \ n_1 + n_2 + n_3 \geq n] \cdot v_j - Pr[n_2 + n_3 + n_4 \geq n$$

$$\& \ n_1 + n_2 + n_3 \geq n] \cdot v_j = Pr[n_1 = n_2 + n_3 + n_4 = n] \cdot 1$$

$$- Pr[n_1 = n_2 + n_3 + n_4 = n] \cdot v_j > 0. \tag{1}^9$$

Since v_j is always less than 1, the above inequality will always hold. Thus, no Type 1 voter has any incentive to deviate from the conjectured equilibrium strategy given his belief that all others are sincere. Notice that the above expression in (1) as well as those in (2), (3) and (4) in subsequent analysis show that we need only examine those cases where a voter's vote is critical for one branch as against another to verify a particular strategy $(2n + 1)$-tuple is an SVE of a 2-stage agenda (Remark 2 in Ordeshook and Palfrey 1988).

Now, consider a Type 4 voter, say voter k. His expected utility

---

equal to n in the second ballot, since $(n + 1)$ voters constitute a majority in the committee of $(2n + 1)$ voters. Therefore, the probability of A winning given his belief and strategy is equal to $Pr[n_1 \geq n \ \& \ n_1 + n_2 \geq n]$. Notice that if the number of Type 1 voters exceeds n, it is needless to say that the total number of Type 1 and 2 voters exceeds n. But I keep the expression $Pr[n_1 \geq n \ \& \ n_1 + n_2 \geq n]$ instead of $Pr[n_1 \geq n]$ for computational purposes in later operations as well as for expositional purposes.

9. $Pr[n_1 \geq n \ \& \ n_1 + n_2 \geq n] - Pr[n_1 \geq n + 1 \ \& \ n_1 + n_2 \geq n] = Pr[n_1 = n \ \& \ n_1 + n_2 \geq n]$ and since $n_1 + n_2 \geq n$ naturally follows from the fact that $n_1 = n$, $Pr[n_1 = n \ \& \ n_1 + n_2 \geq n] = Pr[n_1 = n]$. From the fact that $n_1 + n_2 + n_3 + n_4 = 2n$, it follows that $n_2 + n_3 + n_4 = n$ if $n_1 = n$. Therefore, I get the expression $Pr[n_1 = n_2 + n_3 + n_4 = n]$ in (1). Similar logic establishes that $Pr[n_2 + n_3 + n_4 \geq n + 1 \ \& \ n_1 + n_2 + n_3 \geq n] - Pr[n_2 + n_3 + n_4 \geq n \ \& \ n_1 + n_2 + n_3 \geq n] = Pr[n_1 = n_2 + n_3 + n_4 = n]$.

EU(R) from voting sincerely (a vote for the right-hand branch) equals:

$$Pr[n_1 \geq n + 1 \,\&\, n_1 + n_2 \geq n + 1] \cdot 0 + Pr[n_1 \geq n + 1 \,\&\,$$

$$n_3 + n_4 \geq n] \cdot 1 + Pr[n_2 + n_3 + n_4 \geq n \,\&\, n_1 + n_2 + n_3 \geq n + 1] \cdot v_k$$

$$+ Pr[n_2 + n_3 + n_4 \geq n \,\&\, n_4 \geq n] \cdot 1.$$

His expected utility EU(L) from voting insincerely (a vote for the left-hand branch) equals:

$$Pr[n_1 \geq n \,\&\, n_1 + n_2 \geq n + 1] \cdot 0 + Pr[n_1 \geq n \,\&\, n_3 + n_4 \geq n] \cdot 1$$

$$+ Pr[n_2 + n_3 + n_4 \geq n + 1 \,\&\, n_1 + n_2 + n_3 \geq n + 1] \cdot v_k$$

$$+ Pr[n_2 + n_3 + n_4 \geq n + 1 \,\&\, n_4 \geq n] \cdot 1.$$

He will be sincere at the first stage of voting if $EU(R) - EU(L) \geq 0$

$$\Rightarrow v_k \geq \{(p_3 + p_4)^n - p_4^n\}/\{(p_2 + p_3 + p_4)^n - p_4^n\} \tag{2}$$

Whether the above inequality will hold depends on the probability terms and v_k. However, if n is sufficiently large, the inequality in (2) will necessarily hold for any strictly positive p_2, since the left term will approach 0 as n becomes large.

To establish expression (2), notice that

$$EU(R) - EU(L) = Pr[n_1 \geq n + 1 \,\&\, n_3 + n_4 \geq n] \cdot 1$$

$$- Pr[n_1 \geq n \,\&\, n_3 + n_4 \geq n] \cdot 1 + Pr[n_2 + n_3 + n_4 \geq n$$

$$\&\, n_1 + n_2 + n_3 \geq n + 1] \cdot v_k - Pr[n_2 + n_3 + n_4 \geq n + 1$$

$$\&\, n_1 + n_2 + n_3 \geq n + 1] \cdot v_k + Pr[n_2 + n_3 + n_4 \geq n \,\&\, n_4 \geq n] \cdot 1$$

$$- Pr[n_2 + n_3 + n_4 \geq n + 1 \,\&\, n_4 \geq n] \cdot 1$$

(from the same logic as in note 9)

$$= -Pr[n_1 = n \ \& \ n_3 + n_4 \geq n] \cdot 1 + Pr[n_2 + n_3 + n_4 = n$$

$$\& \ n_1 + n_2 + n_3 \geq n + 1] \cdot v_k + Pr[n_2 + n_3 + n_4 = n \ \& \ n_4 \geq n] \cdot 1.$$

$$Pr[n_1 = n \ \& \ n_3 + n_4 \geq n] = Pr[n_1 = n \ \& \ n_3 + n_4 = n]. \quad (2.1)$$

(From the fact that $n_1 + n_2 + n_3 + n_4 = 2n$, $n_3 + n_4$ should be equal to n if $n_1 = n$.)

$$Pr[n_2 + n_3 + n_4 = n \ \& \ n_1 + n_2 + n_3 \geq n + 1] =$$

$$Pr[n_1 = n \ \& \ n_1 + n_2 + n_3 \geq n + 1].$$

(n_1 should be equal to n if $n_2 + n_3 + n_4 = n$, since $n_1 + n_2 + n_3 + n_4 = 2n$.)

$$= Pr[n_1 = n \ \& \ n_2 + n_3 \geq 1].$$

(Since the number of Type 1 voters is n, there should be at least one Type 2 or Type 3 voter in order to have $n_1 + n_2 + n_3 \geq n + 1$.)

$$= Pr[n_1 = n \ \& \ n_2 + n_3 \geq 0] - Pr[n_1 = n \ \& \ n_2 + n_3 = 0]$$

$$= Pr[n_1 = n] - Pr[n_1 = n \ \& \ n_4 = n]. \quad (2.2)$$

(The fact that $(n_1 = n \ \& \ n_2 + n_3 \geq 0)$ implies that $n_2, n_3,$ and n_4 can be any number satisfying $n_2 + n_3 + n_4 = n$ and the fact that $(n_1 = n \ \& \ n_2 + n_3 = 0)$ means that $n_4 = n$ since $n_1 + n_2 + n_3 + n_4 = 2n$.)

$$Pr[n_2 + n_3 + n_4 = n \ \& \ n_4 \geq n] \cdot 1 = Pr[n_1 = n \ \& \ n_4 = n] \cdot 1. \quad (2.3)$$

(Since $n_1 + n_2 + n_3 + n_4 = 2n$, the fact that $n_2 + n_3 + n_4 = n$ implies $n_1 = n$, and n_4 can only be equal to n, if $n_1 = n$.)

From (2.1), (2.2), and (2.3):

$$-Pr[n_1 = n \ \& \ n_3 + n_4 \geq n] \cdot 1 + Pr[n_2 + n_3 + n_4 = n \ \&$$
$$n_1 + n_2 + n_3 \geq n + 1] \cdot v_k + Pr[n_2 + n_3 + n_4 = n \ \& \ n_4 \geq n] \cdot 1$$
$$= -Pr[n_1 = n \ \& \ n_3 + n_4 = n] \cdot 1 + \{Pr[n_1 = n] - Pr[n_1 = n$$
$$\& \ n_4 = n]\}) \cdot v_k + Pr[n_1 = n \ \& \ n_4 = n] \cdot 1.$$

$$Pr[n_1 = n \ \& \ n_3 + n_4 = n] = (2n!/n!n!)p_1^n(p_3 + p_4)^n. \tag{2.4}$$

$$Pr[n_1 = n] - Pr[n_1 = n \ \& \ n_4 = n]$$
$$= (2n!/n!n!)p_1^n(p_2 + p_3 + p_4)^n - (2n!/n!n!)p_1^n p_4^n. \tag{2.5}$$

$$Pr[n_1 = n \ \& \ n_4 = n] = (2n!/n!n!)p_1^n p_4^n. \tag{2.6}$$

From (2.4), (2.5), and (2.6):

$$-Pr[n_1 = n \ \& \ n_3 + n_4 = n] \cdot 1 + \{Pr[n_1 = n]$$
$$- Pr[n_1 = n \ \& \ n_4 = n]\} \cdot v_k + Pr[n_1 = n \ \& \ n_4 = n] \cdot 1$$
$$= -(2n!/n!n!)p_1^n(p_3 + p_4)^n + \{(2n!/n!n!)p_1^n(p_2 + p_3 + p_4)^n$$
$$- (2n!/n!n!)p_1^n p_4^n)\} \cdot v_k + (2n!/n!n!)p_1^n p_4^n \geq 0$$

$$\Rightarrow v_k \geq \{(p_3 + p_4)^n - p_4^n\}/\{(p_2 + p_3 + p_4)^n - p_4^n\}.$$

So far, I have shown that under any agenda with three alternatives based on the amendment procedure, everyone voting sincerely is an SVE given single-peaked preferences and a sufficiently large n.[10] In particular, under the agenda "A vs C, the winner against B," the Condorcet winner will always be the outcome. Given these results, the natural questions to ask are: (1) If preferences are single-peaked, is everyone being sincere an SVE under any agenda based on the amendment procedure with more than three alternatives given a sufficiently

---

10. The examples in this essay, together with those in Ordeshook and Palfrey (1988) where an alternative that is almost certainly a Condorcet winner cannot be selected if symmetric pure strategies are used, clearly show how sensitive the SVE is to the allowable preference types.

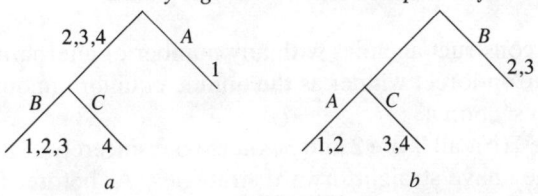

Fig. 2

large n? and (2) Is it possible, if preferences are single-peaked, to construct an agenda based on the amendment procedure with more than three alternatives, where everyone being sincere is an SVE regardless of the size of n?

It turns out that the answers to these questions are both negative and these are proven in the appendix to this essay using examples with four alternatives.

EXAMPLE 2: The second example of the essay mentioned at the beginning of this section is based on the successive procedure. With three alternatives, there exist only three distinct agendas: (*a*) introduce *A* first, (*b*) *B* first, and (*c*) *C* first. Figure 2(a) depicts the agenda where *A* is introduced at the first stage of voting and the second stage of voting is held between *B* and *C* only if *A* fails. And figure 2(b) is the agenda where *B* is introduced first and voting takes place between *A* and *C* only if *B* fails. Results derived from the agenda where *C* is introduced first and voting is held between *A* and *B* if *C* fails can be obtained by appropriate renaming of alternatives and types in figure 2(a), so I omit the analysis of this agenda.

As before, numbers attached to a branch mean that those numbered types have dominant strategies of voting for that branch. In figure 2(a), all Type 1, Type 3, and Type 4 voters have straightforward strategies, because every division in figure 2(a) separates these voters' preference orderings. Therefore, all Type 1, Type 3, and Type 4 voters will vote sincerely throughout the agenda. Type 2 voters have (iterated) dominant strategies of voting sincerely. If a Type 2 voter is decisive at the first stage of voting, this voter gets *B* (the most preferred alternative) by voting for the left-hand branch. This follows because all Type 4 voters vote for the right-hand branch and Type 4 voters alone cannot constitute a majority in case a Type 2 voter is decisive. If a Type 2 voter is not decisive, this voter's strategy does not matter. So every Type 2 voter has a weakly dominant strategy of voting sincerely if all other voters follow their dominant strategies. Therefore, all voters being sincere is the unique SVE under the agenda in figure 2(a). Moreover, the equilibrium outcome is the Condorcet winner. It turns out that this example can be extended to construct agendas with any number of alternatives that still produce the Condorcet winner as the unique equilibrium outcome. This task is left to section 4.

In figure 2(b), all Type 2 and 3 voters vote sincerely at the first stage of voting; they have straightforward strategies. As before, I check only whether everyone being sincere can be an SVE. Consider a specific Type 1 voter, say voter j, who believes that everyone else is sincere. Proceeding in a similar way as in the first example, voter j will be sincere if

$$EU(L) - EU(R) \geq 0 \Rightarrow Pr[n_1 + n_4 = n \ \& \ n_1 + n_2 \geq n] \cdot 1$$

$$- Pr[n_2 + n_3 = n] \cdot v_j \geq 0$$

$$\Rightarrow v_j \leq Pr[n_1 + n_4 = n \ \& \ n_1 + n_2 \geq n]/Pr[n_2 + n_3 = n]$$

$$\Rightarrow v_j \leq Pr[n_1 + n_2 \geq n \mid n_1 + n_4 = n_2 + n_3 = n]. \tag{3)[11]}$$

Likewise, a Type 4 voter, say voter k, will be sincere if $EU(L) - EU(R) \geq 0$

$$\Rightarrow v_k \leq Pr[n_3 + n_4 \geq n \mid n_1 + n_4 = n_2 + n_3 = n]. \tag{4}$$

In general, it is not known whether inequalities (3) and (4) will be satisfied simultaneously. It depends on the number of voters (n), relevant probabilities (p_1, p_2, p_3, p_4), and utilities of the middle ranked alternatives (v). However, if n becomes sufficiently large, any Type 1 voter will be sincere if $p_1 p_2 > p_3 p_4$ and any Type 4 voter will be sincere if $p_1 p_2 < p_3 p_4$.[12]

---

11. $Pr[n_1 + n_4 = n \ \& \ n_1 + n_2 \geq n] = Pr[n_2 + n_3 = n \ \& \ n_1 + n_2 \geq n]$, since the fact that $n_1 + n_2 + n_3 + n_4 = 2n$ implies $n_3 + n_4$ should be equal to $n_1 + n_4$. From the conditional probability formula, $Pr[n_2 + n_3 = n \ \& \ n_1 + n_2 \geq n] / Pr[n_2 + n_3 = n] = Pr[n_1 + n_2 = n \mid n_1 + n_4 = n_2 + n_3 = n]$.

12. To get the desired results, first divide $2n$ voters into two groups such that group 1 contains n voters consisting of Type 1 and 4 voters and group 2 contains n voters consisting of Type 2 and 3 voters. The number of Type 1 voters, M_1, is binomially distributed with probability $q_1 = p_1/(p_1 + p_4)$ in group 1, and the number of Type 2 voters, M_2, is binomially distributed with probability $q_2 = p_2/(p_2 + p_3)$. M_1 and M_2 are distributed independently of each other and if n becomes sufficiently large, M_1 (M_2 respectively) will be normally distributed with mean $nq_1[nq_2]$ and variance $nq_1(1 - q_1)$ [$nq_2(1 - q_2)$]. Therefore, ($M_1 + M_2$) is normally distributed with mean $n(q_1 + q_2)$ and variance $n\{q_1(1 - q_1) + q_2(1 - q_2)\}$. If n becomes sufficiently large, $Pr[n_1 + n_2 \geq n \mid n_1 + n_4 = n_2 + n_3 = n]$ will be equal to $Pr[M_1 + M_2 \geq n]$. Because $Pr[M_1 + M_2 \geq n] = Pr[(M_1 + M_2)/n \geq 1] = Pr[X \geq 1]$ where

This implies that everyone being sincere cannot be an equilibrium if n is sufficiently large.

So far, I have checked only whether everyone being sincere can be an equilibrium. But the implication of the above analysis seems to be that a multiplicity of equilibria are possible except under some specific agendas. The difficulty with several equilibria is that there is no evident way to make a prediction about how voters would choose to play. This, in turn, implies that an agenda setter, in situations where agendas are set monopolistically, faces uncertainty as to what outcome would prevail as the result of strategic voting. Depending on his belief and his attitude toward risk, the agenda setter might well rely on an agenda such as in figure 2(a). Or the agenda setter's main concern might be arriving at a socially desirable and stable outcome, thereby enhancing the possibility of being reelected: if full information is ultimately revealed, there will be a demand in the future for the reconsideration of the issue if an alternative other than the Condorcet winner is the outcome of the present voting, and this will bring discredit on the agenda setter. (This requires a change in the assumption that the payoffs are only dependent on the final outcome.)

Motivated by these examples, I now turn to the central proposition of the essay, viz., that *there exist binary agendas under which the Condorcet winner is supported as the unique equilibrium outcome and voting is sincere*.

4. Condorcet Consistent Binary Agendas under Incomplete Information

Consider the following method of constructing agendas: the first ballot is between two disjoint nonempty subsets of X, $B(L)$, and $B(R)$, such that any alternative in $B(R)$ is higher on the one-dimension than any alternative in $B(L)$; if $B(L)$ wins, the second ballot is between two disjoint

---

$X = (M_1 + M_2)/n$, $Pr[n_1 + n_2 \geq n \mid n_1 + n_4 = n_2 + n_3 = n]$ is equal to $Pr[X \geq 1]$ if n is sufficiently large.

$Pr[X \geq 1] = Pr[\{X - (q_1 + q_2)\}/V^{1/2} \geq \{1 - (q_1 + q_2)\}/V^{1/2}]$, since X is distributed normally with mean $(q_1 + q_2)$ and variance $V = \{q_1(1 - q_1) + q_2(1 - q_2)\}/n$. If n becomes sufficiently large, $P[X \geq 1]$ will approach 0 if $1 - (q_1 + q_2) > 0$, ½ if $1 - (q_1 + q_2) = 0$, and 1 if $1 - (q_1 + q_2) < 0$, since $V^{1/2}$ will approach 0. Since v_j is strictly less than 1, voter j will be sincere, given sufficiently large n, if $1 - (q_1 + q_2) < 0$, implying $p_1 p_2 > p_3 p_4$. It follows from the same logic as above that voter k will be sincere if $p_1 p_2 < p_3 p_4$.

The readers might wonder what happens when $p_1 p_2 = p_3 p_4$. In this case, everyone being sincere can be an equilibrium only if the utilities of middle-ranked alternatives (v) for all Type 1 and 4 voters are less than or equal to 0.5.

nonempty subsets of $B(L)$, $B(L,L)$, and $B(L,R)$, such that any alternative in $B(L,R)$ is higher on the one-dimension than any alternative in $B(L,L)$; if $B(R)$ wins, the second ballot is between two disjoint nonempty subsets of $B(R)$, $B(R,L)$, and $B(R,R)$, such that any alternative in $B(R,R)$ is higher on the one-dimension than any alternative in $B(R,L)$; etc., until a single alternative is reached.

For example, one agenda with 5 alternatives $\{A, B, C, D, E\}$ where $A < B < C < D < E$ might be:

Step 1: Choose between $B(L) = \{A, B\}$ and $B(R) = \{C, D, E\}$.
Step 2a: If $B(L)$ is chosen, choose between $B(L,L) = \{A\}$ and $B(L,R) = \{B\}$.
Step 2b: If $B(R)$ is chosen, choose between $B(R,L) = \{C,D\}$ and $B(R,R) = \{E\}$. If Step 2a is used or $B(R,R)$ is chosen at Step 2b, the process ends.
Step 3: If $B(R,L)$ is chosen at Step 2b, choose between $B(R,L,L) = \{C\}$ and $B(R,L,R) = \{D\}$.

I call the above method of constructing binary agendas as *successive bifurcation method Π*.[13] And an agenda constructed by the successive bifurcation method Π is referred to as the *successive elimination agenda by Π*.

Now I show that under any successive elimination agenda by Π, everyone voting sincerely at every stage of voting is the unique Strategic Voting Equilibrium and the associated equilibrium outcome is the Condorcet winner. First, I prove Lemma 1.

LEMMA 1. *Suppose voters use sincere strategies from the kth to the final ballot. Then the Condorcet winner among the alternatives not eliminated by previous ballots will be the outcome under any successive elimination agenda by Π.*

Proof. To prove this claim, it is sufficient to show that at each relevant ballot the winning branch contains the Condorcet winner. Suppose r alternatives $\{x_i, x_{i+1}, \ldots, x_{r+i-1}\}$ remain at the kth ballot, where $x_i < x_{i+1} < \ldots < x_{r+i-1}$. Without loss of generality, let

$$B(\underbrace{\ldots}_{(k-1)\text{ times}}, L) = \{x_i, \ldots, x_j\} \quad \text{and} \quad B(\underbrace{\ldots}_{(k-1)\text{ times}}, R) = \{x_{j+1}, \ldots, x_{r+i-1}\},$$

---

13. Professor Randall Calvert suggested the term *successive bifurcation method*.

where $i \leq j < r + i - 1$, be the two sets occupying two branches at the kth ballot, where $1 \leq k \leq \lambda$. At $k = 1$, for example, r equals m, the cardinality of the set X. At $k = \lambda$, where λ is the length of the agenda, r must be two. Given the definition of the sincere strategy, any voter whose most preferred alternative among the remaining r alternatives is either $x_i, \ldots,$ or x_j votes for $B(\ldots,L)$ and all others vote for $B(\ldots,R)$. Moreover, these strategies correspond to the sincere strategies obtained by assuming the vote is between x_j and x_{j+1}. Given single-peaked preferences, any voter whose most preferred alternative is in $\{x_i, \ldots, x_j\}$ prefers x_j to x_{j+1} and any voter whose most preferred alternative is in $\{x_{j+1}, \ldots, x_{r+i-1}\}$ prefers x_{j+1} to x_j. If $B(\ldots,L)$ wins against $B(\ldots,R)$ implying x_j wins against x_{j+1}, no alternative in $B(\ldots,R)$ can beat x_j by the assumption of single-peaked preferences. Therefore, the Condorcet winner must be in $B(\ldots,L)$. Similar logic establishes that $B(\ldots,R)$ must contain the Condorcet winner if it wins against $B(\ldots,L)$.

THEOREM 1. *Given any successive elimination agenda by Π, the Condorcet winner will be the final outcome if all voters follow sincere strategies.*

Proof. Set $k = 1$ and apply Lemma 1.

THEOREM 2. *Given any successive elimination agenda by Π, everyone voting sincerely at each ballot is the unique equilibrium.*

Proof. By induction.

i) The λth ballot, if it takes place, is between two alternatives. The division at λth ballot separates all voters' preference orderings.
ii) Now I show that given everyone voting sincerely from the $(k + 1)$th ballot onwards, everyone should be sincere on the kth ballot as well, where $1 \leq k < \lambda$. Without loss of generality, assume as before r alternatives $(x_i, \ldots, x_{i+r-1})$, where $x_i < x_{i+1} < \ldots < x_{i+r-1}$, remain as the result of previous ballots. From the construction of the agenda, the kth ballot should be between $\{x_i, \ldots, x_j\}$ and $\{x_{j+i}, \ldots, x_{i+r-1}\}$, where $i \leq j < i + r - 1$. Since everyone is assumed to be sincere from the $(k + 1)$th ballot onwards, only those cases where a voter vote is critical for one branch as against another need to be examined. If a voter is not decisive at this stage of voting, either the Condorcet winner among $\{x_i, \ldots, x_j\}$ or the Condorcet winner among $\{x_{j+1}, \ldots,$

x_{i+r-1}} wins by Lemma 1, and thus, any strategy can be part of an equilibrium $(2n + 1)$-tuple. I use two inductions.

(1) Any voter whose most preferred alternative among the remaining r alternatives is in $\{x_i, \ldots, x_j\}$ votes for this branch.

(1,a) Any voter whose most preferred alternative is x_i votes sincerely. The division at the kth ballot separates this voter's preference ordering; he prefers, given single-peakedness, any alternative in $\{x_i, \ldots, x_j\}$ to any alternative in $\{x_{j+i}, \ldots, x_{r+i-1}\}$.

(1,b) Given that all the voters with most preferred alternatives $x_i, x_{i+1}, \ldots, x_{g-1}$ vote sincerely, a voter with most preferred alternative x_g, where $i < g \leq j$, should also vote sincerely. This voter prefers, from single-peaked preferences, any alternative in $\{x_g, \ldots, x_j\}$ to any alternative in $\{x_{j+1}, \ldots, x_{r+i-1}\}$. And given that he is decisive at this stage and all voters whose most preferred alternatives are in $\{x_i, \ldots, x_{g-1}\}$ vote sincerely, only an alternative in $\{x_g, \ldots, x_j\}$ can be the outcome if he votes sincerely. To see this, note that, from single-peaked preferences, x_{g-1}, and therefore x_i through x_{g-2} cannot win against x_g since the number of voters who prefer x_{g-1} to x_g can at most be n: the voter in question is decisive and all voters with their most preferred alternatives in $\{x_i, \ldots, x_{g-1}\}$ voted sincerely by the hypothesis. Therefore, no alternative in $\{x_i, \ldots, x_{g-1}\}$ can be the outcome by Lemma 1.

(2) Any voter whose most preferred alternative among the remaining r alternatives is in $\{x_{j+i}, \ldots, x_{i+r-1}\}$ votes for this branch.

(2,a) A voter whose most preferred alternative is x_{i+r-1} votes sincerely. The division at the kth ballot separates this voter's preference ordering; he prefers, given single-peakedness, any alternative in $\{x_{j+i}, \ldots, x_{i+r-1}\}$ to any alternative in $\{x_i, \ldots, x_j\}$.

(2,b) The same logic as those in (1,b) establishes that given all the voters with most preferred alternatives $x_{f+1}, x_{f+2}, \ldots, x_{i+r-1}$ vote sincerely, a voter with most preferred alternative x_f, where $j+1 \leq f < i + r-1$, should also vote sincerely.

Therefore, if preferences are known to be single-peaked,[14] the Condorcet winner is guaranteed to prevail under all binary agendas con-

---

14. It is easy to see that Π can be also applied to the situations where all voters have single-troughed (Vickrey 1960) or single-caved (Inada 1964) preferences.

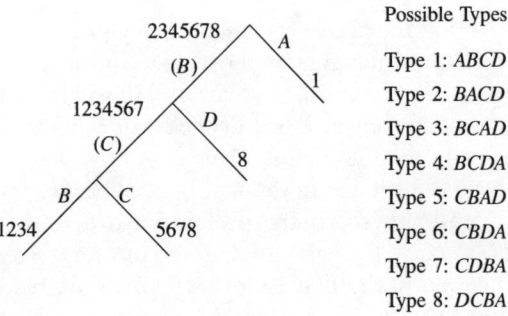

Fig. 3

structed by using successive bifurcation method Π. In any successive elimination agenda by Π, the information that all voters have single-peaked preferences is sufficient to establish a unique equilibrium by, as with complete information, successively eliminating dominated strategies. Moreover, in the equilibrium, all voters are "sophisticatedly sincere" (Austen-Smith, 1987a). These results are illustrated by the following example based on the successive procedure with four alternatives $\{A,B,C,D\}$, where $A > B > C > D$.

EXAMPLE 3: Given single-peaked preferences, only eight types are possible, and these are depicted in figure 3. There are four agendas based on the successive procedure that can be constructed by Π: $(A,B,C,D) = (A,B,D,C)$, $(A,D,B,C) = (A,D,C,B)$, $(D,A,B,C) = (D,A,C,B)$, and $(D,C,A,B) = (D,C,B,A)$. Figure 3 is based on the agenda (A,D,B,C).

As before, numbers alongside a branch mean that those numbered types have dominant strategies of voting for that branch. These dominant strategies correspond to sincere strategies in the definition. These sincere strategies, in turn, correspond to the sincere strategies obtained by assuming that the first ballot is between A and B and the second ballot is between C and D. Now, I check whether the Condorcet winner will be the eventual outcome given these specified strategies.

If A wins in the first ballot, A is surely the Condorcet winner; if A wins against B, A should also win against C and D given single-peaked preferences. If the left-hand branch wins in the first ballot and D in the second ballot, D should be the Condorcet winner; if D wins against C, neither A nor B can win against D given single-peaked preferences. If the third ballot is reached and B is the outcome, it implies B wins against C and this, in turn, means that D cannot win against B given single-peaked preferences. Since B won against A in the first ballot, B should be the Condorcet winner. A similar argument establishes that, if C is the final outcome, C is the Condorcet winner.

I now show that the above specified strategies constitute the unique equilibrium. Similar arguments as those used in the analysis of agenda depicted in figure 2(a) establish that voters will use the above strategies from the second ballot onward. So, I check only whether voters will use sincere strategies in the first ballot. *Type 1, 4, 6, 7, and 8 voters* have to vote for the left-hand branch in the first ballot because the first division of the tree separates these voters' preference orderings. *Type 3 and 5 voters* have dominant strategies of voting sincerely given all Types 8 voters vote sincerely in the first ballot. A Type 3 or 5 voter knows that all Type 8 voters vote for the left-hand branch and, therefore D cannot be the outcome when a Type 3 or 5 voter is decisive and vote for the left-hand branch; the number of Type 8 voters is at most n. If D cannot be the outcome when he (a Type 3 or 5 voter) is decisive, he should vote sincerely since he prefers both B and C to A. *Type 2 voters* should be sincere given all Type 5, 6, 7, and 8 voters are sincere. If a Type 2 voter is decisive, Type 5, 6, 7, and 8 voters together cannot constitute a majority and neither C nor D can be the outcome; only the Condorcet winner can be the outcome. Thus, voting for B yields only B as the outcome when a Type 2 voter is decisive.

Therefore, all voters have dominant strategies of voting sincerely, and these sincere strategies yield the Condorcet winner as the outcome.

As Example 3 shows, successive bifurcation method (Π) can be used to construct agendas with any number of alternatives based on the successive procedure. In any agenda based on the successive procedure, according to the definition of a binary agenda in section 2, all but the last possible ballot are between a nonsingleton subset of X and a singleton, implying that the length of the agenda is $m - 1$. This means that an agenda based on the successive procedure constructed by Π is ex ante inefficient in producing the Condorcet winner in the sense that there is no guarantee, given incomplete information, that voting ends before the $(m - 1)$th ballot. However, Π can also be used to construct binary agendas with the smallest length possible. From the definition of the binary agenda in section 2, it can be easily checked that the length of any binary agenda with m alternatives cannot be less than a number σ such that $2^{\sigma-1} < m \leq 2^\sigma$.[15] The variable σ can be interpreted as the minimum number of ballots to be planned in any binary agenda with m alternatives to reach one definite outcome. To construct agendas with length

---

15. In a binary tree T^* where the order of every terminal node is σ, there are 2^σ terminal branches. Note that T^* is the tree that can contain more alternatives than any other binary trees of length σ. Since, by the definition of the binary agenda in section 2, every element of X should occupy some terminal branch of T^*, the cardinality of the set X, m, should be less than or equal to 2^σ to be fitted into T^*.

σ using Π, it is simply required that the cardinality of each of the two sets of alternatives to be voted against each other at the kth ballot be less than or equal to $2^{\sigma-k}$.[16] For example, one agenda with 11 alternatives might be: $B(L) = \{1,2,3,4,5,6,7\}$, $B(R) = \{8,9,10,11\}$; $B(L,L) = \{1,2,3,4\}$, $B(L,R) = \{5,6,7\}$, $B(R,L) = \{8,9\}$, $B(R,R) = \{10,11\}$; $B(L,L,L) = \{1,2\}$, $B(L,L,R) = \{3,4\}$, $B(L,R,L) = \{5\}$, $B(L,R,R) = \{6,7\}$, $B(R,L,L) = \{8\}$, $B(R,L,R) = \{9\}$, $B(R,R,L) = \{10\}$, $B(R,R,R) = \{11\}$; $B(L,L,L,L) = \{1\}$, $B(L,L,L,R) = \{2\}$, $B(L,L,R,L) = \{3\}$, $B(L,L,R,R) = \{4\}$, $B(L,R,R,L) = \{6\}$, $B(L,R,R,R) = \{7\}$. To arrive at an outcome in this agenda, at most four ($2^3 < 11 \leq 2^4$) ballots are needed.

5. Conclusions

The Gibbard-Satterthwaite theorem (Gibbard 1973; Satterthwaite 1975) states that if individual preferences can be any ordering (a condition called *unrestricted domain*), then every nondictatorial voting mechanism with at least three distinct alternatives will include an incentive for strategic misrepresentation of preferences for at least one preference profile. A voting mechanism is defined as *strategy-proof* if no individual has any positive incentive to indulge in any strategic misrevelation of preferences.

Several relaxations of unrestricted domain conditions have been investigated in an effort to find strategy-proof voting mechanisms. Among them, the assumption that everyone has single-peaked preferences over a one-dimensional issue space is the most well known in a political context. Dummett and Farquharson (1961) have shown that if individuals have single-peaked preferences and if allowable strategies are restricted to the expression *only of single-peaked orderings*, then no one has any incentive to misrepresent his preferences.[17]

As is shown by Blin and Satterthwaite (1976), the restriction of individual strategies to that of expressing single-peaked orderings is

---

16. Let each of the m alternatives occupy exactly one of the 2^σ terminal branches of T^* in note 15, where $2^{\sigma-1} < m \leq 2^\sigma$, and identify the alternatives occupying each branch in T^* by following the definition of the binary agenda in section 2 which states that every branch of T^* is occupied by the alternatives reachable from that branch. In the tree T' obtained by eliminating the empty branches from T^*, it can be easily seen that the cardinalities of the two sets of alternatives to be voted against each other at the kth ballot are both less than or equal to $2^{\sigma-k}$.

17. In Moulin (1980), it is shown that if strategies of voters are to announce their ideal points (peaks) and social choice function picks the median of announced ideal points, then no one has any incentive to misreport his ideal point. The strategies of announcing ideal points in the above context amounts to the restriction of strategies to the expression of single-peaked orderings in the traditional context where strategies take the form of preference orderings.

indispensable for the above result (see also Pattanaik 1976). In most real commitees or legislative bodies, however, decisions are often made by multistage binary procedures where strategies cannot take the form of preference orderings over the whole set of alternatives. Consequently, the restriction of allowable strategies to that of single-peaked orderings is not relevant to many real problems. If no restriction can be placed on allowable strategies, most of the agendas based on some multistage binary procedures are not immune from strategic misrepresentation of individual preferences. For example, agendas based on the amendment procedure are not in general strategy-proof even though the Condorcet winner will be the outcome if all voters are sincere.[18] But the nonexistence of strategy-proof voting mechanisms might not be so discouraging if a voting mechanism yielded an equilibrium of strategic behavior that produced the same outcome as the truthful revelation of preferences would have, since the aim of any collective decision from the normative perspective is to reach an appropriate outcome. Recent literature (cf. Maskin 1985 and citations therein) on the theory of "implementation" are concerned with the above problem of designing game forms or mechanisms the equilibria of which have properties that are desirable according to some specified criteria of social welfare. The Condorcet criterion requiring the social outcome to be the Condorcet winner, if it exists, is widely regarded by many people as embodying the democratic ideal. From this perspective of implementing the Condorcet criterion, any binary voting procedure, if information is complete, is effective in the sense that dominance reduction by working backwards up the tree produces the Condorcet winner as the equilibrium outcome (McKelvey and Niemi 1978; Miller 1980; Moulin 1979). But the examples in this essay show that the Condorcet winner, which is known to exist by the assumption of single-peaked preferences, may not be selected in multistage binary agendas if information is incomplete. Fortunately, the main results in this essay have shown that it is possible to design agendas whereby the Condorcet winner is selected as the outcome of a unique equilibrium even if information is incomplete. In these agendas, the information that all voters have single-peaked preferences is sufficient to establish a unique equilibrium by successively eliminating dominated

---

18. The following example shows that not all agendas based on the amendment procedure are strategy-proof. Assume there are three alternatives $\{A,B,C\}$ where $A < B < C$ and three voters with the following preferences: Individual 1: $A\ B\ C$; Individual 2: $B\ C\ A$; Individual 3: $C\ B\ A$.

Let the agenda be "A vs B, the winner against C." If all voters are sincere, B (the Condorcet winner) will be the outcome. But if individual 3 votes insincerely (votes for A) in the first ballot, C will be the outcome if all others abide by their sincere strategies.

strategies. Moreover, these agendas are strategy-proof: all voters are sincere in the equilibrium.

The results in this essay can be applied at least to two situations. First, in situations in which each voter proposes one alternative, all voters will propose their ideal points if the above agendas are used. For example, agendas based on the successive procedure where alternatives are introduced in decreasing order of magnitude of distance between each alternative and the status quo will induce sincere behavior in the proposal stage. Second, coupled with the institutional structure of "issue-by-issue voting" (Denzau and Mackay 1981; Shepsle 1979; Shepsle and Weingast 1981) in which a committee can only consider and vote one issue at a time, the results in this essay can easily be extended to the usual multidimensional context with incomplete information, *if preferences are known to be separable*—if voters' preferences on one issue do not depend on what occurs on the other issues. If a Condorcet point exists, then issue-by-issue voting under the agendas based on the successive bifurcation method leads to that point. Otherwise, it will lead to the "issue-by-issue median point."

The analysis in this essay is restricted at least in two aspects: (1) The assumption is that all voters have single-peaked preferences and this is common knowledge to all voters; (2) The existence of strategy-proof Condorcet consistent agendas does not imply that these agendas will be used in actual decision making. But the analysis in this essay, based as it is on the assumption that all voters have single-peaked preferences, shows at least that the social outcome is not wholly dependent on individual preferences. Institutional structures such as the kind of agendas used as well as informational aspects affect the social outcome, too. Regarding the second limitation, there might be some reasons as those suggested in section 3 for a monopolistic agenda setter to use these agendas. Or in a model of endogenous agenda formation where voters first propose alternatives to be considered and then choose the structure of the agenda by the procedural voting, these agendas might emerge as the equilibrium outcome.

Appendix

First, I show that for some agenda based on the amendment procedure with more than three alternatives, everyone being sincere cannot constitute an SVE even with a sufficiently large n.

With four alternatives, there exist eight types of voters:

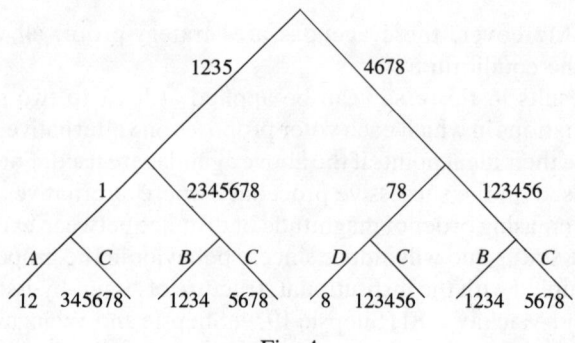

Fig. 4

Type 1: *ABCD*   Type 5: *CBAD*
Type 2: *BACD*   Type 6: *CBDA*
Type 3: *BCAD*   Type 7: *CDBA*
Type 4: *BCDA*   Type 8: *DCBA*.

The agenda "*A* vs *D* in the first ballot, the winner of the first ballot vs *B* in the second ballot, the winner of the second ballot vs *C* in the final ballot" is depicted in figure 4. Numbers alongside a branch mean that sincere strategies of those numbered types are voting for that branch.

I give an example where these specified strategies cannot constitute an SVE. Suppose in the first ballot, the specified strategies resulted in the left-hand branch winning with a margin of one vote against the right-hand branch. Given this, a Type 5 voter in the first ballot was pivotal implying $n_1 + n_2 + n_3 + n_5 = n_4 + n_6 + n_7 + n_8$. This voter in the second ballot should vote for the left-hand branch contrary to the specified sincere strategy of voting for the right-hand branch, since if he is still pivotal in the second ballot given all others abide by the specified strategy, it means that Type 2, 3, and 5 voters do not exist and voting for the right-hand branch will result in *C* as the outcome whereas voting for the left-hand branch produces a lottery between *B* and *C*. In two-stage agendas, only those cases where a voter is pivotal need to be examined to verify that a particular strategy $(2n + 1)$-tuple is an SVE and any revision of beliefs comes too late to affect the final outcome. But with more than two stages, voters might change their beliefs and strategies in later stages by margins of victory observed on previous ballots as well as by what wins or loses (see Ordeshook and Palfrey 1988).

The following example shows that it is not possible to construct agendas based on the amendment procedure where everyone being sincere can be an SVE regardless of the probability terms and the size of

Binary Agendas under Incomplete Information 341

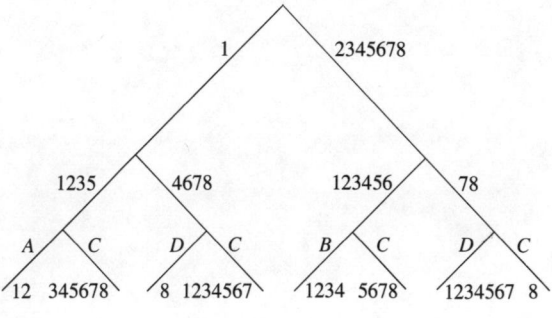

Fig. 5

the committee. These agendas should at least have the structure shown in figure 2(b) from the second stage onward. Only two agendas (1) "A vs B in the first ballot, the winner of the first ballot vs D in the second ballot, the winner of the second ballot vs C in the final ballot" and (2) "C vs D in the first ballot, the winner of the first ballot vs A in the second ballot, the winner of the second ballot vs B in the final ballot" satisfy the condition that the Condorcet winner among the three remaining alternatives will be the outcome from the second stage onward. I only analyze agenda (1) depicted in figure 5, since results from agenda (2) can be obtained by appropriately renaming the alternatives and types in agenda (1). In figure 5, number alongside a branch mean that sincere strategies of those numbered types are voting for that branch.

Since only the Condorcet winner among the remaining alternatives can be the outcome in any SVE from the second stage of voting onward, the only case in which a voter can affect the outcome is when he is decisive in the first stage of voting. Consider a Type 8 voter who believes everyone else is sincere. If he is decisive in the first stage of voting, he can affect the outcome and whether he should vote sincerely or insincerely depends on what the Condorcet winner will be in the two subtrees. Given he is decisive in the first stage of voting ($n_1 = n$), voting for the left-hand branch will result in A if $n_2 \geq 1$, in C if $n_2 = 0$ and $n_3 + n_4 + n_5 + n_6 + n_7 \geq 1$, and in D if $n_8 = n$; whereas voting for the right-hand branch will result in B if $n_2 + n_3 + n_4 \geq 1$, in C if $n_2 = n_3 = n_4 = 0$ and $n_5 + n_6 + n_7 \geq 1$, and in D if $n_8 = n$. Depending on probability terms, his utilities for each alternatives, and the number of voters, he might vote insincerely in the first ballot. If n is sufficiently large, however, he will be sincere, since he cannot expect that there will be no Type 2 voters and in the presence of any Type 2 voter, voting sincerely will result in B being the outcome, whereas voting insincerely will result in A being the outcome.

The Power to Propose

David P. Baron and John Ferejohn

I. Introduction

Since the appearance of Woodrow Wilson's *Congressional Government* more than a century ago, observers of the American Congress have been impressed with the importance of legislative committees. Writing in a period in which committees were not as central in the policy-making process as they were to become half a century later, Wilson argued that most important legislative activity took place in committees and that the parent chambers tended to ratify decisions taken in committee. Reflecting the centrality of committees in Congress, the revival of congressional studies over the past three decades was marked by a series of landmark committee studies as discussed by Richard Fenno in *The Power of the Purse* (1966).[1]

The scholarly focus on the role of committees in congressional decision making led students of Congress to notice that committees differed from one another in various respects. Their policy-making styles varied greatly, with some committees acting in a nonpartisan fashion while others were centers of party disputes. Some committees seemed comprised of subject matter experts while others were populated by distracted and disinterested members. They also differed greatly in the aims and purposes of their members: some committees were composed of members seeking to bring benefits to their districts while others were largely occupied by members apparently interested in wielding power in the parent chamber. Differences among committees were echoed in their relative success in their parent chambers: some committees routinely succeeded in getting their legislation enacted without substantial changes while other committees were much less successful (Fenno 1973).

This research has been supported by National Science Foundation (NSF) grant nos. SES-8310597 and IST-8606157. Thanks are due to Barry Weingast for comments on an earlier version of this essay.

1. For a summary of work to the early 1970s see Richard Fenno, *Congressmen in Committees* (1973).

These differences were reflected in the relative attractiveness of the various committees. A number of studies of transfers to and from various committees suggest that members regard seats on certain committees as much more valuable than seats on others (Shepsle 1978) and that the characteristics of committees as decision-making units help to explain these differences.

Thus, the empirical literature, at least that part of it that focused on the "prereform" Congress, presented a portrait of congressional activity in which important policy-making took place in committee and in which the parent chambers largely deferred to committee decisions. In fact some of the classic studies of this period have to do with the ability of certain committees or committee chairs to thwart the will of chamber majorities. The best known cases concern Judge Smith and the House Rules Committee of the late 1950s (Cummings and Peabody 1969) and Graham Barden and the House Education and Labor Committee during the same period (Fenno 1966).

More recent congressional scholarship, with its renewed focus on congressional rules and procedures, has raised important questions about this portrait. How is it that committees are able to get their way when chamber majorities have different preferences? Why doesn't the majority simply amend committee proposals, or if the committee fails to report legislation, why doesn't the chamber majority use any of a variety of powers available to it to force the committee to report legislation to the floor? And, in view of the apparent powers of chamber majorities, shouldn't committee action be understood as simply anticipating and producing legislation that will satisfy the chamber? In other words, the picture of committee government that emerged from congressional studies might be based on a misunderstanding of the role of committee expectations of floor behavior. Committees might be useful for preparing legislation for chamber consideration but they have little power to deviate from majority preferences, since majorities are free to override their decisions.

But if chamber majorities were to dictate committee decisions, committee members would not find committee work to be very rewarding. Members would not wish to serve on committees and those that did serve would not find it worthwhile to devote much effort to specializing in matters in the committee's jurisdiction. If the chambers do not permit committee members to take some advantage of committee membership, the committee system would not be an effective means for Congress to accomplish its work. Thus, some scholars believe that chamber majorities must find ways to restrain themselves from intervening too much in committee decisions. In other words, for the committee system to work effectively the chambers must provide some assurance that committee decisions will be respected at least some of the time.

One line of research suggests that the chambers adopt rules governing chamber consideration of committee legislation that have the effect of protecting committee proposals from chamber alteration. These rules have the effect of conferring on committees the ability to extract some benefits by establishing "structure-induced" equilibria that advantage the committees relative to the parent chamber. Thus, rules that privilege committee proposals are adopted in order to permit the stable development of a congressional division of labor in which members will find it worthwhile to get on committees and specialize in their subject matter areas (Gilligan and Krehbiel 1987).

In a recent paper, Shepsle and Weingast continue this line of argument by attempting to answer a number of fundamental questions regarding legislative behavior (Shepsle and Weingast 1987). Why are committee proposals changed relatively little on the floors of the two chambers? Why is it that members are willing to serve on committees and devote much of their legislative activities to committee work? What accounts for the central place of committees in legislative decision making in Congress? They might also have asked why it is that the American Congress stands apart from other parliamentary bodies in having such a strong committee system, and why the committee system in the House is more powerful than that in the Senate. Or, they could have posed the problem in a historical form: why are congressional committees apparently less powerful now than they were before the committee reforms of the early 1970s,[2] or why are committees more powerful now than they were in the nineteenth century (Cooper 1970)?

Shepsle and Weingast suggest that the answer to these questions is to be found in particlar aspects of the institutional structure of Congress. They argue that the rules of consideration of committee legislation provide an explanation for committee power in the legislative process. In the same spirit they might also have sought in the rules that govern legislation from different committees, an account of the relative powers and hence the relative attractiveness of these committees. In effect, Shepsle and Weingast seek to find in the rules governing chamber consideration of legislation an explanation of the relative powers of committees in legislative bodies.

---

2. For an examination of the changing powers of committees as policy-making forums see Smith (1986).

Shepsle and Weingast suggest two possible foundations for committee power. First, they argue that congressional committees could possess *ex ante* powers through their control of access to the legislative agenda. One may distinguish two types of ex ante powers: *proposal* power—the right to introduce, before any other member, legislation within their jurisdictions—and *gatekeeping* power—the right to prevent legislative proposals within their jurisdictions from being introduced by noncommittee members.[3]

Shepsle and Weingast argue that neither proposal nor gatekeeping powers can be important bases for committee power.

> ... we demonstrated, in fact, that neither gatekeeping nor proposal power ... could be linked to positive influence over final outcomes. Chamber majorities had sufficient tools to open any gate or alter any proposal. Once a committee made its move, the final outcome was in the hands of floor majorities. We concluded that if gatekeeping and proposal power fully characterized committee power, then committees would not be terribly powerful, and, indeed, that it would be highly unlikely to find members investing their time and energy in committee careers. (Shepsle and Weingast 1987)

Shepsle and Weingast argue that the actual basis of committee power is not to be found in these ex ante powers but is instead found in committee control over the processes by which interchamber differences are reconciled. They claim that committees effectively control who gets on the conference committee and that by controlling the membership of the interchamber conference, the committees are able to determine the content of the conference report which is then presented to each chamber under a "closed rule" so that the chambers are forced to take or to leave the conference recommendation. This effectively gives committees an ex post veto that allows them to prevent enactment of legislation that is not at least as acceptable to committee members as the status quo. Thus, noncommittee members will not find it worthwhile to alter committee proposals during chamber consideration, since the committee will be able to block these alterations in conference or, if that is not possible, to kill the legislation by failing to report a conference agreement.

Shepsle's and Weingast's ex post power may be illustrated in a simple example with a one-dimensional policy space in which members

---

3. The gatekeeping powers of committees are limited by the fact that chamber majorities may "discharge" bills from committees or, in cases of overlapping jurisdictions, receive proposals from competing committees. For an analysis of legislative behavior when committees have gatekeeping powers see Denzau and Mackay (1983).

have "Euclidean preferences."[4] Suppose that the status quo is q, the positions of the median members of the two chambers are x_h and x_s, and that the position of the median members of both committees is x_c. Assume that the chambers have passed bills x_h and x_s, and that these bills are to be reconciled in a conference committee controlled by the committees. Then, according to Shepsle and Weingast, the conference report will be the bill, x, that is closest to x_c subject to the following constraints: x must be "between" x_s and x_h, the committee must prefer x to q, and x must defeat the status quo in both chambers. For example, suppose that the preferences are such that

$$q < x_h < x_s < x_c.$$

Then x will be a point between x_h and x_s at which chamber h is indifferent between q and x. The conference report will then be considered under a closed rule in each chamber. If there is no outcome that defeats q in both chambers and that lies between x_h and x_s, or if the conference committee prefers q to all such outcomes, the conference committee will not report legislation.

Ex post powers are potent in Shepsle's and Weingast's model because they permit committees to put questions to their parent chambers under a "closed rule." By allowing committees to make "final" or closed-rule offers at the conclusion of the legislative process, Shepsle and Weingast argue that the rules governing the consideration of conference reports provide a foundation for committee power. In turn, such powers provide a motivation for members to seek committee positions and to devote themselves to legislative activities on committees. The possession of such powers would also explain why committee legislation is not changed significantly during floor consideration since such changes would simply be overridden in conference (Ferejohn 1986).

Krehbiel (1987) has raised a number of important questions about the degree to which the rules regarding interchamber reconciliation actually have the effect of conferring any sort of veto power on committees. He argues that committee powers are far more circumscribed by chamber majorities than is implied by Shepsle and Weingast. He agrees with those authors that the chambers can discharge legislation from legislative committees and thereby thwart the gatekeeping power. They can also limit the proposal power by permitting noncommittee members to make proposals in a committee's jurisdiction.[5] Furthermore, the cham-

---

4. Each member prefers points closer to his ideal point to those farther away.
5. This practice is occasionally permitted under the Suspension of the Rules procedure in the House of Representatives.

bers can also prevent an ex post veto in various ways. They can prevent commitees from taking legislation to conference, appoint conferees who are in sympathy with floor amendments, or can even discharge legislation from the conference committee. Moreover, chamber rules prevent conferees from making arbitrary changes in chamber-passed legislation. Thus, committees are required to pay considerable respect to the wishes of chamber majorities.

We agree with Krehbiel that chamber rules do not literally confer ex post veto powers on committees. Nevertheless, while not conferring veto power, it is possible that ex post powers might still provide some basis for committee power and therefore that the rules governing reconciliation could help explain committee powers. But we think that ex ante powers may be important as well. In particular, we think that the power to initiate legislative proposals forms an independent basis of committee power. In this essay, we take a small step in the direction of demonstrating this claim. We seek to establish that the ex ante powers of committees, particularly proposal power, provide a foundation for committee power and that the addition of gatekeeping power may increase that power.[6]

The alleged weakness of proposal power is based on the hypothesis that if there is some outcome, $\tilde{x}$, that is preferred to x_c, the committee proposal, by a majority of the chamber, x_c will not be accepted by the chamber but will be amended instead. We shall show that this is not correct. If account is taken of the sequential structure of legislative consideration, there will be an equilibrium committee proposal, x_e, which could be defeated by some other proposal, x, on the floor, but which will be enacted nevertheless.[7] Moreover, we show that the equilibrium proposal is advantageous to committee members, and in this sense the committee's right to originate proposals is a source of committee power that can be established independently of the existence of ex post powers of the type analyzed by Shepsle and Weingast.[8]

We make our argument in the context of two simple legislative models, one of which permits amendments, the other of which does not.

---

6. We do not claim that ex post powers are unimportant or even that they are weaker than proposal power.

7. Moreover, the equilibrium turns out to be "essentially" unique in the sense that while there are several distinct equilibrium proposals, they are unique up to permutation.

8. In a recent paper, Joseph Harrington (1988b) has examined the power of the proposal-maker in a model similar to one of those we analyze in this essay. He focuses on the effects of changing the size of the majority required to pass legislation, changing the degree of impatience, and changing the degree to which members are risk-averse. Our interest is focused more on proposal power in more "congressional" settings and our results are complementary with his.

We make three key assumptions about legislative behavior. The major assumption is that members are unable to commit themselves to undertake future courses of behavior. They cannot credibly promise to vote for some proposal in the future unless such a vote would be consistent with their preferences at the time it is taken. In other words, we restrict our attention to the subgame perfect equilibria of the legislative games. Second, we eliminate weakly dominated strategies from consideration. Third, for reasons discussed below, we restrict attention to "stationary" or history-independent equilibria. These assumptions are enough to endow committee members with significant advantages in legislation even in the absence of ex post powers.

II. Legislative Structure

The task before the legislature is to divide a dollar among its members according to majority rule, and no side payments outside the legislature are permitted. The status quo corresponds to the failure to agree on a division, and so each possible division is weakly preferred to the status quo. Each member is assumed to have selfish, risk-neutral preferences, and those preferences and the legislative rules are assumed to be common knowledge. Although this model is stylized, we think it represents an important range of problems of collective decision making. The division problem is one in which the members have profoundly conflicting preferences and in which there is no majority rule winner so that every proposal may be defeated.

The legislature is governed by a recognition rule that permits the committee to make the initial proposal and allows each member, other than the one who made the previous proposal, an equal chance of being recognized at each stage. Thus, we assume that the legislature adopts a random recognition rule. We acknowledge that random recognition rules are not generally observed in real legislatures. We employ this rule for two reasons. First, because recognition turns out to be valuable in equilibrium, every member will wish to be recognized whenever he may be legally recognized (according to the rules of the legislature), and thus the legislature must resort to some tie-breaking rule for deciding who shall be chosen to make a motion at each time. Second, this rule permits us to examine a situation in which the formal powers of the members are equal (except for proposal power), and this serves to form the benchmark against which to assess the ex post distribution of rewards.

Thus at the beginning of a session, the committee is recognized, and it proposes a bill that specifies how the dollar is to be divided. This is then the motion on the floor. The resolution of that motion depends on the rules of the legislature. Under a *closed rule* the motion must be voted on immediately, and if it is approved the legislature adjourns. Otherwise the legislature continues, and the committee is able to introduce another proposal in the next session.

We consider a variety of procedures under which amendments may be offered. Under an *open rule,* amendments can be offered after the committee makes an initial proposal. That is, after the committee has proposed a bill, another member j is recognized with probability $p_j / \Sigma_{k \neq i} p_k$, where i is the last member recognized, and he or she may either offer an amendment to the bill or move the previous question. For the purposes of this essay a motion of the previous question will be considered the same thing as a motion to impose *cloture.* If the previous question is moved, the legislature votes on whether to accept the proposed division of the dollar. If accepted, the legislature adjourns. If an amendment is offered instead, it is immediately put to a vote against the proposal on the floor, and if it wins, the amendment becomes the proposal on the floor. If the amendment fails, the original bill remains the question on the floor and another member is recognized to make a motion. If the question is put on the bill and the bill fails to win approval, then someone is recognized to propose another bill.[9] The process continues with members proposing amendments or proposing that cloture be imposed until a bill, as subsequently amended, has been accepted.

In addition to the basic open rule in which the committee has proposal power, we also consider cases in which the committee is not empowered to offer amendments and in which, after a bill is defeated, the next member recognized need not be on the committee. Calculation of committee power under these rules permits us to give a more complete assessment of the "pure" power to propose.

Whenever cloture is imposed voting takes place sequentially and in public. That is, there is a fixed order in which each member must announce how he will vote on the question before the body and every other member may observe each vote as it is cast so that members always know the entire history of play whenever they must take an action. In contrast, however, to models in which the agenda is exogenously imposed, and hence all members have perfect information about the sequence of votes to be taken, members in the legislature considered here must form expectations about what future proposals will be made and how the members will vote on them.

---

9. If the committee itself is automatically recognized following the failure of a bill, then we say that the committee has gatekeeping power.

As will be demonstrated, rules governing when the previous question can be moved, or imposing cloture, are important to the magnitude of committee power. In the model of a legislature with an open rule, we consider two different rules for imposing cloture. The first rule imposes cloture if a simple majority agrees. This rule is similar to the one employed in the House of Representatives. In the second rule, cloture requires unanimous consent, which is the rule that was in use in the Senate before the adoption in 1917 of Rule XXII, which allowed a cloture motion to succeed if two-thirds of those present and voting agreed to it.[10] While it is straightforward to consider intermediate cloture rules, the analysis of these two extreme cases is sufficient to allow us to indicate the effects of a variety of rules for imposing cloture.

In order to focus on the impact of proposal power we identify one of the members of the legislature as the committee and assume that he or she has the right to make the initial proposal or bill. The assumption of a single-person committee excludes explicit consideration of the choice problems that arise within committees. If, however, something can be said about procedures within committees, the same method of argument may be extended to examine these issues.

In bilateral bargaining models, members must exhibit some economic impatience for a unique subgame perfect equilibrium to exist (Sutton 1986). If the players are completely patient, they are free to "hold out" indefinitely while waiting for an acceptable offer, and so any division of the dollar is sustainable as a subgame perfect equilibrium. In the legislative setting, the majoritarian structure of the acceptance rule motivates members to be "politically" impatient. If a member fails to accept an offer, he or she may not receive another offer in the future. Thus, we obtain a unique stationary subgame perfect equilibrium without assuming any economic impatience.

Nevertheless, it seems natural in the legislative setting to allow members to display some impatience. As in economic models of bargaining, impatience may arise as an expression of ordinary time preference: a preference for consuming a dollar now rather than waiting to consume it later. But legislators may also exhibit impatience because they must run for election between sessions and, therefore, may not be able to return to the chamber in the future. Thus, we assume that members discount the future using a common discount factor, $0 \leq \delta \leq 1$. In this setting, δ may be interpreted either as a measure of economic time

---

10. In 1975, following years of futile attempts to modify the cloture rule, the Senate adopted the present rule that requires that three-fifths of the entire Senate concur for cloture to be imposed.

preference or as a reelection probability. The fact that δ may be generated by a reelection probability, which is observable, allows us to generate testable predictions.

The process of proposal generation and voting yields an extensive-form game with an infinite game tree. We let X stand for the set of divisions, $x = (x^1, x^2, \ldots, x^n)$, of the dollar and, as a notational convention we say that a member has moved the previous question or proposed to impose cloture if he or she proposes a division x that is identical to the current proposal in the floor. A *history* h_t of the game up until time t is a specification of who had a move at each time, the move selected by each member at every time he had a move to make, and the vote when a vote was required. A strategy in this game is a prescription of what motion to make at each point at which the member is recognized and a prescription of how to vote whenever a vote is required. If H_t denotes the set of histories, then a *pure strategy* for member i is a sequence of functions s_t mapping H_t into his or her available actions at t. Formally, a pure strategy for player i is a sequence of functions that are written as follows:

$$s_t^i : H_t \to X,$$

if i is recognized to make a proposal at time t, and

$$s_t^i : H_t \to \{yes, no\},$$

if t is a time to vote. An outcome of this game is a pair (x, t) where t is the time at which x, a division of the dollar, is enacted. The preferences of member i over outcomes are represented as follows:

$$(x, t) >_i (\hat{x}, \hat{t}) \Leftrightarrow x^i \delta^t > \hat{x}^i \delta^{\hat{t}}.$$

All of the characteristics of the game are assumed to be common knowledge to the members. Thus, everyone knows the rules of procedure as well as the preferences of the other members and knows that everyone knows this, and so on. An important feature of this formulation is that at any time that an agent is to take an action he or she knows which history has occurred, so the game is one of perfect information.

Having specified the structure of the legislative game, the equilibrium concept that will be employed must be specified. We assume that members are not able to make binding commitments either to vote in a particular manner or to offer a particular proposal. Thus, an equilibrium strategy must be "self-enforcing" in the sense that the member would wish to execute it at each point in the game tree at which he has an opportunity to act. Therefore, the equilibrium is required to be subgame perfect. An equilibrium configuration of strategies is *subgame perfect* if the restriction of those strategies to any subgame constitutes an equilibrium in that subgame.

Because of the "coarseness" of voting rules—the fact that if a proposal wins by more than one vote no individual can change the outcome by changing his vote—we must restrict attention to a refinement of the subgame perfect equilibria in which weakly dominated strategies are eliminated. This restriction appears to be essential when analyzing voting games in a noncooperative setting.[11]

Finally, we restrict attention to *stationary* equilibria, which cannot depend on the history of play. In another paper (Baron and Ferejohn 1989), we show that in an infinite-session legislature, any division of the dollar can be supported by a subgame perfect equilibrium. This nonuniqueness depends on the ability of members to play strategies that are extremely contingent or "history dependent." In legislatures in which the membership turns over or changes through time, we believe that such strategies would be very difficult to enforce and would not, therefore, be credible. Thus, we restrict our attention to equilibria with the following property: if, in equilibrium, a member plays some strategy in a subgame, S_{h_t}, that commences after history h_t, then that member plays the same strategy in any subgame, S_{h_τ}, which is identical to S_{h_t}. For example, in the case of the closed-rule model, any subgame that follows the rejection of a bill is identical to the original game, so that whoever is recognized in such a subgame must make a proposal that does not depend on how the game has been played up to that subgame (Baron and Ferejohn 1989).

III. Committee Proposals under a Closed Rule

If the committee has the right to make proposals under a closed rule and can keep other proposals off the legislative agenda, the committee has proposal power coupled with perfect gatekeeping power. The subgame perfect equilibrium proposals then have a particularly simple characterization. Consider first a legislature that will meet for at most two sessions. If session two is reached without a proposal having been accepted, the committee will propose to receive $1 - \epsilon$ and divide ϵ among $(n - 1)/2$ members, where ϵ is small, so that a minimum majority will receive a

---

11. Without it, there are a great number of equilibria that are completely unintuitive and that would never be played.

positive amount. Such a proposal would surely be accepted. Thus, in session one, noncommittee members can expect to receive virtually nothing in the next period and so can demand virtually nothing in the first session. Thus, under a closed rule with two sessions, the committee will propose to take virtually the whole dollar, and this proposal will be immediately approved by a majority vote.

Now, consider a legislature with a closed rule that will terminate at time T if no division has been agreed to, and consider the subgame perfect equilibrium strategies in that game. Backwards induction can be used to establish that (if weakly dominated strategies are eliminated) there is an "essentially" unique subgame perfect equilibrium strategy configuration in which the committee makes the same proposal as it would in a two-period legislature and this initial proposal will be immediately accepted.

It is easy to see that this proposal corresponds to the stationary subgame perfect equilibrium of the infinite session legislative game with perfect gatekeeping power. The argument is this: suppose x is a stationary subgame perfect equilibrium outcome in which member i receives $x^i > 0$, and consider an alternative proposal $\hat{x}$ in which member i receives $\hat{x}^i = x^i/2$ and some other member $j \neq c$ receives $\hat{x}^j = x^j + x^i/4$, and the committee receives $\hat{x}^c = x^c + x^i/4$, and all other members receive the same allocation ($\hat{x}_k = x_k$ for $k \neq i,j,c$). Then, if the committee deviates from the equilibrium by proposing $\hat{x}$ at the beginning of the game and then proposing x at every subsequent stage that it receives recognition, everyone except member i will vote to approve $\hat{x}$ and evidently the committee prefers $\hat{x}$ to x, so the original proposal, x, cannot be an equilibrium.

It is important to recognize that the committee proposal could be defeated in a majority vote by any of a number of other proposals. But, in equilibrium, no one can introduce any of these alternatives. In this case, the committee has both proposal and gatekeeping powers, and these two powers together are sufficient to allow committee members to obtain virtually the whole dollar.

We may now ask whether it is possible to separate the effects of proposal power from that of gatekeeping power. First, we propose a natural measure of the power to propose: it is the difference between the value of the game to the committee when it has proposal power and the value when there is no proposal power. Note that the symmetry of the extensive form implies that the value of the game when the right to make proposals is determined randomly must be equal to $1/n$. Thus, our earlier argument implies that the value of the power to propose and pure gatekeeping is $1 - 1/n$.

Now, consider a case in which the committee has the power to propose but in which it cannot prevent another member from making a proposal if the initial proposal fails. Thus the committee is permitted to make the initial proposal and to keep the gates closed for one period. We may establish the following result: with one-period gatekeeping power, the committee will propose to give δ/n to each of $(n - 1)/2$ other members and keep the remainder to itself, and this proposal will be immediately accepted by a majority. The argument is this: following a rejection of the committee's initial proposal, each member, including the committee, has an equal chance of being recognized, and following recognition each faces an identical set of strategic options. It can be seen that this implies that the continuation value for each member following a rejection of the committee proposal must be equal to $1/n$. Thus, the committee may assure that its initial proposal is accepted by a majority if it offers $(n - 1)/2$ members δ/n and keeps the remaining $1 - \delta(n - 1)/2n$ for itself.[12] Note that for δ near one and n large this implies that the committee receives approximately one-half of the dollar, rather than the whole dollar, which they obtain when they have both proposal and gatekeeping powers. Thus, the value of proposal power combined with one-period gatekeeping is $(2 - \delta)(n - 1)/2n$ which tends to $1 - \delta/2$ for large n. Pure gatekeeping therefore has a value of

$$1 - \frac{1}{n} - \frac{(2 - \delta)(n - 1)}{2n} = \frac{\delta(n - 1)}{2n},$$

which tends to $\delta/2$ for n large.

Now, consider the case in which the committee can keep the gates closed for two periods. Clearly, if its initial proposal were rejected, the committee would be in a situation in which it had a one-period gatekeeping power and the previous result would apply. A noncommittee member would be willing to vote for the committee proposal if and only if he or she would receive at least δ/n. Now consider what a noncommittee member would take to support the committee's initial proposal. The continuation value for a noncommittee member prior to the committee's second proposal is just $\delta/2n$, since the committee need only make a majoritarian proposal and each noncommittee member has a ½ probability of receiving an offer in the committee's first proposal. Therefore, the committee's initial proposal will be immediately accepted if it offers $\delta^2/2n$ to $(n - 1)/2$ nonmembers, and keeps the remainder itself. This argument can be extended to the case in which the

---

12. This result is proved in Proposition 1 in Baron and Ferejohn (1989).

committee can keep the gates closed for $k + 1$ periods: its initial proposal will be to offer $(\delta/2)^k \delta/n$ to $(n - 1)/2$ nonmembers and keep the remainder for itself. Thus, the value to the committee of proposal power together with $(k + 1)$-period gatekeeping power is

$$1 - \frac{n-1}{2}\left(\frac{\delta}{2}\right)^k \frac{\delta}{n} - \frac{1}{n}, \quad \text{or} \quad \frac{(2^{k+1} - \delta^{k+1})(n-1)}{2^{k+1}n}$$

As k gets large and the committee has the power to keep the gates closed for a longer period, the value to the committee converges to one in which case the committee keeps everything for itself. If the committee has simple proposal power—or, the power to make the initial proposal combined with one-period gatekeeping power—then, for δ near one, the committee obtains approximately ½.

IV. Committee Proposals under a Simple Open Rule

With an open rule, motions on the floor may be subject to amendment by noncommittee members, and so the committee no longer controls the legislative agenda (Weingast 1988 and Oleszek 1984).[13] An amendment is itself a proposed allocation of the dollar and may be viewed as a substitute for the motion on the floor. The simplest open rule is one in which no more than one amendment may be on the floor at any time.[14]

We consider several versions of the "simple open rule." The simple open rule with committee proposal and gatekeeping power may be described as follows. The committee is recognized to make the first proposal, which we shall call a *bill*. Then, each of the other members has a $1/(n - 1)$ probability of being recognized to make a motion either to invoke cloture (or move the previous question) or to propose an amendment. If cloture is moved and it is approved by a majority, the bill is voted on and, if approved, the dollar is divided. If the bill is defeated, the next session commences, and committee is recognized first to propose another bill. If an amendment is offered, it must be voted against the bill before another motion is in order.[15] The winner of this vote then becomes the motion on the floor, and another member is recognized. Each member other than the amender then has a probability of $1/(n - 1)$

---

13. The open rules analyzed in this essay are much simpler than those found in Congress, and the reader is referred to the more detailed treatment in Weingast (1988). See also Oleszek (1984).

14. That is, second-degree amendments are not allowed.

15. We assume, for definiteness, that discounting takes place immediately after a subsequent substantive motion—a bill or an amendment—is introduced.

of recognition for the purpose of offering an amendment or moving the previous question. The process continues in this manner until the previous question is moved on a bill and the bill passes. An important feature of this rule is that once a bill has been proposed, followed by an initial amendment, the committee has the same chance to be recognized as any other member (who did not offer the amendment on the floor).

As in our consideration of closed rules we distinguish open rules with varying degrees of gatekeeping power. The simple open rule with one-period gatekeeping is identical to the simple open rule except for the case in which a bill is defeated. In that event, every member has an equal chance of being recognized to offer the next bill. This is the weakest version of gatekeeping power.

We emphasize that the prohibition of second-degree amendments is both a departure from the practices of some real legislatures (such as the Congress) and is also consequential in our analysis. Theoretically, the power of a prohibition on second-degree amendments introduces the authority to force a vote. Once an amendment has been proposed, it must be voted on before another amendment can be considered. The amendment itself may not be subjected to further modification. We offer two defenses for this assumption: first, real legislatures do have degree limitations and so some element of "final" offers is preserved in all such procedures.[16] Second, the rule analyzed here is sufficiently simple to be amenable to analysis.

As important as the prohibition on second-degree amendments is the fact that our procedures permit members to end debate. Members may move the previous question or invoke cloture at any time. As we shall see, this permits the committee to make proposals on which the previous question will be imposed at the first opportunity. The fact that members have the opportunity to impose cloture is part of the source of ex ante proposal power. If someone who is made an acceptable offer is recognized, he will prefer to move the question rather than to offer a substantive amendment.

Under the simple open rule no member will ever be in a position to introduce a bill or an amendment that cannot be amended in one way or another. Thus, whoever proposes a bill or an amendment must take account of the fact that other members may subsequently be recognized to make substantive motions. In particular, the committee proposal

---

16. Thomas Jefferson defended the prohibition of third-degree amendments in the House as follows: "The line must be drawn somewhere and usage has drawn it after the amendment to the amendment." *Constitution, Jefferson's Manual and the Rules of the House of Representatives*, House Document 97-271, 212.

must take into account the fact that other members will be recognized to make amendments.

A difference between an open rule and a closed rule is that the bill (as amended during floor consideration) may be voted on only if the member recognized moves the previous question. Each member who makes a substantive motion therefore faces a tradeoff. If he wants his proposal to be accepted with certainty, it must be sufficiently attractive that whoever is recognized next will wish to move the previous question and vote for the proposal rather than offering an amendment. Making a proposal that is attractive to all members is expensive, however, so the member recognized may prefer to offer a proposal that is attractive only to a majority m of the $n - 1$ members. Then, if one of the m is recognized next, she will move the previous question and the majority will approve it. If one of the $n - 1 - m$ is recognized, she will offer an amendment that will defeat the motion on the floor, and the game will continue. The member recognized thus can determine through the choice of m the probability that his proposal will be accepted.

Intuition suggests that the lower is the (common) discount factor the greater is the incentive to offer a proposal that will be accepted with high probability, since continuing to the next session is costly. The higher is the discount factor the less costly is continuation and the smaller is the majority m to whom an attractive offer is made. In fact, in another essay (Baron and Ferejohn 1989) we show that the size of the majority m to which an acceptable offer is made is a (weakly) decreasing function of δ.

Before presenting our initial results we need some additional notation. Let V_c denote the maximal value of the game to the committee at the beginning of play (before any proposal has been made) assuming that everyone plays optimally from that time forward, and let $V_i(x)$ denote the continuation value (assuming that everyone plays optimally from that point on) to member i at a point at which x is the bill on the floor and i is recognized to make a motion (either an amendment or a motion to impose cloture). To simplify the mathematical exposition, a member who is indifferent between two proposals will be assumed to vote for the one proposed last.[17]

LEMMA. *In a stationary subgame perfect equilibrium $V_i(x) = V_c$.*

Proof: First, note that in a subgame perfect equilibrium, no member will ever make a motion that will fail to obtain a majority. Thus, if x

---

17. Otherwise, the set of amendments that defeat the proposal on the floor is open, and the equilibrium concept has to be weakened to that of an ϵ-equilibrium.

is the bill on the floor and member i offers an amendment, he will choose his amendment from the set of proposals that defeat x. Now, suppose the committee maximizes its expected utility by offering proposal $y = (y^1, y^2, \ldots, y^n)$, resulting in a continuation value V_c, and that member i is recognized. Then, if i moves to amend y by proposing a permutation, y^*, of y such that y^i and y^c are interchanged and the offers to the other members are unchanged, he will be in exactly the same position as the committee and must therefore obtain a continuation value of V_c. Moreover, a majority will vote in favor of amending y to y^*, since every member other than c will vote in favor of y^*. To see that i cannot obtain more than V_c, note that if he could obtain more than V_c by offering x then the committee could have offered a permutation of x as its original bill and obtained more than V_c. Thus, $V_i(x)$ is independent of x, the offer that is currently on the floor, and equals V_c.

This Lemma permits us to describe proposals in a particularly simple fashion. If y is an optimal proposal for some member, then if some other member is recognized, there is a permutation of y that is an optimal proposal for that member. Thus we may restrict ourselves to finding the values y^i of an optimal proposal. Second, we note that when a member is recognized, he will make a proposal such that some subset of members of size $m \geq (n - 1)/2$ will move the previous question. In other words, he must offer $y^i \geq \delta V_i$ to a subset of size m. Given the stationary structure of the game, it is immediate that if m is the size of the subset to which i will make an offer in equilibrium, any other member will make an offer to the same number of members.

We may now present the main result of the present section, which is a characterization of the stationary subgame perfect equilibria of the simple open rule when the committee has proposal power and one-period gatekeeping power. We state and prove this proposition for a three-person committee. The construction is analogous in the case of a larger legislature, but the notation is much less formidable (Baron and Ferejohn 1989).

PROPOSITION 1: In a three-person legislature with a committee with proposal and one-period gatekeeping power, if $\delta \geq \sqrt{3} - 1$ then in any stationary subgame perfect equilibrium the committee proposal is to offer $2\delta/(4 + 2\delta - \delta^2)$ to one noncommittee member and to keep $(4 - \delta^2)/(4 + 2\delta - \delta^2)$ for itself. This proposal is accepted if the member who receives the positive offer is recognized; if the remaining member is recognized, he offers $2\delta/(4 + 2\delta - \delta^2)$ to the noncommittee member and keeps the remainder for himself. If $\delta \leq \sqrt{3} - 1$, the committee offers each of the noncommittee members $\delta/(1 + 2\delta)$ and keeps the remainder for itself.

Proof: First, note that the committee will either offer one member a positive payoff sufficient to induce that member to move cloture if he is recognized, or, it will offer both other members a positive payoff sufficient to induce either of them to move cloture.[18]

Thus, we may write the committee proposal either as $y^+ = (y^a, 1 - y^a, 0)$ or as $y^- = (y^b, (1 - y^b)/2, (1 - y^b)/2)$, and note that V_c must be maximized by a proposal of one of these two forms.

Suppose that the committee proposes y^+. For member i to "accept" the committee proposal (that is, to propose to impose cloture), it must be true that $1 - y^a \geq \delta V_i(y^+) = \delta V_c$ (by the Lemma), and optimality requires that this relation hold with equality.

Furthermore, note that V_c must satisfy the following expression:

$$V_c = \frac{y^a}{2} + \frac{\delta}{2}\left[\frac{\delta}{2} V_c + \frac{1}{2} \cdot 0\right],$$

since y^+ will be accepted if the member receiving the offer of $1 - y^a$ is recognized (which occurs will probability ½) and, if the other member is recognized, he will make a proposal that offers $1 - y^a$ to the non-committee member and 0 to the committee. This offer is accepted if the noncommittee member is recognized; otherwise the committee is recognized and, when it is, it can achieve V_c. We may now combine the expressions and solve for V_c, obtaining

$$V_c = \frac{2}{4 + 2\delta - \delta^2},$$

which implies that

$$1 - y^a = \frac{2\delta}{4 + 2\delta - \delta^2}$$

as was to be shown.

In the second case, when the committee proposal is y^-, both other members receive positive offers, and so we have $V_c = y^b$, and $(1 - y^b)/2 = \delta V_c$. Thus, $V_c = 1/(1 + 2\delta)$.

Putting the two cases together and solving for the critical value of δ

---

18. Since the committee is indifferent to whom it shall make its initial offer, it may randomize at this stage. Indeed, this is the case whenever a member is recognized following the failure of a bill. Consideration of these randomized strategies does not change any of the results reported here in any essential fashion; therefore we ignore them.

indicates that the committee will propose y^+ if $\delta \geq \sqrt{3} - 1$ and will propose y^- otherwise. This completes the proof.

Under a simple open rule with one-period gatekeeping, if there is relatively little discounting, the committee makes an offer to enough other members to form a majority. With probability ½ this offer is accepted and the legislature adjourns. With probability ½ the initial motion is successfully amended and the committee loses any procedural advantage it might have had. Nevertheless, the expected value of being on the committee is still greater than that of not being on the committee. For example, in a three-member legislature with no discounting, the initial proposal has the committee receiving ⅗ and one other member receiving ⅖ and this proposal is accepted with probability ½. Thus, before the game begins, the expected value of being on the committee is ⅖ and is 3⁄10 for each of the nonmembers. Thus, the value of proposal power is ⅖ − ⅓ = 1⁄15. Note that the open rule substantially reduces the proposal power compared to the closed rule. In this example, the value of introducing a closed rule is 4⁄15.

In table 1 we report the value of y^a, the amount that the committee

TABLE 1. Open Rule, Stationary Equilibria

δ	n	$m(\delta,n)$	y^a	V_c	P
1.0	3	1	.6000	.4000	0.5
1.0	5	2	.4359	.2821	0.5
1.0	51	25	.0620	.0375	0.5
1.0	101	50	.0321	.0194	0.5
0.8	3	1	.6774	.4032	0.5
0.8	5	2	.5220	.2987	0.5
0.8	51	25	.0842	.0458	0.5
0.8	101	50	.0440	.0239	0.5
0.6	3	2	.4545	.4545	1.0
0.6	5	2	.4200	.3252	0.5
0.6	51	25	.1143	.0590	0.5
0.6	101	50	.0607	.0313	0.5
0.4	3	2	.5556	.5556	1.0
0.4	5	3	.5238	.3968	0.75
0.4	51	25	.1653	.0835	0.5
0.4	101	50	.0902	.0455	0.5
0.2	3	2	.7143	.7143	1.0
0.2	5	4	.5556	.5556	1.0
0.2	51	25	.2854	.1429	0.5
0.2	101	50	.1665	.0833	0.5

receives in its initial proposal (or bill), $m(\delta,n)$, the number of noncommittee members offered positive amounts in the committee proposal, V_c, the value of the game to the committee, and P, the probability that the initial proposal is accepted by the legislature, for various values of δ and n. We observe the following facts: first, holding n fixed $m(\delta,n)$ is nonincreasing in δ. As δ gets smaller the committee wishes to include more nonmembers in its original bill in order to increase the likelihood that this proposal is accepted. Second, as n increases the relationship between $m(\delta,n)$ and δ "flattens," so that in a large legislature, the committee will make its offer to a bare majority even for small δ.

We may ask whether increasing the gatekeeping power increases the value of the game to the committee. It is clear from the proof of the proposition that it does not. Even if the committee could keep the gates closed indefinitely it would still find the same proposals to be optimal, since the binding constraint on committee proposals results from the open rule. In our equilibrium the committee must make a proposal that at least $(n - 1)/2$ members find sufficiently acceptable that they will move cloture rather than offering an amendment. Thus, unlike the situation in case of the closed rule, once amendments are allowed, variations in the length of time over which the committee may keep others from offering bills do not seem to affect the relative value of committee membership. In this sense, gatekeeping powers seem to be relatively unimportant in a legislature that employs an open rule. Thus, it is useful to emphasize that the value of proposal power does not require that the committee have very much gatekeeping power. As long as the committee can keep the gates closed for one period, there is value to committee membership. Thus, even if the committee can be discharged, as it can in the House of Representatives, as long as the rules give the committee some period in which it may make a proposal, membership remains valuable. Suppose for example that some noncommittee member attempts to employ discharge procedures to bring a particular bill to the floor. House rules require that the discharge petition "lay over" for several days before the discharged bill may come to the floor.[19] In this interval the committee may bring its own proposal to the floor and take advantage of its proposal power. If we interpret the layover requirement as allowing the committee to keep the gates closed for a short period, unlike the situation under the closed rule, proposal power with an open rule and limited gatekeeping powers is just as valuable as it would be with a more extensive gatekeeping power.

---

19. "When 218 members have signed the [discharge] petition, the motion to discharge is put on the Discharge Calendar. After seven days on the calendar, it becomes privileged business on the second and fourth Mondays of the month." Oleszek (1984).

There are several observations that should be made about committee proposals in the present setting. First, the committee proposal is not a majority winner, so it can always be defeated if the set of proposals that can be put against it is unconstrained. Thus, the fact that majority rule is unstable does not undermine committee power even when there is an open rule in effect. Second, in equilibrium, as long as there is not "too much" discounting, there is a significant probability that the committee's initial motion will be overridden (see table 1). Nevertheless, the right of the committee to make the initial proposal is valuable even after account is taken of the fact that sometimes that proposal will be amended in equilibrium.

V. An Open Rule with Unanimous Cloture

The simple open rule was chosen to represent an idealization of amendment procedures in a legislative body that permits cloture by a majority vote. This rule is supposed to approximate one feature of the procedures employed in the House of Representatives. We can use the techniques employed in the previous section to analyze legislative procedures when special majorities are required to invoke cloture. Here we consider an extreme case where unanimity is required to impose cloture. Roughly speaking, this case is supposed to represent a chamber such as the United States Senate in which most of its business is conducted through the use of unanimous consent.

The procedures we model are these. A member is recognized to make an initial motion or bill. Then, as before, each member other than the original one has an equal probability of recognition. When a member is recognized he can offer an amendment that must then be voted on. Then, each member has an equal chance to be recognized to make another amendment. The difference between this procedure and the simple open rule is that no one can move cloture if anyone else has an amendment to offer. In other words, cloture requires unanimous consent.

We may now ask what the committee will propose under an open rule with unanimous cloture. The following proposition illustrates that the unanimous consent feature has the effect of essentially removing all of the advantage of the power to propose.

PROPOSITION 2. *In a three-person legislature with a simple open rule with unanimous cloture, there is a unique subgame perfect stationary equilibrium in which the committee receives $1/(1 + 2\delta)$ and each other member receives $\delta/(1 + 2\delta)$.*

Proof: Let V_c denote the (equilibrium) continuation value of the game to the committee at any node at which it has the ability to make a proposal and let V_i stand for the (equilibrium) continuation value of the game to member i whenever she has the right to make a proposal. With unanimous cloture the committee proposal must be acceptable to all noncommittee members, and so no one must wish to make a proposal. This implies that at the initial node, the committee must offer each other member an amount sufficient to induce her to accept the committee proposal, which requires that $x^i \geq \delta V_i$, for all $i \neq c$, and since the committee is maximizing its payoff these relations must hold with equality. Thus, $V_c = 1 - 2\delta V_i$. Moreover, the lemma states that $V_c = V_i$, since whenever player i is recognized she can achieve the same value as the committee could at the start of the game. Thus, $V_c = 1/(1 + 2\delta)$, which was to be proved.

Note that as the discount factor converges to one, the distribution of rewards converges to an equal division. Thus, in this sense, the value of the power to propose virtually disappears if it is sufficiently difficult to impose cloture. Also, note that since the initial committee proposal will be acceptable to everyone, gatekeeping power will not be valuable in this context. The only remaining source of committee power in this case is the fact that if a proposal is amended each member must bear a cost (or discount factor) before another proposal may be considered. Finally, note that for $\delta \leq \sqrt{3} - 1$, the effect of increasing the proportion of votes needed to impose cloture disappears. A committee with majority rule cloture would make exactly the same proposal as a committee with unanimous cloture, and this proposal would be immediately accepted.

While this result is obtained in a very simple model, we think it might help account for an often-observed difference between the House and Senate. Most empirical observers would agree that committee assignments are more important to House members than they are to senators. Commonly, this difference is attributed to the fact that senators are members of many more committees than are representatives so that each assignment is less consequential to them. Our theory provides an alternative account: the fact that cloture is relatively easy in the House confers more power on its committees than does the relatively difficult cloture rule in the Senate. Of course, the modern Senate need not operate under unanimous consent. Cloture could be imposed much more frequently than it is at present in which case the value of Senate committees would be closer to that of House committees. Before 1917, when Rule XXII was adopted, our model suggests that Senate committees would be less valuable to their members than they are now and much less valuable than House committees.

This result also allows us to suggest a new interpretation of the 1970 decision of the House to guarantee that "previously-noticed amendments"—amendments printed in the *Congressional Record* at least one day before the debate on a bill—receive consideration regardless of any agreements to end debate on the bill (Oleszek 1984). This reform had the effect of introducing something similar to a unanimity requirement for cloture to House procedures, thereby making them more similar to Senate procedures.[20] Thus, the value of being on committees was diminished by the introduction of this rule.

VI. Discussion

There appear to be several possible separate foundations of committee power in Congress. We believe, with Shepsle and Weingast, that ex post powers could be important in some cases and, with Gilligan and Krehbiel, that informational considerations are likely to be significant as well. But, we suggest that proposal and gatekeeping powers may also provide important sources of committee advantage. Our analysis suggests, however, that whether and to what extent proposal power can form a basis for committee power depends in complex ways on the structure of rules by which committee proposals are considered on the floor. If chamber rules do not privilege committees during open rule consideration of legislation and if, as in the Senate, it is difficult to end debate, proposal power will not be an important source of committee power. Gatekeeping power seems important only for legislation considered under a closed rule. In that case, the longer the committee can keep the gates closed, the more value it can extract from the situation. With a simple open rule, variations in gatekeeping power have no effect on what the committee will propose. The fact that other members may offer amendments places stronger limits on committee power than any restrictions on gatekeeping.

Having pointed to several distinct logical bases for committee strength, we suggest that it remains an open question whether variations in ex post versus ex ante powers will in fact be important explanations of variations in committee powers, either cross-sectionally or historically, or whether such variations must be accounted for in some other fashion. The way is open for empirical research to shed light on these issues.

We should also point out that the arguments advanced here have

---

20. Technically, the correspondence between the House rule and the unanimity cloture requirement is only approximate, since members must precommit to the specific wording of a previously noticed amendment, whereas with a unanimous cloture rule they are free to construct an amendment at the time it is to be offered.

broader applications than we have suggested above. First, insofar as committee chairmen have proposal power, our argument has implications for the value of positions within committees. Of course, we cannot give a detailed account of this case without specifying procedures within the committees. Classical committee studies (Fenno 1966; Manley 1970) suggest that the chair sets the committee's agenda but that once a proposal is made it is open to modification. Perhaps the simple open rule may be a useful approximation in this case.

There are also possible applications to House-Senate relations. Traditionally, the House is the originator of bills concerning revenues or appropriations. While the Senate has sometimes maintained that it retains the right to initiate appropriations bills,[21] the constitutional basis for the House claim on tax legislation has not been substantially challenged. The privilege of acting first suggests that the House holds proposal power on certain legislation. Thus, our model would generate predictions as to equilibrium payoffs in this case and would therefore be relevant to the literature on relative institutional power within Congress.

Further, within the government as a whole, the president has proposal power over judicial and other executive branch appointments. In this case, Congress has little capacity to amend a motion once made, so that presidential appointments might be an application of our model of the closed rule.[22] In any case a model of the sort analyzed here will permit the development of equilibrium predictions, and, as was found in the case of the closed rule, one would expect to observe quite asymmetric payoffs.

Finally, the model may have implications for the relationship between Congress and the administrative agencies. When an agency is created, it is given the authority to make policy unless political or judicial authorities intervene. In this sense, agencies have proposal power subject to review by Congress, the president, and the courts. The same sort of analysis that is reported here suggests that the delegation of authority to an agency creates a source of power and that different procedures of political supervision (such as the one- or two-house legislative vetoes recently prohibited by the Supreme Court) will have systematic effects on agency influence.

---

21. *The Authority of the Senate to Originate Appropriation Bills,* Senate Doc. no. 17, 88th Congress, 1st Session (1963), cited in Fenno (1966).

22. In some cases, the practice of clearing nominees with senators from their states appears to contradict this assumption.

References

Abramowitz, Alan. 1980. A comparison of voting for U.S. senators and representatives in 1978. *American Political Science Review* 74:633–40.
Abreu, Dilip. 1986. External equilibria of oligopolistic supergames. *Journal of Economic Theory* 39:191–225.
Acheson, Dean. 1969. Dean Acheson's version of Robert Kennedy's version of the Cuban missile affair. *Esquire* 71:44, 46, 76–77.
Alesina, Alberto, and Alex Cukierman. 1987. The politics of ambiguity. Carnegie Mellon-GSIA Working Paper. Pittsburgh: Carnegie Mellon.
Allison, G. T. 1971. *Essence of decision: Explaining the Cuban missile crisis.* Boston: Little, Brown and Company.
Altfield, Michael, and Bruce Bueno de Mesquita. 1979. Choosing sides in wars. *International Studies Quarterly* 23:87–112.
Ansolabehete, Stephen, David Brady, and Morris P. Fiorina. 1987. The marginals never vanished? Some further thoughts. Graduate School of Business, Stanford University. Manuscript.
Aranson, P. H., and Melvin J. Hinich. 1979. Some aspects of the political economy of election campaign contribution laws. *Public Choice* 34:435–61.
Austen-Smith, David. 1983. The spatial theory of electoral competition: Instability, institutions and information. *Environment and Planning C: Government and Policy* 1 (4):439–60.
———. 1987a. Interest groups, campaign contributions, and probabilistic voting. *Public Choice* 54 (2):123–40.
———. 1987b. Sophisticated sincerity: Voting over endogenous agendas. *American Political Science Review* 81:1323–30.
Austen-Smith, David, and Jeffrey Banks. 1988. Elections, coalitions and legislative outcomes. *American Political Science Review* 82:405–22.
Austen-Smith, David, and William Riker. 1987. Asymmetric information and the coherence of legislation. *American Political Science Review* 81:897–918.
Axelrod, Robert. 1981. The emergence of cooperation among egoists. *American Political Science Review* 75:306–18.
———. 1984. *The evolution of cooperation.* New York: Basic Books.
Bach, Stanley, and Steven S. Smith. 1988. *Managing uncertainty in the House of Representatives: Adaptation and innovation in special rules.* Washington: The Brookings Institution.
Banks, Jeffrey S. 1985. Sophisticated voting outcomes and agenda control. *Social Choice and Welfare* 1:295–306.
———. 1987a. A model of electoral competition with incomplete information. University of Rochester. Manuscript.

———. 1987b. Monopoly agenda control and asymmetric information: Romer-Rosenthal revisited. University of Rochester. Manuscript.

———. 1988. Agency budgets, cost information, and auditing. University of Rochester. Manuscript.

Banks, Jeffrey S., and Farid Gasmi. 1987. Endogenous agenda formation in three-person committees. *Social Choice and Welfare* 4:1–20.

Banks, Jeffrey S., and Joel Sobel. 1987. Equilibrium selection in signaling games. *Econometrica* 55:647–71.

Baron, David P. 1989. Service-induced campaign contributions and the electoral equilibrium. *Quarterly Journal of Economics* 104:45–72.

Baron, David P., and John A. Ferejohn. 1989. Bargaining in legislatures. *American Political Science Review*, forthcoming.

Barro, Robert. 1973. The control of politicians: An economic model. *Public Choice* 14:19–42.

Becker, Gary. 1983. A theory of competition among pressure groups for political influence. *Quarterly Journal of Economics* 98 (3):371–400.

Bental, Benjamin, and Uri Ben-Zion. 1975. Political contribution and policy: Some extensions. *Public Choice* 24:1–12.

Ben-Zion, Uri, and Zeev Eytan. 1974. On money, votes, and policy in a democratic society. *Public Choice* 14:19–42.

Bernhardt, M. Daniel, and Daniel E. Ingberman. 1985. Candidate reputations and the "Incumbency Effect." *Journal of Public Economics* 27:47–67.

Betts, R. K. 1987. *Nuclear blackmail and nuclear balance.* Washington, D.C.: The Brookings Institution.

Binder, John J. 1985. Measuring the effects of regulation with stock price data. *Rand Journal of Economics* 16 (2):167–83.

Binmore, K., and P. Dasgupta. 1987. *The economics of bargaining.* New York: Basil Blackwell.

Black, Duncan. 1958. *The theory of committees and elections.* London: Cambridge University Press.

Black, Fisher, 1972. Capital market equilibrium with restricted borrowing. *Journal of Business* 45:444–55.

Blainey, Geoffrey. 1973. *The causes of war.* New York: Free Press.

Blau, Peter M. 1964. *Exchange and power in social life.* New York: John Wiley and Sons.

Blin, Jean Marie, and Mark A. Satterthwaite. 1976. Strategy-proofness and single peakedness. *Public Choice* 26:51–58.

Brams, Steven, and D. Marc Kilgour. 1987. Threat escalation and crisis stability: A game-theoretic analysis. *American Political Science Review* 81:833–50.

Brams, Steven, and P. Straffin. 1982. The entry problem in a political race. In *Political equilibrium,* ed. P. Ordeshook and K. Shepsle. The Hague, Netherlands: Nijhoff Publishers.

Brito, Dagobert, and Michael Intriligator. 1985. Conflict, war and redistribution. *American Political Science Review* 79:943–57.

Brown, Steven, and John Warner. 1980. Measuring security price performance. *Journal of Financial Economics* 8:205–58.
———. 1985. Using daily stock returns: The case for event studies. *Journal of Financial Economics* 13:3–31.
Bueno de Mesquita, Bruce. 1978. Systematic polarization and the occurrence and duration of war. *Journal of Conflict Resolution* 22:241–67.
———. 1981. *The war trap.* New Haven: Yale University Press.
Bueno de Mesquita, Bruce, and David Lalman. 1986. Reason and war. *American Political Science Review* 80:1113–31.
———. 1988. Arms races and the opportunity for peace. *Synthese* 76:263–83.
Cain, Bruce E. 1978. Strategic voting in Britain. *American Journal of Political Science* 22:639–55.
Calvert, Randall L. 1986. *Models of imperfect information in politics.* Chur, Switzerland: Harwood Academic Publishers.
Campbell, J. E. 1983. Ambiguity in the issue positions of Presidential candidates: A causal-analysis. *American Journal of Political Science* 27 (2):284–93.
Chadwick-Jones, J. K. 1976. *Social exchange theory: Its structure and influence in social psychology.* London: Academic Press.
Chappell, Henry W. 1982. Campaign contributions and congressional voting: A simultaneous probit-tobit model. *Review of Economics and Statistics* 64:77–83.
———. 1988. Information, advertising, and spatial voting. Department of Economics Working Paper. University of South Carolina.
Cho, In-Koo, and David Kreps. 1987. Signaling games and stable equilibria. *Quarterly Journal of Economics* 102:179–222.
Claude, Innis. 1962. *Power and international relations.* New York: Random House.
Cohen, Linda R., and Steven Matthews. 1980. Constrained Plott equilibria, directional equilibria and global cycling sets. *Review of Economic Studies* 47:975–86.
Collie, Melissa. 1981. Incumbency, electoral safety, and turnover in the House of Representatives, 1952–1976. *American Political Science Review* 75:119–31.
Cooper, Joseph. 1970. *The origins of the Standing Committees and the development of the modern House.* Houston: Rice University Studies.
Coughlin, Peter J. 1982. Pareto optimality of policy proposals with probabilistic voting. *Public Choice* 39:427–33.
———. 1984. Davis-Hinich conditions and median outcomes in probabilistic voting models. *Journal of Economic Theory* 34 (1):1–12.
Coughlin, Peter J., and Melvin J. Hinich. 1984. Necessary and sufficient conditions for single-peakedness in public economic models. *Journal of Public Economics* 25:323–41.
Coughlin, Peter J., and Shmuel Nitzan. 1981. Electoral outcomes with probabilistic voting and Nash social welfare maxima. *Journal of Public Economics* 15:113–22.

Cox, G. 1987. Duverger's Law and strategic voting. University of California, San Diego. Manuscript.
Cummings, Milton, Jr., and Robert Peabody. 1969. The decision to enlarge the Committee on Rule: An analysis of the 1961 vote. In *New perspectives on the House of Representatives,* ed. R. Peabody and N. Polsby. Chicago: Rand McNally.
Cyert, R., and M. DeGroot. 1974. Rational expectations and Bayesian analysis. *Journal of Political Economy* 82:521–36.
Davis, Otto, and Melvin J. Hinich. 1966. A mathematical model of policy formation in a democratic society. In *Mathematical applications in political science II,* ed. J. Bernd. Dallas: Southern Methodist University Press.
———. 1967. Some results related to a mathematical model of policy formation in a democratic society. In *Mathematical applications in political science III,* ed. J. Bernd. Charlottesville: University of Virginia Press.
———. 1968. On the power and importance of mean preference in a mathematical model of democratic choice. *Public Choice* 5:59–72.
Davis, Otto, Melvin J. Hinich, and Peter C. Ordeshook. 1970. An expository development of a mathematical model of the electoral process. *American Political Science Review* 64:426–48.
Denzau, Arthur T., and Robert J. Mackay. 1981. Structure-induced equilibria and perfect-foresight expectations. *American Journal of Political Science* 25:762–69.
———. 1983. Gatekeeping and monopoly power of committees: An analysis of sincere and sophisticated behavior. *American Journal of Political Science* 27:740–61.
Denzau, Arthur, T. and Michael Munger. 1986. Legislators and interest groups: How unorganized interests get represented. *American Political Science Review* 80 (1):89–106.
Diehl, Paul F. 1985. Arms races to war: Testing some empirical linkages. *Sociological Quarterly* 26:331–49.
Dinerstein, H. S. 1976. *The making of a missile crisis: October 1962.* Baltimore: Johns Hopkins University Press.
Dougan, William, and Michael Munger. 1989. The rationality of ideology. *Journal of Law and Economics,* forthcoming.
Downs, Anthony. 1957. *An economic theory of democracy.* New York: Harper and Row.
Droop, H. R. 1869. On the political and social effects of different methods of electing representatives. *Papers, London Juridical Society* 3:469–507.
Dummett, Michael, and Robin Farquharson. 1961. Stability in voting. *Econometrica* 16:33–44.
Duverger, M. 1951. *Political parties.* London: Muethen Press.
Enelow, James M., and Melvin J. Hinich. 1981. A new approach to voter uncertainty in the Downsian spatial model. *American Journal of Political Science* 25 (3):483–93.
———. 1982. Nonspatial candidate characteristics and electoral competition. *Journal of Politics* 44:115–20.

---. 1983. Voter expectations in multi-stage voting systems: An equilibrium result. *American Journal of Political Science* 27:820–27.

---. 1984a. Probabilistic voting and the importance of centrist ideologies in democratic elections. *Journal of Politics* 46 (2):459–78.

---. 1984b. *The spatial theory of voting*. New York: Cambridge University Press.

---. Forthcoming a. A general probabilistic spatial theory of elections. *Public Choice*.

---. Forthcoming b. The theory of predictive mappings. In *Readings in the spatial theory of voting*, ed. Enelow and Hinich. New York: Cambridge University Press.

Erikson, Robert. 1972. Malapportionment, gerrymandering, and party fortunes in Congressional elections. *American Political Science Review* 66:1234–45.

Etheridge, L. S. 1985. *Can governments learn?* New York: Pergamon Press.

Fama, Eugene. 1970. Efficient capital markets: A review of theory and empirical work. *Journal of Finance* 25:383–417.

Fama, Eugene, L. Fisher, M. Jensen., and R. Roll. 1969. The adjustment of stock prices to new information. *International Economic Review* 10 (1):1–21.

Farquharson, Robin. 1956. Straightforwardness in voting procedures. *Oxford Economic Papers* 8:80–89.

---. 1969. *Theory of voting*. New Haven: Yale University Press.

Fenno, Richard F., Jr. 1966. *The power of the purse*. Boston: Little, Brown.

---. 1969. The House of Representatives and federal aid to education. In *New perspectives on the House of Representatives*, ed. R. Peabody and N. Polsby. Chicago: Rand McNally.

---. 1973. *Congressmen in committees*. Boston: Little, Brown and Company.

Ferejohn, John A. 1986. Incumbent performance and electoral control. *Public Choice* 50:5–25.

Ferejohn, John A., and Roger G. Noll. 1984. A theory of campaign contributions. Stanford University. Manuscript.

---. 1985. Promise, promises: Campaign contributions and the reputation for services. Working Paper P-85-1. Stanford: Hoover Institution, Stanford University.

---. 1986. Logrolling in an institutional context. In *Congress and policy change*, ed. G. C. Wright, L. N. Rieselback, and L. C. Dodd. New York: Agathon Press.

Fiorina, Morris P. 1977. *Congress: Keystone of the Washington Establishment*. New Haven: Yale University Press.

---. 1981. *Retrospective voting in American national elections*. New Haven: Yale University Press.

Friedman, James W. 1971. A non-cooperative equilibrium of supergames. *International Economic Review* 12:1–12.

Gant, M. M., and D. F. Davis. 1984. Mental economy and voter rationality—The informed citizen problem in voting research. *Journal of Politics* 46 (1): 132–53.

Garthoff, R. L. 1987. *Reflections on the Cuban missile crisis.* Washington, D.C.: The Brookings Institution.

Gibbard, Allan. 1973. Manipulation of voting schemes: A general result. *Econometrica* 41:587–601.

Gilligan, Thomas W., and Keith Krehbiel. 1986. Rules, subjurisdictional choice, and Congressional outcomes: An event study of energy taxation legislation in the 93rd Congress. Social Science Working Paper No. 594. Pasadena: California Institute of Technology.

———. 1987. Collective decision-making and Standing Committees: An informational rationale for restrictive amendment procedures. *Journal of Law, Economics, and Organization* 3:287–335.

———. 1988. Organization of informative committees by a rational legislature. Paper presented at the Annual Meeting of the Midwest Political Science Association, Chicago, Ill.

———. Forthcoming. Asymmetric information and legislative rules with a heterogeneous committee. *American Journal of Political Science.*

Gilpin, Robert. 1981. *War and change in world politics.* Cambridge: Cambridge University Press.

Gochman, Charles S., and Russell Leng. 1983. Realpolitik and the road to war: An analysis of attributes and behavior. *International Studies Quarterly* 27:97–120.

Gochman, Charles S., and Zeev Maoz. 1984. Militarized interstate disputes, 1815–1976: Procedures, patterns, and insights. *Journal of Conflict Resolution* 28:585–615.

Goulder, Alvin W. 1960. The norm of reciprocity: A preliminary statement. *American Sociological Review* 25:161–78.

Green, Jerry. 1973. Information, efficiency and equilibrium. Discussion Paper No. 284. Cambridge, Mass.: Harvard Institute Economic Research.

———. 1977. The non-existence of informational equilibria. *Review of Economic Studies* 44:451–64.

Greenberg, J., and K. Shepsle. 1987. The effect of electoral rewards in multiparty competition with entry. *American Political Science Review* 81 (2): 525–37.

Gretlein, Rodney J. 1983. Dominance elimination procedures on finite alternative games. *International Journal of Game Theory* 12:107–13.

Grossman, Sanford. 1976. On the efficiency of stock markets where traders have diverse information. *Journal of Finance* 31:573–85.

———. 1977. The existence of futures markets, noisy rational expectations and informational externalities. *Review of Economic Sudies* 64:431–49.

———. 1981. An introduction to rational expectations and asymmetric information. *Review of Economic Studies* 48:541–59.

Grossman, Sanford, and Joseph Stiglitz. 1980. On the impossibility of informationally efficient markets. *American Economic Review* 70 (3):393–408.

Haas, E. B. 1953. The balance of power: Prescription, concept, or propaganda? *World Politics* 4:442–77.

Harrington, Joseph E., Jr. 1988a. The power of the proposal maker in a model of endogenous agenda formation. Working Paper. Baltimore: Johns Hopkins University.
———. 1988b. The revelation of information through the electoral process: An exploratory analysis. Manuscript.
Harsanyi, John C. 1967–68. Games with incomplete information played by "Bayesian" players, parts I–III. *Management Science* 14:159–82, 320–34, and 486–502.
Heclo, Hugh. 1977. *A government of strangers*. Washington, D.C.: The Brookings Institution.
Hinich, Melvin J. 1977. Equilibrium in spatial voting: The median voter result is an artifact. *Journal of Economic Theory* 16 (2):208–19.
Hinich, Melvin J., John O. Ledyard, and Peter C. Ordeshook. 1972. Nonvoting and the existence of equilibrium under majority rule. *Journal of Economic Theory* 4:144–53.
———. 1973. A theory of electoral equilibrium: A spatial analysis based on the theory of games. *Journal of Politics* 35:154–93.
Homans, George C. 1961. *Social behavior*. New York: Harcourt, Brace, and World.
Hotelling, Harold. 1929. Stability in competition. *Economic Journal* 39:41–57.
Inada, Ken-ichi. 1964. A note on the simple majority decision rule. *Econometrica* 32:525–31.
Ingberman, D. 1986. Spatial competition with imperfectly informed voters. Ph.D. diss., Carnegie Mellon University, Pittsburgh.
Jacobson, Gary. 1987. The marginals never vanished: Incumbency and competition in elections to the U.S. House of Representatives, 1952–82. *American Journal of Political Science* 31:126–41.
Jacobson, Gary C., and S. Kernall. 1983. *Strategy and choice in Congressional elections*. 2d ed. New Haven: Yale University Press.
Jervis, Robert. 1970. *The logic of images in international relations*. Princeton: Princeton University Press.
———. 1976. *Perception and misperception in international politics*. Princeton: Princeton University Press.
———. 1985. Introduction: Approach and assumptions. In *Psychology and deterrence*, by Robert Jervis, Richard Ned Lebow, and Janice Gross Stein. Baltimore: Johns Hopkins University Press.
———. 1986. From balance to concert. In *Cooperation under anarchy*, ed. K. A. Oye. Princeton: Princeton University Press.
Jervis, Robert, Richard N. Lebow, and Janice G. Stein. 1985. *Psychology and deterrence*. Baltimore: Johns Hopkins University Press.
Johnson, N., and S. Kotz. 1970. *Continuous univariate distributions, vol. 1*. New York: John Wiley and Sons.
Johnston, J. 1963. *Econometric methods*. New York: McGraw-Hill.
Kahn, Herman. 1965. *On escalation: Metaphors and scenarios*. New York: Praeger.

Kaplan, Morton. 1957. *Systems and process in international politics.* New York: John Wiley and Sons.

Kennedy, Paul. 1987. *The rise and fall of the great powers.* New York: Random House.

Keohane, Robert O. 1984. *After hegemony: Cooperation and discord in the world political economy.* Princeton: Princeton University Press.

Kinder, D., and D. Sears. 1982. Political psychology. In *The handbook of political psychology,* ed. G. Lindzey and E. Aronson. Hillsdale, N.J.: L. Erlbaum Associates.

Kissinger, Henry. 1979. *The White House years.* Boston: Little, Brown and Company.

Krehbiel, Keith. 1987. Why are congressional committees so powerful? *American Political Science Review* 81 (3):929–35.

———. 1988. Spatial models of legislative choice. *Legislative Studies Quarterly* 13 (3): 259–319.

Krehbiel, Keith, and John Wright. 1983. The incumbency effect in Congressional elections: A test of two explanations. *American Journal of Political Science* 27:140–57.

Kreps, David M., and Robert Wilson. 1982a. Sequential equilibria. *Econometrica* 50:863–94.

———. 1982b. Reputation and imperfect information. *Journal of Economic Theory* 27:253–79.

Kreps, David M., Paul Milgrom, John Roberts, and Robert Wilson. 1982. Rational cooperation in the finitely repeated Prisoners' Dilemma. *Journal of Economic Theory* 27:245–52.

Lalman, David. 1988. Conflict resolution and peace. *American Journal of Political Science* 32:590–615.

Lebow, R. N. 1981. *Between peace and war: The nature of international crises.* Baltimore: Johns Hopkins University Press.

Ledyard, John O. 1981. The paradox of voting and candidate competition: A general equilibrium analysis. In *Essays in contemporary economics,* ed. G. Howich and J. Quirk. West Lafayette: Purdue University Press.

———. 1984. The pure theory of large two-candidate elections. *Public Choice* 44 (1):7–41.

Leng, Russell J. 1983. When will they ever learn? Coercive bargaining in recurrent crises. *Journal of Conflict Resolution* 27:379–420.

Lintner, J. 1965. The valuation of risk assets and the selection of risky investments in stock portfolios and capital budgets. *Review of Economics and Statistics* (February): 13–37.

Litwak, Robert S. 1984. *Détente and the Nixon doctrine.* Cambridge: Cambridge University Press.

Lott, John. 1986. Brand names and barriers to entry in political markets. *Public Choice* 51:87–92.

———. 1987. Political cheating. *Public Choice* 52:169–86.

Lowi, Theodore. 1979. *The end of liberalism.* New York: W. W. Norton.

Lucas, Robert E. 1972. Expectations and the neutrality of money. *Journal of Economic Theory* 4:103–24.

MacEuen, Michael. 1984. Exposure to information, belief integration, and individual responsiveness to agenda change. *American Political Science Review* 78 (2):372–91.

McKelvey, Richard D. 1970. Ambiguity in political models of policy formation. *Public Choice* 35:385–402.

———. 1976. Intransitivities in multidimensional voting models and some implications for agenda control. *Journal of Economics Theory* 12:472–82.

———. 1979. General conditions for global intransitives in formal voting models. *Econometrica* 47:1085–112.

———. 1986. Covering, dominance, and institution free properties of social choice. *American Journal of Political Science* 30:283–314.

McKelvey, Richard D., and Richard Niemi. 1978. A multistage game representation of sophisticated voting for binary procedures. *Journal of Economic Theory* 18:1–22.

McKelvey, Richard D., and Peter C. Ordeshook. 1972. Symmetrical spatial games without majority rule equilibria. *American Political Science Review* 72: 1172–84.

———. 1985. Elections with limited information: A fulfilled expectations model using contemporaneous poll and endorsement data as information sources. *Journal of Economic Theory* 36 (1):55–85.

McKelvey, Richard D., and Norman Schofield. 1987. Generalized symmetry conditions at a core point. *Econometrica* 55:923–33.

Malinowski, Bronislaw. 1932. *Crime and custom in savage society.* London: Paul, Trench, Trubner.

Manley, John. 1970. *The politics of finance.* Boston: Little, Brown and Company.

Marcet, A., and T. Sargent. 1986. Convergence of least squares learning rules in self referential linear stochastic models. Carnegie Mellon University. Manuscript.

Maskin, Eric. 1985. The theory of implementation in Nash equilibrium: A survey. In *Social goals and social organization,* ed. Leonid. Hurwicz, David Schmeidler, and Hugo Sonnenschein. London: Cambridge University Press.

Matthews, Donald R. 1960. *U.S. Senators and their world.* Chapel Hill: University of North Carolina Press.

Maxwell, Stephen. 1968. *Rationality in deterrence.* London: International Institute for Strategic Studies.

Mayhew, David. 1974a. Congressional elections: The case of the vanishing marginals. *Polity* 6:295–317.

———. 1974b. *Congress: The electoral connection.* New Haven: Yale University Press.

Miller, Nicholas R. 1977. Graph-theoretical approaches to the theory of voting. *American Journal of Political Science* 21:769–803.

———. 1980. A new solution set for tournaments and majority voting: Further

graph-theoretical approaches to the theory of voting. *American Journal of Political Science* 24:68–96.
Morgenthau, Hans J. 1948. *Politics among nations.* New York: Knopf.
Morrow, James D. 1985. A limited information model of crisis bargaining. Paper presented at the Annual Meeting of the American Political Science Association, New Orleans, La.
———. 1987. A limited information model of crisis bargaining. Paper presented at the Annual Meeting of the International Studies Association, Washington, D.C.
———. Forthcoming. Capabilities, uncertainty, and resolve: A limited information model of crisis bargaining. *American Journal of Political Science.*
Mossin, J. 1966. Equilibrium in a capital asset market. *Econometrica* 34:768–83.
Moulin, Hervé. 1979. Dominance solvable voting schemes. *Econometrica* 47:1337–51.
———. 1980. On strategy-proofness and single peakedness. *Public Choice* 35:437–55.
Muth, J. 1961. Rational expectations and the theory of price movements. *Econometrica* 29:315–35.
Myerson, R. B. 1981. Optimal auction design. *Mathematics of operations research.* 6:58–73.
Nalebuff, Barry. 1986. Brinksmanship and nuclear deterrence: The neutrality of escalation. *Conflict Management and Peace Science* 9:19–30.
Nash, J. F. 1950. The bargaining problem. *Econometrica* 18:155–62.
Niou, Emerson M. S., and Peter C. Ordeshook. 1986. A theory of the balance of power in international systems. *Journal of Conflict Resolution* 30 (3): 685–715.
Niou, Emerson M. S., Peter C. Ordeshook, and Gregory F. Rose. Forthcoming. *The balance of power: Stability in international systems.* Cambridge: Cambridge University Press.
Oleszek, Walter. 1984. *Congressional procedures and the policy process.* Washington, D.C.: Congressional Quarterly Press.
Ordeshook, Peter C. 1986. *Game theory and political theory: An introduction.* Cambridge: Cambridge University Press.
Ordeshook, Peter C., and Thomas R. Palfrey. 1988. Agendas, strategic voting, and signaling with incomplete information. *American Journal of Political Science* 32:441–66.
Ordeshook, Peter C., and Thomas Schwartz. 1987. Agendas and the control of political outcomes. *American Political Science Review* 81:179–99.
Organski, A. F. K., and Jacek Kugler. 1980. *The war ledger.* Chicago: University of Chicago Press.
Owen, Guillermo. 1982. *Game theory.* 2d ed. New York: Academic Press.
Page, Benjamin. 1976. *Choices and echoes in presidential elections.* Chicago: University of Chicago Press.
Palfrey, Thomas R. 1984. Spatial equilibrium with entry. *Review of Economic Studies* 51:139–56.

Palfrey, Thomas R., and Howard Rosenthal. 1983. A strategic calculus of voting. *Public Choice* 41:7–53.
———. 1985. Voter participation and strategic uncertainty. *American Political Science Review* 79:62–78.
Palfrey, Thomas R., and S. Srivastava. 1986. Nash implementation using undominated strategies. Social Sciences Working Paper No. 649. Pasadena: California Institute of Technology.
Pattanaik, Prasanta K. 1976. Collective rationality and strategy-proofness of group decision rule. *Theory and Decision* 7:191–203.
Pitkin, Hannah. 1967. *The concept of representation*. Berkeley: University of California.
Plott, Charles R. 1967. A notion of equilibrium and its possibility under majority rule. *American Economic Review* 57:787–806.
Plott, Charles R., and Shyam Sunder. 1982. Efficiency of experimental security markets with insider information: An application of rational expectations models. *Journal of Political Economy* 90:663–98.
Polsby, Nelson W. 1968. The institutionalization of the U.S. House of Representatives. *American Political Science Review* 62:148–68.
Powell, Robert. 1987. Crisis bargaining, escalation, and MAD. *American Political Science Review* 81:717–36.
———. 1988. Nuclear brinksmanship with two-sided incomplete information. *American Political Science Review* 82:155–78.
Rae, D. W. 1971. *The political consequences of electoral laws*. Rev. ed. New Haven: Yale University Press.
Reinganum, Jennifer, and Louis Wilde. 1986. Settlement, litigation, and the allocation of litigation costs. *Rand Journal of Economics* 17:557–66.
Riker, William H. 1962. *The theory of political coalitions*. New Haven: Yale University Press.
———. 1976. The number of political parties: A reexamination of Duverger's Law. *Comparative Politics* 9 (1): 93–106.
———. 1982a. *Liberalism against populism*. San Francisco: W. H. Freeman.
———. 1982b. The two party system and Duverger's Law. *American Political Science Review* 76:753–66.
Riordan, M. H., and D. E. M. Sappington. 1987. Information, incentives, and organizational mode. *Quarterly Journal of Economics* 102 (May): 243–63.
Romer, Thomas, and Howard Rosenthal. 1978. Political resource allocation, controlled agendas, and the status quo. *Public Choice* 33:27–43.
———. 1979. The elusive median voter. *Journal of Public Economics* 12:143–70.
Roth, A. E. 1985. *Game-theoretic models of bargaining*. New York: Cambridge University Press.
Rothschild, Michael, and Joseph Stiglitz. 1970. Increasing risk I: A definition. *Journal of Economic Theory* 2:225–43.
Rubinstein, Ariel. 1982. Perfect equilibrium in a bargaining model. *Econometrica* 50:97–109.

Satterthwaite, Mark A. 1975. Strategy-proofness and Arrow's conditions: Correspondence theorems for voting procedures and social welfare functions. *Journal of Economic Theory* 10:187–217.

Schattschneider, E. E. 1960. *Party government*. New York: Holt, Rinehart and Winston.

Schelling, Thomas C. 1960. *The strategy of conflict*. Cambridge, Mass.: Harvard University Press.

———. 1966. *Arms and influence*. New Haven: Yale University Press.

Schofield, Norman. 1983. Generic instability of majority rule. *Review of Economic Studies* 50:695–705.

———. 1984. Existence of equilibrium on a manifold. *Mathematics of Operations Research* 9:545–57.

Schwert, William. 1981. Using financial data to measure the effects of regulation. *Journal of Law and Economics* 24:121–58.

Sharpe, W. 1964. Capital asset pricing: A theory of market equilibrium under conditions of risk. *Journal of Finance* 19 (3):425–42.

Shepsle, Kenneth A. 1972. The strategy of ambiguity: Uncertainty and electoral competition. *American Political Science Review* 66 (2):555–68.

———. 1978. *Giant jigsaw puzzle*. Chicago: University of Chicago Press.

———. 1979. Institutional arrangements and equilibrium in multidimensional voting models. *American Journal of Political Science* 23:27–60.

———. 1983. Institutional equilibrium and equilibrium institutions. Paper presented at the Annual Meeting of the American Political Science Association, Chicago, Ill.

Shepsle, Kenneth A., and Barry R. Weingast. 1981. Structure-induced equilibrium and legislative choice. *Public Choice* 37:503–19.

———. 1984. Uncovered sets and sophisticated voting outcomes with implications for agenda institutions. *American Journal of Political Science* 28:49–74.

———. 1987. The institutional foundations of committee power. *American Political Science Review* 81 (1):85–104.

Singer, J. David, Stuart Bremer, and John Stuckey. 1972. Capability distribution, uncertainty, and major power war: 1820–1965. In *Peace, war, and numbers*, ed. Bruce Russett. Beverly Hills: Sage Publications.

Siverson, Randolph, and Michael Tennefoss. 1982. Interstate conflicts: 1815–1965. *International Relations* 9:147–78.

Smith, Steven S. 1986. Revolution in the House: Why don't we do it on the floor? Discussion Paper in Governmental Studies No. 5. Washington, D.C.: The Brookings Institution.

Snyder, Glenn H., and Paul Diesing. 1977. *Conflict among nations: Bargaining, decision making, and system structure in international crises*. Princeton: Princeton University Press.

Spafford, D. 1972. Electoral systems and voters' behavior: Comment and a further test. *Comparative Politics* 5:129–34.

Stoessinger, John. 1974. *Why nations go to war*. New York: St. Martin's Press.

Stokes, Donald, and Warren Miller. 1962. Party government and the saliency of Congress. *Public Opinion Quarterly* 26:531–46.
Sutton, John. 1986. Non-cooperative bargaining theory: An introduction. *Review of Economic Studies* 53:709–24.
Taylor, A. J. P. 1954. *The struggle for the mastery of Europe, 1848–1918*. Oxford: Oxford University Press.
Townsend, R. 1978. Market anticipations, rational expectations and Bayesian analysis. *International Economic Review* 19 (2):481–94.
Trachtenberg, M. 1985. The influence of nuclear weapons in the Cuban missile crisis. *International Security* 10:137–203.
Tufte, Edward. 1973. The relationship between seats and votes in two-party systems. *American Political Science Review* 67:540–47.
U.S. Congress. Senate. 1963. *The authority of the Senate to originate appropriation bills*. 88th Cong., 1st sess. S. Doc. 17.
Vickery, William. 1960. Utility, strategy, and social decision rules. *Quarterly Journal of Economics* 74:507–35.
Wagner, R. Harrison. 1982. Deterrence and bargaining. *Journal of Conflict Resolution* 26:329–58.
⸺. 1983. The theory of games and the problem of international cooperation. *American Political Science Review* 77:330–46.
⸺. 1986. The theory of games and the balance of power. *World Politics*, July.
Waltz, Kenneth. 1979. *Theory of international politics*. Reading, Mass.: Addison-Wesley.
Weiner, M. 1957. *Party politics in India: The development of a multiparty system*. Princeton: Princeton University Press.
Weingast, Barry. 1988. The floor in Congress: Committee power under the open rule. Manuscript, Stanford University.
Wilson, R. 1985. Reputations in games and markets. In *Game-theoretic models of bargaining*, ed. Alvin E. Roth. New York: Cambridge University Press.
Wittman, D. 1983. Candidate motivation: A synthesis of alternative theories. *American Political Science Review* 77:142–57.
⸺. Forthcoming. Parties and candidates with policy preferences. In *Readings in the spatial theory of voting*, ed. J. Enelow and M. Hinich. Cambridge: Cambridge University Press.
Woodford, M. 1987. Learning to believe in sunspots. Columbia University. Manuscript.
Wright, Gerald, and Michael Berkman. 1986. Candidates and policy in the U.S. Senate elections. *American Political Science Review* 80:567–88.
Zeckhauser, R. 1969. Majority rule with lotteries on alternatives. *Quarterly Journal of Economics* 83:696–703.

**PROPERTY OF
PUBLIC INTEREST
INSTITUTE**